THE SEVENTEENTH
EARL OF OXFORD
1550—1604

EDWARD DE VERE
17TH EARL OF OXFORD, AGE 25

Probably painted by a Flemish Artist in Paris

THE SEVENTEENTH EARL OF OXFORD
1550—1604

FROM CONTEMPORARY DOCUMENTS

BY B. M. WARD

"For genuine illustration of history, biography, and manners, we must chiefly rely on ancient original papers. To them we must turn for the correction of past errors; for a supply of future materials; and for proof of what hath already been delivered unto us."

EDMUND LODGE,
Illustrations of British History (1791)

LONDON
JOHN MURRAY, ALBEMARLE STREET, W.

FIRST EDITION . . . 1928

Reprinted 1979, by permission of John Murray

TO

B. R. W.

PREFACE

OF all the great Elizabethans who made the Sixteenth Century the heroic age of English History both in action and letters, there is not one so little known and so universally misjudged as Edward de Vere, the seventeenth Earl of Oxford. At the hands of his contemporaries he received both scurrilous abuse and unstinted praise, and therefore it is perhaps not surprising that posterity should have accepted the first and doubted the second. To most Englishmen nowadays he is little more than a name. Even to specialists in Elizabethan history he is hardly more than " Burghley's ill-conditioned son-in-law," as Froude described him, an eccentric of doubtful character and boorish manners, whose contemporary fame as a courtier poet and dramatist was sadly tarnished by his rudeness to his famous rival Sir Philip Sidney on the occasion of the well-known Tennis Court quarrel. Such is his reputation at the present day, but a close examination of the manuscript records of the period, contained in the British Museum, the Public Record Office, and at Hatfield House, reveals a very different story from the one which has been almost universally accepted by historians of the period.

Most of the stories told against the Earl are shown to be without foundation. He did not make away his estate in order to spite his father-in-law because the latter either would not or could not prevent the Duke of Norfolk's execution. The criminal charges made against him in 1581 by Charles Arundel have been generally taken as proved. Not only were they not proved, but strictly speaking they were not charges at all, being really random accusations made in self-defence by the traitor Charles

vii

Arundel, whose treasonable dealings with Spain had been brought to light by the Earl of Oxford himself.

Research into original manuscripts of the period not only shows up the falsity of most of the popular legends that have grown up round Lord Oxford, but it throws a new light on the importance of the part played by him throughout Queen Elizabeth's reign. From 1570 to 1580 he was perhaps second only to the Earl of Leicester as the chief favourite of the Queen. During the same period his reputation as a man of letters was second to none. Although the accusations brought against him by Charles Arundel gave a handle to his rivals to supplant him in the Queen's favour, yet the fact remains that only four years afterwards, i.e. in 1585, he was selected to take charge of the important mission to the Netherlands. In the following year—1586—he received a still more striking proof of Royal favour in the form of £1,000 a year which he received regularly from the Exchequer in four quarterly payments until his death in 1604.

In 1588 he fitted out at his own expense a ship in which he went to sea and played his part in the dramatic victory over the Spanish Armada, indignantly refusing the command of the naval base at Harwich, as a position involving neither service nor credit. On November 24th of that year, when the Queen made a Royal Progress to St. Paul's through the streets of London to render thanks to God for the great victory, Lord Oxford and the Earl Marshal rode on either side of the Queen's chariot through the thronging multitude, and the same two noblemen carried a golden canopy over the Queen's head as she walked up the nave of St. Paul's to take her part in the historic thanksgiving service.

In 1589 Oxford received the most striking testimonial to his literary abilities that was ever bestowed on an Elizabethan man of letters by one of his contemporaries. Although after this date until his death in 1604 he vanishes from the public view except for an occasional appearance —e.g. at the trial of the Earl of Essex in 1601, and as

Lord Great Chamberlain at the coronation of King James
in 1603—we cannot doubt that his life in retirement
was occupied in cultivating those literary and musical
talents which were so highly praised by the men of his day.

A posthumous tribute, written soon after his death
in King James's reign, stating that he was " a man in
mind and body absolutely accomplished with honourable
endowments," is sufficiently impressive to make it well
worth while to glean every record that may have survived
in order to enable us to realise something of the accom-
plishment on which so brilliant a reputation must have
been founded.

During the course of my study of the period I have
carried out certain investigations as to matters of publication and authorship which have led me to arrive at conclusions somewhat at variance from the opinions hitherto
held on these points. I have already published my
reasons for adopting these opinions, and in order to avoid
lengthy discussions in the text of this biography and at
the same time to permit of the verification or criticism
of these opinions by students, I give below a couple of
conclusions I have arrived at, together with a reference
in each case to the publication in which the question is
discussed.

1. That the Earl of Oxford was the editor of an anthology
entitled *A Hundreth Sundrie Flowres*, published in 1573,
and was himself the author of sixteen of the poems published in the book. (Vide Introduction to *A Hundreth
Sundrie Flowres*, published by Etchells and Macdonald
in 1926.)

2. That Oxford's cousin John, Lord Lumley (1532–
1608) was the author of *The Arte of English Poesie*,
published in 1589. (Vide *Review of English Studies*,
July 1925.) The authorship of this work has hitherto
been attributed to one of the two Puttenhams, Richard
or George.

The following chapters are the result of nearly five
years' search among unpublished manuscript records

of the time, every known source of information having been thoroughly examined during that period. The bulk of the biography is based upon contemporary manuscript records. A few questions relating to literature and the drama which cannot be settled on recorded evidence alone have been relegated to a series of Interludes, inserted in the biography proper, but at the same time independent of it. Readers who wish to know the ascertained facts of Lord Oxford's life, and are not interested in subsidiary questions which cannot be definitely settled without further research and criticism, may thus without loss of continuity confine themselves to the biographical chapters, omitting the subsidiary Interludes.

It is my pleasant duty here to acknowledge my indebtedness to the Marquess of Salisbury for permission to examine his unique collection of manuscripts at Hatfield House, and to publish for the first time many important letters which have never before been printed. My thanks are also due to his librarian, the Rev. W. Stanhope-Lovell, for every assistance in transcribing these documents. To Professor Abel Lefranc of the Collège de France I am indebted for very kindly checking my list of French Ambassadors in England with information derived from the records of the French Foreign Office, and to Dr. Van Biema of The Hague for consulting the Dutch State Archives for records of the military expedition of 1585. I should like also to acknowledge my indebtedness to the officials of the British Museum, the Public Record Office, and the Bodleian Library for their courtesy and assistance in my researches through the State Papers, as well as the Lansdowne, Harleian, Rawlinson, and other manuscript collections.

B. M. WARD.

WYVENHOE,
FARNHAM ROYAL,
    BUCKS.
February 28, 1928.

CONTENTS

BOOK THE SECOND

THE COURTIER

CHAPTER IV

1577–1580

INTERLUDE

CHAPTER V

1580–1586

CONTENTS

INTERLUDE

CHAPTER VI
1587–1588

BOOK THE THIRD
THE RECLUSE

CHAPTER VII
1589–1595

INTERLUDE

CHAPTER VIII
1597–1604

CONTENTS

ILLUSTRATIONS

GENEALOGICAL TABLES

(At the end of the volume)

ERRATA

Page 40, last line but nine.   For " Hudson's " read " Hunsdon's."

Page 69, line 12.   For " assemble " read " assembled."

Page 69, last line but one.   For " Bibliotecha " read " Bibliotheca."

Page 82, last line but four.   For " tion " read " action."

Page 111, line 27.   For " time " read " Him."

Page 234, line 4.   For " 1583 " read " 1582."

Page 289, line 7.   For " August " read " the."

Page 289, last line.   For " thither " read " hither."

Page 357, line 11.   For " 26. 6. 84 " read " 26. 6. 86."

Page 365, foot-note 1.   For " *State* " read " *Stage*."

Page 397.   For " Butler, Samuel, 295 n." read " Butler, Samuel, 294 n."

BOOK THE FIRST

THE ROYAL WARD

BOOK THE FIRST

THE ROYAL WARD

" I confess to your Lordship I do honour him (Lord Oxford) so dearly from my heart as I do my own son, and in any case that may touch him for his honour and weal, I shall think him mine own interest therein. And surely, my Lord, by dealing with him I find that which I often heard of your Lordship, that there is much more in him of understanding than any stranger to him would think. And for my part I find that whereof I take comfort in his wit and knowledge grown by good observation."

Lord Burghley to the Earl of Rutland, 1571.

" I am one that count myself a follower of yours now in all fortunes ; and what shall hap to you I count it hap to myself ; or at least I will make myself a voluntary partaker of it. Thus, my Lord, I humbly desire your Lordship to pardon my youth, but to take in good part my zeal and affection towards you, as on whom I have builded my foundation either to stand or to fall . . . so much you have made me yours. And I do protest there is nothing more desired of me than so to be taken and accounted of [by] you."

Earl of Oxford to Lord Burghley, 1572.

" Howsoever my Lord of Oxford be for his own part (in) matters of thrift inconsiderate, I dare avow him to be resolute in dutifulness to the Queen and his country."

Lord Burghley to the Earl of Sussex, 1574.

" I hope your Lordship doth account me now—on whom you have so much bound—as I am : so be you before any else in the world, both through match—whereby I count my greatest stay—and by your Lordship's friendly usage and sticking by me in this time, wherein I am hedged in with so many enemies."

Earl of Oxford to Lord Burghley, 1583.

" Who, in all my causes, I find mine honourable good Lord, and to deal more fatherly than friendly with me, for the which I do acknowledge— and ever will—myself in most especial wise bound."

Earl of Oxford to Lord Burghley, 1590.

" I am sorry that I have not an able body which might have served to attend Her Majesty in the place where she is [i.e. Theobalds, where she was staying with Lord Burghley], being especially there, whither, without any other occasion than to see your Lordship, I would always willingly go."

Earl of Oxford to Lord Burghley, 1597.

CHAPTER I

1066–1561

" What is the most memorablest and most glorious Sun which ever gave light or shine to Nobility ? Our Veres, from the first hour of Cæsar to this present day of King James (which is above a thousand seven hundred years ago) never let their feet slip from the path of nobility, never knew a true eclipse of glory, never found declination from virtue, never forsook their country being wounded, or their lawful King distressed, never were attainted, never blemished, but in the purity of their first garments and with that excellent white and unspotted innocency wherewith it pleased the first Majesty to invest them, they lived, governed, and died, leaving the memory thereof on their monuments, and in the people's hearts ; and the imitation to all the Princes of the World, that either would be accounted good men or would have good men to speak good things of their actions."

GERVASE MARKHAM, in *Honour in his Perfection*, 1624.

§ I. THE HERITAGE

No family has contributed more to English history than the de Veres. For twenty generations, covering a period of nearly six hundred years, they handed on the Earldom of Oxford in unbroken male descent. It is outside the scope of this volume to give an adequate account of this great family ; but a brief outline is, perhaps, desirable in order to see what manner of men they were, with their proud motto *Vero nihil verius*.

The de Veres, although of French origin, settled in England before the Norman Conquest. Alberic or Aubrey de Vere held land under King Edward the Confessor.[1] He evidently sided with his fellow-countryman William the Conqueror in 1066 ; for in the distribution of land that followed the Saxon defeat at Hastings, Aubrey de Vere

---

[1] *Register of Colne Priory*, fol. 18b, quoted in a MS. volume written *circa* 1826 and entitled, *An Account of the Most Ancient and Noble Family of the de Veres, Earls of Oxford*, now preserved in the Colchester Public Library (p. 4).

3

received many estates, notably Chenesiton, now Kensington.[1] He must have been in great favour with the Conqueror, for he married his half-sister Beatrix, niece and heiress of Manasses, Earl of Guisnes.

His grandson, also named Aubrey, took part in the First Crusade, which commenced in 1097 :

In the year of our Lord, 1098, Corborant, Admiral of the Soudan of Perce, was fought with at Antioch and discomfited by the Christians. The night coming on in the chase of this battle, and waxing dark, the Christians being four miles from Antioch, God willing the safety of the Christians showed a white Star or Molette of five points on the Christian host, which to every man's sight did light and arrest upon the standard of Albry the third, there shining excessively.[2]

From this legend arose the origin of the Vere arms : Quarterly gules and or, in the quarter a mullet argent.[3]

When Aubrey returned to England he founded, soon after 1100, the Priory of Colne in Essex, and thus began the long territorial connexion between the Earls of Oxford and that county. He ultimately became a monk in his own religious house, and was buried in the church at Earl's Colne. He was also in high favour with his sovereign King Henry I., the youngest son of the Conqueror, who created him hereditary Lord Great Chamberlain of England. This office, not to be confused with that of Lord Chamberlain, is still in existence to-day. The only duties it involves are in connexion with coronations. It remained in the de Vere family until 1625, when, on the death of the eighteenth Earl of Oxford, it passed through a sister of the seventeenth Earl, into the family of Bertie, Earls of Lindsey. It was probably the religious Aubrey's son,

---

[1] A full account of the de Vere family, from which this outline is taken, will be found in Dugdale's *Baronage* (1675), vol. i, p. 188. It is interesting that names like Aubrey House and Aubrey Walk, found to this day on Camden Hill, Kensington, doubtless owe their origin to Aubrey de Vere.

[2] Leland, *Itinerary*, vol. vi, p. 40.

[3] The " mullet argent " is a silver five-pointed star ; the word " mullet," from the French " molette," being literally the rowel of a spur.

the fourth successive Aubrey, who was created first Earl of Oxford in the reign of King Stephen. He died in the reign of King Richard I.

From Richard I. to Edward IV. is a far cry; and though every generation is a history in itself, we must now pass on to the days when England, torn and bleeding, was in the throes of the Wars of the Roses. The Earls of Oxford were strong supporters of the House of Lancaster; and when Edward IV., a Yorkist, obtained the Crown, one of his first acts was to attaint and execute John the twelfth Earl, and his eldest son, Aubrey. His second son, also John, then aged eighteen, was restored to the Earldom, but he was always looked on with suspicion by the Yorkists. With Warwick, the King maker, he helped to bring about the restoration of King Henry VI. in 1470.

The following year Edward landed in England, and was met by the Lancastrians under Warwick and Oxford at Barnet. Just when defeat seemed certain for the Yorkists a curious accident changed the fortunes of the day. All Oxford's soldiers wore as a distinguishing mark the Vere "mullet argent." The Yorkists carried the insignia of Edward, a sun. In response to a call for assistance from Warwick, Oxford, who had routed the Yorkist left, led his men over to help. It was a misty day, and Warwick's men, mistaking the Oxford star for the Yorkist sun, attacked them. The Earl and his followers, imagining themselves deserted, fled.

For fourteen years Lord Oxford remained an outlaw on the Continent. In 1485 he accompanied the Earl of Richmond, afterwards King Henry VII., when he landed in England; and it was largely due to Oxford that the Lancastrians triumphed at the battle of Bosworth Field. The new sovereign showered favours on his staunch lieutenant to whom he owed so much. He was appointed Captain of the Yeomen of the Guard, Lord Admiral of England, Constable of the Tower of London, and Keeper of the Lions. In 1491 he had the honour, together with

Peter Courtney, Bishop of Winchester, of standing god-
father to Prince Henry, afterwards King Henry VIII.,
when he was christened in the Parish Church at Greenwich.[1]

John, the fourteenth Earl, accompanied King Henry
VIII. in 1520 to the Field of the Cloth of Gold. He
was just twenty-one at the time, and his retinue, we
are told, consisted of three chaplains, six gentlemen,
thirty-three servants, and twenty horses.[2] He married
Anne Howard, daughter of the Duke of Norfolk, but
died without issue at the age of twenty-seven. His
Countess survived him, and was buried on February 22nd,
1558-9, at Lambeth.[3] He was known as "Little John
of Camps," because he resided chiefly at Castle Camps
in Cambridgeshire. At his death in 1526 the Earldom
passed to the fourth successive holder of the name of John.

The fifteenth Earl, who was born about 1490, was
descended from an uncle of the hero of Bosworth Field.
He was elected a Knight of the Garter in 1528, and
carried the Crown at the coronation of Queen Anne Boleyn
on June 1st, 1533 ; and at the dinner after the ceremony—

on the right side of her chair stood the Countess of
Oxford, widow, and on her left side stood the Countess
of Worcester all the dinner season, which divers times in
the dinner time did hold a fine cloth before the Queen's
face when she list to spit, or do otherwise at her pleasure ;
and at the table's end sat the Archbishop of Canterbury,
on the right of the Queen ; and in the middest, between
the Archbishop and the Countess of Oxford, stood the
Earl of Oxford, with a white staff all dinner time ; and at
the Queen's feet under the table sat two Gentlewomen
all dinner time.[4]

He was buried in 1540 in the chancel of the parish church
of Castle Hedingham beneath a black marble monument.
On the top of the tomb is a bas-relief representation of

---

[1] Colchester MS. (cit.), pp. 99-114. Cf. Lysons, vol. iv, p. 430. He died
in 1513 without leaving an heir, and was succeeded by his nephew John.

[2] Colchester MS. (cit.), p. 120.

[3] Lysons, *Environs of London*, vol. i, p. 297.

[4] Stow, *Annals* (ed. 1631), p. 567.

the Vere arms, and beneath them the Earl himself kneeling opposite his wife Elizabeth Trussell, the only daughter and heiress of the wealthy Edward Trussell, who died a minor shortly after her birth in 1496. On his right arm is carved the Garter, and on either side of the tomb are represented their four sons and four daughters. They were John, afterwards sixteenth Earl of Oxford ; Aubrey, ancestor of the nineteenth Earl ; Robert, who died in 1598 [1] ; and Geoffrey, father of Francis and Horatio Vere, two famous soldiers in the reign of Queen Elizabeth. The daughters were Elizabeth, who married Thomas Lord Darcy ; Anne, who married Edmund Lord Sheffield ; Frances, who married Henry Howard, the poet Earl of Surrey ; and Ursula.

§ II. CASTLE HEDINGHAM

John, the sixteenth Earl of Oxford, married first,[2] about 1537, Dorothy Neville, a sister of the fourth Earl of Westmorland. By her he had one daughter, Katherine, who was afterwards the wife of Edward, third Baron Windsor. He married secondly Margaret Golding, as is evidenced by the following entry in the Parish Register of Belchamp St. Paul's, Essex :

Ao. Domini 1548. The wedding of my Lord John de Vere, Earl of Oxenford, and Margery, the daughter of John Goulding Esquire, the first of August.

By her he had two children, Edward and Mary. We shall meet Lady Mary Vere, who was younger than her brother, later on as the wife of Lord Willoughby de Eresby ; while Edward is the subject of this biography.

The evidence afforded as to the second marriage of the

---

[1] A brass in Charlton Parish Church records that " here lyeth buried Robert Veer Esquire, third son of John de Veer, Earl of Oxford, which said Robert deceased the 2nd April 1598 " (Mill Stephenson, *A List of Monumental Brasses in the British Isles* (1926), p. 214). By his will, proved May 27th, 1598, he left all his property to " Jone Veer my well beloved wife," but makes no mention of any children. (P.C.C. 36 Lewyn.)

[2] Colchester MS. (cit.), p. 126.

Earl of Oxford on August 1st, 1548, is important as it
enables us to clear Edward and Mary from a charge of
illegitimacy which was brought against the former by
Edward, the third Baron Windsor, some time during
Edward de Vere's minority and Wardship at Cecil House,
and again by Thomas, the seventh Baron Windsor in
1660. Why the former raised the question is not clear,
but Thomas, Lord Windsor in 1660 petitioned the Crown
for the office of Lord Great Chamberlain on the ground
that the sixteenth Earl's second wife had not been lawfully
married to him, so that he had left " Katherine his only
daughter and heir (by Dorothy, daughter of the Earl of
Westmorland, his only lawful wife) who was married to
Edward, Lord Windsor, great grandfather of the Peti-
tioner." [1]

A letter dated June 27th, 1547, from Lord Oxford's
brother-in-law Sir Thomas Darcy to William Cecil [2] enables
us to see how the scandal first arose. A love affair was
apparently in progress between Lord Oxford and a certain
" gentlewoman . . . Mistress Dorothy late woman to
my Lady Katherine his daughter." Banns had been
already twice called in church, but Sir Thomas Darcy
thought it very expedient to put a stop to it. He seems to
have succeeded, as there is no record of a marriage having
taken place ; and indeed the evidence of Lord Oxford's
marriage to Margery Golding on August 1st, 1548, is fairly
conclusive proof that no marriage to Mistress Dorothy
ever did take place. It would seem that the tradition of
a previous marriage was handed down in the Windsor
family, and that they were unaware of the record of the
Golding marriage preserved in the Parish Register at
Belchamp St. Paul's. It is curious to see how scandal
accompanied Edward de Vere into the world ; and we
shall find as the story develops that the voice of scandal
steadily pursued him throughout his life, and has continued
to pursue his memory during the three hundred years
that have elapsed since his death. One of the results of

[1] *The Ancestor*, January, 1903, p. 28.　　　[2] Ibid., p. 24.

examining the contemporary documents dealing with
his life is to show the utter baselessness of all these insinuations. It is therefore satisfactory at the very outset of his
career to be able by means of an official entry in a Parish
Register to nail the first of these lies to the counter, and
thus to clear the way for the record of his life.

Edward de Vere, afterwards the seventeenth Earl of
Oxford, was born on April 12th, 1550, at Castle Hedingham
in Essex.[1] The name Edward, which is unique in the
Vere family, was probably given to him as a compliment
to King Edward VI., who was then reigning. He was
styled Viscount Bulbeck, one of the subsidiary titles
borne by the Earls of Oxford. His father, who took
little part in Court life during the troublous reign of
Queen Mary, was an enthusiastic sportsman. An amusing
story, illustrative of his prowess in the hunting field, is
told of him when he was in France in 1544 :

By reason of his warlike disposition, we read, he was
invited to the hunting of a wild boar, a sport mixed with
much danger and deserving the best man's care for his
preservation and safety. Whence it comes that the
Frenchmen, when they hunt this beast, are ever armed
with light arms, mounted on horseback, and having chasing
staves like lances in their hands. To this sport the Earl
of Oxford goes ; but no otherwise attired than as when he
walked in his own private bedchamber, only a dancing
rapier by his side ; neither any better mounted than on
a plain English Tracconer, or ambling nag. Anon the boar
is put on foot (which was a beast both huge and fierce),
the chase is eagerly pursued, many affrights are given,
and many dangers escaped. At last the Earl, weary of
the toil or else urged by some other necessity, alights from
his horse and walks alone by himself on foot ; when
suddenly down the path in which the Earl walked came
the enraged beast, with his mouth all foamy, his teeth
whetted, his bristles up, and all other signs of fury and
anger. The gallants of France cry unto the Earl to run
aside and save himself ; everyone holloed out that he was
lost, and (more than their wishes) none there was that

[1] Hatfield MSS. Cal. (XIII. 142).

durst bring him succour. But the Earl (who was as
careless of their clamours as they were careful to exclaim)
alters not his pace, nor goes an hair's breadth out of his
path ; and finding that the boar and he must struggle
for passage, draws out his rapier and at the first encounter
slew the boar. Which, when the French nobility perceived,
they came galloping in unto him and made the wonder
in their distracted amazements, some twelve times greater
than Hercules twelve labours, all joining in one, that it
was an act many degrees beyond possibility. . . . But the
Earl, seeing their distraction, replied : " My Lords, what
have I done of which I have no feeling ? Is it the killing
of this English pig ? Why, every boy in my nation would
have performed it. They may be bugbears to the French :
to us they are but servants." . . . And so they returned
to Paris with the slain beast, where the wonder did neither
decrease nor die, but to this day lives in many of their
old annals." [1]

With such a father we may be sure that riding, shooting,
and hawking were among the earliest accomplishments
learned by the young Lord Bulbeck. But Lord Oxford's
interests were by no means confined to out-door recrea-
tions. His family circle linked him with many of the
most famous scholars and poets of the day. Arthur
Golding was his brother-in-law and his son's tutor : Sir
Thomas Smith, the well-known statesman, scholar, and
author, was another of his son's tutors : one of his sisters,
Frances Vere, married the poet Earl of Surrey, and herself
wrote verse [2] : another sister, Anne Vere, married Lord
Sheffield.[3] And he was, at this time, one of the small
but ever increasing band of noblemen who kept a company
of actors. In the summer these men would travel round
the country making what money they could by giving
performances in the courtyards of inns. But in the winter,

[1] Gervase Markham, *Honour in his Perfection.*
[2] Cf. *Surrey's Poetical Works,* J. Yeowell (1908), p. xxiv.
[3] Lord Sheffield (1521–1549) became the Earl of Oxford's ward in 1538.
" Great his skill in music, who wrote a book of sonnets according to the
Italian fashion." (Fuller : cf. *D.N.B.,* art. Sheffield, Sir Edmund). His
sonnets are all apparently lost. He was killed while helping to suppress
Ket's rebellion.

particularly between Christmas and Lent, they would be
at Castle Hedingham helping to provide entertainment
for the long evenings.

These facts tell us quite plainly that the sixteenth Earl
of Oxford and his family circle took an unusual interest
in literature and the drama. It was among people of
this calibre that the young Lord Bulbeck was brought up.
Youthful impressions rarely die ; and when in after-years
we find him becoming famous as a poet and a dramatist
we may safely trace back his artistic ability and interest
to these early years at Castle Hedingham.

With the accession of Queen Mary the sixteenth Earl
of Oxford, who remained true to the Reformed Faith, was
obliged to retire from Court life and live in seclusion at
Castle Hedingham. Even so he narrowly escaped being
compromised in the anti-Catholic conspiracy of 1556,
for his name heads a list of Noblemen " vehemently
suspected " of complicity in that plot.[1] It was, no doubt,
during this period that Sir Thomas Smith, another staunch
Protestant, became for a time the young Lord Bulbeck's
tutor. We may therefore safely surmise that Edward de
Vere's early upbringing was in the tenets of the Reformed
Church.

In November 1558, while still in his ninth year, Edward
de Vere matriculated as an " impubes " fellow-commoner
of Queens' College, Cambridge. This quite exceptional
precocity was but a foretaste of what was to come. It
was principally to his uncle Arthur Golding, who with
Sir Thomas Smith had been responsible for his early
education, that he owed the grounding in scholarship
that this achievement implies. Golding's place in Elizabethan literature is too well known to need repeating
here. His most famous work was a translation of Ovid's
Metamorphoses, which Shakespeare drew on largely in
after-years. Edward de Vere must, therefore, have made
an early acquaintance with his tutor's favourite Latin
author.

[1] S.P. Dom. Mary, VII. 24.

In the same month Queen Mary died ; and with the passing of the Catholic reaction the Earl of Oxford emerged from his enforced retirement. He was one of the peers who accompanied the Princess Elizabeth from her semi-prison at Hatfield to her throne in London on November 23rd. At the same time Margery, Countess of Oxford, was appointed Maid of Honour to the new Queen ; and she and her husband seem to have spent the year 1559 at the Court.[1]

Lord Oxford was now in high favour, and in the autumn of this year he was chosen to meet the Duke of Finland, second son of the King of Sweden, who had come to England to attempt to negotiate a marriage between Queen Elizabeth and his elder brother, Prince Eric. The Duke landed at Harwich—

about the end of September, and was there honourably received by the Earl of Oxford and the Lord Robert Dudley, and by them conducted from thence to London. He had in his own train about fifty persons well mounted ; the Earl of Oxford also, and the Lord Robert Dudley were followed with a fair attendance both of gentlemen and yeomen.[2]

The Swedish Royal family at this time were Protestants, and the fact that Lord Oxford was selected to meet the Duke of Finland shows that he was a recognised pillar of the Reformed Church.

In 1561, a year before his death, the Earl of Oxford entertained the Queen for five days at Castle Hedingham.[3] Lord Bulbeck was then aged eleven, and it must have been a thrilling experience for the boy to see the young Queen who had so honoured his father and mother, and about whom he had heard so much. She was then twenty-eight, and her beauty and accomplishments made her one

---

[1] Nichols's *Progresses*, vol. i, p. 37.

[2] Sir John Hayward, *Annals of Queen Elizabeth* (Camden Soc., 1840), p. 37.

[3] Nichols's *Progresses*, vol. i, pp. 92–104. The Queen was at Castle Hedingham from August 14th to 18th.

of the most striking personalities in Europe at that time. The great procession of suitors had already started arriving—and going away empty-handed. In response to a request from her first Parliament that she should marry, she had graciously replied that she would consider it ; but she had added that as Queen she was already wedded to her country. She was never tired of saying that she gloried in being " mere English," a phrase which delighted the vast majority of her loyal subjects who were weary of a half foreign Queen and a totally foreign King-Consort. " Mere English " she was indeed—a Tudor on her father's side and a Boleyn on her mother's. With her youthful vivacity and freshness, with her love of all English outdoor sports, and with her quick wit and deep learning, she was, in 1561, the very embodiment of that wonderful spirit of nationalism, which, under her stimulus, was to break the power of Spain, and create that glorious wealth of literature that can never grow old or be forgotten.

We are not told what entertainments were provided for her Majesty ; but we may be certain that hunting and hawking figured largely in the outdoor programme, while in the evenings the guests were no doubt diverted with masques and stage plays. All this young Edward saw, and must have thought how wonderful it was.

But he was not destined to live much longer at Castle Hedingham ; for he left it in the following year, to find new friends and new surroundings in the stately Westminster home of his father's friend Sir William Cecil.

CHAPTER II

1562–1571

" Such virtues be in your honour, so haughty courage joined with great skill, such sufficiency in learning, so good nature and common sense, that in your honour is, I think, expressed the right pattern of a noble gentleman."

Thomas Underdoune to the Earl of Oxford, 1569.

" Your Honour hath continually, even from your tender years, bestowed your time and travail towards the attaining of learning : as also the University of Cambridge hath acknowledged in granting and giving unto you such commendation and praise thereof, as verily by right was due unto your excellent virtue and rare learning."

John Brooke, of Ashe, to the Earl of Oxford, 1577.

§ I. CECIL HOUSE

ON August 3rd, 1562, the sixteenth **Earl of Oxford** died at Castle Hedingham ; and on the—

31st day of August was buried in Essex the good Earl (of Oxford) with three Heralds of Arms, Master Garter, Master Lancaster, Master Richmond, with a standard and a great banner of arms, and eight banner rolls, crest, target, sword and coat armour, and a hearse with velvet and a pall of velvet, and a dozen of scutcheons, and with many mourners in black ; and a great moan (was) made for him.[1]

In his will, dated July 28th, 1562, after various legacies to his family, he leaves " ten pounds and one of my great horses " to " my very good Lord Sir Nicholas Bacon," and the same to " my trusty and loving friend Sir William Cecil," and asks them to assist his executors. It seems not unlikely that when the Queen was entertained at Castle Hedingham in the previous year the question of young Edward's future as a Royal Ward in Sir William Cecil's

[1] *Machyn's Diary* (ed. Nichols, Camden Soc., 1848).

household, in the event of his father's death, had been
discussed.　Cecil had just been appointed Master of the
Wards, and Machyn in his *Diary* tells us that :

> On the 3rd day of September came riding out of Essex
> from the funeral of the Earl of Oxford his father, the
> young Earl of Oxford, with seven score horse all in black ;
> through London and Chepe and Ludgate, and so to Temple
> Bar . . . between 5 and 6 of the afternoon.

And for the next eight and a half years we shall find him
in Cecil House in the Strand.　It is perhaps worth mentioning that this ride up to London was very likely made in
the company of George Gascoigne, the poet, who was
connected with Lord Oxford by marriage.　We shall
come across these two—Gascoigne and the young Earl—
many times in the course of the next fifteen years ; and
it may perhaps have been from Gascoigne that Oxford
first received the poetic and dramatic impulse in this
very year.[1]
Cecil House stood on the north side of the Strand
almost opposite the site of the present Hotel Cecil, and
half a mile or so outside the City walls.[2]　In those days the
river was the main traffic highway, and most of the great
houses situated along its north bank had private water-
gates and stairs at which to embark and land.　Here the
public " watermen " in their boats plied for hire exactly
as taxis do in the London streets to-day.　Cecil House,
however, had no outlet on to the river ; but it was situated
only a few hundred yards from the public wharf at the
bottom of Ivy Lane.
Let us pause for a moment and picture the dwelling
in which Lord Oxford was destined to spend the remainder
of his minority.

[1] This argument will be found set out at length in my introduction to
the 1926 edition of *A Hundreth Sundrie Flowres*.

[2] It is interesting to see how this corner of London from Whitehall to
the Temple, then a separate town called Westminster and quite distinct
from the City, is a reflection of the sixteenth century.　The Cecil Hotel,
Somerset House, Surrey Street, Norfolk Street, Arundel Street, and Essex
Street are all named after the houses of the Tudor nobility.

Cecil House sometime belonged to the parson of St. Martin's-in-the-Fields, and by composition came to Sir Thomas Palmer, knight, in the reign of Edward VI., who began to build the same of brick and timber, very large and spacious ; but of later time it hath been far more beautifully increased by the late Sir William Cecil, baron of Burghley. . . . Standing on the north side of the Strand, a very fair house raised with bricks, proportionably adorned with four turrets placed at the four quarters of the house ; within it is curiously beautified with rare devices, and especially the Oratory, placed in an angle of the great chamber.[1]

One of the chief features of Cecil House was its garden. The grounds in which the house stood must have covered many acres, and were more extensive than those of any of the other private houses in Westminster. John Gerard, well known as the author of *Herbal, or General History of Plants* (1597), was for twenty years Sir William Cecil's gardener [2] ; and Sir William himself evidently took a great pride in his garden, because he had his picture painted riding in it on his " little Mule." [3] Indeed, it is not unlikely that he deliberately chose an inland site without a water-gate because the congestion of existing houses along the river bank only allowed of comparatively small and narrow strips of garden.

Although no description of the garden at Cecil House has come down to us, there exists a contemporary account by the German traveller, Paul Hentzner, of the grounds at Theobalds, Cecil's country seat. The garden here was also laid out by John Gerard, and was, no doubt, similar in many respects to that at Cecil House.

We left London in a coach—writes Hentzner—in order to see the remarkable places in its neighbourhood. The first was Theobalds, belonging to Lord Burghley, the Treasurer. In the Gallery was painted the genealogy of

[1] Wheatley, *London Past and Present* (1891). Quoting from Stow and Norden.

[2] *The Shakespeare Garden*, Esther Singleton, p. 33.

[3] Now in the Bodleian Library.

the Kings of England. From this place one goes into the garden, encompassed with a moat full of water, large enough for one to have the pleasure of going in a boat and rowing between the shrubs. Here are great variety of trees and plants, labyrinths made with a great deal of labour, a *jet d'eau* with its basin of white marble and columns and pyramids of wood and other materials up and down the garden. After seeing these we were led by the gardener into the summer-house, in the lower part of which, built semi-circularly, are the twelve Roman Emperors in white marble and a table of touch-stone. The upper part of it is set round with cisterns of lead, into which the water is conveyed through pipes so that fish may be kept in them, and in summer time they are very convenient for bathing. In another room for entertainment near this, and joined to it by a little bridge, was an oval table of red marble.[1]

Cecil imbued his sons and the Royal Wards under his charge with his own keenness in horticulture. Sir Robert Cecil, who was afterwards created Earl of Salisbury,

placed his splendid garden at Hatfield under the care of John Tradescant, the first of a noted family of horticulturalists. John Tradescant also had a garden of his own in South Lambeth, " the finest in England " every one called it.[2]

And Lord Zouch, who was a Royal Ward from 1569 to 1577, filled his garden at Hackney with plants he had collected while travelling in Austria, Italy, and Spain. No record has survived to tell us what Lord Oxford's gardens in London and Hackney were like, but we may conjecture that they bore the stamp of his nine years' wardship at Cecil House.

On July 14th, 1561, just a year before Lord Oxford's arrival in London, the Queen had honoured her Principal Secretary by supping at Cecil House " before it was fully finished " ; so that when the young Earl came to live there it must have been one of the most up-to-date mansions in

[1] Singleton, op. cit., p. 27. Hentzner's account was written in 1598.
[2] Singleton, op. cit., p. 35.

3

Westminster. Sir William, we are told, maintained a household of eighty persons " exclusive of those who attended him at Court," and his expenses were £30 a week in his absence, and between £40 and £50 when he was present. His stables cost 1,000 marks a year.[1]

The story of Queen Elizabeth's great minister, Cecil, is too well known to need more than a passing reference here. For forty years he was her constant and most trusted adviser. The vast collection of papers and letters preserved in the family seat at Hatfield bears eloquent testimony to his untiring diligence and sagacity. But the very success of his unique career has somewhat weakened our appreciation of the fierce struggle he went through to retain his Sovereign's confidence at the beginning of her reign. When Lord Oxford came to London in 1562 the Privy Council was sharply divided into two groups. On the one side were ranged most of the members of the old aristocracy who adhered to the traditional English foreign policy of friendship with Spain against the old enemy, France. Opposed to them stood two men only, Cecil and Bacon, who advocated an alliance with France, open war with Spain, and active support of the Reformed Church, both at home and on the Continent. That two self-made men, with nothing but their own abilities behind them, should have dared to oppose all the hereditary leaders of England is a sufficient proof of their courage and patriotism. Although the aristocracy had lost ground under the first four Tudors, the country folk still looked on the great families like the Howards, the Fitzalans, and the Stanleys as their natural leaders. And they, in turn, despised and detested the new men, who, borne on the

---

[1] Wheatley, op. cit. A mark was about 13s. 4d.; Cecil's stables, therefore, ran him up a bill of over £600 a year. It must be remembered, however, that as Principal Secretary he was one of the Queen's most responsible and confidential servants, which made it necessary for him to keep a stableful of horses and messengers ready at a moment's notice to take Her Majesty's despatches to all parts of the kingdom. So that part, at least, of the expenses of his stables and household would have been borne by the Exchequer.

crest of the wave of the Reformation, were now steadily working their way into the most confidential positions round the Queen.   The old families, moreover, were nearly all either openly or secretly Catholics.   This was not so much for reasons of conscience, but from the natural antipathy with which any ruling class regards a change.

Over these two warring factions presided the enigmatic figure of the Queen.   Still under thirty, she had inherited the immense personal power that her father had wrenched from the aristocracy and invested in the Crown.   It was impossible to say how she would shape her policy.   So far on one point only had she given a decision.   This was that in matters of religion England was to be neither Catholic nor Genevan, but, with herself as supreme head of the Church, toleration and moderation were to be the watchwords.   It has become the practice among many modern historians to decry Elizabeth, and attribute all her successes to her ministers, and all her failures to her own weakness and vacillation.   There can be no doubt that at times her capriciousness was the despair and exasperation of the Council ; but to assume that England's achievements during her reign were due to them and in spite of her, is to commit a grave injustice.   No commander-in-chief can win a battle without loyal and skilful subordinates ; but to transfer the honour of the victory from the leader to the lieutenants is to ignore the fact that it is on the commander alone that the responsibility of choosing, training, and issuing orders to his subordinates rests.   Moreover, he is a poor psychologist who can imagine a Tudor meekly taking orders from servants.   The daughter of " King Harry the Eighth of glorious memory " may have had her faults and weaknesses, but she was emphatically mistress of England, of her Government, and of her own mind and inclinations.

Lord Oxford's daily routine as a minor in Cecil House has been preserved for us in a document entitled " Orders for the Earl of Oxford's exercises."   In it we read that he is to " rise in such time as he may be ready to his exercises by 7 o'clock." The hours of work were :

7–7.30.	Dancing,
7.30–8.	Breakfast,
8–9.	French,
9–10.	Latin,
10–10.30.	Writing and Drawing.

Then Common Prayers, and so to dinner.

1–2	Cosmography,
2–3.	Latin,
3–4.	French,
4–4.30.	Exercises with his pen.

Then Common Prayers, and so to supper.[1]

On Holy Days this was modified, for we are told that he is to " read before dinner the Epistle and Gospel in his own tongue, and in the other tongue after dinner. All the rest of the day to be spent in riding, shooting, dancing, walking, and other commendable exercises, saving the time for Prayer."

His tutor at Cecil House was Lawrence Nowell, Dean of Lichfield, brother of the learned Alexander Nowell, Dean of St. Paul's. In June 1563 Lawrence Nowell wrote a Latin letter to Lord Burghley, drawing his attention to the slip-shod manner in which the cartographers and geographers of England were doing their work. " I have, moreover, noticed," he writes, " that those writers who have taken up the work of describing the geography of England have not been satisfactory to you in any way " ; the reason being " that without any art or judgment . . . they jumble up together haphazard in their maps imaginary sites of localities." He goes on to ask Lord Burghley that to him may be entrusted the task of compiling an accurate map because " I clearly see that my work for the Earl of Oxford cannot be much longer required." [2]

That a scholar of Lawrence Nowell's attainments should speak thus of his pupil, then aged 13½, argues a precocity

---

[1] S.P. Dom. Eliz., 26. 50.   [2] Lansdowne MSS., 6. 54.

quite out of the ordinary. This is further borne out by a letter dated August 23rd, 1563, written to Lord Burghley in French by Lord Oxford :

MONSIEUR TRÈS HONORABLE,
    Monsieur, j'ai reçu vos lettres plaines d'humanité et courtoisie, et fort resemblantes à votre grand amour et singulier affection envers moi, comme vrais enfants devement procrées d'une telle mère pour laquelle je me trouve de jour en jour plus tenu à v.h. vos bons admonestements pour l'observation du bon ordre selon vos appointements. Je me délibère (Dieu aidant) de garder en toute diligence comme chose que je cognois et considère tendre especialment à mon propre bien et profit, usant en celà l'advis et authorité de ceux qui sont auprès de moi, la discretion desquels j'estime si grande (s'il me convient parler quelquechose à leur avantage) qui non seulement ils se porteront selon qu'un tel temps le requiert, ains que plus est feront tant que je me gouverne selon que vous avez ordonné et commandé. Quant à l'ordre de mon étude pour ce qu'il requiert un long discours à l'expliquer par le menu, et le temps est court à cette heure, je vous prie affectueusement m'en excuser pour le présent, vous assurant que par le premier passant je le vous ferai savoir bien au long. Cependant je prie à Dieu vous donner santé.

EDWARD OXINFORD.[1]

In the spring of this year Lord Burghley and the other trustees of the late Earl of Oxford's will had written to the Dowager Countess, enquiring as to the reason for the delay in obtaining probate. To this she replied on April 30th:

I gathered generally that complaints had been brought to my Lord of Norfolk's grace and to my Lord Robert Dudley [who were supervisors of the will] by sundry, that the only let why my Lord's late will hath not been proved or exhibited hath been only in me and through my delays.

[1] Lansdowne MSS., 6. 25. For a facsimile reproduction see *A Hundreth Sundrie Flowres* (1926), opp. p. xxxiv.

She then goes on to excuse herself :

I confess that a great trust hath been committed to me of those things which, in my Lord's lifetime, were kept most secret from me.   And since that time the doubtful declaration of my Lord's debts hath so uncertainly fallen out that . . . I had rather leave up the whole doings thereof to my son (if by your good advice I may so deal honourably) than to venture further, and uncertainly altogether, with the will. . . . And what my further determination is touching the will, yet loth to determine without your good advice, for that I mean the honour or gain (if any be) might come wholly to my son, who is under your charge.[1]

This mention of " my son, who is under your charge," without any message of love or affection, seems to indicate that the widowed Countess handed him over to Cecil as a Royal Ward without a pang ; and her anxiety to be cleared of all responsibility in her late husband's affairs can be explained by her marriage shortly after his death to Charles Tyrrell, one of the Queen's Gentlemen Pensioners.   The allusion to the late Earl's legacy of debts, and the significant hint contained in the words " the honour or gain *if any be*," should be remembered when we deal with Lord Oxford's financial embarrassments, which began from the day he took over his patrimony on coming of age.

§ II.   CAMBRIDGE, OXFORD, AND GRAY'S INN

Lawrence Nowell's statement, already quoted, that Lord Oxford would soon be ripe for new tutors was no exaggeration ; for a year later we find him receiving his degree at Cambridge University, at the early age of $14\frac{1}{2}$ years.   This event occurred on August 10th during the Queen's progress to the University.[2]

That he left his mark on the University as a student of considerable ability we have on the testimony of John Brooke, himself a graduate of Trinity College :

[1] Lansdowne MSS., 6. 20.   [2] Nichols's *Progresses*, vol. i, p. 180.

I understanding right well that your honour hath continually, even from your tender years, bestowed your time and travail towards the attaining of [learning], as also the University of Cambridge hath acknowledged in granting and giving unto you such commendation and praise thereof, as verily by right was due unto your excellent virtue and rare learning. Wherein verily Cambridge, the mother of learning and learned men, hath openly confessed : and in this her confessing made known unto all men, that your honour being learned and able to judge, as a safe harbour and defence of learning, and therefore one most fit to whose honourable patronage I might safely commit these my poor and simple labours.[1]

We read in Nichols's *Progresses* that the Earl of Oxford was lodged at St. John's College. It is natural that as a Royal Ward he should have studied there because his guardian, Sir William Cecil, had been at that College from 1535 to 1541.

In view of Lord Oxford's subsequent interest in the drama, it is worth recording that the first entertainment in honour of Her Majesty's visit was the acting of the *Aulularia* of Plautus in King's College Chapel.[2]

Earlier in the same year, while Lord Oxford was up at Cambridge, his uncle and erstwhile turor, Arthur Golding, dedicated to him *Th' Abridgement of the histories of Trogus Pompeius*, published in May :

It came to my remembrance [writes the translator of Ovid] that since it hath pleased Almighty God to take to his mercy your noble father (to whom I had long before vowed this my travail) there was not any who, either of duty might more justly claim the same, or for whose estate it seemed more requisite and necessary, or of whom I thought it should be more favourably accepted, than of your honour. For . . . it is not unknown to others, and I have had experience thereof myself, how earnest a desire your honour hath naturally graffed in you to read, peruse, and communicate with others as well the histories of ancient

---

[1] *The Staffe of Christian Faith* . . . by John Brooke of Ashe next Sandwiche . . . 1577. (B.M. 3901, b. 19.)

[2] Nichols's *Progresses*, vol. i. ; and *The Times*, March 11th, 1924.

times, and things done long ago, as also of the present
estate of things in our days, and that not without a certain
pregnancy of wit and ripeness of understanding. The
which do not only now rejoice the hearts of all such as
bear faithful affection to the honourable house of your
ancestors, but also stir up a great hope and expectation
of such wisdom and experience in you in times to come,
as is meet and beseeming for so noble a race.

He goes on to quote the examples of Epaminondas,
Prince of Thebes, and Arymba, King of Epirus, who
cultivated not only the martial arts of war, but also
excelled in learning and the arts of peace :

Let these and other examples encourage your tender
years . . . to proceed in learning and virtue . . . and yourself
thereby become equal to any of your predecessors in
advancing the honour of your noble house : whereof, as
your great forwardness giveth assured hope and expectation, so I most heartily beseech Almighty God to further,
augment, establish and confirmate the same in your
Lordship with the abundance of his grace.
                    Your Lordship's humble Servant,
                              ARTHUR GOLDYNG.

It is interesting to learn from his own uncle that Lord
Oxford took especial delight in history, both past and
present. It may therefore help us better to understand
his character if we consider for a moment the events which
were then taking place in Europe.

In England, after the quiet transition from Catholicism
had been effected, the great question of the moment was
that of the Royal succession. Unless the Queen were to
have a direct descendant of her own, it seemed as if at
her death the horrors of civil war must start afresh.
We find, for example, on January 12th, 1563, Parliament
presenting a petition to the Queen begging her to marry.
It was one of many such appeals.

We are, perhaps, inclined to forget that the Englishman
of the fifteen-sixties was not gifted with prophetic vision.
He could hardly in his most optimistic moments imagine

that his frail Queen, who was continually falling sick, would outlast the century. To him the prominent and fascinating Mary Stuart, the Countess of Lennox, and the heads of the great houses of Hastings, Seymour, and Stanley, were centres round whom the future Wars of the Roses would be fought. This was the burning question of the hour ; and it was not till the next decade, when the Catholic plots began to be discovered, that the religious controversy superseded in importance that of the succession.

In France, the first War of Religion had come to an end by the Peace of Amboise in March 1563. By the murder of the Duc de Guise in the previous month, Catherine de Medici had become the mistress of the Catholic Party. Against her stood Admiral Coligny, the Huguenot leader. The stage was now set for the miserable tragedy of an endless succession of civil wars and hollow truces, only to culminate in that veritable holocaust on St. Bartholomew's Day in Paris in 1572.

In Scotland equally important events were taking place. In 1561, on the death of her husband, Francis II., King of France, Mary Stuart returned to Scotland to take up her queenly heritage. During the next two years, in spite of her determination to reintroduce Catholicism, she gradually won favour with the nobility and the people ; and in 1563 she sent Maitland to London to claim her right of succession after Queen Elizabeth. Elizabeth's reply was to propose the Earl of Leicester as her husband. Mary pretended to interest herself in the proposal, but in 1565 she married the Earl of Darnley. Two years later he was murdered, and Mary married the Earl of Bothwell, thus losing at a blow all the popularity she had so laboriously built up. The following year, 1568, defeated and deserted, she took refuge in England, where she remained a prisoner until her execution in 1587.

In Central Europe the dominating feature was the struggle of the Empire against the ever-increasing encroachments of the Turks. Year by year the Crescent was steadily pushing the Cross westwards ; but eight years later, in 1571, the position was materially eased by the complete defeat of the Turkish navy by Don John of Austria at Lepanto.

Most ominous of all to England, however, was the gradual shaping of Spain's policy under her vigorous King, Philip II. Almost alone of all the European kings and princes, Philip saw his objectives clearly. These were the counter Reformation, and the development of the Spanish Empire in the New World. We shall see, as the years unfold, how the attention of England was riveted more and more on to Spain. For the moment the Spanish threat had hardly begun to make itself felt. The first move took place in 1567, when Philip sent the Duke of Alva to the Netherlands with definite orders to re-establish the Roman Church. How this led, step by step, to the defeat of the Armada in 1588, and finally to the Peace in 1604, must be told as the story unfolds.

Such was the state of Europe as Lord Oxford saw it as he studied history at St John's College in his fifteenth year.

During the next eighteen months nothing definite is known as to his movements beyond the fact that in 1565 he and his fellow Royal ward and cousin, the Earl of Rutland,[1] acted as pages at the wedding of Ambrose Dudley, Earl of Warwick, and Lady Anne Russell, eldest daughter of the Earl of Bedford:

For the honour and celebration of this noble marriage [writes Holinshed] a goodly challenge was made and observed at Westminster ; at the tilt, each one six courses : at the tournay, twelve strokes with the sword and three pushes with the puncheon staff : and twelve blows with the sword at barriers, or twenty if any were so disposed.

[1] Edward Manners, 3rd Earl of Rutland (1549–87), came as a Royal Ward to Cecil House on the death of his father in 1563. He had a distinguished legal career, and would have succeeded Sir Thomas Bromley as Lord Chancellor but for his sudden death six days after Bromley's. Camden describes him as " a profound lawyer and a man accomplished with all polite learning," which is in itself a tribute to the excellent education Lord Burghley provided for the Wards under his charge.

No doubt he spent this year partly at Cecil House in London and partly at Oxford University; for in 1566 we find him in the train of Her Majesty during her progress to this University. It was here, on September 6th, in company with other "nobles and persons of quality," that he was created Master of Arts in a convocation held in the public refectory of Christ Church College, in the presence of Robert, Earl of Leicester, Chancellor of the University.[1]

His university studies completed, the law next claimed his attention; and in a list of members admitted to Gray's Inn in 1567 we find the names of Lord Oxford, Philip Sidney, and John Manners, a younger brother of the Earl of Rutland.[2] This brought him into touch once more with George Gascoigne, who in addition to studying for the bar was occupying his leisure time with the drama. Two of his plays were acted about this time by the Gentlemen of the Inn : *The Supposes*, a translation from the Italian of Ariosto, which was the first prose play represented in English, and afforded the foundation for part of *The Taming of the Shrew* ; and *Jocasta*, from the *Phœnissœ* of Euripides, in which Gascoigne collaborated with two other fellow students, Francis Kinwelmersh and Christopher Yelverton. This was the first adaptation of a Greek play to the English stage.[3] The exact date of these performances is not known ; but Fleay conjectures that the expression " St. Nicholas' feast " (*Supposes*, Act I., Scene 2,) points to a Christmas performance.[4] If this be so, the plays were acted only about five weeks before Lord Oxford's admission to Gray's Inn. It is probable that he actually saw the performances ; but, at any rate, he would certainly have heard all about them from his old friend the author.

[1] Nichols, *Progresses*, vol. i, p. 215 ; Anthony Wood, *Fasti Oxonienses*, vol. iii, col. 178.

[2] Harleian MSS., 1912. Lord Oxford's admission is dated Feb. 1st, 1566–7.

[3] Cf. Fleay, *Chronicle History of the London Stage*, p. 65.

[4] *Chronicle of the English Drama*, vol. ii, p. 238.

To Gray's Inn Burghley introduced his two sons, Thomas and Robert, founders of the noble houses of Exeter and Salisbury ; his sons-in-law, Lord Wentworth and Edward de Vere, Earl of Oxford [1] ; while Nicholas Bacon brought his five sons, all of whom had distinguished careers before them, and one, the youngest of the family, was destined to be the most famous man of his time. Around this family circle Burghley grouped within the walls of Gray's Inn the most brilliant young men of that day, every one of whom played some part, small or great, in that age of adventures which so often ended in tragedies. Two of them lost their lives by being involved in the cause of Mary, Queen of Scots—Thomas Howard, fourth Duke of Norfolk, and Henry Percy, eighth Earl of Northumberland. More fortunate was the lot of Sir Philip Sidney, who came to the Inn with a double tie, for he was the son of Sir Henry Sidney, and the son-in-law of Sir Francis Walsingham. After him came Henry Wriothesley, third Earl of Southampton, Roger Manners, Earl of Rutland, and William Herbert, Earl of Pembroke. These names brought the Inn into touch with Shakespeare, who borrowed hints from Sidney's *Arcadia*, and is believed to have taken Southampton, Rutland, and Pembroke as the models whom he reproduced under the names of Bassanio, Gratiano, Romeo, Benedict, Florizel, and Valentine.[2]

" About this time," writes Burghley in his Diary, under date July 1567, " Thomas Brincknell, an under-cook, was hurt by the Earl of Oxford at Cecil House in the Strand, whereof he died ; and by a verdict found *felo-de-se* with running upon a point of a fence sword of the said Earl's." [3]

§ III. Thomas Churchyard

When Charles the Fifth, Holy Roman Emperor, old and broken in health, surrendered the sovereignty of the

[1] Actually at the time Lord Oxford was Burghley's Ward, not son-in-law, because he did not marry Anne Cecil till 1571.

[2] *Lectures on Gray's Inn*, by Sir D. Plunket Barton, late Judge of the High Court of Justice, Ireland, and Treasurer and Resident Bencher of Gray's Inn, 1922. Reported in *The Times*, May 26th, 1925.

[3] Murdin, *State Papers*, p. 764.

Spanish Netherlands to his son Prince Philip at Brussels in 1555, it is said that tears sprang to the eyes of the Dutch nobles and deputies as they listened to their beloved sovereign reading his abdication. While he was speaking he rested his arm affectionately on the shoulder of a young man of twenty-two. The name of this young man was William of Nassau, afterwards Prince of Orange. A dozen years later these two Princes, to whom the care and government of the country had been entrusted, were mortal enemies. . . .

It was in 1567 that Philip, now King of Spain, determined to stamp out heresy in his Dutch dominions. He committed this task to the foremost Spanish soldier, the Duke of Alva ; but before Alva reached Brussels the Prince of Orange had withdrawn to one of his German estates at Dillenburg near Cologne. He was outlawed and his Dutch estates confiscated ; to which he replied by raising troops in Germany and attacking Alva. The long struggle against Spanish tyranny, to which he was to devote the rest of his life, had begun.

These events were watched with the keenest interest at Cecil House, the headquarters in England of the " Common Cause " of Protestantism against the Roman Church ; and it was no doubt with the object of securing first-hand information of the doings of the Prince of Orange that we find Thomas Churchyard, then in the Earl of Oxford's employ, being sent to Dillenburg by his master's orders.[1] We do not know when Churchyard first became attached to Lord Oxford's household. He was now nearly fifty, having started life as a page in the service of Henry Howard, Earl of Surrey, Oxford's uncle by marriage. After Surrey's execution he led an adventurous life as a soldier of fortune in Scotland, Ireland, and France until 1564. He returned from his mission to Dillenburg after a few months' absence, when a breach

[1] Churchyard, *A True Discourse Historical*, 1602, p. 10. As Oxford was only seventeen years old, it is probable that Cecil was the real instigator of Churchyard's mission, though he would not be unwilling that the expense should be borne by his Ward.

occurred between him and the young Earl.[1] In 1570 he
was employed by Cecil to report on the movements of
Catholic recusants at Bath.[2] His pen was busy on a
wide range of subjects for the next twenty years, and he
was patronised by many courtiers, including Sir Christopher
Hatton. In 1590 we shall meet him once again in Lord
Oxford's employ.

On December 2nd, 1568, " Margaret, widow of John,
16th Earl, wife of Charles Tyrrell, Esq., and mother of the
17th Earl," died and was buried at Earl's Colne.[3] Her
husband did not long survive her, for he died in the spring
of 1570. Although in his will [4] he bequeaths " unto the
Earl of Oxford one great horse that his lordship gave
me," the fact remains that never in after-years did Lord
Oxford mention his stepfather other than contemptuously.
Tyrrell seems to have been an insignificant character, and
he took no part, great or small, in the life and activities
of the Court. It is safe to assume that his mother's second
marriage offended her son, who saw in it perhaps a slight,
not only to the memory of his father, but also to the great
de Vere lineage, to which he was so proud to belong.

In 1569, just before the Rebellion in the North, Thomas
Underdoune [5] dedicated " To the Right Honourable
Edward de Vere, Lord Bulbeck, Earl of Oxenford, Lord
Great Chamberlain of England," his translation of *An
Æthiopian History*, from the Greek of Heliodorus :

I do not deny [he writes] but that in many matters,
I mean matters of learning, a nobleman ought to have a
sight ; but to be too much addicted that way, I think it
is not good. Now of all knowledge fit for a noble gentleman, I suppose the knowledge of histories is most seeming.
For furthering whereof I have Englished a passing fine and
witty history, written in Greek by Heliodorus ; and for

[1] Churchyard, *A General Rehearsal of all Wars*, 1579.
[2] Lansdowne MSS., 11. 56.
[3] *History of Essex*, Morant, vol. ii.
[4] P.C.C. 15, Lyon.
[5] Thomas Underdoune was a poet and translator ; he published *The
excellent history of Theseus and Ariadne*, 1566 ; Heliodorus' *Æthiopian
History*, 1569 ; and *Ovid Against Ibis*, with an appendix of legends, 1569.

right good cause consecrated the same to your honourable
Lordship. For such virtues be in your honour, so haughty
courage joined with great skill, such sufficiency in learning,
so good nature and common sense that in your honour is,
I think, expressed the right pattern of a noble gentleman.
. . . Therefore I beseech your honour favourably to
accept this my small travail in translating Heliodorus,
which I have so well translated as he is worthy, I am persuaded that your honour will well like of. . . . [1]

Lord Oxford was now nineteen ; and it is clear from
Underdoune's outspoken caution against noblemen becoming too addicted to learning, that the young Earl's interests
were becoming more and more centred in books and study.
This is just what we should expect from the report of his
doings at the two Universities ; and ten years later we
shall find him being reproved for the same tendency by
his old friend Gabriel Harvey, the Cambridge scholar and
writer.

§ IV. Two old Account Books

An interesting side light on the customs of the time is
to be found in a document endorsed in Lord Burghley's
own handwriting, " A summary of the charges of the
apparel of the Earl of Oxford, 1566." It is in reality Lord
Oxford's tailor's bills for the first four years of his wardship. The total amount—over six hundred pounds—is
most remarkable. In later years we shall find Lord
Burghley continually upbraiding Lord Oxford for his
extravagance. When he does so, it will be well for us
to remember these bills—vouched for by Burghley himself—which were incurred by Oxford when he was between
the ages of twelve and sixteen. As Lord Burghley allowed
his ward to spend about £1,000 a year, expressed in terms
of modern money, on his clothes, it is hardly reasonable
for him to complain that when he grew up he had developed
extravagant habits. The document runs as follows:

[1] " The first edition of Underdoune's translation is undated . . . (but)
it is conjectured to be the end of the 10th Book of Heliodorus' *Æthiopian
History*, which Francis Caldecke obtained a licence to print in 1569."
(*The Abbey Classics*, vol. xxiii.)

For the apparel, with Rapiers and Daggers, for my Lord of Oxenford, his person, viz :

1562 and 63—In the first year and twenty-six odd days, beginning the 3rd of September, and ending the 28th of September, Anno Reginae Elizabeth 5th	154	5	6
1563 and 64—Item, in the second year, beginning on the 29th of September, Anno 5th, and ending 30th of September, Anno 6th	106	15	11
1564 and 5—Also in the third year beginning the last of October, Anno 6th, ending the 29th of September, Anno 7th . .	191	10	8
1565 and 6—More for the 5th year beginning the 30th Day of September, Anno 7th, and ending the 28th Sept. Anno 8th .	175	12	1
1566—Sum of these 4 years . . . . [1]£627	15	0	

Before we leave Cecil House and follow Lord Oxford to the wars, let us linger for a moment over another old account book where various sums of money paid on behalf of the Royal Wards were recorded. It is headed " Payments made by John Hart, Chester Herald, on behalf of the Earl of Oxford from January 1st to September 30th, 1569/70." [2] The following extract is from the first quarter's account :

To John Spark, draper, for fine black [cloth] for a cape and a riding cloak . . .	6	5	0
To Myles Spilsby, tailor, for one doublet of cambric, one of fine canvas, and one of black satin ; and the furniture of a riding cloak	12	13	0
To John Martin, hosier, for one pair of velvet hose black	10	9	2
To Philip Eunter, upholsterer, for one fine wool bed bolster, and pillows of down .	2	7	0
To Brown, my Lord's servant, for ten pairs of Spanish leather shoes, and three pairs of Moyles	1	5	0
To John Maria, cutler, for a rapier, dagger and girdle	1	6	8

[1] S.P. Dom. Eliz., 42. 38.   [2] S.P. Dom. Add., 19. 38.

To William Seres, stationer, for a Geneva
  Bible gilt, a Chaucer, Plutarch's works in
  French, with other books and papers   .   2   7 10
To George Hill, saddler, for collars and girths
  for my Lord's horse   5   0
To Riche, the apothecary, for potions, pills
  and other drugs, for my Lord's diet in
  time of his sickness 15 15   4
To William Bishop, for wood and coals for
  victuals for my Lord and his men in the
  time of his said diet, for a comocase furnished, for two Italian books, for house
  rent, for the hire of a hothouse, for horse
  hire, boat hire, carriages and other .   .   30 16   0
To Chester Herald, for six sheets of fine holland, six handkerchiefs and six others of
  cambric, and for four yards of velvet, and
  four others of satin, for to guard and border a Spanish cape 15 10   8
More to him for certain other articles for my
  Lord, during his being sick at Windsor,
  for rewards to his physician, and others,
  for servants' wages . . . and for the
  charges of keeping in the stable and
  shoeing of four geldings for my Lord's
  service   36   5   4
And for the board and diet of my Lord with
  his tutors and servants at Cecil House for
  14 days of this quarter at £3 a week   .   6   0   0
  Summa Totalis 145 17   4

In the next quarter we find an item :

To William Tavy, capper, for one velvet hat,
  and one taffeta hat ; two velvet caps, a
  scarf, two pairs of garters with silver at
  the ends, a plume of feathers for a hat,
  and another hat band £4   6   0

In the third quarter his library is further augmented,
because a payment is made :

To William Seres, stationer, for Tully's and
  Plato's works in folio, with other books,
  paper and nibs £4   6   4
4

From his portraits and these two quaint old account
books we can picture very vividly the nineteen-year-old
Earl of Oxford when he lived at Cecil House in the Strand
in the year 1569. Rather below medium height, he was
sturdy with brown curly hair and hazel eyes. On his
head a velvet cap with a plume of pheasants' feathers
fastened on one side. A black satin doublet, velvet
breeches, and silk stockings supported by silver buckled
garters. On his feet the broad-toed, flat-footed, soft
leather shoes of the period. At his side a light rapier,
passed through a silver-studded belt. Thus clad he
would be taken by his guardian down to the river stairs
at the bottom of Ivy Lane. The liveried watermen would
be ready waiting at the steps with the canopied barge.
And so they would go upstream, perhaps, to the Palace at
Richmond, where the Queen had sent for "her Turk,"
as she playfully called Lord Oxford, to dance with her,
or to play on the virginals.

On another morning perhaps he would order one of
his "four geldings," and having discarded the Court
silks and satins for the more serviceable cloths and cam-
brics, he would ride out from Cecil House westward along
the Strand past St. Martin's Church, with a hawk on his
wrist. Here he would canter along the soft turf at the side
of the narrow country lane till he came to the little village
of Kensington. An hour's hawking, with its wild gallops
over fields and through woods ; and so back to London
with the bag of partridges and herons tied to his saddle.

And then in the evening, tired with the day's chase,
we may picture him in his library surrounded by the books
he loved so well. His uncle, Arthur Golding, had no
doubt introduced him to Plato, to Cicero, to his own
translation of Ovid, and to the Geneva Bible, for Golding
had strong Calvinistic leanings. But we may be sure that
his active mind was more attracted by the wealth of
Renaissance literature that was then beginning to flood
England. In later years Lord Oxford spent many months
travelling in Italy ; and his enthusiasm for that country

originated no doubt from the Italian books he had read,
perhaps surreptitiously, while he was a Royal Ward.

§ V. The Rising in the North

Although, as we have seen, the transition from Catholicism to Protestantism had been carried out in 1559 almost
without incident, the position by 1569 had materially
altered. At the Court, the Feudal aristocracy whose
sympathies were mainly Catholic, led by the Duke of
Norfolk and the Earl of Arundel, was numerically far
stronger than the Protestants under the leadership of
Sir William Cecil. In the country, and particularly in the
north, Catholicism was daily growing in strength. Moreover, the King of Spain's policy in the Netherlands,
coupled with the Scottish Queen's flight into England
the previous year, had led the Catholics to believe that
the moment had come to strike a blow.

Elizabeth and Cecil, however, were not caught napping.
In March 1569 Mary had been removed from the north
to Tutbury, where she was placed under the charge of
George Talbot, sixth Earl of Shrewsbury. In May a
commission was sent to the Sheriffs of Counties to prepare
" muster rolls " of all able-bodied men fit to bear arms,[1]
and the loyal Earl of Sussex, one of the ablest soldiers in
the country, was appointed Lord-Lieutenant of the North.
On October 25th Mary was again removed secretly by night
from Tutbury to Coventry, so that she should be well
out of the reach of any insurgents from the north. While
these preparations were being carried out, the Catholic
leaders were engaging in secret intrigues. Their design
was to seize the Queen of Scots, marry her to the Duke
of Norfolk, and place her on the English throne. The
Earls of Northumberland and Westmorland were to raise
the revolt in the north, Lord Derby was to join them from
the north-west, the Duke of Norfolk from the east, and
it was confidently hoped that Southampton and Montague

---

[1] S.P. Dom. Eliz., 49. 71.

would also assist. Unfortunately for them their leader, the
Duke, was a poor conspirator. He was more than once
on the verge of launching the enterprise when he drew back
in fear. Thus the summer wore on, and opportunity after
opportunity slipped through the grasp of the Catholics.

Early in November the Earls of Northumberland and
Westmorland, tired of waiting for the Duke, raised the
standard of revolt on their own account. Gathering
round them about four thousand of their retainers, they
celebrated a solemn Mass in Durham Cathedral and
marched south towards Tutbury. For a time the position
was serious. Sussex, too weak in cavalry to meet them
in the field, was obliged to remain behind the walls of
York. The ill-concerted rebellion, however, collapsed
as dramatically as it had begun. The followers of the
two Earls, seeing that the midlands were not going to
rise, melted away ; and Northumberland and Westmorland, deserted by all but a handful of men, fled across the
Border, pursued by the Lord-Lieutenant.

Meantime the Queen and Cecil had not been idle.
Directly news reached London that the revolt had begun,
the machinery prepared in May was set in motion. Three
thousand horse and twelve thousand foot, all from the
more dependable and populous southern counties, were
called up and mobilised. They were placed under the
orders of Charles Howard and Edward Horsey respectively,[1]
and divided into two columns which were gradually con-
centrated at Leicester and Lincoln, under arrangements
made by the Earl of Warwick and Lord Clinton,[2] who

[1] S.P. Dom. Eliz., 59. 68. Charles Howard (1536–1624) was the eldest
son of William, Lord Howard of Effingham, who was at this time Lord
Chamberlain. He was a brilliant soldier, sailor and statesman, his greatest
achievement being the defeat of the Spanish Armada in 1588. Edward
Horsey (d. 1583) was at this time Captain of the Isle of Wight, where many
of the levies were raised. He was knighted in 1577.

[2] Ambrose Dudley, Earl of Warwick, was the elder brother of the
famous Robert, Earl of Leicester. He had seen service in France against
the Catholics, and was at this time about forty years of age. Edward
Fiennes, Lord Clinton, was a man of nearly fifty, and one of Elizabeth's
most trusted warriors. He had been appointed Lord Admiral on her
accession. He was created Earl of Lincoln in 1572.

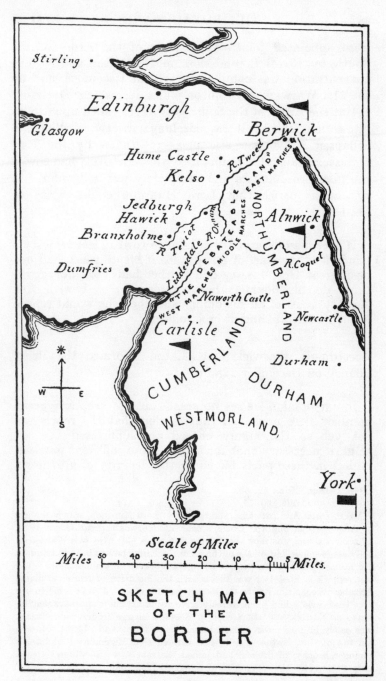

Stirling ·

Edinburgh

Glasgow

Berwick

Hume Castle ·
R. Tweed
Kelso ·

Jedburgh
Hawick ·
Branxholme ·
R. Teviot
R. Liddesdale
R. Esk
THE DEBATEABLE LAND
EAST MARCHES
NORTHUMBERLAND

Alnwick

Dumfries ·
WEST MARCHES
MIDDLE MARCHES
R. Coquet

Naworth Castle
Newcastle

Carlisle

CUMBERLAND

Durham ·

DURHAM

WESTMORLAND

York ·

Scale of Miles

Miles 50 40 30 20 10 0 5 Miles.

SKETCH MAP
OF THE
BORDER

37

were appointed joint commanders of the Army of the South by Royal Commission on November 29th.[1] The concentration was completed early in December, and on the 21st Warwick and Clinton joined forces near Durham.[2]

But the Army of the South was never called upon to go into action, for while it was marching north the rebellion had collapsed. The energetic measures taken by the Earl of Sussex against the remnants of the rebel army had cowed the northern counties and completely restored order. It was with justice that Lord Hunsdon could write to Cecil:

If ever man deserved thanks or reward at Her Majesty's hands it is the Earl of Sussex, for if his diligence had not been great Her Majesty had neither had York nor York-shire at this hour at her command. . . . I wish Her Majesty knew of all his doings and then she would repose in such a faithful and discreet officer. [3]

Accordingly Warwick and Clinton informed the Privy Council on December 22nd:

In our opinion we see no great cause to keep any great numbers here now . . . [but] seeing that the rebels are not yet so thoroughly chased nor suppressed . . . we think it necessary that for a time some sufficient garrison be left in these parts for the better security of all things,

[1] S.P. Dom. Eliz., 59. 53.
[2] S.P. Dom. Eliz., 60. 34.
[3] S.P. Dom. Add., 15. 49. Henry Carey, Lord Hunsdon, was a nephew of Anne Boleyn and the Queen's cousin. He was a great favourite of Elizabeth's, and was now about forty-five years old. He was Warden of the East Marches, but on the outbreak of the Rising he had been in London. He hurried back to his post, arriving at York on November 24th. The last remark in his letter was made with the intention of trying to dispel Elizabeth's suspicions as to the integrity of his chief. It had come to her ears that Sussex had been secretly advocating the marriage between the Duke of Norfolk and the Queen of Scots, a charge from which Sussex was easily able to clear himself later. (S.P. Dom. Add., 17. 94, 95, 96.) On top of this, however, news had arrived that Egremont Radcliffe, a younger brother of Sussex, had joined the rebels, a fact which did not help to decrease the difficulties of the Lord-Lieutenant.

which we refer to your Lordships' better order and judge-
ment.[1]

Elizabeth was nothing loth to save the heavy charges
of maintaining an army in the field, and orders were issued
for its discharge. At the same time it was left to the
discretion of the commanders on the spot to retain any
men who might be required for garrison duty. By
December 30th over half the army had been disbanded, and
Warwick and Clinton were able to inform the Privy
Council :

Whereas once the Lord of Sussex required of us certain
companies of Shot [2] to be bestowed in sundry places, afterwards, upon intelligence of the Earl of Northumberland's
taking, and the dispersing of all the rest, he wrote unto
us that it should be unneedful to leave any garrison at all ;
whereupon we resolved to discharge our whole force, except
four or five hundred Shot to attend upon us till we be
going hence.[3]

By the middle of January, their commissions ended and
their men disbanded, Warwick and Clinton returned to
their homes.

While these events were in progress Lord Oxford had
been sick, for on November 24th he writes thus to Cecil :

Sir, Although my hap hath been so hard that it hath
visited me of late with sickness, yet, thanks be to God . . .
I find my health restored, and I find myself doubly beholden
unto you both for that and many good turns which, I have
received before of your part. . . . I am bold to desire
your favour and friendship that you will suffer me to be
employed, by your means and help, in this service that is
now in hand.

He goes on to remind his guardian that it has always been
his wish to see " the wars and services in strange and

---

[1] S.P. Dom. Eliz., 60. 45. Froude, always anxious to belittle Elizabeth,
has asserted that she ordered the disbanding of the Army of the South
against the advice of Warwick and Clinton, a statement that is completely
at variance with the facts.

[2] I.e., arquebusiers.

[3] S.P. Dom. Eliz., 60. 61.

foreign parts," and asks him to " do me so much honour
as that, by your purchase of my licence, I may be called
to the service of my Prince and country, as, at this present
troublous time, a number are." [1]

His request was not granted immediately ; but on
March 30th, 1570, Cecil wrote to Sir William Dansell, the
Receiver-General of the Court of Wards and Liveries :

" . . . As the Queen's Majesty sendeth at this present
the Earl of Oxford into the north parts to remain with my
Lord of Sussex, and to be employed there in Her Majesty's
service ; these are to require you to deliver unto the said
Earl . . . the sum of £40. . . ." [2]

As Lord Oxford took part in Sussex's campaign in
Scotland in April and May, some account of it will be of
interest here.

When the Army of the South had been disbanded Sussex
was left once more with the normal garrison to guard the
frontier. His headquarters were at York, and his forces
were organised into three commands : the East Marches
under Lord Hunsdon at Berwick, the Middle Marches
under Sir John Forster at Alnwick, and the West Marches
under Lord Scrope at Carlisle.[3] The only remaining
storm centre on English territory was Naworth Castle
in Cumberland, the home of Leonard Dacre, the last male
representative of the great northern family of that name.[4]

---

[1] Lansdowne MSS., 11. 121.

[2] S.P. Dom. Add., 19. 37.

[3] Sir John Forster, then aged about fifty, was a veteran of the Border,
having fought at Solway Moss and Pinkie, and having been Warden
of the Middle Marches since 1560. Henry, Lord Scrope (1534–92) was
another experienced frontiersman, having been Warden of the West
Marches since 1562. His son and successor married Lord Hudson's
daughter, Philadelphia Carey.

[4] His nephew, George Lord Dacre, had died at the age of nine in May
1569. Camden says that Leonard " stomached it much that so goodly
an inheritance descended by law to his nieces, whom the Duke of Norfolk
their father-in-law had betrothed to his sons, and had commenced a suit
against his nieces : which, when it went not to his desire, he fell to
plotting and practising with the rebels." He died an exile in Flanders
in 1573.

For some time he had been a confederate of the Earls of Northumberland and Westmorland, who confidently expected his support when they launched their enterprise ; but instead of joining them he went to London and placed himself at the Queen's command. He was given a commission to raise men and oppose the rebels, which he undertook to do. There can be little doubt, however, that he was really acting treacherously and intended to use the men he raised to further the rising. Unfortunately for him, the rebellion had collapsed before he could return north ; and he therefore shut himself up in Naworth Castle, which he put in a state of defence.

The task of rounding him up was entrusted to Lord Hunsdon and Sir John Forster, and Sussex was sent for to London to make his report. Hunsdon arrived at the Castle at dawn on February 20th with 1,500 Horse and Foot. Dacre's force was drawn up outside, and Hunsdon's reconnaissance showed him that he was outnumbered by two to one. He accordingly decided to retire on Carlisle, about ten miles distant, and gather reinforcements from Lord Scrope ; but Dacre, seeing his advantage, followed and attacked. Hunsdon's account of the ensuing action is brief but graphic :

His footmen gave the proudest charge upon my Shot that ever I saw. Whereupon, having left Sir John Forster with five hundred horse for my back, I charged with the rest of my horsemen upon his footmen, and slew between three and four hundred, and have taken two or three hundred prisoners, such as they are. And Leonard Dacre being with his horsemen, was the first man that flew, like a tall gentleman, and, as I think, never looked behind him till he was in Liddlesdale ; and yet one of my company had him by the arm, and if he had not been rescued by certain Scots, whereof he had many, he had been taken.[1]

This brilliant little exploit overjoyed the Queen. " I doubt much, my Harry," she wrote, " whether that the

[1] S.P. Dom. Add., 17. 107.

victory which were given me more joyed me, or that you were by God appointed the instrument of my glory." [1]

By the middle of the next month it was becoming more and more apparent that the position across the Border was taking a turn for the worse. Since the assassination of the Regent in January [2] the supporters of Mary Queen of Scots had become bolder, and had made many daring raids into the northern counties, burning and destroying villages, and carrying off cattle. Their numbers had been increased by the English rebels, who, having fled across the Border and hearing of the severity with which their comrades had been treated, dared not return to their homes. Moreover, on March 2nd, Sir Thomas Gargrave, Sussex's second-in-command at York, had reported:

Lord Hume has forsaken religion and hears two or three Masses daily with Lady Northumberland; so being revolted and joined with Buccleugh and the Carrs, Lords Maxwell and Herries may join them, and with the assistance of the rebels, they will hurt the frontiers unless prevented. [3]

Sussex was still in London, and at a meeting of the Privy Council held there on March 14th, it was decided that the Border garrisons should be reinforced by 1,000 horse and 3,000 foot, with which Sussex should make an extensive raid into Scotland. There was ample justification for this action. It was an open secret that many of the Scottish lairds who dwelt near the Border had been harbouring the English fugitives, and had been the instigators of the raids into England. Sussex was therefore enjoined to proclaim that the invasion of Scotland was being undertaken with the double purpose of appre-

---

[1] S.P. Dom. Add., 17. 113.

[2] James Stuart, Earl of Moray, half-brother of Mary, Queen of Scots. He had been appointed Regent of Scotland in the name of Mary's infant son, James, in 1567. He was a Protestant and a staunch friend of Elizabeth's. He governed Scotland with a Council known as the " King's Lords," so called because their policy was to replace Mary on the throne by Prince James. Opposed to them were the " Queen's Lords," who supported the cause of the captive Mary Stuart.

[3] S.P. Dom. Add., 18. 2.

hending the fugitives and avenging the damage done in England.[1]

Ten days later Sussex was back at York, and Lord Hunsdon was disgusted to hear that Elizabeth was still harbouring suspicions about her Lord-Lieutenant :

I am sorry to see [he wrote bluntly to Cecil], my Lord-Lieutenant come down with no countenance ; for his lieutenancy, it is for her [the Queen's] service. I assure you it rather hinders her service than furthers it ; for I know the world looked for his being of the Privy Council at the least, which had been more beneficial to her service [than] any commodity to him. . . . God send her many so well able to serve her in all respects, whereof she surely hath small store.[2]

Sussex was too good a soldier to take offence at the mean way he had been treated in London, and at once set about the task before him. On April 5th he held a conference with his three Wardens at Newcastle, when the plan of campaign was decided on. On the 10th he wrote to Cecil to say that he trusts—

before the light of this moon be past to leave a memory in Scotland whereof they and their children shall be afraid to offer war to England.[3]

By the 17th the preliminary moves had been completed ; and that night the army crossed the Border simultaneously at three places.

The main column consisted of 700 horse and 1,700 foot, and was under the personal direction of Sussex himself, with Hunsdon as his lieutenant. They entered Scotland just east of Kelso, and marched up the valley of the Teviot—

burning on both hand at the least two mile, leaving neither Castle, town, nor tower unburnt till we came to Jedburgh.[4]

This district belonged to Buccleuch, one of Mary's adhe-

---

[1] Cal. S.P. Scot., pp. 95 and 115.   [2] S.P. Dom. Add., 18. 15.
[3] Cal. S.P. Scot., p. 110.
[4] Sharpe, *Memorials of the Rebellion*, p. 238.

rents ; and among other places they destroyed a " proper tower " of Buccleuch's called " Mose Howse."

We had that day only three small skirmishes . . . the Lord Hume and Leonard Dacre were in the field but durst not come near.[1]

Meanwhile, a second column under Sir John Forster, consisting of 200 horse and 800 foot, had crossed the Border at the source of the River Coquet. He moved down the valley of the Oxnam, burning and destroying as he went, and joined Sussex on the evening of the 18th at Jedburgh.

An early start was made the next morning on either bank of the Teviot towards Hawick. Sussex's column took the north side, and destroyed three castles belonging to three of the " Queen's Lords "—Ferniehurst, Huntly, and Bedroul. Sir John Forster followed the right bank and rejoined his chief that night at Hawick. As they approached the town the inhabitants, in order to forestall them, took the roofs off their houses and themselves set fire to the inflammable thatch, hoping by this means to save their town. Sussex, however, was in time to quench the flames, and by using the unconsumed thatch succeeded in burning the whole town with the exception of one house.

The following morning the foot-soldiers, who had marched over thirty miles in less than forty-eight hours, were rested ; while Sussex with a band of horsemen rode over to Branxholme, Buccleuch's principal mansion. Finding it also burnt before his arrival, he completed its destruction by blowing up the walls with gunpowder, and cutting down the fruit-trees in the orchard. That afternoon the whole army marched back to Jedburgh.[2]

Next day, the 21st, Sussex and Hunsdon returned to Kelso, where they spent the night. A few miles to the north was situated Hume Castle, the stronghold of Lord Hume, one of the most active supporters of the Queen of

---

[1] Sharpe, *Memorials of the Rebellion*, p. 238.
[2] Cal. S.P. Foreign, p. 228.

Scots. Sussex had intended to assault it on the 22nd, but owing to a miscarriage of orders the artillery had returned to Berwick. Sussex, however, profited by this mistake, which may indeed have been a deliberate ruse. He was particularly anxious to capture the many refugees that Hume was sheltering; but he knew that unless he could come upon them by surprise they would elude him by scattering in the country. Accordingly he sent Hume a message to say that although he had it in his power to take the castle, he would forbear to do so, in the hope that by this act of clemency Hume might be persuaded " to amend his fault." Having thus lulled the defenders of the castle into a sense of security, he made his way back ostentatiously to Berwick.[1]

The third column of 100 horse and 500 foot under Lord Scrope had passed into Scotland by way of Carlisle on the evening of the 17th. He marched to within a mile of Dumfries, burning and destroying the towns and villages on his way. Here he encountered the principal landowner, Lord Maxwell, at the head of a greatly superior force. A sharp skirmish ensued in which the English horse were roughly handled. The timely arrival of reinforcements in the shape of 150 shot, however, enabled him to extricate his cavalry. He saw it would be dangerous with his small numbers to linger on Scottish soil, and therefore returned to Carlisle on the 21st.[2]

On the morning of the 28th, Sussex, by means of a night march, appeared again suddenly outside Hume Castle with his siege train, and opened a bombardment. At one o'clock in the afternoon Lord Hume sent out a request for a parley. Sussex, whose powder was beginning to run short, consented to meet his envoy; and an agreement was arrived at by which the defenders were permitted to retire unmolested, provided they laid down their arms and left all their belongings in the castle. A garrison of 200 men was left there, pending Elizabeth's decision as to

[1] Cal. S.P. Scottish, p. 115.
[2] Ibid., p. 130.

its ultimate fate.[1]   Before returning to Berwick, another stronghold belonging to Lord Hume, Fast Castle, was captured and destroyed.

While these operations were in progress, the Earl of Lennox, who was on his way from London to Edinburgh to take over the Regency, was lying ill at Berwick.   By the 12th May he was sufficiently recovered to resume his journey ; and on the 13th, escorted by a detachment of English troops under Sir William Drury, Marshal of Berwick, he entered Edinburgh.   Although Drury's mission had been solely to convey Lennox in safety to the Scottish capital, he was persuaded to accompany the Earls of Morton and Mar, who were on the point of setting out to relieve Glasgow.   After assisting them in this and other services, he returned to Berwick on June 2nd.[2]

Meanwhile the news of these doings in Scotland had reached Paris, where it aroused considerable indignation. The King of France, through his ambassador La Mothe Fénelon, requested Elizabeth to withdraw her troops, and behind this request a veiled threat was plainly discernible.   Now the one thing Elizabeth dreaded above all others was lest her policy should drive France and Spain into alliance with each other against her.   At this time she was by way of being on friendly terms with the " most Christian King," Charles IX.   Although she returned a typically evasive answer to Fenelon, she deemed it advisable to order Sussex with some asperity to recall Drury immediately [3] ; but as soon as she had soothed the French King, she disclosed her real feelings in a letter to the Lord Lieutenant dated June 11th :

Right trusty and well-beloved cousin, we greet you well. Although we have not in any express writing to you declared our well liking of your service at this time, yet we would not have you think but we have well considered that therein you have deserved both praise and thanks.   For indeed we have not known in our time, nor heard of any former, that such entries into Scotland, with such acts

[1] Cal. S.P. Scot., pp. 145 and 197.   [2] Ibid., p. 198.   [3] Ibid., p. 183.

of avenge have been so attempted and achieved with so
small numbers, and so much to our honour, and the small
loss or hurt of any of our subjects ; therefore we have
good cause hereby to continue and confirm the opinion
we have of your wisdom in governing . . . of your
painfulness in executing the same, and of your faith-
fulness towards us in your direct proceeding to make all
your said actions to end with our honour and contentation. And as we know that in such causes, the foresight
and order is to be attributed to a general, so we are not
ignorant that the concurrency of the wisdom, fidelity
and activity of others having principal charge with you,
has been the furtherance of our honour ; and therefore
knowing very well the good desert of our cousin of Hunsdon,
we have written at this time a special letter to him of
thanks. And, for the Marshal to whom you committed
the charge of the last entry into Scotland, we now see him
by his actions both in fidelity, wisdom and knowledge
to be the same that we always conceived to be, and think
him worthy of estimation and countenance ; and so we
pray you to let him understand of our allowance of him,
and to give the others who now served with him in our
name such thanks as we perceive they have deserved, and
especially (besides other their deserts) as they have so
behaved themselves in Scotland—as by living in order
without spoil of such as are our friends—they have given
great cause to have our nation commended, and our
friends to rest satisfied.[1]

That Elizabeth, who was seldom fulsome in her thanks
or praise, should have written in this strain to her Lord-
Lieutenant is an eloquent testimony to the greatness of
the service he had rendered his country. Modern historians
almost unanimously describe Sussex's campaign in Scotland as " wanton " and " brutal " ; but even if we cannot
wholly endorse the suffering he inflicted on hundreds of
innocent people, we can at least endeavour to picture the
Scottish problem as it appeared in the eyes of the Elizabethans. To us the Tweed is just a river, to be crossed in
a train or a motor-car. To them it was a curtain behind
which lurked marauders, bandits, and the Queen's enemies ;

[1] Cal. S.P. Scot., p. 205.

and through which at any moment a French army might
appear. Sussex had made no idle boast when he said on
April 10th that he intended to leave such a memory in
Scotland that " they and their children shall be afraid to
offer war to England." By his energy and generalship he
did for Elizabeth's turbulent frontier what another English
general, Lord Roberts, did for another English Queen in
India over 300 years later.

We do not know for certain what part Lord Oxford
played in the campaign ; but his rank and his youth make
it probable that he served on Lord Sussex's staff. We do
know, however, that for the next thirteen years he was
the staunchest supporter Sussex possessed at Court.
He was to Sussex what Philip Sidney was to the Earl of
Leicester. The long and bitter feud between the two older
men, that more than once brought them to blows in the
Council-chamber, was pursued on one memorable occasion
with no less intensity by Oxford and Sidney.

It is not always easy to follow the tortuous intrigues of
the various factions at Gloriana's Court. Alliances were
made, broken, and mended again, friends became foes,
and foes were reconciled. But throughout it all two
men remained constant enemies—Sussex and Leicester.
To Sussex the swarthy Leicester was the Queen's evil
genius, who did not scruple to play upon her passions in
order to raise himself to the position of King-Consort.
The family stamps the man, and Sussex may have detected in Robert Dudley the mirror of his father, the
Duke of Northumberland, who had been brought to the
scaffold in 1554 for seeking to become the father-in-law
of a Queen. It is possible for us to look back, after the
passage of ten generations, and admire the qualities of both
men ; but with them it was war to the knife. When, in
1583, Sussex lay dying of consumption brought on by the
rigours and hardships of his campaigns, his last words
were : " Beware of the Gipsy ; you do not know the beast
as well as I do." [1]

[1] Naunton, *Fragmenta Regalia.*

How long Lord Oxford remained on the Border is not known, but he probably returned to London in the late summer or early autumn. It may have been on the occasion of his home-coming that Stow describes him riding into London—

and so to his house by London Stone, with four score gentlemen in a livery of Reading tawny, and chains of gold about their necks, before him ; and one hundred tall yeomen in the like livery to follow him, without chains, but all having his cognizance of the Blue Boar embroidered on their left shoulder.[1]

London Stone is probably a fragment of the old Roman defences of the City, and is still in existence, having been built into the south wall of St. Swithin's Church, just south of the Mansion House.

Holinshed (who was followed by Shakespeare in 2 *Henry VI.*, Act IV, scene 6) tells us that when Cade, in 1450, forced his way into London, he first of all proceeded to London Stone, and having struck his sword upon it said, in reference to himself and in explanation of his own action, " Now is Mortimer lord of this city." [2]

The house Stow refers to was called Vere House, and he tells us that it was—

A fair and large built house sometime pertaining to the prior of Tortington in Sussex, since to the Earl of Oxford, now to Sir John Hart, alderman. Which house hath a fair garden thereunto, lying on the west side thereof.[3]

It was Lord Oxford's principal London dwelling until 1589, when Sir John Hart bought it. It had been originally granted in 1540 to the sixteenth Earl by King Henry VIII. on the dissolution of Tortington Priory ; and in 1573 the Queen renewed the grant to the seventeenth Earl in consideration of a yearly rent of thirty shillings.[4]

During this winter Lord Oxford made the acquaintance

---

[1] Stow, *Annals*, p. 34.   [2] *Encyc. Brit.*, vol. xvi, p. 956.
[3] Cf. Wheatley, *London Past and Present*, vol. ii, p. 620.
[4] Pat. Roll. 1101, mem. 31, 15 Eliz.

of Dr. Dee, Queen Elizabeth's famous astrologer. The
details are not known, but in 1592 Dee published *A Com-
pendious Rehearsal*, which was in reality his defence against
charges of witchcraft and sorcery that had been preferred
against him. His defence took the form of citing the many
noblemen and gentlemen who had patronised him ; and
among them he quotes " the honourable the Earl of
Oxford, his favourable letters, anno 1570." Dee used
to be consulted in his astrological capacity by many of the
highest people in the land. Elizabeth herself had gone to
him when Queen Mary had died and had asked him to
choose an hour and a date for her coronation when the
stars would be favourable. We, living in a more sophisti-
cated age, may be inclined to smile at this ; but we must
at least admit the coincidence that Gloriana's reign did
turn out to be one of the most successful in our history.
The Earls of Leicester and Derby, and Sir Philip Sidney
were among his many patrons.

While on the subject of astrology it may be worth
mentioning that Lord Oxford certainly practised this
ancient science. In a small volume of doggrel poems
entitled *Pandora*, published by John Soouthern [1] and
dedicated to the Earl of Oxford in 1584, he speaks of his
patron thus :

> For who marketh better than he
>   The seven turning flames of the sky ?
> Or hath read more of the antique ;
>   Hath greater knowledge of the tongues ?
> Or understandeth sooner the sounds
>   Of the learner to love music ?

The " seven turning flames of the sky " are of course the
planets ; and we may conjecture that it was in 1570 that
he studied astrology under Dr. Dee. We shall meet
these two again in later years working together as " adventurers," or speculators, in Martin Frobisher's attempts
to find a North-West Passage to China and the East Indies.

[1] John Soouthern was probably a Frenchman who had settled permanently in England. He was at this time in the household of the Earl
of Oxford.

§ VI. Parliament

Monday, April 2nd, 1571, was a great day in London, for the Queen was to open Parliament in State. There had been no session for five years, during which time many notable events had occurred that were bound to loom large at discussions in both Houses. Foremost, of course, was the question of the Queen of Scots ; then there was the Bull of Excommunication that Pope Pius V. had pronounced against Elizabeth ; and lastly the great Catholic rising, so long threatened, had come and gone with the complete discomfiture of the rebels. But these matters alone would not have been sufficient to ·induce the Queen to call her Parliament together. With true Tudor distaste for all forms of democracy, she never summoned Parliament unless compelled to do so. But in one respect she was in their hands. She was dependent on their good-will for the replenishment of her depleted Treasury. The ordinary revenues of the State had proved inadequate to bear the heavy charges of the Northern Rising, the war in Ireland, and the maintenance of the Navy. She was therefore reluctantly compelled to call upon her Lords and Commons to make some additional provision to meet these liabilities.

The procession to Westminster was led by the fifty Gentlemen Pensioners all mounted and carrying their gilt battle-axes. After them followed, in order, the Knights of the Bath, the Barons of the Exchequer, the Judges, the Master of the Rolls, the Attorney and Solicitor-General, the Lords Spiritual, the Lords Temporal, and finally the Archbishop of Canterbury. Then came the Officers of State ; the Marquess of Northampton with the Hat of Maintenance ; Lord Admiral Clinton, who was acting Lord Steward for the day ; the Earl of Oxford, Lord Great Chamberlain ; and the Earl of Worcester, who deputised as Earl Marshal in the enforced absence of the Duke of Norfolk.

Her Majesty sat in her coach in her imperial robes, with a wreath or coronet of gold set with rich pearls and stones

over her head ; her coach drawn by two palfreys, covered
with crimson velvet, drawn out, embossed and embroidered
very richly.[1]

Behind the coach rode the Earl of Leicester, who, as
Master of the Horse, led Her Majesty's palfrey.   And
finally the Maids of Honour, also mounted, with the
Bodyguard riding on either side of them.

After attending a service in Westminster Abbey the
Queen, with her train borne by the Earl of Oxford, was
conducted to the House of Lords.   Behind her followed the
Lords Spiritual and Temporal, who took their places accord-
ing to their degree.   The order of precedence of the great
Officers of State had been laid down in 1540 :

The Lord Vice Regent shall be placed on the Bishop's
side above them all.
Then the Lord Chancellor,
        the Lord Treasurer,
        the Lord President of the Privy Council,
        the Lord Privy Seal.
These four being of the degree of a Baron or above shall
sit in the Parliament, in all assemblies of Council, above
Dukes not being of the Blood Royal, viz. the King's brother,
uncle, or nephews, etc.
And these six :
        the Lord Great Chamberlain of England,
        the Lord High Constable of England,
        the Earl Marshal of England,
        the Lord Admiral of England,
        the Lord Great Master or Steward of the King's House,
        the Lord Chamberlain of the King's Household.
These six are placed in all assemblies of Council after
the Lord Privy Seal, according to their degrees and estates :
so that if he be a Baron, to sit above all Barons ; and if
he be an Earl, above all Earls.[2]

The Lord Chancellor and the Lord Treasurer were Sir
Nicholas Bacon and Lord Burghley respectively.[3]   The

---

[1] D'Ewes, *Journals*, p. 136.

[2] W. Segar, *Honor Military and Civil* (1602), p. 243.

[3] Sir Nicholas Bacon was officially known as " Lord Keeper of the Great
Seal," but his duties were those of Lord Chancellor.

latter had received his Barony two months previously ; and
the power that his position now gave him, ranking as he
did above all the rest of the nobility, may well be imagined.
The offices of Lord President of the Council and Lord Privy
Seal appear to have been in abeyance, but in 1572 Lord
Howard of Effingham was given the latter appointment.

Lord Oxford was the Great Chamberlain, by virtue of
which he took precedence above all Earls. There was no
High Constable, the Duke of Norfolk was Earl Marshal,
Clinton was Lord Admiral, and seems also to have acted as
Lord Steward,[1] and Lord Howard of Effingham, father
of the hero of the Armada, was Lord Chamberlain.

When all were assembled the Queen called on her Lord
Keeper to read the Speech from the Throne. My Lord
Keeper, with the memory of the crushed rebellion behind
him, was in fighting mood, and did not spare the feelings
of the many Catholic Lords who faced him. He referred
in general terms to the great benefits that the Queen had
conferred on the country for upwards of ten years, three of
which he dealt with in greater detail. First, and in his
opinion most important, was that " we are delivered and
made free from the bondage of the Roman tyranny."
Secondly the earnestness with which Her Majesty had
sought peace, " the richest and most wished-for ornament
of any public weal." But, he added, " the same might by
God's grace have continued twenty years longer had not
the Raging Romanist Rebels entertained the matter. . . ."
Lastly, the great benefit of clemency and mercy. " I
pray you," he asked the House, " hath it been seen or read
that any Prince of this Realm, during whole ten years'
reign and more, hath had his hands so clean from blood ?
If no offence were, Her Majesty's wisdom in governing
was the more to be wondered at ; and if offences were,
then Her Majesty's clemency and mercy the more to be
commended."

---

[1] Cal. Rutland MSS., I. 92. The Lord Stewardship was vacant from the
death of the Earl of Pembroke, in 1570, until the appointment of the Earl
of Derby in 1585.

He then drew attention to the heavy expenses that had been incurred of late—expenses, he was careful to point out, that were solely due to the rebellious behaviour of the Queen's disloyal subjects in England, Scotland, and Ireland. He called upon both Houses to seek some way of providing for the replenishment of the empty Treasury.[1]

But if the Upper House seemed to exhibit too great a partiality towards Catholicism, it soon became apparent that the Lower House threatened to go too far in the opposite direction. A significant step was taken on April 4th when, from the Bar of the House of Lords, Christopher Wray, who had just been elected Speaker in the Commons, appealed to Her Majesty to grant them the privilege of free speech. To this request the Lord Keeper gave a somewhat reluctant consent ; but at the same time he warned them " that they should do well to meddle with no matters of State but such as were propounded unto them " ; and advised them to " occupy themselves in other matters concerning the Commonwealth." [2]

But the Commons were in no temper to heed warnings or to take advice. They at once brought forward seven bills all advocating a further reformation of the Church so as to bring it more into line with Geneva, and a more vigorous policy against the Catholics. The Queen, who was trying to steer a middle course between the extremists of both parties, was most indignant, and affected to see in their proceedings an insult to her supremacy as head of the Church. She accordingly ordered the arrest of one of the most outspoken members. The Commons, however, were in no mood to submit, and succeeded in securing his release. But at the dissolution, which took place on May 29th, they were severely informed by the Lord Keeper that " the Queen's highness did utterly disallow and condemn their folly in meddling with things not appertaining to them, nor within the capacity of their understanding." [3]

---

[1] D'Ewes, pp. 137–139.   [2] Ibid., p. 141.
[3] Lingard, *History of England*, vol. iii, p. 123.

Although Lord Oxford took no part other than in the ceremonial of this Parliament, the speeches and proceedings which he listened to and voted on form part of the framework in which his life must be set. His first attendance at Parliament was of itself an important event in his career. But more important still perhaps is the fact that he was witnessing the opening scenes of the great struggle that finally culminated in the Civil War and the Puritan Revolution. As a member of the old aristocracy his instincts would be all on the side of feudalism and the *ancien régime*. As a member of Sir William and Lady Mildred Cecil's household his education had been conducted entirely on pro-Reformation lines. More and more the Reformation was coming into conflict with the feudal ideals. The descendants of the hereditary nobility—the Howards, the Fitzalans, the Percys, and the rest—were being elbowed out of the government by the new men like Cecil and Bacon. In spite of the admiration that we know he had for his guardian, we shall see later that for a time his instincts won the day, and he broke away from his Cecil associations, and chose the more congenial companionship of men like Lord Surrey, Lord Henry Howard, and Lord Lumley.

It was probably about this time that Edmund Elviden dedicated *The most excellent and pleasant Metaphoricall Historie of Peisistratus and Catanea* to the Earl of Oxford. He apologises for having " boldly or rather impudently offered to your honour this present rude and gross conceit . . . for your honour's recreation and avoiding of tedious time, after your weighty affairs finished . . . sufficiently intending to satisfy the humour of your wise disposition."

There is no date on the title-page of the book, which is " set forth this present year," but as Elviden is only known to have written two other books, *The Closit of Counsells* in 1569, and *A Neweyeres gift to the Rebellious Persons in the North partes of England* in 1570, it seems not unlikely that the *Metaphoricall Historie* belongs to the same

period.[1] But it is time now to pass from the stern work
of Parliament and watch the younger members of both
Houses at play.

§ VII. A TOURNAMENT

The first, second, and third of May 1571 was holden at
Westminster, before the Queen's Majesty, a solemn joust
at the tilt, tournay, and barriers. The challengers were
Edward Earl of Oxford, Charles Howard, Sir Henry Lee,
and Christopher Hatton, Esq., who all did very valiantly;
but the chief honour was given to the Earl of Oxford.[2]

These tournaments, which were such a feature of
Elizabeth's reign, had been revived in 1562 by Sir Henry
Lee, who had established himself as Her Majesty's
champion against all comers. Sir William Segar, Garter
King at Arms, in his *Honor Military and Civil* (1602),
gives an account of what were probably the five greatest
tournaments held under Gloriana's auspices. They were
all held in connexion with some special celebration, and
were additional to the Annual Accession Day tournaments
on November 17th, at which Sir Henry Lee, and later the
Earl of Cumberland, acted as the Queen's champions.

The following is Sir William Segar's list :

1. (January 1st ?) 1559. To celebrate the Queen's
accession. The challengers were the Duke of Norfolk,
the Earl of Sussex, Lords Scrope, Darcy, and Hunsdon,
and Lords Ambrose and Robert Dudley.

2. May 1st to 3rd, 1571.

3. June 1572. To celebrate the installation of the Duc
de Montmorenci as a Knight of the Garter. The challengers were Walter Earl of Essex, and Edward Earl of
Rutland. Lord Oxford took no part in this tournament,
his share in helping to entertain the Queen's French guests

---

[1] I am indebted to the Librarian of the Henry E. Huntington Library,
San Marino, California, for the foregoing information about the *Metaphoricall Historie*. So far as is known, there is no other copy of this
book. Nothing is known of Edmund Elviden beyond the fact that he was
the author of the three books given above.

[2] Stow, *Annals*, p. 669.

being the organisation of a display of Arquebusiers and Artillery in St. James's Park.[1]

4. January 1st, 1581. In honour of Elizabeth's suitor the Duc d'Anjou, who had recently arrived in England. The challengers were Anjou himself, the Prince d'Ausine, the Comte St. Aignon, MM. Chamvallon and de Bacqueville ; and the Earls of Sussex and Leicester.

5. January 22nd, 1581. To celebrate Philip Howard Earl of Surrey's succession to the Earldom of Arundel. He himself, assisted by Sir William Drury, was the challenger. The prize was given to the Earl of Oxford, who was one of the defendants.

There was also the famous " triumph "—not described by Segar—which was held on May 15th and 16th, 1581, probably also in honour of the Duc d'Anjou.[2] The challengers were the Earl of Arundel, Lord Windsor, Philip Sidney, and Fulke Greville. This was perhaps the occasion on which Philip Sidney won the prize, as he tells us in one of his Sonnets :

> Having this day my horse, my hand, my lance,
> Guided so well that I obtained the prize,
> Both by the judgment of the English eyes,
> And of some sent by that sweet enemy France.

Lord Oxford at the time was in the Queen's disfavour.

It is a remarkable tribute to Lord Oxford's skill at arms and horsemanship that he was given the prize at the only two great tournaments in which he was a competitor. Let us then pause for a moment and hear from the lips of Sir William Segar, who was afterwards Garter King-at-Arms, how these festivities were conducted.

The King's pleasure being signified unto the Constable and Marshal, they caused Lists, or rails, to be made ; and set up in length three score paces, and in breadth forty paces. . . . At either end of the Lists was made a

---

[1] Agnes Strickland, *Queens of England*, vol. vi, p. 361. Montmorenci was elected K.G. May 16th, landed at Dover June 9th, and was installed at St. George's Chapel, Windsor, June 18th (Camden, p. 187 ; Holinshed, p. 284).

[2] An account is given by E. K. Chambers, *Elizabethan Stage*, vol. iv, p. 63.

gate . . . with a strong bar to keep out the people. . . . One gate opened towards the east, and the other towards the west, being strongly barred with a rail of seven foot long, and of such height as no horse could pass under or over the same.

Before the tournament began the pledges, or hostages, of the Challengers and Defendants were brought in and placed below the royal box, where they remained until redeemed by the valour of their champion.

The Challenger did commonly come to the east gate of the Lists. . . . Beholding the Challenger there, the Constable said : " For what cause art thou come hither thus armed ? And what is thy name ? " Unto whom the Challenger answered thus : " My name is A.B. and I am hither come armed and mounted to perform my challenge against C.D., and acquit my pledges." . . . Then the Constable did open the visor of his headpiece to see his face, and thereby to know that man to be he that makes the challenge.

The same ceremony took place at the west gate when the Defendant appeared ; after which the Constable measured their lances, and administered the first oath :

The Constable, having caused his clerk to read the Challenger's bill . . . said : " Dost thou conceive the effect of this bill ? Here is also thine own gauntlet of defiance. Thou shalt swear by the Holy Evangelists that all things therein contained be true ; and that thou maintain it so to be upon the person of thine adversary, as God shall help thee and the Holy Evangelists."

When both Challenger and Defendant had taken the first oath, the Constable administered the second oath, which was to the effect that they had not brought into the Lists any illegal " weapon . . . engine, instrument, herb, charm, or enchantment " ; and that neither of them should put " trust in any other thing than God."

The Heralds then cleared the Lists, and warned the crowd against uttering " any speech, word, voice, or countenance, whereby either the Challenger or Defendant

may take advantage.   The Constable then did pronounce
with a loud voice, ' Let them go, let them go, let them
go.' " [1]

The rules as to scoring, and the award of the prize, were
those laid down by John Tiptoft, Earl of Worcester, in
the reign of Edward IV. :

First, whoso breaketh most spears, as they ought to
be broken, shall have the prize.

Item, whoso hitteth three times in the height of the
helm shall have the prize.

Item, whoso meeteth two times, cournall to cournall
(i.e. parry and return), shall have the prize.

Item, whoso beareth a man down with the stroke of a
spear, shall have the prize.

The method of scoring " broken spears " was as follows :

First, whoso breaketh a spear between the saddle and
the charnell of the helm (i.e. a body thrust) shall be allowed
for one.

Item, whoso breaketh a spear from the charnell upwards
(i.e. a head thrust) shall be allowed for two.

Item, whoso breaketh a spear so as he strike his adversary
down . . . shall be allowed as three spears broken.

Then follow the disqualifications for fouls :

First, whoso striketh a horse shall have no prize.

Item, whoso striketh a man his back turned, or dis-
garnished of his spear, shall have no prize.

Item, whoso hitteth the tilt three times shall have no
prize.

Item, whoso unhelmeth himself two times shall have no
prize, unless his horse do fail him. [2]

In the Tournament held in May 1571 the Defendants
opposed to Lord Oxford were, Lord Stafford, Thomas
Cecil, Henry Knollys, Thomas Knyvett, Robert Colsell,
Thomas Bedingfield, and Thomas Coningsby.[3]

---

[1] Sir William Segar, *Honor Military and Civil*, 1602, p. 132.
[2] Ibid.   [3] Harleian MSS., 6064. 87.

This Triumph continued three days.   The first at Tilt ;
the second at Tournay ; and the third at the Barriers.
On every of the Challengers Her Majesty bestowed a
prize, for the receiving whereof they were particularly
led, armed, by two ladies into the Presence Chamber ;
Oxford himself receiving a tablet of diamonds.[1]

Lord Oxford's display in this famous tournament was
the subject of much comment at the Court.   In a letter
to the Earl of Rutland, George Delves, himself one of the
Defendants, says : " Lord Oxford has performed his
challenge at tilt, tournay, and barriers, far above expectation of the world, and not much inferior to the other
three challengers," a handsome tribute seeing that Oxford
was a novice, while the other three were not only older
men, but were veterans at the game.   " The Earl of
Oxford's livery," Delves continues, " was crimson velvet,
very costly ; he himself, and the furniture, was in some
more colours, yet he was the Red Knight. . . . There is
no man of life and agility in every respect in the Court
but the Earl of Oxford." [2]

A graceful tribute to the young Earl's skill in horsemanship was paid to him by Giles Fletcher in Latin verses :

But if at any time with fiery energy he should call up a
mimicry of war, he controls his foaming steed with a light
rein, and armed with a long spear rides to the encounter.
Fearlessly he settles himself in the saddle, gracefully
bending his body this way and that.   Now he circles
round ; now with spurred heel he rouses his charger.   The
gallant animal with fiery energy collects himself together,
and flying quicker than the wind beats the ground with
his hoofs, and again is pulled up short as the reins control
him.

Bravo, valiant youth ! 'Tis thus that martial spirits
pass through their apprenticeship in war.   Thus do
yearling bulls try the feel of each other's horns.   Thus
too do goats not yet expert in fighting begin to butt one

[1] Harleian MSS., 6064. 87 ; Segar, *The Book of Honour*, 1590, p. 94.
[2] Cal. Rutland MSS., George Delves to the Earl of Rutland, May 14th
and June 24th, 1571.

against the other, and soon venture to draw blood with
their horns.

The country sees in thee both a leader pre-eminent in
war, and a skilful man-at-arms. Thy valour puts forth
leaves, and begins to bear early fruit, and glory already
ripens in thy earliest deeds.[1]

But for the moment other thoughts were beginning to
fill his mind, for next month he became engaged to be
married to Anne Cecil, the eldest daughter of his guardian,
who had been created Baron Burghley earlier in the year.

§ VIII. Mistress Anne Cecil

As early as 1569 the project of a match between Anne
Cecil and Philip Sidney, then aged thirteen and fifteen
respectively, had been mooted. Sidney's uncle, the Earl
of Leicester, whose fortune, in default of an heir of his
own, would descend to his nephew Philip, had been a prime
mover in the proposals. He had, moreover, promised to
endow the couple handsomely. It is not clear why these
negotiations came to nothing. It may, perhaps, be
attributable partly to the well-known enmity between
Leicester and Burghley, partly to a financial deadlock,
and partly to the extreme youth of the parties concerned.
But the death-blow to the proposals was finally delivered
in the summer of 1571, when Burghley accepted on his
daughter's behalf a marriage proposal from the Earl of
Oxford.

Let us listen to what Burghley and the Court have to
say about this engagement.

The first intimation we get is in a letter written by Lord
St. John to the Earl of Rutland, who was in Paris :

The Earl of Oxford hath gotten him a wife—or at the
least a wife hath caught him ; this is Mistress Anne
Cecil ; whereunto the Queen hath given her consent, and
the which hath caused great weeping, wailing, and sorrowful
cheer of those that had hoped to have that golden day.

[1] Eclogue, *In nuptias clarissimi D. Edouardi Vere*. Hatfield MSS.
(Cal. XIII. 109).

Thus you may see whilst that some triumph with olive branches, others follow the chariot with willow garlands.[1]

This piece of gossip must have been of particular interest to Rutland, who, a year older than his cousin Lord Oxford, had also been a Royal Ward at Cecil House, and of course knew both bride and bridegroom intimately. We may well picture the " sorrowful cheer " of the disappointed Maids of Honour, many of whom, no doubt, had secretly aspired to marry the popular young courtier.

A fortnight later Burghley sends the news officially to Lord Rutland :

I think it doth seem strange to your Lordship to hear of a purposed determination in my Lord of Oxford to marry with my daughter ; and so before his Lordship moved it to me I might have thought it, if any other had moved it to me himself. For at his own motion I could not well imagine what to think, considering I never meant to seek it nor hoped of it.   And yet reason moved me to think well of my Lord, and to acknowledge myself greatly beholden to him, as indeed I do. Truly, my Lord, after I was acquainted of the former intention of a marriage with Master Philip Sidney, whom always I loved and esteemed, I was fully determined to have of myself moved no marriage for my daughter until she should have been near sixteen, that with moving I might also conclude. And yet I thought it not inconvenient in the meantime, being free to hearken to any motion made by such others as I should have cause to like. Truly, my Lord, my goodwill serves me to have moved such a matter as this in another direction than this is, but having more occasion to doubt of the issue of the matter, I did forbear, and in mine own conceit I could have as well liked there as in any other place in England. Percase your Lordship may guess where I mean, and so shall I, for I will name nobody.[2] Now that the matter is determined betwixt my Lord of Oxford and me, I confess to your Lordship I do honour him so dearly

---

[1] Cal. Rutland MSS., July 28th, 1571.

[2] Query, is this a reference to Rutland himself, who may have formed a boy-and-girl attachment with Anne, during his seven years' wardship in Cecil House ?

from my heart as I do my own son, and in any case that may touch him for his honour and weal, I shall think him mine own interest therein.   And surely, my Lord, by dealing with him I find that which I often heard of your Lordship, that there is much more in him of understanding than any stranger to him would think.   And for my own part I find that whereof I take comfort in his wit and knowledge grown by good observation.[1]

It was evidently expected that the marriage would take place in September, for on the 21st Hugh Fitz-William writes from London to the Countess of Shrewsbury :

They say the Queen will be at my Lord of Burghley's house beside Waltham on Sunday next, where my Lord of Oxford shall marry Mistress Anne Cecil his daughter.[2]

The Queen and Court were in progress at this time, and reached Theobalds, Lord Burghley's country house, on the 22nd ; but the wedding was postponed, perhaps in order to wait until the Court returned to London.

Lord Hunsdon, who had been on service against the northern rebels with Oxford, evidently approved, for he writes to Lord Burghley that he is " glad to hear of the Earl of Oxford's marriage."

On Wednesday, December 19th, the marriage took place in Westminster Abbey, the Queen herself being present ; and in the afternoon a great feast was held at Cecil House.

" Last Tuesday," writes de la Mothe Fénelon to the King of France, " I had audience with the Queen ; and on Wednesday she took me with her to dine with Lord Burghley, who was celebrating the marriage of his daughter with the Earl of Oxford." [4]

At this dinner, he tells us, he met the Earl of Leicester, and had a long talk with him about the proposed marriage between the Queen herself and the Duc d'Anjou ; all of

---

[1] Cal. Rutland MSS., August 15th, 1571.
[2] Joseph Hunter, *Hallamshire*, p. 83.
[3] Cal. S.P. Foreign, November 22nd, 1571.
[4] *Correspondance . . . de Bertrand de Salignac de la Mothe Fénelon* (1840), vol. iv, p. 315.

which goes to show that the wedding was an unusually
brilliant one, graced as it was by the presence of the Queen
and her chief Courtier. And, of course, being Elizabethans,
the ceremony would not have been complete without a
rhapsodist, who composed, and perhaps recited, an Eclogue
in Latin hexameters :

Fortunate art thou as a father-in-law, witnessing the
marriage of thy daughter, and happy art thou as a son-
in-law, and thou maiden in thy husband, and, last of all,
happy bridegroom in thy bride. Not as an oath-breaker
doth Hymen join these bands, for both the bridegroom and
the bride possess that which each may love, and every
quality which may be loved. For like a river swelling its
banks, by means of intercourse and sympathy love will
arise, and the glory of rank, and children recalling the
qualities of both parents; for the valour of the father
and the prudence of the mother will come out in the
offspring. . . . Hail to thee, Hymen, hail ! [1]

In the evening Lord Burghley, tired but happy, wrote
a long letter to Francis Walsingham, who was then Ambassador at Paris. His obvious pleasure at the success of
the whole ceremony is well expressed in his own words :

. . . I can write no more for lack of leisure, being
occasioned to write at this time divers ways, and not
unoccupied with feasting my friends at the marriage of
my daughter, who is this day married to the Earl of
Oxford, to my comfort, by reason of the Queen's Majesty,
who hath very honourably with her presence and great
favour accompanied it.[2]

[1] Hatfield MSS. (Cal. XIII. 109). The writer, Giles Fletcher the elder,
held several civil appointments in Elizabeth's reign. He went as envoy
to Russia in 1588. He was the father of two poets—Phineas and Giles
the younger—and uncle of John Fletcher, the dramatist. The latter is
well known as the collaborator with Francis Beaumont in many plays,
and with Shakespeare in *King Henry VIII*.

[2] Sir Dudley Digges, *The Compleat Ambassador*, p. 164.

CHAPTER III

1572–1576

" I overtook, coming from Italy,
    In Germany, a great and famous Earl
Of England ; the most goodly fashion'd man
I ever saw : from head to foot in form
Rare and most absolute ; he had a face
Like one of the most ancient honour'd Romans
From whence his noblest family was deriv'd ;
He was beside of spirit passing great,
Valiant and learn'd, and liberal as the sun,
Spoke and writ sweetly, or of learned subjects,
Or of the discipline of public weals ;
And 'twas the Earl of Oxford."
        GEORGE CHAPMAN, in *The Revenge of Bussy d'Ambois.*

§ I. THOMAS HOWARD, 4TH DUKE OF NORFOLK

MENTION has already been made of the Catholic plot, the
first act of which was played in the northern counties in
November 1569. The premature rebellion of the Earls
of Northumberland and Westmorland had been stamped
out ; but the Catholics, though momentarily off their
balance, were not disheartened. Throughout 1571 the
Duke of Norfolk and the Queen of Scots had carried on
a secret correspondence, the purport of which was still
their marriage, and the establishment of Mary on the throne
of England.   In justice to Norfolk it must be said that at
his trial he stoutly denied any intended treason against
Her Majesty.   But he was found guilty, and in January
1572 was sentenced to death.   For five months Elizabeth
kept on signing his death warrant, and then at the last
moment revoking it.   Finally she made up her mind and
on June 2nd he was executed.

This execution had a profound effect on Lord Oxford,
who was not only Norfolk's first cousin but one of his

6   65

greatest friends.   For after his conviction Norfolk wrote as follows to his eldest son, Philip Howard :

Although my hap hath been such that my kin have had cause to be ashamed of me, their kinsman ; yet I hope when I am gone nature will so work in them that they will be in good will to you, as heretofore they have been to me.   Amongst whom I will begin as high as I unworthy dare presume, with my cousin of Oxford.[1]

On December 10th, 1571, the French Ambassador sent the Sieur de Sabran to Paris with secret despatches. Some of the information was too secret to be committed to writing, as the following extract shows :

The good affection that the nobility of this realm bear towards the King [of France] will be shown in a letter that one of them, Sr. Lane [Ralph Lane], wrote to me in Italian, the contents of which, as well as certain other matters Sr. Lane confided in me, will be explained to the King by de Sabran ; and he will also tell him of a certain proposal recently made by the Earl of Oxford to some of his friends,[2] and what came of it.[3]

Now the Duke of Norfolk had been arrested in September ; and although Lord Oxford's " proposal " was not on this occasion committed to writing, the whole story leaked out two years later in an unexpected way. In 1574 a petition was submitted to the Privy Council headed " A poor woman's complaint " ; and in it we read the following curious account of a plot engineered by Lord Oxford having as its object the rescue of the Duke of Norfolk from his prison :

Certain conspiracies that of force I have been acquainted, touching Your Majesty. . . . At the time that the late Duke of Norfolk was removed out of the Tower to the Charter-house, my husband being prisoner in the Fleet, the Earl of Oxford provided a ship called " The Grace of God," and £10 was earnest thereupon, and £500 more was to be

[1] *Catholic Record Society*, vol. xxi, p. 7, January 28th, 1572.

[2] . . . ce que le comte d'Oxford a naguères proposé en une compagnie où il estoit. . . ."

[3] *Correspondance . . . de la Mothe Fénelon*.   Ralph Lane was afterwards the first Governor of Virginia.

paid to me, my husband's liberty granted, and the ship to be given him with £2,000 in ready money, the one half to be paid here, the other to be delivered to him at the arrival of the Duke in Spain. My husband opened these dealings to me, and offered me £900 of the first payment. . . . But I utterly refused such gain to receive ; I had a care of the duty I owe to your Majesty, as also I feared it would be the utter destruction of my husband. . . . And so that enterprise was dashed.[1]

From the foregoing it seems probable that Lord Oxford's " proposal " mentioned in Fénelon's letter was nothing more nor less than the forcible rescue of his cousin the Duke, and his conveyance to Spain. That he regarded with contempt Norfolk's tame submission in allowing himself to be arrested instead of putting up a fight is borne out by another document in the Public Record Office. It is a long rigmarole purporting to be indiscreet statements made on various occasions by Lord Oxford for many years past ; the object of its compilers, Lord Henry Howard and Charles Arundel, being to endeavour to incense Her Majesty against the Earl. The following extracts speak for themselves :

Railing at my Lord of Norfolk for his coming at the Queen's commandment, contrary to his (Oxford's) counsel as he said in a letter he wrote.

Continual railing on the Duke for coming up when he was sent for.

My Lord of Norfolk worthy to lose his head for not following his counsel at Lichfield to take arms.[2]

At any rate we know that the attempted rescue, which probably took place in November 1571, failed ; and in December Oxford's mind was occupied with his marriage.

The political significance of this marriage, as well as of another that took place about the same time, was not lost on Guerau Despes, the Spanish Ambassador. He also was deeply implicated in the Ridolphi plot, and was eventually expelled from England ; but before this occurred he wrote thus to the King of Spain :

[1] S.P. Dom. Eliz., 95. 92. [2] Ibid., 151. 46–49.

Lord Burghley is celebrating with great festivity at the palace the marriage of his daughter with the Earl of Oxford. The son of the Earl of Worcester is married also to the sister of the Earl of Huntingdon, which means taking two families away from the Catholics.[1]

But if these celebrations appeared to the Spaniards to presage the loss of two English families to Catholicism, to Lord Oxford his union with the daughter of the Queen's Secretary of State seemed like the key with which to release his cousin Norfolk from the Tower ; and as soon as the wedding was over, he begged Burghley to intervene and save the Duke's life :

The Papists in the Low Countries—writes one of Burghley's agents, John Lee, from Antwerp on March 18th, 1572—hope some attempt shortly against the Queen, for they hear that the French King has manned twenty ships of war, and that the Duke of Alva has sent into Germany to take up bands of Horse and Foot. They further affirm that there was like to have been a meeting there the 27th of last month, when it was thought that the Duke of Norfolk should have passed[2]; so that they be fully persuaded that the Queen dare not proceed further therein, and also affirm that the Duke has secret friends and those of the best, and such as may do very much with the Queen ; and that the Earl of Oxford (who has been a most humble suitor for him) has conceived some great displeasure against you for the same, whereupon he hath, as they say here, put away from him the Countess his wife.[3]

---

[1] Cal. S.P. Spanish (1568–79), 358. Edward Somerset (1550–1628) succeeded his father as fourth Earl of Worcester in 1589. He married Elizabeth Hastings, fourth daughter of the second Earl of Huntingdon. The Hastings family was so strongly Protestant that, like the Cecils, Don Guerau despaired of their ever being induced to return to the old faith. Lord Worcester was elected K.G. in 1593, was appointed Deputy Master of the Horse in 1597, and Master of the Horse and Earl Marshal in 1601.

[2] I.e., been executed.

[3] S.P. Dom. Add., 21. 23. Dugdale in his *Baronage* has elaborated this story by saying that the Earl, in order to revenge himself on his father-in-law, dissipated his heritage by selling it at ludicrously low prices, thus ruining himself and his wife. That this idea is pure invention can be seen by a reference to Appendix B, where a complete list of all sales of land he made during his lifetime is given. It will be seen that out of 56 sales only two occurred before 1576, the earliest taking place in 1573.

Bitter as Oxford's feelings undoubtedly were against his father-in-law, he quickly realised that there was nothing further to be done.   And we shall next meet him in happier circumstances accompanying the Queen in her progress through Warwickshire two months later.

§ II.   Warwick Castle

Be it remembered [writes a contemporary chronicler] that in the year of our Lord 1572, and in the fourteenth year of our Sovereign Lady Queen Elizabeth, the 12th day of August in the said year it pleased our said Sovereign Lady to visit this borough of Warwick in her person.[1]

On the appointed day all the chief citizens were assemble outside the town :—

in order, first the bailiff, then the recorder, then each of the principal burgesses in order kneeling ;   and behind Mr. Bailiff kneeled Mr. Griffyn, preacher.

About three o'clock the procession approached ;

Her Majesty in her coach, accompanied with the Lady of Warwick in the same coach . . . the Lord Burghley, lately made Lord Treasurer of England, the Earl of Sussex, lately made Lord Chamberlain to Her Majesty, the Lord Howard of Effingham, lately made Lord Privy Seal, the Earl of Oxford, Lord Great Chamberlain of England, the Earl of Rutland, the Earl of Huntingdon, lately made Lord President of the North, the Earl of Warwick, the Earl of Leicester, Master of the Horse, and many other lords, bishops, and ladies.

The Recorder then made a long speech about the history of Warwick, and recited certain Latin verses, composed by Mr. Griffyn.   When this was finished—

the Bailiff, Recorder, and principal burgesses, with their assistants, were commanded to their horses . . . and in order rode two and two' together before Her Majesty . . . till they came to the Castle gate, where the said principal burgesses and assistants stayed . . . making a lane . . .

[1] *Black Book of Warwick.*   Printed in *Bibliotecha Topographica Britannica,* vol. iv.

where Her Majesty should pass; who, passing through them and viewing them well, gave them thanks, saying withal: " It is a well favoured and comely company."

For a week the Queen was in the neighbourhood, spending her time partly with the Earl of Leicester at Kenilworth Castle, and partly with Thomas Fisher at Warwick Priory. On Sunday, August 18th, the Queen having returned to Warwick Castle :

it pleased her to have the country people resorting to see her dance in the Court of the Castle . . . which thing, as it pleased well the country people, so it seemed Her Majesty was much delighted, and made very merry.

In the evening, after supper—

there was devised on the Temple ditch a fort, made of slender timber covered with canvas. In this fort were appointed divers persons to serve the soldiers ; and therefore so many harnesses as might be gotten within the town were had, wherewith men were armed and appointed to shew themselves ; some others appointed to cast out fireworks, as squibs and balls of fire. Against that fort was another castle-wise prepared of like strength, whereof was governor the Earl of Oxford, a lusty gentleman, with a lusty band of gentlemen. Between these forts, or against them, were placed certain battering pieces, to the number of twelve or fourteen, brought from London, and twelve fair chambers, or mortar pieces, brought also from the Tower, at the charge of the Earl of Warwick. These pieces and chambers were by trains fired, and so made a great noise, as though it had been a sore assault ; having some intermission, in which time the Earl of Oxford and his soldiers, to the number of two hundred, with calivers and arquebusses, likewise gave divers assaults ; they in the fort shooting again, and casting out divers fires, terrible to those that have not been in like experiences, valiant to such as delighted therein, and indeed strange to them that understood it not. For the wild fire falling into the river Avon would for a time lie still, and then again rise and fly abroad, casting forth many flashes and flames, whereat the Queen's Majesty took great pleasure. . . . At the last, when it was appointed that the over-throwing

of the fort should be, a dragon flying, casting out huge
flames and squibs, lighted upon the fort, and so set fire
thereon, to the subversion thereof ; but whether by
negligence or otherwise, it happened that a ball of fire fell
on a house at the end of the bridge. . . .

A man and his wife were asleep in this house and were with
difficulty rescued by the Earl of Oxford and Fulke Greville,
who seems to have been his opponent in the mimic battle.

And no small marvel it was that so little harm was done,
for the fire balls and squibs cast up did fly quite over the
Castle, and into the midst of the town ; falling down some
on the houses some in courts . . . and some in the street. . . .
Four houses in the town and suburbs were on fire at once,
whereof one had a ball come through both sides, and made
a hole as big as a man's head, and did no more harm.

It is comforting to read, a little further on, that the poor
man whose house on the bridge was burned down received
£25 12s. 8d. from the Queen and her Courtiers on the
following morning.

In September the Court returned to London. But
in the meantime news had reached England of the massacre
of St. Bartholomew. The horror with which all Englishmen regarded this ghastly orgy is brought out in a letter
endorsed September 1572 from Lord Oxford to his father-
in-law. The letter begins with certain business details
regarding his property ; and it is noteworthy that the
Earl's anger over Norfolk's execution seems to have quite
blown over, for he assures Burghley that " both in this
[i.e. matters relating to his estates], as in all other things,
I am to be governed and commanded at your Lordship's
good devotion."

I would to God [Lord Oxford continues] your Lordship
would let me understand some of your news which here
doth ring doubtfully in the ears of every man, of the
murder of the Admiral of France, and a number of noblemen and worthy gentlemen, and such as greatly have in
their lifetime honoured the Queen's Majesty our Mistress ;
on whose tragedies we have a number of French Æneases
in this city that tell of their own overthrows with tears

falling from their eyes, a piteous thing to hear but a cruel and far more grievous thing we must deem it then to see. All rumours here are but confused of those troops that are escaped from Paris and Rouen where Monsieur hath also been, and like a Vesper Sicilianus, as they say, that cruelty spreads all over France, whereof your Lordship is better advertised than we are here. And sith the world is so full of treasons and vile instruments daily to attempt new and unlooked for things, good my Lord, I shall affectionately and heartily desire your Lordship to be careful both of yourself and of her Majesty, that your friends may long enjoy you and you them. I speak because I am not ignorant what practices have been made against your person lately by Mather, and later, as I understand by foreign practices if it be true. And think if the Admiral in France was an eyesore or beam in the eyes of the papists, that the Lord Treasurer of England is a blot and a crossbar in their way, whose remove they will never stick to attempt, seeing they have prevailed so well in others. This estate hath depended on you a great while as all the world doth judge, and now all men's eyes not being occupied any more on these lost lords are, as it were on a sudden bent and fixed on you, as a singular hope and pillar, whereto the religion hath to lean. And blame me not, though I am bolder with your Lordship than my custom is, for I am one that count myself a follower of yours now in all fortunes ; and what shall hap to you I count it hap to myself ; or at least I will make myself a voluntary partaker of it. Thus, my Lord, I humbly desire your Lordship to pardon my youth, but to take in good part my zeal and affection towards you, as one on whom I have builded my foundation either to stand or to fall. And, good my Lord, think I do not this presumptuously as to advise you that am but to take advice of your Lordship, but to admonish you, as one with whom I would spend my blood and life, so much you have made me yours. And I do protest there is nothing more desired of me than so to be taken and accounted of you. Thus with my hearty commendations and your daughter's we leave you to the custody of Almighty God.

Your Lordship's affectionate son-in-law,

EDWARD OXEFORD.[1]

---

[1] Harleian MSS., 6991. 5.

The next letter, written shortly afterwards, is in the same friendly strain. The letter is addressed " To my singular good Lord the Lord Burghley, and Lord Treasurer of England, give this at the Court," and is endorsed September 22nd, 1572 :

My Lord, I received your letters when I rather looked to have seen yourself here than to have heard from you ; sith it is so that your Lordship is otherwise affaired with the business of the Commonwealth than to be disposed to recreate yourself, and repose you among your own, yet we do hope after this—you having had so great a care of the Queen's Majesty's service—you will begin to have some respect for your own health, and take a pleasure to dwell where you have taken pains to build. My wife, whom I thought should have taken her leave of you if your Lordship had come, till you would have otherwise commanded, is departed unto the country this day : [and my]self as fast as I can get me out of town to follow. If there were any service to be done abroad, I had rather serve there than at home, where yet some honour is to be got. If there be any setting forth to sea, to which service I bear most affection, I shall desire your Lordship to give me and get me that favour and credit that I might make one. Which, if there be no such intention then I shall be most willing to be employed on the sea coasts to be in a readiness with my countrymen against any invasion. Thus remembering myself to your good Lordship, I commit you to God ; from London this 22nd of September, by your Lordship to command.

EDWARD OXENFORD.[1]

Lord Oxford's keenness to serve in the Navy was due no doubt to the comparatively recent discovery of the New World, and to the possibilities it had opened up. The sea made a vivid appeal to the more imaginative and adventurous young men in Elizabethan England. But it was not until 1588, when the Spanish Armada was sailing up channel, that Oxford's wish to see service afloat was gratified.

[1] Lansdowne MSS., 14. 84.

§ III. CHRISTOPHER HATTON

At this point a new character, Christopher Hatton, steps on to the scene ; and as he will occupy a prominent position for many years to come, it will be well to say a few words about him.

Born in 1540 in Northamptonshire, he was ten years older than Lord Oxford. He came to London with the object of studying for the bar about 1560, and in 1564 was made one of the Queen's Gentlemen Pensioners. Attracted by his handsome figure and graceful bearing, the Queen kept him by her side and showered favours on him. Sir John Perrot, her Majesty's half-brother, said of him that " he danced his way into the Queen's favour in a galliard." In 1571 he became a Member of Parliament, and the next year was appointed Captain of the Bodyguard. This rapid rise had fired his ambition, and he consulted Edward Dyer, the poet, and friend of Philip Sidney, as to the best way of maintaining and improving his position at Court.

The best and soundest way in my opinion [Dyer replied on October 9th] is . . . to use your suits towards Her Majesty in words, behaviour, and deeds ; to acknowledge your duty, declaring your reverence which in heart you bear, and never seem to condemn her frailties, but rather joyfully to commend such things as should be in her, as though they were in her indeed : hating my Lord of Crm in the Queen's understanding for affections sake, and blaming him openly for seeking the Queen's favour. . . . Marry, thus much would I advise you to remember, that you use no words of disgrace or reproach towards him to any ; that he, being the less provoked, may sleep, thinking all safe, while you do awake and attend to your advantages.[1]

In the following year Hatton, pursuing Dyer's tactics, wrote one of his curious love-letters to the Queen. He was then on the Continent convalescing after an illness,

---

[1] Harleian MSS., 787. 88. Printed by Sir H. Nicolas, *Life and Times of Sir Christopher Hatton* (1847), p. 18.

and had evidently just received a present from his Royal
Mistress :

God bless you for ever; the branch of the sweetest bush
I will wear and bear to my life's end : God witness I feign
not.   It is a gracious favour most dear and welcome
unto me : reserve it to the Sheep, he hath no tooth to bite,
where the Boar's tusk may both raze and tear.

The " Sheep " was the Queen's nickname for Hatton,
while the " Boar " obviously refers to Oxford, the de Vere
crest being a Blue Boar.   This unmistakeable reference
to the existence of rivalry between Hatton and Oxford
enables us to identify the Earl as " my Lord of Crm " in
the previous letter with some confidence.[1]

We shall see later that Hatton carried out Dyer's cynical
piece of advice with conspicuous success.   But the chief
interest in the letter lies in Dyer's reference to the Earl of
Oxford.   Hatton is advised to cultivate a deliberate and
secret enmity against him, for no reason apparently other
than that Oxford stood high in Her Majesty's favour, a
position coveted by Hatton himself.   These Machiavellian
tactics, as we shall see, were to lead later into a welter of
intrigue.

The falsity of the legend that the execution of the Duke
of Norfolk on June 2nd, 1572 caused a permanent breach
between Lord Burghley and his son-in-law is clearly shown
by the affectionate tone of Lord Oxford's letters to his
father-in-law in the following September.   But two men
so different in outlook and character, could not exist for
long without some misunderstandings and differences
arising between them.   The following letter addressed to
" The right honourable my singular good Lord, the Lord
Treasurer," and endorsed 1572, shows Oxford protesting to

[1] It may be pointed out that Dyer's letter of October 9th containing
the phrase " my Lord of Crm " is only preserved in a copy in Hatton's
letter-book.   Is it possible that the original may have been badly written
and that Hatton's secretary, in making the transcript, read " Crm " for
" Oxon " ?   They would not be dissimilar in badly written script.   " My
Lord of Crm " was evidently some name in the original, and I can think
of no better explanation for this apparently meaningless phrase.

his father-in-law that he should not be too ready to believe sinister reports about himself :

My Lord, Your last letters, which be the first I have received of your Lordship's good opinion conceived towards me, which God grant so long to continue as I would be both desirous and diligent to seek the same, have not a little, after so many storms passed of your heavy grace towards me, lightened and disburdened my careful mind. And, sith I have been so little beholden to sinister reports, I hope now, with your Lordship in different judgment, to be more plausible unto you than heretofore; through my careful deeds to please you, which hardly, either through my youth, or rather my misfortune, hitherto I have done. But yet lest those, I cannot tell how to term them but as backfriends unto me, shall take place again to undo your Lordship's beginnings of well meaning of me, I shall most earnestly desire your Lordship to forbear to believe too fast, lest I, growing so slowly into your good opinion, may be undeservedly of my part voted out of your favour—the which thing to always obtain, if your Lordship do but equally consider of me, may see by all the means possible in me, I do aspire. Though perhaps by reason of my youth, your graver and severer years will not judge the same. Thus therefore hoping the best in your Lordship, and fearing the worst in myself, I take my leave, lest my letters may become loathsome and tedious unto you, to whom I wish to be most grateful. Written this 31st day of October by your loving son-in-law from Wivenhoe,

                                        EDWARD OXFORD.

This bearer hath some need of your Lordship's favour which when he shall speak with your Lordship, I pray you for my sake he may find you the more his furtherer and helper in his cause.[1]

Thus closed the first year of Lord Oxford's married life. It was not an auspicious beginning. Almost before the wedding bells had ceased chiming, a rift caused by Norfolk's execution had opened between the Earl and his father-in-law; and although this rift was not so wide and permanent as has been generally supposed, it is clear that two such men as Burghley and Oxford could not live in

---

[1] Lansdowne MSS., 14. 85.

close proximity and at the same time in complete harmony with one another for more than a very short period.

If Oxford could have realised his desire to see active service abroad, things might have turned out much more happily ; but he was destined to kick his heels idly at home. Not that opportunities for active service were lacking. The massacre of St. Bartholomew, and the King of Spain's ferocious policy against the Protestants in the Low Countries, had intensified the already bitter religious hatreds. The first band of English volunteers under Sir Roger Williams had landed in the Netherlands, and were measuring their strength with the Spanish army, in " His most Catholic Majesty's " dominions. The Spanish menace had begun. Small wonder that Lord Oxford was urging his father-in-law to obtain for him some service " in defence of his Prince and Country."

So, too, thought his uncle, Arthur Golding, for in 1571 he had translated and published *John Calvin's version of the Psalms of David*, which he dedicated in the following words to his nephew :

But you, perchance, according to the noble courage and disposition of your years, do look I should present unto you some History of the Conquests and affairs of mighty Princes, some treatise of the Government of Common Weals, some description of the platte of the whole Earth, or some discourse of Chivalry and Feats of Arms. These things are indeed meet studies for a nobleman, and in their season right necessary for the Commonwealth : but as now I present unto your honour much greater things : that is to wit, true Religion, true Godliness, true Virtue, without the which neither force, policy, nor friendship are of any value, neither can any Commonweal, any City, any household, or any company be well governed or have any stable and long continuance. These be the things wherein your Lordship may do God, your Prince, and your Country best service, and which do give true nobility, or rather are the very nobility itself. The greater that you are of birth and calling, the more do these things belong unto you. The greater gifts of Nature, the more graces of mind, the more worldly benefits that God hath bestowed

upon you, the more are you bound to be thankful unto
him. But thankful you cannot be without the true
knowledge of him, neither can you know him rightly but
by his word. For his word is the lantern of your feet, and
the light of your steps. Whosoever walketh without it
walketh but in darkness, though he were otherwise as
sharp-sighted as Linceus or Argus, and had all the sciences,
arts, cunning, eloquence, and wisdom of the world.[1]

This preface was dedicated to Oxford by his uncle and
former tutor on October 20th, 1571, a few weeks before
his marriage in December of that year. It would seem to
have been a last effort on the part of his tutor to influence
his pupil in the direction of Puritanism. But such efforts
were doomed to disappointment. The movement of the
time that appealed to Oxford was not the Reformation but
the Renaissance, not the ideals of church government propounded by John Calvin but the ideals of honour, justice,
and chivalry so eloquently preached by Balthasar
Castiglione in his treatise on the Perfect Courtier.

§ IV. Il Cortegiano

Lord Oxford's request to be employed on active service
was refused, and once again the old round of court life
begins anew.

My Lord of Oxford is lately grown into great credit
[writes Gilbert Talbot to his father the Earl of Shrewsbury
on May 11th], for the Queen's Majesty delighteth more
in his personage and his dancing and his valiantness than
any other. I think Sussex doth back him all that he can.
If it were not for his fickle head he would pass any of them
shortly. My Lady Burghley unwisely hath declared herself, as it were, jealous, which is come to the Queen's ear :
whereat she hath been not a little offended with her, but
now she is reconciled again. At all these love matters my
Lord Treasurer winketh, and will not meddle in any way.[2]

[1] *The Psalms of David*, Arthur Golding, 1571.
[2] *Illustrations of British History*, Lodge, 1791, vol, ii. p. 100. Lord
Shrewsbury was then employed in guarding Mary, Queen of Scots ; his
son was aged twenty, and at the Court.

But the Court with its dancing, feasting, and revelry, was far from fulfilling Lord Oxford's ideal of life ; and as he had perforce to remain in London, we find him beginning to seek a new outlet for his activities. This outlet, destined to play so great a part in his life, was literature.

That he should have turned to literature when active service abroad was denied him was natural. We have seen him taking his degree at Cambridge when only fourteen and a half ; and we know that by the time he was twenty his library included the works of Chaucer, Plutarch, Cicero and Plato, besides " other books and papers." We have also seen, on the evidence of his tutor Arthur Golding, that he took a keen interest in " the present estate of things in our days, and that not without a certain pregnancy of wit and ripeness of understanding." It is therefore not surprising to find him eager to support and encourage writers whose enthusiasms corresponded with his own.

All the great movements of the sixteenth century had by this time fully declared themselves. *The Courtier*, by Castiglione,[1] was published at Venice in 1528 ; *The Prince*, by Machiavelli, in 1532 ; Calvin's *Institutes of the Christian Religion* appeared in 1536, and in 1541 he had been recalled from exile to direct the Puritan State of Geneva.   In that same year, 1541, Ignatius Loyola was elected General of the new Society of Jesus. Castiglione had been the friend of Raphael, and of Cardinal Bembo, the Platonist and finished Latin scholar. He represented the æsthetic side of the Renaissance, to which he added all that was best in the old mediæval tradition of chivalry and honour. Machiavelli, on the other hand, had little sympathy with the past ; he freed the State from moral law, and advocated the use of force and fraud as essential elements of government.

Calvin looked upon the State as a divine institution, and Geneva was ruled in accordance with Christian principles

---

[1] Baldassare Castiglione (1478–1529) was an Italian statesman and man of letters.

with a rod of iron. Ignatius Loyola represented the Counter-Reformation.

Oxford's upbringing in Burghley's Protestant household had failed to influence him in the direction of Puritanism, and left his mind open to the ideas of the Counter-Reformation, to which a few years later he succumbed for a time. The real influence which his university career and subsequent reading had left upon his mind was, however, the glory of the classical languages, more especially of Latin, and the beauty of the old ideas of aristocracy and chivalry. In a word, the movements represented by Machiavelli and Calvin did not interest him at all ; and although later on he was destined to feel some sympathy for the old form of religion which had been in vogue during his youth, it was to Balthasar Castiglione that his heart really went out. When, therefore, he found his old Cambridge tutor, Bartholomew Clerke, engaged on a translation from Italian into Latin of his much-admired author, he took the greatest interest in the progress of the work, and decided on the occasion of its publication to give it as powerful a send-off as possible by contributing an appreciative and enthusiastic preface. As this preface seems to have been Oxford's first serious incursion into literature, and as he never seems to have deserted the principles here enunciated by him, it is important that it should be given in full. The following is a translation of this eloquent piece of Latin prose :

Edward Vere, Earl of Oxford, Lord Great Chamberlain of England, Viscount Bulbeck and Baron Scales and Badlesmere to the Reader—Greeting.

A frequent and earnest consideration of the translation of Castiglione's Italian work, which has now for a long time been undertaken and finally carried out by my friend Clerke, has caused me to waver between two opinions : debating in my mind whether I should preface it by some writing and letter of my own, or whether I should do no more than study it with a mind full of gratitude. The first course seemed to demand greater skill and art than I can lay claim to, the second to be a work of no less good-will and application. To do both, however, seemed to combine a task of delightful industry with an indication of special good-will.

I have therefore undertaken the work, and I do so the more willingly, in order that I may lay a laurel wreath of my own on the translation in which I have studied this book, and also to ensure that neither my good-will (which is very great) should remain unexpressed, nor that my skill (which is small) should seem to fear to face the light and the eyes of men.

It is no more than its due that praises of every kind should be rendered to this work descriptive of a Courtier. It is indeed in every way right and one may say almost inevitable that with the highest and greatest praises I should address both the author and translator, and even more the great patroness of so great a work, whose name alone on the title-page gives it a right majestic and honourable introduction.

For what more difficult, more noble, or more magnificent task has anyone ever undertaken than our author Castiglione, who has drawn for us the figure and model of a courtier, a work to which nothing can be added, in which there is no redundant word, a portrait which we shall recognise as that of the highest and most perfect type of man. And so, although nature herself has made nothing perfect in every detail, yet the manners of men exceed in dignity that with which nature has endowed them ; and he who surpasses others has here surpassed himself, and has even outdone nature which by no one has ever been surpassed. Nay more, however elaborate the ceremonial, whatever the magnificence of the Court, the splendour of the Courtiers, and the multitude of spectators, he has been able to lay down principles for the guidance of the very Monarch himself.

Again, Castiglione has vividly depicted more and even greater things than these. For who has spoken of Princes with greater gravity ? Who has discoursed of illustrious women with a more ample dignity ? No one has written of military affairs more eloquently, more aptly about horse-racing, and more clearly and admirably about encounters under arms on the field of battle: I will say nothing of the fitness and the excellence with which he has depicted the beauty of chivalry in the noblest persons. Nor will I refer to his delineations in the case of those

7

persons who cannot be Courtiers, when he alludes to some notable defect, or to some ridiculous character, or to some deformity of appearance. Whatever is heard in the mouths of men in casual talk and in society, whether apt and candid, or villainous and shameful, that he has set down in so natural a manner that it seems to be acted before our very eyes.

Again, to the credit of the translator of so great a work, a writer too who is no mean orator, must be added a new glory of language. For although Latin has come down to us from the ancient city of Rome, a city in which the study of eloquence flourished exceedingly, it has now given back its features for use in modern Courts as a polished language of an excellent temper, fitted out with royal pomp, and possessing admirable dignity. All this my good friend Clerke has done, combining exceptional genius with wonderful eloquence. For he has resuscitated that dormant quality of fluent discourse. He has recalled those ornaments and lights which he had laid aside, for use in connexion with subjects most worthy of them. For this reason he deserves all the more honour, because that to great subjects—and they are indeed great—he has applied the greatest lights and ornaments.

For who is clearer in his use of words ? Or richer in the dignity of his sentences ? Or who can conform to the variety of circumstances with greater art ? If weighty matters are under consideration, he unfolds his theme in a solemn and majestic rhythm ; if the subject is familiar and facetious, he makes use of words that are witty and amusing. When therefore he writes with precise and well-chosen words, with skilfully constructed and crystal-clear sentences, and with every art of dignified rhetoric, it cannot be but that some noble quality should be felt to proceed from his work. To me indeed it seems, when I read this courtly Latin, that I am listening to Crassus, Antonius, and Hortensius, discoursing on this very theme.

And, great as all these qualities are, our translator has wisely added one single surpassing title of distinction to recommend his work. For indeed what more effective tion could he have taken to make his work fruitful of good results than to dedicate his *Courtier* to our most illustrious and noble Queen, in whom all courtly qualities are personified, together with those diviner and truly celestial virtues ?   For there is no pen so skilful or powerful, no kind of speech so clear, that is not left behind by her own surpassing virtue. It was therefore an excellent display of wisdom on the part of our translator to seek out as a patroness of his work one who was of surpassing virtue, of wisest mind, of soundest religion, and cultivated in the highest degree in learning and in literary studies.

Lastly, if the noblest attributes of the wisest Princes, the safest protection of a flourishing commonwealth, the greatest qualities of the best citizens, by her own merit, and in the opinion of all, continually encompass her around ; surely to obtain the protection of that authority, to strengthen it with gifts, and to mark it with the superscription of her name, is a work which, while worthy of all Monarchs, is most worthy of our own Queen, to whom alone is due all the praise of all the Muses and all the glory of literature.

Given at the Royal Court on the 5th of January 1571.[1]

This preface was reprinted in all subsequent editions of Clerke's translation of *The Courtier*. It must have been well known to all educated Elizabethans, to whom Latin was a perfectly familiar language. Six years later—in 1578—Gabriel Harvey alludes to it as a well-known example of Oxford's literary eminence. " Let that courtly epistle, more polished even than the writings of Castiglione himself, witness how greatly thou dost excel in letters." [2]

But it is not only remarkable as an eloquent piece of Latin prose. It seems to indicate a determination on the part of its author to do something more for literature than merely to accept dedications from authors. For the first time in our annals we find a nobleman taking immense trouble to recommend a book in which he is interested. We shall find Oxford in the following year not only doing the same thing again, but actually paying for the publication of the book himself. Here was a literary patron indeed, and there would seem to be little doubt that the initial impulse came from the Queen who is so magnificently eulogised in the closing words of the Preface.

[1] I.e., 1572, N.S.   [2] *Gratulationes Valdinenses*, lib. iv, 1578.

§ V. Thomas Bedingfield

The following year, 1573, we find that a sum of £10 11s. 8d. is due to the Hospital of the Savoy " from Edward, Earl of Oxford " on account of " part rent of two tenements within the Hospital." [1] The Savoy at this time was a well-known haunt of literary men, who were given rooms in it by their patrons. We shall meet here, later on, such men as Gabriel Harvey and John Lyly, the latter in his capacity of secretary and actor-manager to Lord Oxford's company of players, and the former as the Earl's friend and contemporary at Oxford University.

Other writers were seeking his patronage, among them Thomas Twyne [2] ; not, as the following dedication shows, merely because he was a rich nobleman, but because, as Twyne puts it, " your honour taketh singular delight " in " books of Geography, Histories, and other good learning." But we must read it all, and not in extracts, in order to appreciate it to the full.

To the Right Honourable Edward de Vere, Lord Bulbeck, Earl of Oxford, Lord Great Chamberlain of England : Tho. Twyne wisheth long life, perfect health, increase of honour, and endless felicity.

Nobility is a precious gift, which so glittereth in the eyes of all men, that there is no one corporal thing in this world whereof we make a greater account. For so it is esteemed of all, desired of all, and reverenced by all virtue, saith Tully, and before him Plato : if it might be seen with our bodily eyes doubtless it would procure marvellous love, and good liking unto itself, the show thereof would appear so fair and amiable.

The uniting of which two most noble graces, with all other furniture of Nature and Fortune within your person, Right Honourable and my very good Lord, hath so bent my judgment, and brought me into such liking and

---

[1] W. J. Loftie, *Memorials of the Savoy* (1878), p. 125.

[2] Thomas Twyne (1543–1613), physician; Fellow of Corpus Christi College, Oxford, 1564 ; M.A. 1568 ; M.D. Oxford 1593 ; M.D. Cambridge ; practised at Lewes ; author of several works. He completed Phaer's translation of the *Æneid* into blank verse.

admiration thereof, that I have rested no small time, not
only not satisfied in being one of the admirators, but also
desirous to be one of the participators of those your honour's
most laudable dispositions, whereunto I do now humbly
submit myself.   And in token of my dutiful meaning
herein, am so hardy as to present your honour with this
simple travail, which I so term, in respect of my pains in
translating the same.   Howbeit I am persuaded that it
cost Master Lhuyd, who first and not long since wrote the
same in Latin, no small labour and industry in the gathering
and the penning.

Regarding your honour to be among the rest a very
fit person for it, in consideration that being, as yet, but in
your flower and tender age and generally hoped and
accounted of in time to become the chiefest stay of this your
commonwealth and country you would receive into your
safe tuition the written name and description of that
Britain, which, as it is in part your native soil, so your duty
biddeth you to defend and maintain it.   Hereon, when your
honour shall be at leisure to look, bestowing such regard as
you are accustomed to do on books of Geography, Histories, and other good learning, wherein I am privy your
honour taketh singular delight, I doubt not but you shall
have cause to judge your time very well applied.   And so
much the rather for that in the study of Geography it is
expedient first to know exactly the situation of our own
home, where we bide, before that we shall be able to judge
how other countries do lie unto us, which are far distant
from us, besides that it were a foul shame to be inquisitive
of the state of foreign lands and to be ignorant of our
own.   As your honour being already perfectly instructed
is not now to learn at my hand.   But for my part it shall
be sufficient that your honour should deign to accept this
small present, or rather therein my hearty good will, which
being no otherwise able to gratify the same, shall never
cease to pray to God that he would always direct you in the
commendable race of your virtue and learning which you
have begun, augment your honour with many degrees,
and in the end reward you with immortal felicity.

Your honour's most humble at commandment,

THOMAS TWYNE.[1]

---

[1] *The Breviary of Britain.   Written in Latin by Humphrey Lhuyd . . .
and lately Englished by Thomas Twyne, gentleman,* 1573.

Another of Lord Oxford's friends in the literary world
was Thomas Bedingfield.[1] They had known each other
some time before this date, because, it will be remembered,
Bedingfield had been one of the Defenders opposed to
Oxford in the Tournament of 1571. Just before this
Tournament Bedingfield had completed the manuscript
of his translation of *Cardanus' Comfort*. Lord Oxford had
evidently asked to be allowed to read it ; for in his covering
letter sending it to him, Bedingfield says :

My good Lord, I can give nothing more agreeable to
your mind and fortune than the willing performance of
such service as it shall please you to command me unto.
And therefore rather to obey than to boast of my cunning,
and as a new sign of mine old devotion, I do present the
book your Lordship so long desired, . . . because most
faithfully I honour and love you.

He goes on with a playful allusion to the title of the
book :

A needless thing I know it is to comfort you, whom
nature and fortune hath not only inured but rather upon
whom they have bountifully bestowed their grace : notwithstanding sith you delight to see others acquitted by
[of] cares, your Lordship shall not do amiss to read some
part of Cardanus' counsel : wherein considering the
manifold miseries of others, you may the rather esteem
your own happy estate with increase of those noble and
rare virtues which I know and rejoice to be in you. Sure
I am it would have better beseemed me to have taken
this travail in some discourse of arms (being your Lordship's chief profession and mine also) than in philosopher's
skill to have thus busied myself : yet sith your pleasure
was such, and your knowledge in either great, I do
(as I will ever) most willingly obey you. And if
any either through skill or curiosity do find fault with
me, I trust notwithstanding for the respects aforesaid

---

[1] Thomas Bedingfield (*d.* 1613) was a son of Queen Elizabeth's jailer,
Sir Henry Bedingfield. He was a Gentleman Pensioner, and the author
of various miscellaneous works.

to be holden excused. From my lodging this first of
January, 1571.[1]
            Your Lordship's always to command,
                        Thomas Bedingfield.

Although at the moment other matters were occupying
his attention, Lord Oxford did not forget the manuscript
he had read and enjoyed.   And it happened that when he
turned his whole attention in 1573 to literature, he remembered Bedingfield's work, and decided to undertake its
publication in defiance of its author's wishes.   In due
course it appeared, the title-page reading, *Cardanus' Com-
forte, translated into Englishe. And published by com-
maundement of the right honourable the Earle of Oxenforde.
Anno Domini* 1573.

Oxford himself wrote a prefatory letter and a poem,
which appeared in the book, both of which are given
below :

To my loving friend Thomas Bedingfield Esquire, one of
Her Majesty's Gentlemen Pensioners.

After I had perused your letters, good Master Bedingfield, finding in them your request far differing from the
desert of your labour, I could not choose but greatly
doubt whether it were better for me to yield to your desire,
or execute mine own intention towards the publishing
of your book.   For I do confess the affections that I have
always borne towards you could move me not a little.
But when I had thoroughly considered in my mind, of
sundry and diverse arguments, whether it were best to
obey mine affections, or the merits of your studies ; at
the length I determined it were better to deny your
unlawful request than to grant or condescend to the
concealment of so worthy a work.   Whereby as you have
been profited in the translating, so many may reap
knowledge by the reading of the same that shall comfort
the afflicted, confirm the doubtful, encourage the coward,
and lift up the base-minded man to achieve to any true

[1] Although it might appear at first sight that this date should be 1572
New Style, 1571 is probably correct, because January 1st was spoken of as
New Year's Day.   Compare the lists of New Year's presents given to the
Queen on January 1st every year. (Nichols, *Progresses*.)

sum or grade of virtue, whereto ought only the noble thoughts of men to be inclined.

And because next to the sacred letters of divinity, nothing doth persuade the same more than philosophy, of which your book is plentifully stored, I thought myself to commit an unpardonable error to have murdered the same in the waste bottom of my chests ; and better I thought it were to displease one than to displease many ; further considering so little a trifle cannot procure so great a breach of our amity, as may not with a little persuasion of reason be repaired again. And herein I am forced, like a good and politic captain, oftentimes to spoil and burn the corn of his own country, lest his enemies thereof do take advantage. For rather than so many of your countrymen should be deluded through my sinister means of your industry in studies (whereof you are bound in conscience to yield them an account) I am content to make spoil and havoc of your request, and that, that might have wrought greatly in me in this former respect, utterly to be of no effect or operation. And when you examine yourself, what doth avail a mass of gold to be continually imprisoned in your bags, and never to be employed to your use ? Wherefore we have this Latin proverb : *Scire tuum nihil est, nisi te scire hoc sciat alter.* What doth avail the tree unless it yield fruit unto another ? What doth avail the vine unless another delighteth in the grape ? What doth avail the rose unless another took pleasure in the smell ? Why should this tree be accounted better than that tree but for the goodness of his fruit ? Why should this rose be better esteemed than that rose, unless in pleasantness of smell it far surpassed the other rose ?

And so it is in all other things as well as in man. Why should this man be more esteemed than that man but for his virtue, through which every man desireth to be accounted of ? Then you amongst men, I do not doubt, but will aspire to follow that virtuous path, to illuster yourself with the ornaments of virtue. And in mine opinion as it beautifieth a fair woman to be decked with pearls and precious stones, so much more it ornifieth a gentleman to be furnished with glittering virtues.

Wherefore, considering the small harm I do to you, the great good I do to others, I prefer mine own intention to discover your volume, before your request to secret same ;

wherein I may seem to you to play the part of the cunning
and expert mediciner or physician, who although his
patient in the extremity of his burning fever is desirous
of cold liquor or drink to qualify his sore thirst or rather
kill his languishing body ; yet for the danger he doth
evidently know by his science to ensue, denieth him the
same. So you being sick of so much doubt in your own
proceedings, through which infirmity you are desirous to
bury and insevill [1] your works in the grave of oblivion :
yet I, knowing the discommodities that shall redound to
yourself thereby (and which is more unto your countrymen) as one that is willing to salve so great an inconvenience,
am nothing dainty to deny your request.

Again we see, if our friends be dead we cannot show or
declare our affection more than by erecting them of tombs,
whereby when they be dead in deed, yet make we them
live as it were again through their monument. But with
me behold it happeneth far better ; for in your lifetime I
shall erect you such a monument that, as I say, in your
lifetime you shall see how noble a shadow of your virtuous
life shall hereafter remain when you are dead and gone.
And in your lifetime, again I say, I shall give you that
monument and remembrance of your life whereby I may
declare my good will, though with your ill will, as yet
that I do bear you in your life.

Thus earnestly desiring you in this one request of mine
(as I would yield to you in a great many) not to repugn
the setting forth of your own proper studies, I bid you
farewell. From my new country Muses of Wivenhoe,[2]
wishing you as you have begun, to proceed in these virtuous
actions. For when all things shall else forsake us, virtue
will ever abide with us, and when our bodies fall into the
bowels of the earth, yet that shall mount with our minds
into the highest heavens.

From your loving and assured friend,

E. OXENFORD.

THE EARL OF OXFORD TO THE READER OF BEDINGFIELD'S
" CARDANUS' COMFORT "

The labouring man that tills the fertile soil,
And reaps the harvest fruit, hath not indeed
The gain, but pain ; but if for all his toil
He gets the straw, the lord will have the seed.

---

[1] From the French *ensevelir*, meaning "to bury."
[2] Wivenhoe is on the Essex coast, at the mouth of the river Colne.

The manchet fine falls not unto his share ;
  On coarsest cheat his hungry stomach feeds.
The landlord doth possess the finest fare ;
  He pulls the flowers, the other plucks but weeds.

The mason poor that builds the lordly halls,
  Dwells not in them ; they are for high degree ;
His cottage is compact in paper walls,
  And not with brick or stone, as others be.

The idle drone that labours not at all,
  Sucks up the sweet of honey from the bee ;
Who worketh most to their share least doth fall,
  With due desert reward will never be.

The swiftest hare unto the mastiff slow
  Oft-times doth fall, to him as for a prey ;
The greyhound thereby doth miss his game we know
  For which he made such speedy haste away.

So he that takes the pain to pen the book
  Reaps not the gifts of golden goodly muse ;
But those gain that, who on the work shall look,
  And from the sour the sweet by skill shall choose ;
For he that beats the bush the bird not gets,
  But who sits still and holdeth fast the nets.

It is not difficult when we read these two eloquent pieces of prose in *The Courtier* and *Cardanus' Comfort* to see that literature was already bidding fair to become the master passion of Lord Oxford's life. His new home by the sea in Essex has been christened his " new country Muses," and literary men were already finding in him not merely a patron willing to be the passive recipient of a dedication, but one who took a keen interest in reading their manuscripts. Best of all, he was ready to pay for the publication, for this is the only construction we can put upon the phrase " published by commandment of the right honourable the Earl of Oxenford."

In May we hear of three of Lord Oxford's men holding up two of their former associates on Gad's Hill, near Rochester. The two latter submitted a complaint, which is sufficiently curious to warrant inclusion. It is addressed

" to the Right Honourable the Lord Burghley, Lord
Treasurer of England," and endorsed " Fawnt and Wotton,
May 1573 from Gravesend."

The dutiful regard we owe to your honour, and the due
confidence we have in this case, doth stay us to address
our complaint to any but to your lordship, because the
matter doth near touch the honour of my late good Lord
and master, of whom publicly to hear complaint of raging
demeanour would grieve your honour and myself to make
it, if there were any other means for our security.   So it
is, Right Honourable, Wootton and myself riding peace-
ably by the highway from Gravesend to Rochester, had
three calivers charged with bullets, discharged at us by
three of my Lord of Oxford's men ; Danye Wylkyns,
John Hannam, and Deny the Frenchman, who lay privily
in a ditch awaiting our coming with full intent to murder
us ; yet (notwithstanding they all discharging upon us
so near that my saddle having the girths broken fell with
myself from the horse and a bullet within half a foot of
me) it pleased God to deliver us from that determined
mischief ; whereupon they mounted on horseback and fled
towards London with all possible speed.   The consideration hereof doth warn us to provide for our safety, insomuch
as we plainly see our lives are sought, for otherwise the
forenamed parties would not have pursued us from London.
Who in like manner yesterday beset our lodging, for which
cause and to preserve my Lord's favour in time, we left
the city and chose the country for our safeguard, where we
find ourselves in no less peril of spoil than before ; and now
seeing that neither city nor country is a sufficient protection
from their malice, humbly appeal to your honour, whom
we never knew but a maintainer of justice and punisher
of abuses (. . .) generally to the counsel as your honour
liketh best, they (have now) given us great advantage of
them, which surely we would pursue to the uttermost of
it, wer't not in respect of our late noble Lord and master,
who with pardon be it spoken, is to be thought as the
procurer of that which is done.   And so consider, Right
Honourable, if we have offended the laws of the realm or
our late noble Lord, as (which we have not) we remain here
in Gravesend to abide condign punishment, from whence we
dare not depart before we be assured of our security, and

order taken for them.　Thus beseeching God to preserve your Honour; from Gravesend this present Thursday.

By your Honour's ever to command,

WILLM FFAUNT.　JOHN WOTTON.[1]

Towards the end of the year Oxford's old longing to see " strange and foreign parts " broke out afresh.　We cannot say actually how near he was to going; but we know that Sir William Cordell, the Master of the Rolls, was told to settle the necessary financial arrangements, which he did on September 2nd.　The biggest problem was the question of the Earl's debts.　" To determine what my debts are certainly," Lord Oxford replied to one of Cordell's interrogations, " it is not possible, and because as yet I cannot have the right of them all; but my debts to the Queen's Majesty are these which I have gathered together considered.　I have just cause to think that the sum of my debts will be £6,000 at the least."　For the payment of this sum he agrees to set aside between £400 and £500 a year.　He then goes on to outline his family arrangements.　" For my wife to live on during my absence I have assigned £300; and for her jointure £669 6s. 8d. . . . For myself, to serve my turn beyond the seas, £1,000; . . . and for my sister £100." [2]

Nothing, however, came of this project and he continued at Court for the remainder of the year, both the Queen and Lord Burghley being, as we know, very much opposed to the idea of foreign travel.

§ VI.　THE LOW COUNTRIES

The opening month of 1574 brings us in touch once more with Ralph Lane.　The French Ambassador had in 1571 associated him with Lord Oxford, in connexion with the scheme to rescue the Duke of Norfolk from the Tower.　On January 17th Lane wrote to Burghley about various matters, including "the protection of Portugal's traffic."　This was no doubt a proposal to bolster up Portugal against the ever-increasing power of Spain—a proposal which was

[1] S.P. Dom. Eliz., 91. 36.　　　　[2] Hatfield MSS. (Cal. II. 58).

fully justified by after-events.   For six years later Spain
absorbed Portugal, thus at one stroke almost doubling her
Empire, her Navy, and her Mercantile Marine.

There is no clue as to Oxford's connexion with this project beyond the endorsement of Lane's letter in Burghley's
own hand, which runs, " 17th Jan. 1573.   Raff Lane ;
Er. Oxf : L. Edwd. Sem ; Guerras." [1]

In March Oxford accompanied the Queen when she visited
the Archbishop of Canterbury, for on the 19th he vacated
his quarters at Lambeth Palace, which were then allotted
to Christopher Hatton.[2]

On June 27th Lord Burghley wrote to the Earl of Sussex,
who was Lord Chamberlain :

My good Lord, I heartily thank you for your gentle
remembrance of my daughter of Oxinforde, who, as I
think meaneth as her duty is, to wait on Her Majesty at
Richmond, except my Lord her husband shall otherwise
direct her.   And so I take my leave.

Your Lordship's assuredly
W. BURGHLEY.[3]

Sussex, as Lord Chamberlain, was responsible for the
allotment of rooms when the Court was situated in one of
the Royal Palaces.   It was no doubt on this account that
Lord Burghley wrote on behalf of his daughter and his
son-in-law.

Suddenly, in the midst of all this peace and quiet, a
bombshell was exploded in the Court.   We hear of it in
a letter from Henry Killigrew, then Ambassador at
Edinburgh :

My Lord of Oxford [he wrote to Walsingham on July
18th] and Lord Seymour are fled out of England, and
passed by Bruges to Brussels.[4]

---

[1] Hatfield MSS. (Cal. II. 68).

[2] E. K. Chambers, *Elizabethan Stage*, vol. iv, p. 90.

[3] Quoted in Colchester MS. (cit.), p. 150.   No authority is given, and the
original seems to have disappeared.

[4] Cal. S.P. Foreign.   Oxford had been abroad at least three weeks
before this letter was written.

The consternation this news caused at the Court can well be imagined when we remember that the Earl of Westmorland, who had been attainted for his part in the rebellion of 1569, was then an exile in Brussels.   It must have seemed, in the absence of definite news, that the Lord Treasurer's son-in-law had thrown in his lot with the Queen's enemies.

There was a great triumph among the northern rebels ... when they heard of the Earl of Oxford's coming over ; it was said that he was flying, and that the Earl of Southampton had fled to Spain.   In a council held at Louvain, it was concluded that the Earl of Westmorland should ride to Bruges to welcome him, and persuade him not to return ; but the Earls did not meet.   It were a great pity such a valiant and noble young gentleman should communicate with such detestable men.[1]

The Queen was furious and instantly despatched Thomas Bedingfield with orders to fetch him home.   On July 15th Lord Burghley wrote anxiously to the Earl of Sussex, who, as Oxford's friend, was trying to smooth the troubled waters :

I must heartily thank your Lordship for your advertisement of my Lord of Oxford's cause, wherein I am sorry that Her Majesty maketh such haste. . . .   My Lord, howsoever my Lord of Oxford be for his own part [in] matters of thrift inconsiderate, I dare avow him to be resolute in dutifulness to the Queen and his country.[2]

Lord Burghley proved right ; within a fortnight Oxford was back in England.

Of my Lord of Oxford's return [writes Sir Walter Mildmay on July 27th] I am glad to hear.   I trust this little journey will make him love home the better hereafter. It were a great pity he should not go straight, there be so many good things in him, to serve his God and Prince.[3]

----

[1] Cal. S.P. Dom. Add. Edward Woodshaw to Lord Burghley, September 3rd, 1574 ; from Antwerp.

[2] Cotton MSS., Titus B. 2. 298.

[3] *Queen Elizabeth*, Wright (1838), p. 507.

On July 29th Lord Burghley and Lady Oxford went to
London to meet the Earl, and the following day all three
went down to Theobalds. Here they waited to hear Her
Majesty's pleasure. The Court was then in progress and
by August 1st had reached Woodstock. On this date
Sir Francis Walsingham wrote to Lord Burghley :

I find Her Majesty graciously enough inclined towards
the Earl of Oxford, whose peace I think will be both easily
and speedily made, for that Her Majesty doth conceive
that his evidence in his return hath [countered ?] the contempt of his departure ; and the rather than avow his
honourable and dutiful carriage of himself towards the
rebels . . . an argument of his approved loyalty, which,
as appears to-night, shall serve.[1]

Burghley replied at some length in an earnest appeal
to Walsingham on behalf of his son-in-law :

Sir, Yesternight your letters came to Master Benigfeld [2]
and me signifying Her Majesty's pleasure that my Lord of
Oxford should come to Gloucester now at Her Majesty's
being there. Whereof he being advertised by us was very
ready to take the journey, showing in himself a mixture of
contrary affections, although both reasonable and commendable. The one, fearful and doubtful in what sort he
shall recover Her Majesty's favour because of his offence
in departure as he did without licence ; the other, glad
and resolute to look for a speedy good end because he had
in his abode so notoriously rejected the attempts of Her
Majesty's evil subjects, and in his return set apart all his
own particular desires of foreign travel and come to
present himself before Her Majesty, of whose goodness
towards him he saith he cannot count. Hereupon he and
Master Benigfeld departed this afternoon to London,
where the Earl, as I perceive, will spend only two days or
less to make him some apparel meet for the Court, although
I would have had him forbear that new charge, considering
his former apparel is very sufficient, and he not provided
to increase a new charge.

I must be bold by this my letter to require you in my
name most humbly to beseech Her Majesty that she will

---

[1] Harleian MSS., 6991. 50.   [2] Presumably Thomas Bedingfield.

regard his loyalty and not his lightness in sudden joy over his confidence in her goodness and clemency, and not his boldness in attempting that which hath offended her. And finally so to order him both in the order and speed of his coming to Her Majesty's pleasure, that Her Majesty's enemies and rebels which sought by many devices to stay him from returning, may perceive his returning otherwise rewarded than they would have had him imagined, and that also his friends, that have advised him to return, may take comfort thereof with himself, and he not repent his dutifulness in doing that which in this time none hath done—I mean of such as have either gone without licence, and not returned in their due time. . . . I think it is sound counsel to be given to Her Majesty, that this young nobleman, being of such a quality as he is for birth, office, and other notable valours of body and spirit, he may not be discomforted either by any extraordinary delay or by any outward sharp or unkind reproof . . . and that her favourable accepting of his submission may be largely and manifestly declared unto him, to the confirmation of him in his singular loyalty. . . . If he shall not find comfort now in this amendment of his fault, I fear the malice of some discontented persons, wherewith the Court is overmuch sprinkled, [may] set to draw him to a repentance rather of his dutifulness in thus returning, than to set in him a contentation to continue in his duty. . . .

I cannot well end, neither will I end, without also praying you to remember Master Hatton to continue my Lord's friend, as he hath manifestly been, and as my Lord confesseth to me that he hopeth assuredly so to prove him. . . . I pray you so to deal with my Lords that are to deal with my Lord of Oxford, that this my letter to you prove as an intercession to them from me for my Lord ; and I doubt not but Master Secretary Smith will remember his old love towards the Earl when he was his scholar.[1]

The reference to Hatton is interesting. It is clear that neither Burghley nor Oxford had any idea that Hatton was secretly jealous of the Earl's high favour, or that Dyer in 1572 had advised him to " use no words of disgrace or reproach towards him to any ; that he being the less provoked may sleep, thinking all safe, while you do awake and

[1] S.P. Dom., 98. 2.

attend to your advantages." Hatton's apparent befriend-
ing of Lord Oxford at this juncture need not therefore
surprise us.   It was quite in accordance not only with
Dyer's cynical advice, but also with the time-honoured
methods adopted by the court " reptilia," as Lord
Willoughby called the social climbers who were seeking
their own advancement.

By August 7th Lord Oxford had made his peace with
the Queen. A copy of a letter exists in the Domestic
State Papers in which the writer says :

. . . I am sure you are not inadvertised how the Earl
of Oxford is restored to Her Majesty's favour, in whose
loyal behaviour towards Her Majesty's rebels in the Low
Country who sought conference with him, a thing he utterly
refused, did very much qualify his contempt in departing
without Her Majesty's leave. The desire of travel is not
yet quenched in him, though he dare not make any motion
unto Her Majesty that he may with her favour accomplish
the said desire. By no means he can be drawn to follow
the Court, and yet there are many cunning devices used
in that behalf for his stay. . . .[1]

The Earl, however, did stay at the Court during the
progress, for Burghley notes that from August 5th to
September 16th " he was absent in the Progress."   On this
latter date he returned to Theobalds, where many supper
parties were held, among the guests being Lady Lennox, the
Earl and Countess of Northumberland, and Lady Hunsdon.[2]

Three days before Lord Oxford arrived at Theobalds the
Countess of Oxford wrote to Lord Chamberlain Sussex :

My good Lord, Because I think it long since I saw Her
Majesty, and would be glad to do my duty after Her
Majesty's coming to Hampton Court,[3] I heartily beseech
your good Lordship to show me your favour in your order
to the ushers for my lodging ; that in consideration that
there is but two chambers, it would please you to increase

---

[1] S.P. Dom. 98. 5.   The Calendar, noting that it is only a copy, suggests
Walsingham as the writer.
[2] Hatfield MSS. (Cal. XIII. 144).
[3] The Queen returned to Hampton Court on October 1st.

8

it with a third chamber next unto it, which was reserved last time for my Lord Arundel's men, and, as I was informed by my Lord Howard, he had it when he lay in the same lodging. I shall think myself greatly bound to you for it, for the more commodious my lodging is the willinger I hope my Lord my husband will be to come thither, thereby the oftener to attend Her Majesty. Thus trusting in your Lordship's favourable consideration I leave to trouble your Lordship any further, with my most hearty commendations to my good Lady your wife.[1] From my father's house at Theobalds.

Your lordship's poor friend
ANNE OXENFORDE.[2]

This curious little appeal by the Countess of Oxford in order to make court life more attractive to her husband is most interesting. It shows us clearly that the Earl had little inclination for court routine, but preferred his " new country Muses " and his " lewd friends," as Lord Burghley called his literary companions. It is not recorded whether the Countess was granted her request, but it is probable ; for Burghley in his diary tells us that the Earl and his Countess spent October at Hampton Court.

Lord Oxford's brief trip to the Low Countries had coincided with an important military operation in the war between the Dutch and the Spaniards. Bommel was a place of great strategical importance, forming an outpost in the defence of Flanders. From June till October 1574 a Spanish force under Hierges laid siege to it, but it was successfully defended by Van Haeften, who eventually forced the enemy to raise the siege by cutting the dykes.

Lord Oxford, as we have seen, was deeply interested in all military matters, and he must have visited the Spanish lines outside Bommel in July. He took great delight in after years in recounting this adventure, and, when flushed with wine, allowed his imagination to run riot in

---

[1] Lady Sussex was Sir Philip Sidney's aunt, and the foundress of Sidney-Sussex College.

[2] Quoted in Colchester MS. (cit), p. 150. No authority is given. From internal evidence, and from its being placed next to Lord Burghley's letter quoted from this MS., it evidently belongs to this year.

the most fantastic, but nevertheless amusing way.   Reference has already been made to the attempts in 1581 on
the part of Charles Arundel to disgrace the Earl in the
Queen's eyes.   This he did by collecting all the scandal
and slander he could lay hands on.   One of these items
was headed " details of three notable lies."   As they throw
an illuminating light not only on Oxford's after-dinner talk
but also on his escapade in the Low Countries, the first
of these, as recounted by Charles Arundel, is given below :

At his [Oxford's] being in Flanders, the Duke of Alva,[1]
as he [Oxford] will constantly affirm, grew so much to
affect him for the several parts he saw in him, as he made
him his Lieutenant General over all the army then in the
Low Countries, and employed him further in a notable
piece of service, where according to his place he commanded and directed the Ambassador of Spain [2] that is
now here, Mondragon, Santio d'Avila, and the rest of the
captains ; but these who I have named, as he will say of
all others, were most glad to be commanded by him.
And so valiantly he behaved himself as he gained great
love of all the soldiers, and in less admiration of his valour
of all sorts.   And in this journey he passed many straits
and divers bridges kept by the enemy, which he let them
from [3] with the loss of many a man's life.   But still he
forced them to retire, till at the last he ·approached the
place that he went to besiege ; and using no delay the
cannon was planted and the battery continued the space
of ten days, by which time he had made such a breach as
by a general consent of all his captains he gave an assault,
and to encourage his soldiers this valiant prince led them
thereto, and through the force of his murdering arm many
were sore wounded, but more killed.   Notwithstanding
being not well followed by the reiters [and] others, he was

---

[1] The Duke of Alva (1508–1582) was sent by Philip II. to the Low
Countries in 1567 with orders to restore the Catholic religion.   But the
determined resistance offered by the Burghers was too much for him,
and he returned to Spain, a broken man, in December 1573.   It will therefore be seen that he was not actually in the Netherlands at the time of
Lord Oxford's visit, which makes it all the more incomprehensible why
Charles Arundel should have put forward this story seriously.

[2] Bernardino de Mendoza.

[3] I.e., captured from them.

repulsed, but determining to give a fresh and general assault the next day Master Beningefeld, as the devil would have it, came in upon his swift post-horse, and called him from this service by Her Majesty's letters, being the greatest disgrace that any such general received. And now the question is whether this noble general were more troubled with his calling home, or Beningefeld more moved with pity and compassion to behold this slaughter, or his horse more afeared when he passed the bridges at sight of the dead bodies—whereat he started and flung in such sort as Beningefeld could hardly keep his back. Whether this hath passed him I leave it to the report of my Lord Charles Howard, my Lord Windsor, my Lord Compton, my Lord Harry Howard and my Lord Thomas Howard, Rawlie, George Gifford, Waddose, Neell and Southwell, and divers other gentlemen that hath accompanied him.[1] And if in his soberest moods he would allow this, it may easily be gathered what will pass him in his cups.[2]

It seems ludicrous in the extreme that Arundel should have brought forward this story seriously, as it is so obviously reminiscent of a convivial evening. But we must remember that Arundel was fighting for his life. Oxford had accused him of complicity with Spain, an accusation that proved in the end to be correct. By bringing a host of frivolous counter-charges, mostly imaginary, against his accuser he secured for himself breathing space ; and so contrived to escape to Paris, where he joined the English fugitives and was paid as a spy by the King of Spain.

§ VII. France and Italy

By this time it must have been abundantly clear to the Queen and Lord Burghley that they could no longer deny Lord Oxford his wish to travel on the Continent ; and so at last Her Majesty gave the long-sought-for licence permitting the Earl to leave England and journey overseas.

By the New Year all family and financial arrangements had been completed. A fresh list of his debts was compiled, a modification in the entail of his property was laid

[1] I.e., dined with.   [2] S.P. Dom. Eliz., 151. 45.

down, so as to prevent, in case of his death, the whole
estate passing to his sister Mary, and the " impoverishment
of the ancient Earldom." [1] To this end certain lands
were to be set apart for his cousins, among whom we
find the names Francis and Horatio Vere, who have come
down in history as " the fighting Veres," because of their
long and devoted service in the Queen's armies in the
Netherlands.

On January 7th Lord Oxford took his leave of the
Court with Paris as his first destination ; and he took with
him in his retinue " two gentlemen, two grooms, one
payend, a harbinger, a housekeeper, and a trenchman,"
as we know from a note in Lord Burghley's own hand.[2]

By March 7th he had already been some time in Paris,
for on that date, in a letter to Burghley, Valentine Dale,
the English Ambassador, says :

. . . . I presented my Lord of Oxford also unto the
King and Queen, who used him honourably.   Amongst
other talk the King asked whether he was married.   I
said he had a fair lady.   " Il y a donc ce " dit-il " un beau
couple." [3]

Paris was only a temporary resting-place on the way to
the greater attractions of Italy, the home of the Renaissance, and the centre of culture and learning.   Just a
week later we find Dr. Dale writing to the Lord Treasurer :

. . . I had all passports and commissions for post-horses
and letters for my Lord of Oxford that he could require ;
and indeed he was well liked of, and governed himself very
honourably while he was here.   I got the Ambassador of
Venice's letters for him, both unto the State, and unto the
Ambassador's particular friends.   He did wisely to cumber
himself with as little company as he might.[4]

But before he could leave Paris important news reached
the Earl from his father-in-law.   This was that the Countess

[1] Hist. MSS. Comm., 14th Report.
[2] Hatfield MSS. 146. 13.
[3] S.P. Foreign, 33. 38 (Cal. 1575-7, p. 25).
[4] Ibid., 33. 45 (Cal. 1575-7, p. 29).

of Oxford was about to have a child.   To this Lord Oxford
answered in great spirits on March 17th :

My Lord, Your letters have made me a glad man, for
these last have put me in assurance of that good fortune
which you formerly mentioned doubtfully.   I thank God
therefore, with your Lordship, that it hath pleased Him
to make me a father, where your Lordship is a grandfather ;
and if it be a boy I shall likewise be the partaker with you
in a greater contentation.   But thereby to take an occasion
to return I am off from that opinion; for now it hath pleased
God to give me a son of my own (as I hope it is) methinks
I have the better occasion to travel, sith whatsoever
becometh of me I leave behind me one to supply my duty
and service, either to my Prince or else my country.

Lord Burghley, who was always opposed to foreign travel,
had evidently urged Oxford to return on account of his
wife's pregnancy.   The Earl's reply makes it clear that he
will not be denied the long-wished-for journey to Italy.

For fear of the inquisition [the letter continues, after
thanking his father-in-law for sending him money] I dare
not pass by Milan, the Bishop whereof exerciseth such
tyranny ;   wherefore I take the way of Germany, where
I mean to acquaint myself with Sturmius, with whom—
after I have passed my journey which now I have in hand
—I mean to pass some time.   I have found here this
courtesy : the King hath given me his letters of recommendation to his Ambassador in the Turk's Court ; likewise the Venetian Ambassador that is here, knowing my
desire to see those parts, hath given me his letters to the
Duke [1] and divers of his kinsmen in Venice, to procure
me their furtherances to my journey, which I am not
yet assured to hold ; for if the Turks come—as they be
looked for—upon the coasts of Italy or elsewhere, if I
may I will see the service ; if he cometh not, then perhaps
I bestow two or three months to see Constantinople, and
some part of Greece.

No doubt as he wrote this Lord Oxford was thinking
of the great battle of Lepanto, which had taken place in

[1] Doge.

1571, and hoping that it might be his good fortune to
take part in such another sea-fight against the Infidel
while he was in Venice.

The English Ambassador here [he continues] greatly
complaineth of the dearness of this country, and earnestly
hath desired me to crave your Lordship's favour to consider the difference of his time from them which were
before him. He saith the charges are greater ; his ability
less.[1] The account announces long and oft the causes of
expense augmented ; his allowance not more increased.
But as concerning these matters—now I have satisfied his
desire—I refer them to your Lordship's discretion, that is
better experienced than I, perhaps, informed in the difficult
negotiations of Ambassadors.

We may sympathise with Dr. Dale, who was by no means
the only sufferer from Queen Elizabeth's parsimony.
History does not relate if his request was conceded, but
it is unlikely. The letter concludes with an appeal for
more money :

My Lord, whereas I perceive by your Lordship's letters
how hardly money is to be gotten, and that my man writeth
he would fain pay unto my creditors some part of that
money which I have appointed to be made over unto me ;
good my Lord, let rather my creditors bear with me awhile,
and take their days assured according to that order I left,
than I so want in a strange country, unknowing yet
what need I may have of money myself. My revenue is
appointed, with the profits of my lands, to pay them as I
may ; and if I cannot yet pay them as I would, yet as I
can I will, but preferring my own necessity before theirs.
And if at the end of my travels I shall have something
left of my provision, they shall have it among them ;
but before I will not defurnish myself. Good my Lord,
have an eye unto my men that I have put in trust. Thus
making my commendations to your Lordship and my Lady,
I commit you to God ; and wherever I am I rest at your
Lordship's commandment. Written the 17th March from
Paris.

EDWARD OXENFORD.

[1] I.e., his ability to meet the cost.

In a postscript he adds :

My Lord, this gentleman, Master Corbeck, hath given me great cause to like of him both for his courtesies he hath shown me in letting me understand the difficulties as well as the safeties of my travel, and also I find him affected both to me and your Lordship. I pray your Lordship that those who are my friends may seem yours, as yours I esteem mine.[1]

A few days later Lord Oxford left Paris for Strasburg, and Dr. Dale, who had evidently been favourably impressed by the young Earl, wrote thus to Lord Burghley :

. . . I will assure your Lordship unfeignedly my Lord of Oxford used himself as orderly and moderately as might be desired, and with great commendation, neither is there any appearance of the likelihood of any other. God send him a Raphael always in his company, which I trust he verily so hath, for Mr. Lewyn is both discreet and of good years, and one that my Lord doth respect. . . . If the skill of this painter here be liked, I suggest he would be induced to come thither, for he is a Fleming, and liketh not over well of his entertainment here. It seemeth to us he hath done my Lord of Oxford well. My Lord's device is very proper, witty and significant.[2]

The last paragraph is presumably a reference to a picture of himself that the Earl had painted in Paris, and sent to the Countess ; for in a note in his own hand Burghley remarks :

March 17th. The Earl departed from Paris and wrote to his wife, and sent her his picture and two horses.[3]

At Strasburg Lord Oxford visited the famous Sturmius,[4]

[1] Hatfield MSS. (Cal. II. 29).
[2] S.P. Foreign, 33. 47 (Cal. 1575–7, p. 32).
[3] Hatfield MSS. (Cal. XIII. 144).
[4] John Sturmius (1507–89) was *Rector Perpetuus* of Strasburg University. In 1578 this University comprised more than a thousand scholars, including three Princes, and two hundred of the nobility. It included students from all parts of Europe, such as Portugal, Poland, Denmark, France, and England. Robert Sidney, the younger brother of Sir Philip Sidney, was for some years placed under the charge of Sturmius. " The method of Sturmius's teaching became the basis of that of the Jesuits, and through them of the public school instruction of England " (*Encyc. Brit.*, 11th ed., vol. xxvii, p. 763). " His Latin Gymnasium at Strasburg became the model which the German schools of Protestant Europe strove to imitate " (Ibid., vol. viii, p. 958).

and was much impressed, but only two connexions between them have come down to us. Two years later Sturmius wrote Lord Burghley a letter, in which he makes the remark :

" . . . As I write I think of the Earl of Oxford, and his Lady too understands Latin, I think." [1]

The other connexion is in a letter from William Lewyn to Sturmius, in which he says that the Earl of Oxford " had a most high opinion of you, and had made most honourable mention of you : which things afforded me the greatest pleasure." [2]

On " April 26th the Earl of Oxford departed from Strasburg " [3] ; and in May " the Earl left Germany accompanied by Ralph Hopton, a son of the Lieutenant of the Tower " [4] ; and later in the same month reached Padua.

I sent a gentleman of mine [writes Sir Richard Shelley to Burghley from Venice in May] with a letter to him [Lord Oxford] to give him *hora buona* of his welcome and safe arrival, offering him then a house furnished that should have cost him nothing, and to have provided him with the like against his coming hither to Venice, with all the fervour that I was able. . . . His Lordship thanks me by a letter for my courtesy, praying me nevertheless very earnestly to forbear the sending of him either letters or messages, till he should know how I was thought of by the Queen's most excellent Majesty ; which affection and wariness, albeit I liked very well in so great a subject, yet on the other side it appalled me much that I, for all my wariness and fidelity, should be in jealousy, as it were of a fugitive.[5]

[1] Cal. S.P. Foreign, 1577–8, p. 350.

[2] Zurich letters, 2nd Series (1845), September 8th, 1576.

[3] Hatfield MSS. (Cal. XIII. 144).

[4] Cal. S.P. Spanish. The Calendar says " left *for* Germany " ; clearly a misprint.

[5] Harleian MSS., 6992. 4. The letter is not the original, but is a copy made in 1582, when it was evidently used as evidence to prove Shelley's loyalty to the Queen. He was not without justice suspected of being a Catholic. " There met at Rome the year of Jubilee, which was 1575, divers Englishmen to treat of their common cause, as namely Sir Richard Shelley, . . . etc. . . . etc. . . . All these wished well the conversion of their country, but agreed not well in the means or manner of consultation." (*Cath. Rec. Soc.*, 1906, vol. ii.)

William Lewyn had, in the meantime, for some reason
not known, become detached from the Earl's retinue,
for in July he writes to Lord Burghley that he does not
know whether Lord Oxford has started for Greece, or
whether he is still in Italy, but that he understands there
is an English nobleman at Venice who has a companion
who was with Sir Philip Sidney. These, he adds, may be
the Earl and Ralph Hopton.[1]

From the above it seems not unlikely that Oxford, on his
way out, met Sidney on his way back. This may well
have happened at Strasburg, for we know that Philip's
brother, Robert, was later confided to Sturmius's care.
At any rate, Ralph Hopton seems to have left Sidney's
entourage and joined Lord Oxford's.

By September the Earl had reached Venice. There had
evidently been some hitch in the payment of his money,
which was to have been sent out from England every six
months. This appears in a letter to Lord Burghley
from Clemente Paretti, a banker, to whom Lord Oxford's
money had been consigned :

Right Honourable, My most humble duty remembered.
I am sorry that afore this time I could not, according to
duty, write to your honour of my Lord's success and good
disposition in this his travel. But my daily and continual
service about my Lord hath rather hindered than furthered
my good intention and service which always hath been and
is employed to obey your honour's commandment. At this
present your honour shall understand my Lord's better
disposition, God be thanked, for now last coming from
Genoa his Lordship found himself somewhat altered by
reason of the extreme heats ; and before his Lordship
hurt his knee in one of the Venetian galleys, but all is past
without further harm. Of any other reports that your
honour hath understood of my Lord, no credit is to be
given unto. It is true that a while ago at Padua were
killed unawares (in a quarrel that was amongst a certain
congregation of Saffi and students) two noble gentlemen of
Polonia, and the bruit ran *Gentiluomini Inglesi.* . . .[2]

---

[1] Cal. S.P. Foreign, 1575–7, p. 80.
[2] Hatfield MSS. (Cal. II. 114. September 23rd, 1575).

The next day, September 24th, Lord Oxford received letters from England acquainting him, amongst other things, that on July 2nd the Countess, his wife, had given birth to a daughter. He wrote the following long letter to his father-in-law on the same day :

My good Lord, Having looked for your Lordship's letters a great while, at length when I grew to despair of them, I received two packets from your Lordship. Three packets, which at sundry times I had sent this summer towards England returned back again, by reason of the plague being in the passages none were suffered to pass, but as they came were returned back ; which I came not to the knowledge of till my return now to Venice, where I have been grieved with a fever ; yet with the help of God now I have recovered the same, and am past the danger thereof, though brought very weak thereby, and hindered from a great deal of travel, which grieves me most seeing my time [is] not sufficient for my desire ; for although I have seen so much as sufficeth me, yet would I fain have time to profit thereby.

He goes on to answer his father-in-law's questions about Italy :

Your Lordship seems desirous to know how I like Italy, what is mine intention in travel, and when I mean to return. For my liking of Italy, my Lord, I am glad I have seen it, and I care not ever to see it any more, unless it be to serve my Prince and country. For mine intention to travel, I am desirous to see more of Germany, wherefore I shall desire your Lordship, with my Lord of Leicester, to procure me the next summer to continue my licence, at the end of which I mean undoubtedly to return. I thought to have seen Spain, but by Italy I guess the worst. I have sent one of my servants into England with some new disposition of my things there, wherefore I will not trouble your Lordship in these letters with the same. If this sickness had not happened unto me, which hath taken away this chiefest time of travel at this present, I should not have written for further leave, but to supply the which I doubt not Her Majesty will not deny me so small a favour.

Then follow more financial troubles and difficulties :

By reason of my great charges of travel and sickness I have taken up of Master Baptiste Nigrone five hundred crowns, which I shall desire your Lordship to see them repaid, hoping by this time my money which is made of the sale of my land is all come in. Likewise I shall desire your Lordship that whereas I had one Luke Atslow that served—who is now become a lewd subject to Her Majesty and an evil member to his country—which had certain leases of me—I do think according to law he loseth them all to the Queen, since he is become one of the Romish Church, and there hath performed all such ceremonies as might reconcile himself to that charge ; having used lewd speeches against the Queen's Majesty's supremacy, legitimation, government and particular life ; and is here, as it were, a practiser upon our nation. Then this is my desire : that your Lordship—if it be so as I do take it— would procure those leases into my hands again, where, as I have understood by my Lord of Bedford, they have hardly dealt with my tenants. Thus thanking your Lordship for your good news of my wife's delivery, I recommend myself unto your favour ; and although I write for a few months more, yet, though I have them, so it may fall out I will shorten them myself. Written this 24th September, by your Lordship's to command,

                                        EDWARD OXEFORD.[1]

A curious little relic, which belongs to this date, is preserved among the Hatfield MSS.[2] It is a Latin poem of ten lines, stated to have been copied from the fly-leaf of a Greek Testament, once in the possession of the Countess of Oxford. It is addressed " To the illustrious Lady Anne de Vere, Countess of Oxford, while her noble husband, Edward Vere, Earl of Oxford, was occupied in foreign travel." The poem, which is mainly a series of puns on the words *Vera* and *veritas*, may be translated as follows :

Words of truth are fitting to a Vere ; lies are foreign to the truth, and only true things stand fast, all else is fluctuating and comes to an end. Therefore, since thou, a Vere, art wife and mother of a Vere daughter, and seeing that thou mayest with good hope look forward to being

---

[1] Hatfield MSS. (Cal. II. 114).   [2] Ibid. (Cal. XIII. 362).

mother of an heir of the Veres, may thy mind always glow with love of the truth, and may thy true motto be *Ever Lover of the Truth*.   And that thou mayest the better attain to this, pray to the Author of all Truth that His Word may teach thee ; that His Spirit may nourish thy inner life.   So that, thus alleviating the absent longings of thy dear husband, thou, a Vere, mayest be called the true glory of thy husband.

In view of Lord Oxford's great desire to have a son expressed in a previous letter, it seems not improbable that he wrote the lines himself in a Greek Testament when he heard of the birth of his daughter Elizabeth.   This is of course surmise, as the Testament has been lost ; but the nature of the poem makes the Earl's authorship seem not unlikely.

By November Lord Oxford had reached Padua, whence he wrote a hurried note to Lord Burghley about the sale of his lands :

My Lord, having the opportunity to write, by this bearer, who departeth from us here in Padua this night, although I cannot make so large a write as I would gladly desire, yet I thought it not fit to let so short a time slip. Wherefore, remembering my commendations to your good Lordship, these shall be to desire you to pardon the short-ness of my letter, and to impute it at this present to the haste of this messenger's departure.   And as concerning mine own matters, I shall desire your Lordship to make no stay of the sales of my land ; but that all things—according to my determinating before I came away with those that I appointed last by my servant William Booth—might go forward according to mine order taken without any other alteration.   Thus recommending myself unto your Lord-ship again, and to my Lady your wife, with mine, I leave further to trouble your Lordship. From Padua 27th November, your Lordship's to command,

EDWARD OXENFORD.[1]

On December 11th Lord Oxford received his money from Pasquino Spinola at Venice, and left for Florence on the

---

[1] Hatfield MSS. (Cal. II. 122).

following day. Meanwhile, his creditors at home were proving recalcitrant, and it is in a despondent mood that we find him writing to Lord Burghley on January 3rd from Siena :

My Lord, I am sorry to hear how hard my fortune is in England, as I perceive by your Lordship's letters ; but knowing how vain a thing it is to linger a necessary mischief—to know the worst of myself, and to let your Lordship understand wherein I would use your honourable friendship—in short, I have thus determined. That, whereas I understand the greatness of my debt and greediness of my creditors grows so dishonourable and troublesome unto your Lordship, that that land of mine which in Cornwall I have appointed to be sold, according to that first order for mine expenses in this travel, be gone through and withal. And to stop my creditors' exclamations— or rather defamations I may call them—I shall desire your Lordship by the virtue of this letter, which doth not err, as I take it, from any former purpose—which was that always upon my letter to authorise your Lordship to sell any portion of my land [1] that you will sell more of my land where your Lordship shall think fittest, to disburden me of my debts to Her Majesty, my sister, or elsewhere I am exclaimed upon.

He goes on to ask Burghley, in conjunction with Lewyn, Kelton, and the auditor, to make a " view " of the lands he inherited, and also to discharge from his service one Hubbard, who has been defrauding him, and who " deserveth very evil at my hands."

In doing these things [the letter continues] your Lordship shall greatly pleasure me, in not doing them you shall as much hinder me ; for although to part with land your Lordship hath advised the contrary, and that your Lordship for the good affection you bear unto me could not wish it otherwise, yet you see I have no other remedies, I have no help but of mine own, and mine is made to serve me and myself, not mine.

---

[1] A marginal note in Lord Burghley's hand beside this reads : " no such authority."

His determination not to be drawn from his travel by these difficulties is brought out in the next paragraph :

Whereupon, till all such incumbrances be passed over, and till I can better settle myself at home, I have determined to continue my travel, the which thing in no wise I desire your Lordship to hinder, unless you would have it thus : *ut nulla sit inter nos amicitia.* For having made an end of all hope to help myself by Her Majesty's service—considering that my youth is objected unto me, and for every step of mine a block is found to be laid in my way—I see it is but vain *calcitrare contra li busse* ; and the worst of things being known, they are the more easier to be provided for to bear and support them with patience. Wherefore, for things passed amiss to repent them it is too late to help them, which I cannot but ease them. That I am determined to hope for anything, I do not ; but if anything do happen *preter spem*, I think before that time I must be as old as [1] my son, who shall enjoy them, must give the thanks ; and I am to content myself according to the English proverb that it is my hap to starve while the grass doth grow.

After hoping that plain speaking may clear up all misunderstandings he concludes :

Thus I leave your Lordship to the protection of Almighty God, whom I beseech to send you long and happy life, and better fortune to define your felicity in these your aged years [2] than it hath pleased time to grant in my youth. But of a hard beginning we may expect a good and easy ending. Your Lordship's to command during life. The 3rd of January from Siena.

EDWARD OXEFORD.[3]

For the next three months his movements are not known ; but he seems to have visited Sicily, probably via Rome, as the following extract from a book published fourteen years later plainly shows :

Many things I have omitted to speak of, which I have seen and noted in the time of my troublesome travel. One

---

[1] I.e., that.   [2] Burghley was only forty-nine !
[3] Hatfield MSS. (Cal. II. 83).

thing did greatly comfort me which I saw long since in Sicilia, in the city of Palermo, a thing worthy of memory, where the Right Honourable the Earl of Oxford, a famous man of Chivalry, at what time he travelled into foreign countries, being then personally present, made there a challenge against all manner of persons whatsoever, and at all manner of weapons, as Tournaments, Barriers with horse and armour, to fight a combat with any whatsoever in the defence of his Prince and Country. For which he was very highly commended, and yet no man durst be so hardy to encounter with him, so that all Italy over he is acknowledged the only Chevalier and Nobleman of England.   This title they give unto him as worthily deserved.[1]

One other item of interest which belongs to this period is to be found in a play written by George Chapman. The play itself was not published till 1613, though it was written some years before; but Chapman, who evidently knew Oxford, must have been thinking of the Earl's travels on the Continent when he put the following eulogy into the mouth of one of his characters, Clermont d'Ambois :

> CLER. I overtook, coming from Italy,
> In Germany, a great and famous Earl
> Of England ; the most goodly fashion'd man
> I ever saw : from head to foot in form
> Rare and most absolute ; he had a face
> Like one of the most ancient honour'd Romans
> From whence his noblest family was deriv'd ;
> He was beside of spirit passing great,
> Valiant and learn'd, and liberal as the sun,
> Spoke and writ sweetly, or of learned subjects,
> Or of the discipline of public weals ;
> And 'twas the Earl of Oxford.[2]

Some time in March Lord Oxford was at Lyons, at Carniv'al time, on his way home, and on March 31st

---

[1] *The Travels of Edward Webbe* (1590). Edward Webbe was a Master Gunner. This appointment was one of importance, as its holder was a senior officer in the Army, and consequently a man of standing and repute.

[2] *The Revenge of Bussy d'Ambois.*

Dr. Dale reported his arrival in Paris, together with a
certain William Russell, to Lord Burghley.[1]   The Venetian
Ambassador also reported his arrival to the Signory :

The Earl of Oxford, an English gentleman [he writes],
has arrived here.   He has come from Venice, and according
to what has been said to me by the English Ambassador
here resident [2] speaks in great praise of the numerous
courtesies which he has received in that city ; and he
reports that on his departure from Venice your Serenity
had already elected an Ambassador to be sent to the
Queen, and the English Ambassador expressed the greatest
satisfaction at the intelligence.   I myself, not having
received any information from your Serenity, or from any
of my correspondents, did not know what answer to give
concerning the matter.   From Paris, April 3rd, 1576.[3]

We must now leave Lord Oxford for the moment in
excellent spirits in Paris ; and turn our attention to
certain events which had in the meantime been happening
in England.

§ VIII.   The Crisis of 1576

The Countess of Oxford, as we have seen, gave birth
to a daughter on July 2nd, 1575.   Lord Oxford's two letters,
the first from Paris when he heard she was about to become
a mother, and the second from Venice when he had heard
of her safe delivery, have been quoted in full.   They both
express his whole-hearted joy at the news.   There is no
hint of suspicion or mistrust from beginning to end.   These
letters are important in view of subsequent developments,
and should be borne in mind.

We must now go back to London.   On the very day—
March 7th, 1575—that Lord Oxford was being introduced
to the King and Queen of France, and receiving their
congratulations on behalf of himself and his wife ; on that
very day Queen Elizabeth was holding an audience with
one of her physicians, Dr. Richard Masters, in the presence

[1] Cal. S.P. For., 1575-7, p. 294.   [2] Dr. Dale.
[3] Cal. S.P. Venetian, 1558-80, p. 548.

9

chamber at Richmond. Masters wrote a full account of
his interview in the evening to Lord Burghley, and the
purport of this letter is so remarkable that we must read
it in his own words :

To the right honourable the Lord Burghley, the Lord
Treasurer of England.

After my duty it may please your Lordship to understand
that having Her Majesty this Monday morning in the
chamber at the gallery and next to the Green sitting alone,
I said " Seeing it hath pleased your Majesty oftentimes
to enquire tenderly after my Lady of Oxford's health, it
is now fallen out so (God be thanked) that she is with child
evidently ; and albeit it were but an indifferent thing for
Her Majesty to hear of, yet it was more than indifferent
for your Lordship to signify the same unto her." Here-
withal she arose, or rather sprang up from the cushion,
and said these words : " Indeed, it is a matter that concerneth my Lord's joy chiefly ; yet I protest to God that
next to them that have interest in it, there is nobody that
can be more joyous of it than I am." Then I went forth
and told her that your Lordship had a privy likelihood of
it upon your coming from the Court after Shrovetide,[1]
but you concealed it. . . .

Her Majesty asked me how the young lady did bear the
matter. I answered that she kept it secret four or five
days from all persons and that her face was much fallen
and thin with little colour, and that when she was comforted and counselled to be gladsome and so rejoice, she
would cry : " Alas, alas, how should I rejoice seeing he that
should rejoice with me is not here ; and to say truth [I]
stand in doubt whether he pass upon me and it or not " ;
and bemoaning her case would lament that after so long
sickness of body she should enter a new grief and sorrow of
mind. At this Her Majesty showed great compassion
as your Lordship shall hear hereafter. And repeated my
Lord of Oxford's answer to me, which he made openly in
the presence chamber of Her Majesty, viz., that if she were
with child it was not his. I answered that it was the common answer of lusty courtiers everywhere, so to say. . . .
Then she asking and being answered of me [who] was in
the next chamber, she calleth my Lord of Leicester and

---

[1] Lord Oxford left England over a month before Shrovetide.

telleth him all. And here I told her that though your Lordship had concealed it awhile from her, yet you left it to her discretion either to reveal it or to keep it and lose. And here an end was made, taking advantage of my last words, that she would be with you for concealing it so long from her. And severally she showed herself unfeignedly to rejoice, and in great offence with my Lord of Oxford, repeating the same to my Lord of Leicester after he came to her. Thus much rather to show my goodwill than otherwise desiring your Lordship, that there may a note be taken from the day of the first quickening, for thereof somewhat may be known noteworthy. From Richmond the 7th of March, 1574 [i.e., 1575 N.S.].

By your Lordship's most bounden,

RICHARD MASTERS.[1]

How can we reconcile the statement made by Dr. Masters that Lord Oxford had denied the parentage of the child with the Earl's own obvious pleasure when he heard a few days later that the Countess was about to become a mother? Moreover, Masters insinuates that Oxford had denied the parentage of the child before he went abroad on January 7th; and yet Masters himself, Lady Oxford's own physician, only discovers on March 7th that she is going to have a child. Clearly someone is spreading scandalous reports. Who is it?

The seeds of suspicion had now been sown in the minds of the Queen and Lord Burghley, and as is customary with weeds, they quickly took root and flourished.

Meanwhile, in July the child had been born, and in September the Earl wrote to his father-in-law expressing his pleasure at his wife's safe delivery.

On January 3rd, 1576, the poison was once more at work in Burghley's mind. He was puzzled, and to help him clear his thoughts, he took pen and paper. This is what he wrote :

He [Oxford] confessed to my Lord Howard that he lay not with his wife but at Hampton Court, and that then the child could not be his, because the child was born in July which was not the space of twelve months.[2]

[1] Lansdowne MSS., 19. 83.   [2] Hatfield MSS. (Cal. XIII. 144).

The reasoning is certainly peculiar, but the appearance
of Lord Henry Howard is interesting. When did Oxford
make this " confession " to Lord Henry ? Not before
he went abroad in January, because it was not till
March that the Countess was found to be with child.
Lord Henry, moreover, was in England all this time, so
they cannot possibly have met after January. Then
again, why should Oxford make this obviously untrue
" confession " to Lord Henry ? It may help us to understand the case better if we examine for a moment this new
character who has stepped on to the stage.

Lord Henry Howard was the second son of the poet Earl
of Surrey, and therefore Oxford's first cousin. He was
now thirty-five years old. His many-sided personality
makes him one of the most remarkable, and at the same
time sinister, figures in Elizabethan England. He shared
with Lord Lumley the distinction of being the most learned
nobleman of his day. He made little or no attempt to conceal his pro-Spanish and Catholic leanings, nor his support of
the Queen of Scots. This attitude was plainly incompatible
with genuine loyalty to his sovereign ; and although he
repeatedly expressed his entire devotion to the person of
Elizabeth, this was mere lip service, and it is not surprising
that he spent many years either in prison or under restraint.
But he was a master of subtle intrigue and dissimulation,
and it is not the least remarkable of his achievements that
he succeeded in avoiding anything worse than imprisonment between 1570 and 1587. He was a bitter and lifelong
enemy of Lord Burghley.

His relations with Lord Oxford are less easy to define.
Their mutual love of literature and learning generally
would naturally cause them to gravitate together. It seems
probable that prior to 1576 they had been fairly close
friends. But any sympathy Oxford may have had for
Lord Harry in the past was turned to hatred and disgust
when he heard of the latter's vile lies and insinuations about
the Countess. His opinion of him after this particularly
foul behaviour is terse and to the point. We are told that

he was wont to " affirm to divers that the Howards were
the most treacherous race under heaven " ; and that " my
Lord Howard [was] the worst villain that lived in this
earth." [1]

There is little doubt that in Lord Henry Howard we
have found the Iago of the piece. But Burghley at the
time evidently believed Lord Henry, for he continued to
puzzle it all out on the bit of paper before him. This is
what he wrote :

Anno XVI Eliz. (1574) 29th July.   Lord Burghley went
to London with his daughter, the Countess of Oxford.

30th July.   Earl of Oxford went to Theobalds with his
wife.

3rd Aug.   Earl of Oxford at the hunting of the stag.

1574. 16th Sept.   Earl of Oxford at Theobalds when
the Progress from farm ties [sic].

19th Sept. Sunday.   Lady Lennox, Earl of Oxford,
Lord Northumberland, Lady Northumberland.

20th Sept. Monday.   Lady Margaret Lennox, Earl of
Oxford, Lady Lennox, Lady Hunsdon.

21st Sept.   Lady Lennox, Lord Northumberland, and
my Lady.[2]

October at Hampton Court.   The Countess fell sick at
Hampton Court.   (Afore November.)

7th Jan.   The Earl departed overseas.

6th March.   The Earl presented to the French King.

17th March.   The Earl departed from Paris and wrote
to his wife and sent her his picture and two horses.

26th April. The Earl of Oxford departed from Strasburg.

2nd July.   The Countess delivered of a daughter.

24th Sept.   The letter of the Earl by which he gives
thanks for his wife's delivery.   Mark well this letter.

3rd Jan.   The Earl wrote to me.[3]

Lord Burghley was puzzled. And in the meantime
Oxford without a shadow of suspicion, was eagerly
anticipating the wonders of Rome, as he journeyed south
from Siena.

[1] S.P. Dom., 151. 46.
[2] These notes, I imagine, refer to dinner or supper parties.
[3] Hatfield MSS. (Cal. XIII. 144).

Before this digression we left Lord Oxford, it will be remembered, on April 3rd, 1576, at Paris on his way home. He seems to have been in excellent spirits, and to have visited both Dr. Dale and the Venetian Ambassador.

Next day the bomb exploded.

In an overwhelming passion he started for England at once ; on the way over his ship was attacked by pirates and all his goods stolen ; he refused to land at Dover, where his brother-in-law, Thomas Cecil, had gone to meet him, and he landed in the Thames with Gascoigne's old companion in arms, Rowland Yorke, and was met by Burghley and the Countess of Oxford ; he refused to speak to them, and brushing them aside, he went straight to the Queen. This was on April 20th.[1]

Lord Burghley was staggered.

By April 23rd he was desperate. He had drawn up, and now submitted to the Queen, a piteous appeal :

Most sovereign lady, As I was accustomed from the beginning of my service to your Majesty until of late by the permission of your goodness and by occasion of the place wherein I serve your Majesty, to be frequently an intercessor for others to your Majesty, and therein did find your Majesty always inclinable to give me gracious audience ; so now do I find in the latter end of my years a necessary occasion to be an intercessor for another next to myself, in a cause godly, honest and just ; and therefore, having had proof of your Majesty for most favours in causes not so important, I doubt not but to find the like influence of your grace in a cause so near touching myself as your Majesty will conceive it doth. . . .

To enter to trouble your Majesty with the circumstances of my cause, I mean not for sundry respects but chiefly for two ; the one is that I am very loth to be more cumbersome to your Majesty than need shall compel me ; the other is for that I hope in God's goodness, and for reverence borne to your Majesty, that success thereof may have a better end than the beginning threateneth. But your Majesty may think my suit will be very long where I am so long ere I begin it ; and truly, most gracious sovereign

1 Hatfield MSS. (Cal. II. 131).

lady, it is true that the nature of my cause is such as I
have no pleasure to enter into it, but had rather seek
means to shut it up for them to lay it open, not for lack
of the soundness thereof on my part, but for the wickedness
of others from whom the ground work proceedeth.

My suit therefore shall be presently to your Majesty
but in general sort, that whereas I am, by God's visitation
with some infirmity and yet not great, stayed from coming
to do my duty to your Majesty at this time, and my
daughter, the Countess of Oxford, also occasioned to her
great grief to be absent from your Majesty's Court, and
that the occasion of her absence may be diversly reported
to your Majesty, as I said before, by some of ignorance by
some percase otherwise, it may please your Majesty—
because the ground and working thereupon toucheth me as
nearly as any worldly cause in my concept can do—of
me as of an old worn servant that dare compare with the
best, the greatest, the oldest and the youngest, for loyalty
and devotion, giving place to many others in other worldly
qualities, as your Majesty shall prefer any before me ;
and of my daughter, your Majesty's most humble young
servant, as of one that is towards your Majesty in dutiful
love and fear, yea, in fervent admiration of your graces
to contend with any her equals, and in the cause betwixt
my Lord of Oxford and her, whether it be for respect of
misliking in me or misdeeming of hers whereof I cannot
yet know the certainty, I do avow in the presence of God
and of his angels whom I do call as ministers of his ire,
if in this I do utter any untruth.

I have not in his absence on my part omitted any
occasion to do him good for himself and his causes, no,
I have not in thought imagined anything offensive to him,
but contrariwise I have been as diligent for his causes to
his benefit as I have been for my own, and this I pronounce
of knowledge for myself, and therefore if, contrary to my
desert, I should otherwise be judged or suspected, I should
receive great injury for my daughter, though nature will
make some . . . to speak favourably ; yet now I have
taken God and His angels to be witnesses of my writing,
I renounce nature, and protest simply to your Majesty.
I did never see in her behaviour in word or deed, nor ever
could perceive by any other means, but that she hath
always used herself honestly, chastely, and lovingly

towards him ; and now upon expectation of his coming so filled with joy thereof, so desirous to see the time of his arrival approach, as in my judgment no young lover rooted or sotted in love of any person could more excessively show the same with all comely tokens ; and when, at his arrival, some doubts were cast of his acceptance of her true innocency, seemed to make her so bold as she never cast any care of things, but wholly reposed herself with assurance to be well used by him. And with that confidence, and importunity made to me, she went to him, and there missed of her expectation, and so attendeth, as her duty is, to gain of her hope some recompense.

And now, lest I should enter further into the matter, and not meaning to trouble your Majesty, I do end with this humble request ; that in anything that may hereof follow, whereof I may have wrong with dishonesty offered me, I may have your Majesty's princely favour to seek my just defence for me and mine ; not meaning for respect of my old service, nor of the place whereunto your Majesty hath called me (though unworthy) to challenge any extraordinary favour, for my service hath been but a piece of my duty, and my vocation hath been too great a reward. And so I do remain constant to serve your Majesty in what place so ever your Majesty shall command, even in as base as I have done in great.[1]

Two days later he had partially recovered, and characteristically sat down and wrote out three pages of notes " touching the Earl of Oxford." The story as told by Burghley is just what we should expect : that the Countess was financially embarrassed during her husband's absence ; that the Earl expressed his pleasure on receiving the news of his daughter's birth ; that he suddenly changed in Paris on April 4th ; that he refused to speak with any of his wife's family when he landed in England ; and finally that Lord Henry Howard was keeping Burghley in touch with Lord Oxford's actions.[2]

These notes are disjointed, and evidently written under stress of great emotion, but the last item is particularly

[1] Lansdowne MSS., 102. 2. Unsigned, but in Lord Burghley's hand. Endorsed," A copy of a letter delivered by Mr. Edw. Cavir of the Chamber."
[2] Hatfield MSS. (Cal. II. 131).

illuminating. Lord Henry Howard's intervention can
only have been in the direction of mischief-making, for
although he seems to have succeeded in deceiving Lord
Burghley, we may easily guess the part this subtle intriguer
was playing.

Two days later, on April 27th, Burghley received his
first communication from his son-in-law since the bursting
of the storm :

My Lord, Although I have forborne in some respect,
which should [be] private to myself, either to write or
come unto your Lordship, yet had I determined, as
opportunity should have served me, to have accomplished
the same in compass of a few days. But now, urged thereto
by your letters, to satisfy you the sooner, I must let your
Lordship understand this much : that is, until I can better
satisfy or advertise myself of some mislikes, I am not
determined, as touching my wife, to accompany her. What
they are—because some are not to be spoken of or written
upon as imperfections—I will not deal withal. Some that
otherwise discontented me I will not blaze or publish until
it please me. And last of all, I mean not to weary my life
any more with such troubles and molestations as I have
endured ; nor will I, to please your Lordship only, dis-
content myself.

The fact that Lord Oxford distinctly states that his
anger arises from more than one cause is important. It
is reasonable to suppose that Lord Henry Howard's cruel
slanders about the Countess affected him most deeply.
But there were also other reasons not without their
significance. Annoyance with Lord Burghley (quite unjust perhaps) for his slowness in raising ready money ;
misunderstandings between them over the question of
certain of the Earl's followers ; failure to have his licence
to continue travelling renewed ; and, most important of
all, Oxford's discovery of the plot against his book, *A
Hundreth Sundrie Flowres*, which will be dealt with in
the following Interlude.

The letter continues :

Wherefore—as your Lordship very well writeth unto

me—that you mean, if it standeth with my liking, to receive her into your house, these are likewise to let your Lordship understand that it doth very well content me; for there, as your daughter or her mother's, more than my wife, you may take comfort of her; and I, rid of the cumber thereby, shall remain well eased of many griefs. I do not doubt but that she hath sufficient proportion for her being to live upon and to maintain herself.

This might have been done through private conference before, and had not needed to have been the fable of the world if you would have had the patience to have understood me; but I do not know by whom, or whose advice it was to run that course so contrary to my will or meaning, that made her so disgraced to the world [and] raised suspicions openly that, with private conference, might have been more silently handled, and hath given me more greater cause to mislike.

Wherefore I desire your Lordship in these causes—now you shall understand me—not to urge me any further; and so I write unto your Lordship, as you have done unto me, this Friday, 27th April. Your Lordship's to be used in all things reasonable,

EDWARD OXEFORD.[1]

Modern historians unanimously characterise Lord Oxford's treatment of his wife in 1576 as " brutal," " ill-tempered," " churlish," and many similar epithets. Further, they all echo each other in attributing all the trouble to the Earl and his " ungovernable temper "; while Lord Burghley and the Countess become the objects of sympathy and pity. But is this view borne out by the facts, many of which are published here for the first time?

Let us look back at the matter from Lord Oxford's point of view. He had never really got on well with Lord Burghley, and he cordially detested his mother-in-law. He had had an exasperating time with financial and other petty affairs while he was travelling. And now, on April 4th at Paris, he hears that the English Court is laughing at him for a cuckold. Surely it is hardly surprising that

[1] Hatfield MSS. (Cal. II. 132).

he displays a considerable outburst of rage. His wife has disgraced him ; therefore he washes his hands of her for ever ; that is his line of argument. Hasty and harsh perhaps, nevertheless intensely human.

This uncompromising letter from his son-in-law left Lord Burghley no nearer the solution of the mystery. The Earl said practically nothing definite except the fact that he flatly refused to have anything to do either with his father-in-law or his wife. But almost immediately afterwards Lord Burghley seems to have received another letter, this time with definite allegations against his parents-in-law. The letter has been lost ; but we can reconstruct its contents from a page of notes written by Burghley on April 29th, and endorsed, " The communication I had from my Lord of Oxford."

The allegations against Lord Burghley are : not providing him with sufficient money ; ill-treating his followers ; purposely rousing the Queen's indignation against him (Oxford) ; while Lady Burghley is accused of having declared she wished him dead ; of undermining his wife's affection for him ; and of slandering him. But as for Lady Oxford, Lord Burghley writes that the Earl " meaneth not to discover anything of the cause of his misliking " ; and that " until he understand further of it," he " meaneth not to visit her."

With this Lord Oxford relapsed into stony silence. May wore on into June, and still the Lord Treasurer of England was peremptorily forbidden to bring his daughter, the Countess of Oxford, to the Court.

On June 12th Lord Burghley broke the silence. The letter he wrote has been lost, but a rough draft in his own hand has been preserved, from which we may gather its gist. It is headed " 12th June, 1576. To be remembered."

The time now past [is] almost of two months without certainty whereupon to rest arguments of unkindness both towards my daughter, his wife, and me also.

Rejecting of her from his company.

Not regarding his child born of her.

His absence from the Court in respect to avoid his offence, and her solitary lying.

He goes on to declare that there is " no proof nor particularity advanced " by the Earl in his accusations against him.   On the contrary, he calls to witness " my care to get him his money when his bankers had none ; my endeavour to have his land sold to the truest advantage, or else not to be sold ; my dealing with his creditors to stay their clamours for their debt ; and my particular suits to Her Majesty for his advancement to place of service, namely to be Master of the Horse, as Her Majesty can testify."

There was also the old question as to Lord Oxford's legitimacy, and Burghley points out that " I preferred his title to the Earldom, the Lord Windsor attempting to have made him illegitimate."   He also points out that " I did my best to have the jury find the death of the poor man, whom he killed in my house, *se defendendo*."

Lord Burghley concludes his notes as follows :

I desire that his Lordship will yield to her, being his wife, either that love that a loving and honest wife ought to have, or otherwise to be so used as all lewd and vain speeches may cease of his unkindness to her.   And that, with his favour and permission, she may both come to his presence and be allowed to come to do her duty to Her Majesty, if Her Majesty shall therewith be content ; and she shall bear, as she may, the lack of the rest, or else that his Lordship will notify some just cause of her not observing such favour, and that she will be permitted to make her answer thereto, before such as Her Majesty may be pleased to appoint.[1]

Still there was no answer from Lord Oxford.

On July 10th Lord Burghley made another appeal, his rough draft once again being our only authority :

Although I both hope and assure myself that my Lord of Oxford doth now understand that the conception which he had gathered to think unkindness in me towards him was grounded upon untrue reports of others, as I have

[1] Hatfield MSS. (Cal. II. 170–171).

manifestly proved them, yet because I understand that
of late the same untruths are still continued in secret
reports to others—whereby some which have no cause to
speak amiss of me may, by giving credit to the same,
think otherwise of the truth than I deserve, or than one of
my place or fealty ought to be thought of without manifest
cause known—upon such report, I hear, is lately made
untruly and falsely ; I do as followeth not only avow the
same to be untruths, but the maintainers and devisers of
them to be liars and malicious backbiters, and such as
will so lightly credit such slanders of me to be light in
consideration and judgment, and if they will not hear the
trial of the falsehood thereof, I must think them furtherers
of untruths, and unworthy for my poor good will or
friendship.[1]

This paragraph is most interesting, for here we have
the first indication that not only Lord Burghley, but his
son-in-law also, have at last recognised that " the untrue
reports of others " are at the bottom of the whole trouble.
Although no names are mentioned, we may be sure that
Lord Harry Howard was in Burghley's mind as he wrote
these words.

The letter continues with a refutation of the same
allegations that we have heard before. He denies that he
prevented the enrolment in Chancery of Lord Oxford's
book of entail ; and he asserts, no doubt with truth,
that so far from stopping the Earl's money when he was
abroad, he advanced over £2,000 of his own, when the
former's resources ran dry.

To this appeal Lord Oxford responded so far as to
interview Burghley on July 12th. At this meeting he
agreed, with certain reservations, to allow his father-in-law
to bring the Countess to Court. The following day he wrote
to Lord Burghley :

My very good Lord, Yesterday, at your Lordship's
earnest request, I had some conference with you about
your daughter. Wherein, for that Her Majesty had so
often moved me, and that you dealt so earnestly with me,
to content her as much as I could, I did agree that you

[1] Hatfield MSS. (Cal. I. 474, where it is wrongly dated 1570).

could eft bring her to the Court, with condition that she should not come when I was present, nor at any time have speech with me, and further that your Lordship should not urge further in her cause.   But now I understand that your Lordship means this day to bring her to the Court, and that you mean afterwards to prosecute the cause with further hope.   Now if your Lordship shall do so, then shall you take more in hand than I have, or can, promise you ; for always I have, and I will still, prefer mine own content before others. And observing that wherein I may temper or moderate for your sake, I will do [so] most willingly.   Wherefore I shall desire your Lordship not to take advantage of my promise till you have given me your honourable assurance by letter or word of your performance of the condition ; which being observed, I could yield, as it is my duty, to Her Majesty's request, and I will bear with your fatherly desire towards her.   Otherwise all that is done can stand to no effect.

From my lodging at Charing Cross this morning.

Your Lordship's to employ,

EDWARD OXEFORD.[1]

Though this eased a situation that threatened to become well-nigh intolerable, the wound was by no means healed. The shock that the scandal had caused left Lord Oxford stunned. He absolutely declined to live with his wife. Arrangements were drawn up for her separate maintenance. The Earl allowed her their country house at Wivenhoe and her lodgings in the Savoy; and in Lord Burghley's own words, " hath promised the Queen's Majesty to be wholly advised by me." Lord Burghley also says in the same letter, " I perceive he would make the sons of the younger uncle [2] his heirs male if he could, which I think he cannot, of the Earldom."[3]

Francis and Horatio Vere were then aged sixteen and eleven respectively, and it is interesting that Lord Oxford attempted to make them his successors in the

[1] Hatfield MSS. (Cal. II. 135).

[2] Francis and Horatio, afterwards famous as " the fighting Veres," sons of Geoffrey de Vere.

[3] Hatfield MSS. (Cal. II. 170).   The letter is undated, but it probably refers to 1576, and not 1577, as conjectured in the Calendar.

Earldom, to the exclusion of the descendants of his elder
uncle, Aubrey.[1]   We know that Francis and Horatio were
his favourite cousins, and that they continued to be so
to the end of his life.   It was to Francis that he entrusted the administration of his estate, and Horatio—
then known as Sir Horatio Vere—took charge of the Earl's
son Henry, while campaigning during King James's reign
in the Palatinate and Low Countries.

In time Lord Oxford and his wife became reconciled.
Two more daughters were born, and outwardly they seemed
to have quite forgotten the terrible days of April and
May 1576.   But beneath this outward display, it is safe
to say that never again were relations quite the same
between husband, wife, and father-in-law.

This domestic tragedy had its reaction on Lord Oxford's
literary activities.   Up till now his writings—both prose
and verse—had been care-free and serene.   But his poems
of 1576 show a very different temper.   Loss of good name
and irretrievable disgrace are the themes he harps on now.
The example given below is taken from *The Paradyse of
Dainty Devises*, which was published in this year.

Fram'd in the front of forlorn hope past all recovery
I stayless stand, to abide the shock of shame and infamy.
My life, through ling'ring long, is lodg'd in love of loathsome ways ;
My death delay'd to keep from life and harm of hapless days.
My sprites, my heart, my wit and force, in deep distress are drown'd ;
The only loss of my good name is of these griefs the ground.

And since my mind, my wit, my head, my voice and tongue are weak,
To utter, move, devise, conceive, sound forth, declare and speak,
Such piercing plaints as answer might, or would my woeful case,
Help crave I must, and crave I will, with tears upon my face,
Of all that may in heaven or hell, in earth or air be found,
To wail with me this loss of mine, as of these griefs the ground.

Help Gods, help saints, help sprites and powers that in the heaven do dwell,
Help ye that aye are wont to wail, ye howling hounds of hell,
Help man, help beasts, help birds and worms, that on the earth do toil ;
Help fish, help fowl, that flocks and feeds upon the salt sea soil,
Help echo that in air doth flee, shrill voices to resound,
To wail this loss of my good name, as of these griefs the ground.

E. O.

---

[1] This attempt failed, because ultimately Aubrey's grandson succeeded
as 19th Earl of Oxford.

Although Lord Oxford's Italian trip had ended so disastrously, the memory of it had its lighter side, with which it may be fitting to conclude this chapter. The same vivid imagination that had transformed his fortnight in the Low Countries into a military campaign of unsurpassed ferocity and excitement was busy conjuring up marvellous stories about his doings in Italy. We are told that, under the heightened exhilaration of wine and company, he would dilate on the mythical wonders of the home of the Renaissance. Not the least amusing part of these stories is the fact that they were brought up, in all seriousness, by Charles Arundel, when he was defending himself against a charge of treason preferred against him by Lord Oxford.

I have heard him often tell [relates Arundel] that at his being in Italy, there fell discord and disunion in the city of Genoa between two families; whereupon it grew to wars, and great aid and assistance [was] given to either party. And that for the fame that ran throughout Italy of his service done in the Low Countries under the Duke of Alva, he was chosen and made General of 30,000 that the Pope sent to the aid of one party; and that in this action he showed so great discretion and government as by his wisdom the matters were compounded, and an accord made; being more for his glory than if he had fought the battle.

His third lie [continues Arundel] is [about] certain excellent orations he made, as namely to the state of Venice, at Padua, at Bologna, and divers other places in Italy, and one which pleased him above the rest [was] to his army, when he marched towards Genoa; which, when he had pronounced it, he left nothing to reply, but everyone to wonder at his judgment, being reputed for his eloquence another Cicero, and for his conduct a Cæsar.

Arundel then calls on Lord Henry Howard, Francis Southwell, William Vavasour, and others to bear witness. " Let these examples plead ! " he cries indignantly :

That the cobblers' wives of Milan are more richly dressed every working day than the Queen at Christmas.

That St. Mark's Church is paved at Venice with diamonds and rubies.

That a merchant at Genoa hath a mantle of a chimney of more price than all the treasure of the Tower.[1]

One cannot help feeling sorry that Charles Arundel should have seen fit shortly afterwards to run away to the Continent, and in the service of the King of Spain to take up arms against his fellow-countrymen. His delightfully ingenuous manner makes him one of the most interesting witnesses we have as to Lord Oxford's personality. Unfortunately, like most people devoid of any sense of humour, he soon becomes tedious, and his statements degenerate into weary reiterations of scurrilous abuse.

One other incident in connexion with Lord Oxford's travels in Italy may be noted here. We read in Stow's *Annals* (p. 868) that at this time—

Milliners or Haberdashers had not any gloves embroidered, or trimmed with gold or silk, neither gold nor embroidered girdles and hangers, neither could they make any costly wash or perfume ; until about the fourteenth or fifteenth year of the Queen the right honourable Edward de Vere, Earl of Oxford, came from Italy, and brought with him gloves, sweet bags, a perfumed leather jerkin, and other pleasant things ; and that year the Queen had a pair of perfumed gloves trimmed only with four tufts, or roses of coloured silk ; the Queen took such pleasure in those gloves that she was pictured with those gloves upon her hands, and for many years after it was called the Earl of Oxford's perfume.

[1] S.P. Dom., 151. 46.

10

INTERLUDE: "THE CROWN OF BAYS"

I will now rehearse unto your Majesty such a strange and cruel *Metamorphosis* as I think must needs move your noble mind unto compassion. There were two sworn brethren which long time served (Diana) called *Deep Desire* and *Due Desert*, and although it be very hard to part these two in sunder, yet is it said that she did long sithens convert *Due Desert* into yonder same *Lawrell* tree. The which may very well be so, considering the *etymology* of his name, for we see that the *Lawrel branch* is a token of triumph, in all *Trophies*, and given as a reward to all victors, a dignity for all degrees, consecrated and dedicate to *Apollo* and the *Muses* as a worthy flower, leaf, or branch, for their due deserts.

George Gascoigne to Queen Elizabeth, 1575.

> A crown of bays shall that man wear
> That triumphs over me ;
> For black and tawny will I wear,
> Which mourning colours be.

Earl of Oxford, 1576.

IN the early half of 1573 was published a poetical anthology called *A Hundreth Sundrie Flowres*. It marked a most important step in the history of English poetry. It was the first of a series of famous anthologies which appeared during the reign of Queen Elizabeth. As it was probably edited and published by Lord Oxford, and contained sixteen of his own lyrics, some details of it will be given here.

Forty-five of the hundred poems that it contains were by George Gascoigne, whom we have already come across in an earlier chapter. In March 1572 he had gone as a volunteer to help the Dutch against the Spaniards in the Low Countries, under Sir Roger Williams, where he remained till November 1574. We know for certain that there were four other contributors. I have shown elsewhere that three of these were almost certainly Lord Oxford himself, Christopher Hatton, and Gervase Holles,

who all appear under pseudonyms.[1] Lord Oxford's
pseudonym, *Meritum petere grave*, appears as the signature
of sixteen of the poems. That it was his is revealed by
the fact that one of the poems entitled " The absent lover
in ciphers deciphering his name craveth some speedy
relief as followeth," contains the name EDWARD DE VERE
interwoven through it.[2] This Latin posy, *Meritum petere
grave*, also appears on the title-page in the space usually
reserved for the author's name, from which it seems safe
to assume that the Earl of Oxford was closely concerned
with the publication of *A Hundreth Sundrie Flowres*, just
as he had been in the case of Bedingfield's *Cardanus'
Comfort*, published by his commandment in this very year.
The manuscripts of the poems were originally collected in
or before 1572 by a certain " G. T."—probably George
Turbervile the poet—from his friends, including Hatton
and Gascoigne. In August of that year he handed over
his collection to another friend, " H. W.," with strict
injunctions that they were on no account to be printed.
Shortly afterwards Turbervile went to Antwerp, almost
certainly in connexion with the publication there in
January of a political satire directed against Lord Burghley
and Sir Nicholas Bacon, which had been written secretly
by Lord Henry Howard; but the very nature of its contents
made its publication, even anonymously, impossible in
England.[3] In the ensuing June Turbervile was joined
there by Hatton, who was also concerned in Lord Henry's
propaganda.[4]

[1] Cf. *A Hundreth Sundrie Flowres*, Etchells and Macdonald (1926),
Introduction; and *The Library*, June 1927. Gervase Holles (1547–1628),
grandfather of the antiquary, was a nephew by marriage of Lord Oxford's
aunt, Lady Anne de Vere, who had married the poet, Lord Sheffield.

[2] Dr. Greg, in *The Library*, December 1926, p. 279, makes the following
comment : " In this [poem] we are expressly told that a name is concealed,
and the acrostic found is an excellent one. I should be reluctant to believe
that its presence could be due to chance."

[3] This book was called *A Treatise of Treasons*, etc. (see *Short Title
Catalogue*, Pollard and Redgrave, 1926, p. 169). I hope shortly to publish
the evidence that it was written by Lord Henry Howard. This evidence
is to be found in B.M., G. 5443. 2, and S.P. Dom. Eliz., 147. 4 and 6.

[4] *Review of English Studies*, January 1928.

It was probably during the absence on the Continent of the three persons most concerned—Gascoigne, Hatton, and Turbervile—that Lord Oxford got hold of the collection from " H. W.," who may have been Henry Wotton.[1] We cannot say for certain if " H. W." connived at the publication, or if Oxford carried it through without his consent. At any rate the onus was ostensibly laid on the shoulders of the " printer," a transparent device that could have deceived nobody at the time.[2] Finally, we have seen that Lord Oxford included certain of his own poems which were printed together with the rest of Turbervile's collection. In so doing he committed an action the significance of which requires some explanation.

In the sixteenth century, although many courtiers wrote poetry, it was an unwritten law that nothing of theirs should be printed while they were alive. Tottel's *Miscellany*, which appeared in 1557, contained poems by Sir Thomas Wyat, Lord Surrey, and Lord Vaux, who had died in 1541, 1547, and 1556 respectively. Sir Philip Sidney, another of the great Elizabethan courtier poets, died in 1586 ; but it was not till 1590 that any of his poems appeared in print. But Lord Oxford, in the first flush of his youth and enthusiasm for literature and poetry, was too impatient to allow his work to wait in manuscript till after his death. In deference, however, to the usage of his times, he veiled the authorship of his own poems, as well as those by Hatton and Holles, behind pseudonyms ;

[1] The only facts definitely known about Henry Wotton are that he came of a Norfolk family, and that in 1578 he published a book called *A Courtlie Controversy.*

[2] Many of the anonymous books which were published during Queen Elizabeth's reign contain prefaces in which the " printer " says that the manuscripts came " accidentally " into his hands, and that he has effected the publication with total disregard as to the author's wishes. The following remark in *The Arte of English Poesie* (1589) sufficiently explains the real meaning of these prefaces :

" . . . I know very many notable gentlemen in the Court that have written very commendably and suppressed it again, or else suffered it to be published without their own names to it ; as [if] it were a discredit for a gentleman to seem learned, and to show himself amorous of any good art."

and only allowed Gascoigne's name to appear undisguised
in the book.

It is a truism to say that any man who has the hardihood
to go against the customs of his day is met with opposition,
envy, and even hatred.   There can be no doubt that the
identity of *Meritum petere grave* was an open secret at the
Court, and that Oxford incurred a full share of disapproval
from the conservative elements in that quarter.   But he
was too keen a pioneer to be deterred by ridicule or abuse.
Although it is anticipating a little, it may perhaps be
remarked that in 1576 seven more of his poems appeared
in the second Elizabethan anthology entitled *A Paradise
of Dainty Devices*.   This time his identity was even more
flagrantly disclosed, because the poems were signed
" E. O."   Even so, we have unfortunately only got a few
fragments of what must have been a very considerable
literary output from " his new country Muses at Wivenhoe."
In 1578 Gabriel Harvey, addressing him in Latin, says :

. . . Let that courtly epistle, more polished even than
the writings of Castiglione himself, witness how greatly
thou dost excel in letters ; I have seen many Latin
verses of thine : yea even more English verses are extant :
thou hast drunk deep draughts not only of the Muses of
France and Italy, but hast learned the manners of many
men, and the arts of foreign countries.[1]

There can be little doubt, as we shall see, that when
Hatton came home and discovered that many of his poems
had been printed he was not unnaturally indignant with
Lord Oxford.   One of the items in the *Flowres* was a
prose tale interspersed with lyrics called *The Adventures
of Master F. I.*   This story was founded on fact.   " Master
F. I." (or Fortunatus Infœlix) has been identified with
Christopher Hatton on the strength of a marginal note to
that effect by Gabriel Harvey in one of his books.   The
lyrics around which the tale was woven were all signed
" F. I.," which means presumably that they were by
Hatton himself ; while the prose portions, which were all

¹ See p. 157, *post.*

signed " G. T." were probably written by George Turbervile. A brief summary of this story will now be given.

The scene of " Master F. I.'s " adventures is laid in the
north of England. The story tells of a love affair that he
conducted with a certain "Mistress Elinor," and it evidently refers to an early period in Hatton's life when he
was living in Northamptonshire. The opening paragraphs
run as follows :

The said F. I. chanced once in the north parts of this
realm [1] to fall in company of a very fair gentlewoman whose
name was Mistress *Elinor*, unto whom bearing a hot
affection, he first adventured to write this letter following.
                                                          G. T.

Mistress, I pray you understand that being altogether
a stranger in these parts, my good hap hath been to behold
you to my no small contentation, and my evil hap accom-
panies the same, with such imperfection of my deserts,
as I find always a ready repulse in mine own frowardness.
. . . And let this poor paper (besprent with salt tears and
blown over with scalding sighs) be saved of you as a safeguard of your sampler, or a bottom to wind your sewing
silk, that when your last needleful is wrought, you may
return to reading thereof and consider the care of him
who is
                More yours than his own,
                                                          F. I.

This letter by her received (as I have heard him say)
her answer was this. She took occasion one day, at his
request, to dance with him, the which doing she bashfully
began to declare unto him that she had read over the
writing which he delivered unto her, with like protestation
that (as at delivery thereof she understood not for what
cause he thrust the same into her bosom) so now she could
perceive thereby any part of his meaning, nevertheless
at last seemed to take upon her the matter, and though
she disabled herself yet gave him thanks as etc. Whereupon he brake the brawl, and walking abroad devised
immediately these few verses following.
                                                          G. T.

[1] Hatton was born and brought up in Northamptonshire.

Fair Bersabe the bright once bathing in a well,
With dew bedimm'd King David's eyes that ruled Israel.
And Solomon himself, the source of sapience,
Against the force of such assaults could make but small defence.
To it the stoutest yield and strongest feel like woe,
Bold Hercules and Sampson both did prove it to be so.
What wonder seemeth then, when stars stand thick in skies,
If such a blazing star have power to dim my dazzled eyes ?

L'envoie.

To you these few suffice, your wits be quick and good,
You can conject by change of hue what humours feed my blood.

F. I.

I have heard the author say that these were the first verses that ever he wrote upon like occasion. . . . And thereupon recompting her words, he compiled these following, which he termed *Terza Sequenza,* to sweet Mistress SHE.

G. T.[1]

As the story develops it becomes more and more intimate, and, though amusing and inoffensive enough as a private manuscript, its appearance in print put an entirely new complexion on the matter. Although I have not been able to trace who " Mistress Elinor " was, her identity would have been no secret to her contemporaries ; and this cavalier treatment of her good name must have been extremely trying both to herself and Hatton. The perpetrator of the outrage was Lord Oxford. When, therefore, he went abroad, Hatton set to work to devise a scheme by which he would be able not only to dissociate himself and her from the story, but also to turn the tables on Lord Oxford.

It must be remembered that the only author whose name appeared openly in *A Hundreth Sundrie Flowres* was George Gascoigne, the poet. And when Oxford left England on January 7th, 1575, Hatton must have approached Gascoigne, who had returned from Holland two months before, and between them they hatched a most ingenious plot.

Oxford had scarcely left the country before the first

---

[1] Cf. *A Hundreth Sundrie Flowres* (cit.).

step was taken. Gascoigne wrote an open letter dated
January 31st, 1575, in which he claimed that he himself
was really the author of everything in *A Hundreth Sundrie
Flowres*, and expresses great regret for certain " wanton
places " in the story about " Master F. I." He admitted
that he wrote the story, but is now heartily sorry, particularly as the idea seems to have got about that in it
" sundry persons in high places " had been maligned.
" How could this be," he cries in tones of injured innocence,
" seeing that it is really only a translation from one of
Bartello's riding tales ! " [1]

This lame explanation was of course totally inadequate,
and it was indeed only the beginning of a ruse which
developed later. In the first place, no such person as
Bartello ever existed ; and if we are to understand that
Gascoigne meant Bandello, the Italian novelist, it is an
indisputable fact that he wrote no " riding tale " or other
story even remotely resembling *The Adventures of Master
F. I.* with its English characters and English setting. But
Gascoigne's letter was only a preliminary move, and later
in the year he and Hatton began to unfold their plot.

In July we find Gascoigne being employed by the Earl
of Leicester to help entertain the Queen at the famous
Kenilworth celebrations. He dressed himself up in the
character of Sylvanus, an old man of the woods, and
declaimed before Her Majesty a long and somewhat
tedious speech that he had composed. The following
significant sentence need only be noted here :

. . . we see that the Laurel branch is a token of triumph
in all trophies, and given as a reward to all victors, a
dignity for all degrees, consecrated and dedicate to Apollo
and the Muses as a worthy flower, leaf, or branch for their
due deserts.[2]

His friends too seem to have been hard at work praising
his exceptional worth as a poet, because in a dedication

[1] *Epistle to the Reverend Divines.* (Cunliffe, *Works of George Gascoigne,*
1910, vol. i.)
[2] Cunliffe, op. cit., vol. ii, p. 126.

signed May 2nd, 1576, he refers to a time " now almost
twelve months past," which would be just about the time
of the Kenilworth pageant, when they—

had sundry times served me as an Echo with praises and
common suffrages, affirming that I deserved a Laurel
Garland, with sundry other plausible speeches not here to
be rehearsed.[1]

During September the Queen, then on a progress,
visited Woodstock, where Gascoigne was introduced to
her presence. He took the occasion to recite to her a
little moral story called the *Tale of Hemetes the Heremite*,
supposed to have been written by the Bishop of Thebes,
and now translated by him. The Queen, who always
took delight in learned discourses, expressed her pleasure;
and complimented Gascoigne on this and no doubt on his
other contributions to English literature.[2]

Thus encouraged, Gascoigne prepared for Her Majesty
a beautifully illuminated copy of the *Tale of Hemetes*
translated into four languages, English, Latin, Italian, and
French. He designed a frontispiece for it in which she
was depicted seated upon her throne with himself kneeling
before her presenting his book. Above his head is suspended the Laurel Wreath, evidently the Laureate Crown
of English poetry.[3] In the dedication to " The Queen's
most excellent Majesty " which precedes the *Tale* he refers
to the frontispiece in the following significant manner :

Behold here (learned Princess) not Gascoigne, the idle
poet, writing trifles of the Green Knight, but Gascoigne,
the satirical writer, meditating each Muse that may
express his reformation. Forget (most excellent Lady) the
poesies which I have scattered in the world, and I vow to
write volumes of profitable poems wherewith your Majesty
may be pleased. Only employ me (good Queen) and I

[1] Cunliffe, op. cit., vol ii, p. 212.
[2] Cunliffe, vol. ii, pp. 474, 583.
[3] A reproduction of this picture will be found in Cunliffe, vol. ii, and
in *A Hundreth Sundrie Flowres*.

trust to be proved as diligent as Clearchus, as resolute as Mutius, and as faithful as Curtius.[1]

Nothing could be clearer from all these references to the Laurel Wreath and from the picture just described than that Gascoigne has been asking the Queen to make him her Poet Laureate. John Skelton, who died in 1529, had been created Poet Laureate by both Universities and probably by the King.[2] The memory of Skelton, the first Poet Laureate, would be fresh in people's minds at this time, for in 1568 the first complete edition of his works had appeared under the title " Pithy pleasant and profitable works of Master Skelton, Poet Laureate. Now collected and newly published."

But in 1575 there was no official Poet Laureate, and the plot engineered by Hatton and Gascoigne was nothing more nor less than to get Gascoigne recognised by the Queen as Skelton's successor in the Laureateship. In this they were successful, for although there is no official document appointing him to the office, any more than there is in the case of Skelton, we know that the Queen was graciously pleased to receive his picture of himself crowned with laurel as a New Year's gift on January 1st, 1576. This interesting little book, with its remarkable frontispiece, is still to be found amongst the Royal Manuscripts in the British Museum.[3]

A moment's thought, moreover, will show that it is obvious that the Queen's consent to receive Gascoigne as her Laureate must have been obtained before he made the presentation on New Year's Day. The mere idea of Gascoigne, a soldier-adventurer by profession, casually strolling into the royal presence, without any authority or previous permission, is ludicrous in the extreme. It is quite evident that someone had been pulling strings behind the scenes, and we may make a shrewd guess that this person was Christopher Hatton, the Captain of the Queen's

---

[1] Cunliffe, vol. ii, p. 477.
[2] D.N.B., art. Skelton, John.
[3] B.M. Royal MSS., 18, A. 48 and 18, A. 61.

Bodyguard and the personal favourite of his royal mistress.[1]

The next move followed swiftly. On the following day, January 2nd, 1576, the new Poet Laureate announced his intention of bring out a revised edition of *A Hundreth Sundrie Flowres*. This, he asserts, is necessary because he, the sole author, was abroad when it was published. He called the new edition *The Posies of George Gascoigne, Esquire*.[2] The subject-matter of the book, except for the addition of a long poem describing his soldiering exploits in Holland, is in all essential respects, save one, exactly the same as in the *Flowres*. This one exception was the *Adventures of Master F. I.*

The story is now called *The Fable of Ferdinando Jeronimy*. We are once again assured that it is a translation from Bartello, though who Bartello was or where the original is to be found is discreetly passed over. As it was recognised that it would be most improbable that an Italian

---

[1] Walter Hamilton, *The Origin of the Office of Poet Laureate*, gives the following as Poets Laureate in Queen Elizabeth's reign :

Name.	Date of Birth.	Date of Appointment.	Date of Death.
Richard Edwards	1523	1561	1566
Edmund Spenser	1552	1590	1599
Samuel Daniel	1562	1599	1619

It will be seen that an interregnum exists between the death of Richard Edwards in 1566 and the appointment of Edmund Spenser in 1590. It seems probable that Gascoigne held the laureateship from January 1576 to October 1577. Now, in 1579, " E. K." wrote a prefatory epistle to Spenser's *Shepherd's Calendar*, his first published work. In this epistle Spenser is frequently referred to as " our new poet," and is compared to the " old famous poet Chaucer," who was the first holder of the title of Laureate. I suggest that " E. K." is hinting that Spenser should be appointed to the post of Poet Laureate, left vacant by Gascoigne's death two years before. Actually, however, Spenser was not officially recognised until 1590, in which year the first three books of the *Faery Queen* were published.

[2] A note of defiance can be detected in this title. " The *Posies* of George Gascoigne " means the Latin tags or " posies " with which Gascoigne signed the poems which had been attributed to " sundry gentlemen " in *A Hundreth Sundrie Flowres*. There is little doubt that Gascoigne's claim to these poems was quite false.

writer would choose an English setting for his story, a
mass of minute alterations have been made.   Lombardy
is substituted for England, Venice for London, and
" Mistress Elinor " becomes Leonora de Valasco.   Most
significant of all, the offending initials G. T., with which
the prose portions had been signed by Turbervile in the
Flowres, do not appear once.   In fact anyone reading it who
had not seen the original, or did not know of the mythical
nature of " Bartello," could have no reason to suppose
that it was not exactly what it purported to be, viz. an
innocent translation of an Italian " riding tale."

Exactly when Lord Oxford first saw or heard of the
capture of his book by Gascoigne is not known.   But we
may surmise that it took place on or about April 4th in
Paris.   It was on that date, it will be remembered, that
" he suddenly changed."   He left Paris for England in a
violent hurry and a furious temper.   It is noteworthy that
he refused to land at Dover, where Thomas Cecil had gone
to meet him, but went round to the Thames and landed at
Rowland Yorke's house instead.   He seems to have stayed
some days with Rowland Yorke and his brother Edward
Yorke.[1]

Now the significance of this lies in the fact that Rowland
Yorke was a great friend of Gascoigne.   The two men had
sailed together to the Netherlands as volunteers in March
1572, and had served as captains of companies under Sir
Roger Williams and Colonel Chester until they were
captured by the Spaniards at Leyden in July 1574.   When
we read, therefore, that Oxford landed at Yorke's house,
that he was supping with Edward Yorke, and that he
meant to have nothing to do with his wife or her people
till he had carried out certain unspecified enquiries, it
certainly looks very much as though *The Posies of George
Gascoigne, Esquire*, had been partly the cause of the
trouble.

It is perhaps a fair surmise that Oxford, with his great
literary interests and attainments, had secretly aspired to

[1] Hatfield MSS. (Cal. II. 131, 132).

become Skelton's successor as Poet Laureate of England. We may even be able to trace in Gascoigne's allegory of the two brothers " Deep Desire " and " Due Desert "— quoted at the head of this Interlude—a reference to the Earl and himself competing for " Apollo's Laurel Crown." But Oxford could not of course say so openly, because it would have been considered a terrible disgrace for a nobleman to adopt " bald rhyming " as his profession. But whether or no he had hoped in the long run to convert the Queen, who was a true friend of the Muses and all good learning, to his way of thinking, it is obvious that he had been completely forestalled by Gascoigne on New Year's Day, 1576. And he opened his heart in an unmistakeable way in a poem signed " E. O.," which appeared in *A Paradise of Dainty Devices* later on in the same year. It was called " The complaint of a lover wearing black ' and tawny." The allusion to Gascoigne's Laurel Crown and his own failure to obtain the Laureateship seem hardly to admit of dispute.

> A crown of bays shall that man wear
>   That triumphs over me ;
> For black and tawny will I wear,
>   Which mourning colours be.
>
> The more I follow on,
>   The more she fled away,
> As Daphne did full long ago,
>   Apollo's wishful prey.
>
> The more my plaints I do resound
>   The less she pities me ;
> The more I sought the less I found,
>   Yet mine she meant to be.
>
> Melpomene, alas, with doleful tunes help then ;
> And sing *Bis, woe* worth on me, forsaken man.[1]

Though the capture of his book and the failure to become the Queen's Poet Laureate almost certainly contributed to Lord Oxford's " sudden change " in Paris on April 4th, 1576, it was not the primary cause. This great crisis in his life was unquestionably accomplished by the diabolical plot engineered by Lord Henry Howard, with the disastrous results that have already been described.

[1] Melpomene is the Muse of Tragedy and of Lyric Poetry.

The whole story of the catastrophe, so far as we shall probably ever know it, has now been told. With it a definite chapter in the story of Lord Oxford's life closes and a new one begins. But before we pass on it will not be out of place to make a few reflections on the tangled skein that we have attempted to unravel.

It would be presumptuous on our part to place our finger on any particular event, and say that this incident or that was the cause of the whole unhappy business. Lord Oxford himself in his letters to his father-in-law deliberately declines to specify his " mislikings," and Burghley for his part is obviously puzzled and groping in the dark throughout. Ostensibly, it may be argued, the cause of the trouble was faithlessness on the part of the Countess to her husband, that at least has been the echo of all Oxford's biographers from Isaac D'Israeli to Sir Sidney Lee. But against this must be set the certain fact that neither the Earl nor Burghley really believed for an instant that Lady Oxford had been untrue to her marriage vows. The paternity of Elizabeth Vere was never seriously questioned either at the time of her birth or in after years. In spite of this, however, it is an undeniable fact that for the next six years Oxford positively refused to live with his wife, or to have anything to do with her family. There was evidently something amiss that rankled in his mind and led him to take such drastic action against his wife, whom he knew to be innocent. What was this unknown grievance ?

We must remember, in the first place, that in Lord Oxford we are not dealing with a normal, humdrum man. His views, for example, on literature were sufficiently unorthodox to outrage the feelings of so conventional a man as Lord Burghley. We cannot doubt that, as his mind developed, he chafed more and more at his virtual imprisonment in Cecil House. His marriage, which may at first have seemed to him the key to his independence, only resulted in drawing the shackles still closer. There is little doubt that, but for his hare-brained escapade when

he ran away to the Low Countries in 1574, the Queen
and Lord Burghley would never have given him permission
to achieve his great ambition of foreign travel. To
Burghley, France and Italy were sinks of iniquity and vice
that contaminated anyone who had the misfortune to
come into contact with them. To Oxford, they represented
all the beauty and culture of the Renaissance, a veritable
fairy-land, compared with which Cecil House and the Court
were like squalid slums. How could two such men live
harmoniously together ?

Surely, then, when the Earl began to hear whispers
emanating from his father-in-law that were as untrue as
they were foolish, he would not be slow to see that Burghley
was playing into his hands. His violent reaction to the
Lord Treasurer's ill-timed insinuations reduced that unhappy man to a pitiable condition. It was in vain that
he withdrew everything he had uttered, and pleaded that it
was a slanderous lie of others, notably of Lord Henry
Howard, that had led him to harbour such unworthy
suspicions. The initiative had now passed into Lord
Oxford's hands, and he was determined at whatever cost
to retain it. Liberty was what he wanted, and liberty was
only possible by making a complete break with the whole
Cecil clan. It was a ruthless action and in many ways
a tragic one. It broke his wife's heart, and for a time at
any rate, estranged his truest friends. And his ultimate
reconciliation with his wife and Lord Burghley was tinged
with a bitterness that never could be quite overcome.

But for the moment he was free. With all the zest of his
impetuous nature he threw himself into the new life that
seemed to open so gloriously before him. To make the
break with Cecil House more complete, he chose for his
companions wild spirits like Lord Surrey, Charles Arundel,
Francis Southwell, and Walter Ralegh. He turned Catholic,
and then Atheist, though this did not appear openly.
At length, sickened by Howard treachery and Ralegh
arrogance, he re-entered once more the portals of Cecil
House. But this is anticipating our story.

The great upheaval left an even more permanent mark
on his literary exploits and ambitions. It is possible that
his failure to obtain the Laureateship roused in him the
determination never again to allow his name to appear in
print. There can be no doubt that he continued to write
and take a keen interest in poetry and the drama till the
day of his death. Men like Harvey, William Webbe,
Francis Meres, and others, are unanimous in testifying that
he stood supreme from 1578 till 1598, both as poet and
dramatist. But whether or no his writings still exist, it
is abundantly clear that they were not printed under his
own name.

BOOK THE SECOND

THE COURTIER

BOOK THE SECOND

THE COURTIER

" I may not omit the deserved commendations of many honourable
and noble Lords and Gentlemen in Her Majesty's Court, which, in the rare
devices of poetry, have been and yet are most skilful ; among whom the
right honourable Earl of Oxford may challenge to himself the title of the
most excellent among the rest."

WILLIAM WEBBE, 1586.

CHAPTER IV

1577–1580

" For a long time past Phœbus Apollo has cultivated thy mind in the arts. English poetical measures have been sung by thee long enough. Let the Courtly Epistle—more polished even than the writings of Castiglione himself—witness how greatly thou dost excel in letters. I have seen many Latin verses of thine, yea, even more English verses are extant."
Gabriel Harvey to the Earl of Oxford, 1578.

§ I. Her Majesty's Letters Patent

THE year 1577 opened without any improvement in the relations between the Earl of Oxford and his wife, and Lord Burghley took the opportunity of making a fresh appeal to his son-in-law to relent :

My Lord, My silence and forebearing of speech to your Lordship (now a good time) in a cause of that weight to me as concerneth so nearly my dearest beloved daughter, your Lordship's wife, hath hitherto proceeded, partly in hope that after some space of months some change to the better might follow, partly to avoid the offending of you in whom I have seen some change from your old wonted countenance. But considering with myself, and that seriously, how long both I as a father to your afflicted wife (and be it spoken without offence of comparison) for my part as loving and as well deserving a friend towards you, since I first knew you, as any whosoever of any degree ; and also (how long) your loving, faithful, and dutiful wife hath suffered the lack of your love, conversation and company : though in several respects desired, yea, in some sort due by several deserts to us.

I cannot, my Lord, see this old year passed with such disgraces, and a new entered meet to record a concourse of graces, nor feel the burden of the griefs to grow as they daily do without appearance of amendment, but assay by reasonable means to seek relief ; specially for my daughter, whose grief is the greater and shall always be inasmuch as her love is most fervent and addicted to you, and because she cannot, or may not, without offence be suffered to come to your presence, as she desireth, to offer the sacrifice of her heart ; nor can I find opportunity in open places, where we sometimes meet, to reveal my griefs both for myself but especially to relieve them for my daughter. I do heartily by this my instant letter beseech your Lordship (and by contestation of your honour do require you to assent) that I may have some time convenient to speak with your Lordship in your own chamber or in some other meet place ; meaning not to move anything to your Lordship but that shall proceed from a ground of mere love towards you, and that shall be agreeable to your honour and calling, to your profit and comfort, and not unmeet for either of us both. And if your Lordship shall for any respect though unknown to me like to have any person of noble or other degree present, I shall not refuse of any such to be named by your Lordship's self. And to this my request, my Lord, I pray you give me answer by this bearer as it shall please you by speech or by writing, having made nobody privy with this my letter.

Your Lordship's truly affected,

W. BURG.[1]

The Earl's answer is not recorded ; indeed, it is doubtful if he deigned a reply, for in July his whole attention seems to have been devoted to a suit he was trying to persuade the Queen to grant him.

It may further please your Lordship to be advertised [writes John Stanhope to Burghley on July 25th] that my Lord of Oxford giveth his diligent attention on Her Majesty, and earnestly laboureth his suit, the which he was once persuaded and had yielded to leave ; but now renewing it with intent to proceed therein for his own good, some unkindness and strangeness proceed therein between my Lord of Surrey,[2] my Lord Harry, and his Lordship. It is

---

[1] Lansdowne MSS., 238. 129.

[2] Philip Howard, grandson of the poet Earl of Surrey and son of the late Duke of Norfolk. He was Oxford's first cousin, and was now twenty years old. The " strangeness " referred to was overcome later, because in 1579 Surrey and Oxford were associated in a Court Masque. He succeeded Henry Fitzalan, 12th Earl of Arundel (his maternal grandfather) as Earl of Arundel in 1580. He was an ardent Catholic. In 1589 he was tried and convicted by his peers, Lord Oxford being one, for having, among other things, heard a Mass at which the success of the Spanish Armada was prayed for. He died in the Tower in 1595. He was beatified in 1886 by the Roman Catholic Church.

said Her Majesty hath promised to give him the fee simple
of Rysing, and as much more of those lands in fee farm as
shall make up the sum of £250.[1]

The Manor of Rysing originally belonged to the Duke of
Norfolk, and had been confiscated by the Crown on his
attainder and execution.   In 1578 the Queen conveyed
it to Lord Oxford, as foreshadowed in Stanhope's letter.
The fact that it had belonged to Surrey's father would
account for the " strangeness " mentioned by Stanhope.
The wording of this grant by the Queen to Lord Oxford is
interesting :

The Queen to all to whom these present letters may come,
Greeting.   Know you that We, as well in consideration of
the good, true, and faithful service done and given to Us
before this time by Our most dear cousin Edward Earl of
Oxford, Great Chamberlain of England, as for divers other
causes and considerations moving Us ;   by Our special
grace, and out of Our certain knowledge and mere motion,
We gave and granted, and by these presents for Us, Our
heirs, and successors do give and grant to the above named
Edward Earl of Oxford, all that Our Lordship or Manor of
Rysing. . . .[2]

It is difficult to see exactly what " good, true, and faithful
service " Lord Oxford could have performed on the Queen's
behalf.   We know, of course, that she was very fond of
him, and that he had been a diligent courtier.   But, on the
other hand, it is indisputable that he had never held any
official appointment at Court.   The hereditary title of Lord
Great Chamberlain held by the Earls of Oxford was in no
sense comparable to appointments like those of Lord
Chamberlain, Lord Steward, or Master of the Horse.   Lord
Great Chamberlain was merely a rank which entitled the
holder to a specified seat in the House of Lords, and a place
in Royal Processions.   The only duties it involved were in
connexion with Coronations.

It is most unusual to find Her Majesty bestowing lands

[1] Hatfield MSS. (Cal. II. 157).
[2] Patent Roll 1165. m. 34. 20 Eliz. (1578).   Latin.

on a courtier who was not also an official of the Royal
Household. Leicester, Essex, Hatton, and Ralegh all
received lavish gifts of land from her ; but all, at one time
or another, had held highly responsible posts. Moreover,
gifts of land to State Officials cannot primarily be regarded
as personal presents to be enjoyed according to the
recipient's pleasure. They were, in part at least, intended
to be used in defraying the cost of such appointments.
The official salary was seldom if ever adequate. A typical
example—that of Francis Walsingham when he was
appointed Ambassador at the French Court in 1570—may
be quoted :

Surely if Her Majesty make choice of any of my mean
calling and ability, she must also resolve to enable them
some way whereby they may bear the burden. Sir Henry
Norris [Walsingham's predecessor] whose living is known
to be very great hath found the charge very heavy, and
therefore unfit for the shoulders of any other of my mean
calling.[1]

The normal method by which Elizabeth " enabled "
her officials to " bear the burden " was by gifts of land or
monopolies to supplement their meagre salaries. But gifts
only followed services ; and we may be quite sure that the
" good, true, and faithful service " that Lord Oxford had
performed in the past, and was no doubt then performing,
was no sinecure. But it does not transpire in any official
correspondence what its nature was. We shall have
occasion in a later chapter to discuss in greater detail this
and other mysterious gifts to Lord Oxford by the Queen.

It may be added that the conception of most modern
historians that Elizabeth gave indiscriminate presents to
her so-called " favourites " because they looked handsome
or danced well is so universally believed that it will not
be easily dispelled. That she took pleasure in the personal
attractions of men like Leicester, Essex, Hatton, and Ralegh
is as natural as it is undeniable. But they worked hard

---

[1] Walsingham to Cecil. Printed by Conyers Read, *Sir Francis Walsingham*, vol. i, p. 105.

for their presents.   Leicester was her Commander-in-Chief
and was seldom absent from the Council-table : Essex
was one of her ablest Generals, her Master of the Horse,
and Earl Marshal ; Hatton was successively her Bodyguard
Commander, Vice-Chamberlain, and Lord Chancellor ;
and Ralegh, besides commanding her Bodyguard for many
years, spent his money freely in founding her Colonial
Empire.   We may be quite sure that Oxford, for his part,
had certain definite duties to perform in return for a gift
of land worth £250 a year.

§ II.   " THE BRAVE LORD WILLOUGHBY "

> " The fifteenth day of July,
>   With glistering spear and shield,
> A famous fight in Flanders
>   Was foughten in the field ;
> The most courageous officers
>   Were English Captains three :
> But the bravest man in battel
>   Was brave Lord Willoughby." [1]

" My Lord Willoughby was one of the Queen's best swordsmen. . . . I
have heard it spoken that had he not slighted the Court, but applied
himself to the Queen, he might have enjoyed a plentiful portion of her
grace ; and it was his saying—and it did him no good—that he was none
of the Reptilia : intimating that he could not creep on the ground, and
that the Court was not his element.   For, indeed, as he was a great soldier,
so he was of amiable magnanimity, and could not brook the obsequiousness
and assiduity of the Court." (Sir Robert Naunton, in *Fragmenta Regalia*.)

In July 1577 Lady Mary Vere, Lord Oxford's sister and
a Maid of Honour, became engaged to be married to
Peregrine Bertie.   This match met with the strong disapproval of Peregrine's mother, who had been married
when quite a girl to Charles Brandon, Duke of Suffolk.
The Duke died in 1545, leaving her a childless widow, and
she had then married Richard Bertie, a zealous Protestant.
Their only son, Peregrine, had derived his name from the
fact that he had been born on the Continent during his
parents' enforced exile on account of the Marian perse-

---

[1] From an old English ballad (c. 1585–90) published in Percy's *Reliques*.

cutions.[1]   The Duchess of Suffolk expressed herself forcibly
in a letter to Lord Burghley dated July 2nd :

It is very true that my wise son has gone very far with
my Lady Mary Vere, I fear too far to turn.   I must say to
you in counsel what I have said to her plainly, that I
had rather he had matched in any other place ; and I told
her the causes.   Her friends made small account of me ;
her brother did what in him lay to deface my husband and
son ; besides, our religions agree not, and I cannot tell
what more.   If she should prove like her brother, if an
empire follows her I should be sorry to match so.   She said
that she could not rule her brother's tongue, nor help
the rest of his faults, but for herself she trusted so to use
her[self] as I should have no cause to mislike her.   And
seeing that it was so far forth between my son and her, she
desired my good will and asked no more.   ' That is a seemly
thing,' quoth I, ' for you to live on ; for I fear that Master
Bertie will so much mislike of these dealings that he will
give little more than his good will, if he give that.   Besides,
if Her Majesty shall mislike of it, sure we turn him to the
wide world.'   She told me how Lord Sussex and Master
Hatton had promised to speak for her to the Queen, and
that I would require you to do the like.   I told her her
brother used you and your daughter so evil that I could
not require you to deal in it.   Well, if I would write, she
knew you would do it for my sake ; and since there was
no undoing it, she trusted I would, for my son's sake, help
now.

The Duchess goes on to say that the Queen has found
fault with her for keeping Peregrine away from the Court—

But God knows I did it not so but for fear of this marriage
and quarrels.   Within this fortnight there was one spoke
to me for one Mistress Gaymege, an heir of a thousand
marks land, which had been a meeter match for my son.[2]

A fortnight later the Duchess wrote again to Lord Burghley.   She was evidently most anxious to stop the marriage,

[1] He was born on October 12th, 1555, at Wesel (Collins, *Peerage*, vol. ii,
p. 55).
[2] Hatfield MSS. (Cal. XIII. 146).

and in the absence of her husband was turning to the
Lord Treasurer for advice :

My good Lord, I received this letter here enclosed
yesterday from my husband wherein your Lordship may
perceive his head is troubled, as I [can] not blame him.
But if he knew as much as I of my good Lord of Oxford's
dealings it would trouble him more. But the case standing
as it doth I mean to keep it from him. . . . I cannot express
how much this grieveth me, that my son, in the weightiest
matter, hath so forgotten himself to the trouble and dis-
quiet of his friends, and like enough to be his own undoing
and the young lady's too. For if my Lord of Oxford's
wilfulness come to my husband's ears I believe he would
make his son but small marriage.

I wot not what to do therein. If I should stay for Her
Majesty's good will in it, and my husband far off from it,
you know he cannot take that well at my hand, that I
should seek to bestow his son as it were against his will . . .
and so I am dead at my wit's end. And yet I think if
Her Majesty could be won to like it, I am sure my husband
would be the easier won to it, if my Lord of Oxford's great
uncourteousness do not too much trouble him.

My good Lord, I cannot tell what to do or say in this ;
but as my good Lord and very friend I commit myself
and the case to your good advice and counsel and help. . . .
From Willoughby House, this 14th of July,

K. SUFFOULK.[1]

A hitch seems to have occurred in the autumn, for on
November 11th, in a letter to the Earl of Rutland, Thomas
Screven says :

The marriage of the Lady Mary Vere is deferred until
after Christmas, for as yet neither has Her Majesty given
licence, nor has the Earl of Oxford wholly assented thereto.[2]

But if outside forces were trying to prevent the marriage
the two persons most nearly concerned were equally
determined on their union. In an affectionate letter to
his fiancée Peregrine assures her that he " makes more
account of her than myself or life," adding that he writes

[1] Hatfield MSS. (Cal. II. 156).   [2] Cal. Rutland MSS., I. 115.

to let her know " how uncourteously I am dealt with by my Lord your brother, who, as I hear, bandeth against me and sweareth my death." The letter ends " yours more than his own and so till death." [1]

The wedding took place soon after Christmas, for in a letter to Lord Burghley in the ensuing March the Duchess of Suffolk requests a bill off impost for two tun of wine on behalf of her daughter Mary and her husband.[2] But the marriage did not prove a happy one. In September we find Sir Thomas Cecil in a letter to his father speaking of an " unkindness " that had grown up between them ; adding that he thinks the Lady Mary " will be beaten with that rod which heretofore she prepared for others." [3]

Subsequent evidence shows that Lord Oxford's " uncourteous " behaviour towards his brother-in-law did not last after the wedding had taken place. Their differences were evidently religious in origin ; but in 1582, after the Earl had returned to Protestantism, we shall meet the two men again and find their quarrels amicably settled. Moreover, in 1599 Robert Bertie, the eldest son of Peregrine and Lady Mary, wrote in a very friendly way to his uncle, which would have been impossible had his father and Lord Oxford remained enemies.

We now return to the matrimonial troubles of Lord and Lady Oxford. Lord Burghley's new year appeal did not have the effect he had hoped. The Earl and his Countess remained separated. In December 1577 the Duchess of Suffolk devised an ingenious and very kindly meant scheme to try and bring them together :

My very good Lord [she writes to Burghley], Upon Tuesday last Harry Cook being here and my daughter [4] entering in to talk with him of my Lord of Oxford, of his sister, of my Lady his wife, and the young Lady his daughter, at the last he uttered these speeches : that he

---

[1] Cal. Ancaster MSS.   [2] Hatfield MSS. (Cal. II. 205).   [3] Ibid.
[4] Susan Bertie, who married Reginald Grey, 5th Earl of Kent. He died in 1573.

thought my Lord would very gladly see the child [1] if he could devise how to see her and not to go to her. My daughter said she thought if it might so like him my Lady your wife would send the child to him ; but to that he answered my Lord would not be known of it that he so much desired to see it. So because it was a young man's words I took no great hold of it.

On Thursday I went to see my Lady Mary Vere. After other talks she asked me what I would say to it if my Lord her brother would take his wife again. 'Truly,' quoth I, ' nothing could comfort me more, for now I wish to your brother as much good as to my own son.' 'Indeed,' quoth she, ' he would very fain see the child, and is loth to send for her.' 'Then,' quoth I, ' an you will keep my counsel we will have some sport with him. I will see if I can get the child hither to me, when you shall come hither ; and whilst my Lord your brother is with you I will bring in the child as though it were some other child of my friend's, and we shall see how nature will work in him to like it, and tell him it is his own after.' 'Very well,' quoth she ; so we agreed hereon. Notwithstanding, I mean not to delay in it otherwise than it shall seem good to your Lordship, and in that sort that may best like you. I will do what I can either in that or anything else what may anyway lay in me. If it be clear about your house here in London I think if it may so please you it were good that both my Lady of Oxford and the child were there, and so the child might be quickly brought hither at my Lord's being there. I would wish speed that he might be taken in his good mood. I thank God I am at this present in his good favour. For one other besides his sister and Harry Cook told me that my Lord would fain have the child a while in my house with his sister, and no doubt of it if he be not crossed in this his liking he will sure have me laid to, and then I trust all things will follow to your desire. I hear he is about to buy a house here in London about Watling Street, and not to continue a Courtier as he hath done ; but I pray you keep all these things secret or else you may undo those that do take pains to bring it to pass if my Lord's counsel should be betrayed before he list himself. And above all others my credit should be lost with him if he should know I

[1] Elizabeth Vere, then aged two and a half.

dealt in anything without his consent ; and therefore my good Lord I pray you keep it very secret, and write me two or three words what you would have me do in it.

And thus with my very hearty commendation I commit your Lordship to God, whom I pray to work all things to your comfort. From Willoughby House this 15th of December.

Your Lordship's very assured friend,

K. SUFFOULK.[1]

History does not relate what came of the Duchess of Suffolk's scheme to bring about a reunion between Lord and Lady Oxford. But it is pleasant to think that it may, perhaps, have been the first step which led to their ultimate reconciliation.

After a distinguished military career Lord Willoughby died in 1601 and was buried at Spilsby in Lincolnshire. The following is taken from the inscription on his tomb :

This presents unto you the worthy memory of the Right Honourable Sir Peregrine Bertie, knight, Lord Willoughby of Willoughby, Beake, and Eresby ; deservedly employed by Queen Elizabeth as General of her forces in the Low Countries and in France ; as Ambassador into Denmark ; and lately as Governor of Berwick, where he died in the forty-seventh year of his age, anno 1600.[2]

§ III. GABRIEL HARVEY

In July 1578 the Queen paid another visit to Cambridge University. She was accompanied by the whole Court, among whom were Lord Burghley, the Earls of Leicester and Oxford, Sir Christopher Hatton, who had recently been knighted and appointed Vice-Chamberlain of the Household, and Philip Sidney. It was on this occasion that Gabriel Harvey met the Court at Audley End and presented the Queen and her courtiers with a series of Latin verses he had written in their honour. The portion addressed to Lord Oxford was entitled :

An heroic address to the [Earl of Oxford], concerning

[1] Lansdowne MSS., 25. 27.
[2] Canon Gilbert George Walker, *A Great Elizabethan* (1927), p. 27.

the combined utility and dignity of military affairs and of warlike exercises.

Harvey's tribute to Lord Oxford's learning and scholarship, and the statement that " I have seen many Latin verses of thine, yea, even more English verses are extant," is important as showing us how far the Earl had progressed along the path of literature :

This is my welcome ; this is how I have decided to bid All Hail ! to thee and to the other Nobles.

Thy splendid fame, great Earl, demands even more than in the case of others the services of a poet possessing lofty eloquence. Thy merit doth not creep along the ground, nor can it be confined within the limits of a song. It is a wonder which reaches as far as the heavenly orbs. O great-hearted one, strong in thy mind and thy fiery will, thou wilt conquer thyself, thou wilt conquer others ; thy glory will spread out in all directions beyond the Arctic Ocean ; and England will put thee to the test and prove thee to be a native-born Achilles. Do thou but go forward boldly and without hesitation. Mars will obey thee, Hermes will be thy messenger, Pallas striking her shield with her spear shaft will attend thee, thine own breast and courageous heart will instruct thee. For a long time past Phœbus Apollo has cultivated thy mind in the arts. English poetical measures have been sung by thee long enough. Let that Courtly Epistle [1]—more polished even than the writings of Castiglione himself— witness how greatly thou dost excel in letters. I have seen many Latin verses of thine, yea, even more English verses are extant ; thou hast drunk deep draughts not only of the Muses of France and Italy, but hast learned the manners of many men, and the arts of foreign countries. It was not for nothing that Sturmius himself was visited by thee ; neither in France, Italy, nor Germany are any such cultivated and polished men. O thou hero worthy of renown, throw away the insignificant pen, throw away bloodless books, and writings that serve no useful purpose ; now must the sword be brought into play, now is the time

---

[1] Lord Oxford's letter " to the reader " prefixed to Bartholomew Clerke's *Courtier* (see p. 80).

for thee to sharpen the spear and to handle great engines of war. On all sides men are talking of camps and of deadly weapons ; war and the Furies are everywhere, and Bellona reigns supreme.

Gabriel Harvey was no false prophet. The Spanish menace had begun in earnest. Protestantism and England were standing on the threshold of the great struggle that lasted to the end of Elizabeth's reign.

Now may all martial influences [he continues] support thy eager mind, driving out the cares of Peace. Pull Hannibal up short at the gates of Britain. Defended though he be by a mighty host, let Don John of Austria come on only to be driven home again. Fate is unknown to man, nor are the counsels of the Thunderer fully determined. And what if suddenly a most powerful enemy should invade our borders ? If the Turk should be arming his savage hosts against us ? What though the terrible war trumpet is even now sounding its blast ? Thou wilt see it all ; even at this very moment thou art fiercely longing for the fray. I feel it. Our whole country knows it. In thy breast is noble blood, Courage animates thy brow, Mars lives in thy tongue, Minerva strengthens thy right hand, Bellona reigns in thy body, within thee burns the fire of Mars. Thine eyes flash fire, thy countenance shakes a spear ; who would not swear that Achilles had come to life again ? [1]

Gabriel Harvey, who was almost exactly the same age as Oxford,[2] was at this time a fellow of Trinity Hall, Cambridge. Prior to this he had been at Christ's College, where he had taken his B.A. in 1570. It was as an undergraduate that he had first met Lord Oxford, because he tells us that—

In the prime of his (i.e. Lord Oxford's) gallantest youth he bestowed Angels upon me in Christ's College in Cambridge, and otherwise vouchsafed me many gracious

---

[1] *Gratulationes Valdinenses*, libri quatuor, 1578.

[2] Cf. McKerrow, *Works of Thomas Nashe*, vol. v, p. 69, where the date of his birth is given as 1550 or 1551.

favours at the affectionate commendation of my cousin
Master Thomas Smith, the son of Sir Thomas. . . .[1]

It is evident that a genuine friendship between the Earl
and Harvey sprang up as a result of their early acquaintance
and it is equally evident that literature must have been the
common ground on which they met. Although it is
probable that they kept in touch with each other during
the intervening years, this cannot be proved. But their
reunion at Audley End may have been the cause of a
visit Harvey paid to London in 1579 when he first met
John Lyly, who was the Earl's private secretary and was
engaged in writing his famous novel *Euphues*, which he
dedicated to Lord Oxford. Harvey tells us that Lyly was
then living in the Savoy, and it is more than likely that his
rooms there were provided for him at Lord Oxford's
expense.[2]

Let us return now to Audley End and examine more
critically the address to Lord Oxford. Even if we discard
much of the fulsome praise as mere flattery we are left
with one indisputable fact. This is that Lord Oxford was
well known to have written a great number of poems both
in Latin and English, the majority in the latter tongue.
Eight poems only subscribed by his name had appeared
in print prior to this date, viz. one prefixed to Bedingfield's
Cardanus' Comfort (1573), and seven in the *Paradise of*

[1] Gabriel Harvey, *Foure letters* . . . 1592. (Bodley Head Quartos, 34.)
Thomas Smith, claimed as a cousin by Harvey, was the natural son of the
Queen's Principal Secretary Sir Thomas Smith. It is not unlikely that
when Sir Thomas was Lord Oxford's tutor in the previous reign his son had
been young Edward de Vere's playfellow. In 1571 Sir Thomas received
a grant of land in the long narrow peninsula on the north-east coast of
Ireland known as The Ardes. He sent over his son to administer the
estate, where he remained as Colonel of the district until about 1580.

[2] Cf. Bond, *Works of John Lyly*, vol. i, pp. 17, 24. "[in the dedication to
Euphues and his England] we have the first authentic indication of Lyly's
connexion with Burleigh's son-in-law, a connexion which may have begun
in the Savoy where, as we saw, Oxford rented ' two tenements,' but which
Lyly must in any case have owed to Burleigh's recommendation. The
nature of the connexion is to be inferred from Lyly's own letter of 1582
and from Harvey's *Advertisement to Pap Hatchet*. He was engaged as
private secretary to the Earl and admitted to his confidence."

Dainty Devices (1576). If we add the sixteen lyrics rescued
from their anonymity in *A Hundreth Sundrie Flowres*
(1573) we are still left with only twenty-four in English
and none in Latin. This number is quite incompatible
with Harvey's description of the Earl's poetical output.
It is therefore evident that he must have been privileged
to read Oxford's poems in manuscript—a privilege that
must also have been extended to others in the Court, because Harvey makes no secret of their existence in his open
address. These facts are important and confirm what
we are told by other, and no less credible witnesses than
Harvey, that Lord Oxford stands supreme amongst his
contemporary poets and dramatists.

Another interesting feature of Harvey's address is his
evidently sincere appeal to Lord Oxford to give up his
preoccupation in literature and prepare himself for the
coming war. Everybody in England knew that war was
inevitable, and leadership in war was the heritage of the
nobility. There can be no doubt that Harvey was sincerely
distressed that his friend, who held one of the proudest
titles in the realm, was obviously unconcerned with martial
matters. Harvey no doubt considered that it was an
excellent thing for a nobleman to display a reasonable
interest in culture and the Muses, but here was a nobleman who had exceeded all bounds of moderation and was
making literature his one occupation to the exclusion of
everything else. This, says Harvey, is quite wrong ;
and his engaging frankness helps to give us a very life-
like picture of Lord Oxford's character as judged by his
contemporaries at Gloriana's Court.

Another episode that occurred during this Progress may
be related here. We will let the Spanish Ambassador,
Bernardino de Mendoza, tell us the story in his own words :

This Queen [Elizabeth] has greatly feasted Alençon's
Ambassador,[1] and on one occasion when she was enter-

---

[1] M. de Bacqueville, who had been sent to England by Alençon in connexion with his marriage and affairs in the Low Countries. Alençon had
been created Duc d'Anjou in 1576, but he was indiscriminately known by
both titles at this time, though the latter is more strictly correct.

taining him at dinner she thought the sideboard was not
so well furnished with pieces of plate as she would have
liked the Frenchman to have seen it ; she therefore called
the Earl of Sussex, the Lord Steward, who had charge of
these things, and asked him how it was there was so little
plate. The Earl replied that he had, for many years,
accompanied her and other Sovereigns of England in their
Progresses, and he had never seen them take so much plate
as she was carrying then. The Queen told him to hold
his tongue, that he was a great rogue, and that the more
good that was done to people like him the worse they got.
She then turned to a certain North,[1] who was there in the
room, and asked him whether he thought there was much
or little plate on the sideboard, to which he replied there
was very little, and threw the blame on Sussex. When
North left the Queen's Chamber Sussex told him that he
had spoken wrongly and falsely in what he said to the
Queen ; whereupon North replied that if he (Sussex) did
not belong to the Council he would prove what he said to
his teeth. Sussex then went to Leicester and complained
of the knavish behaviour of North, but Leicester told
him the words he used should not be applied to such
persons as North. Sussex answered that, whatever he
might think of the words, North was a great knave ; so
that they remained offended with one another as they had
been before on other matters. This may not be of importance, but I have thought well to relate it to you [2] so that
you may see how easily matters here may now be brought
into discord, if care be taken on one side to ensure support
against eventualities. The next day the Queen sent twice
to tell the Earl of Oxford, who is a very gallant lad, to
dance before the Ambassadors ; whereupon he replied
that he hoped Her Majesty would not order him to do so,
as he did not wish to entertain Frenchmen. When the
Lord Steward took him the message the second time he
replied that he would not give pleasure to Frenchmen,
nor listen to such a message, and with that he left the
room. He is a lad who has a great following in the country,

---

[1] Roger, 2nd Baron North (1530–1600). The Queen visited him at his
seat, Kirtling, on this Progress. He was the Earl of Leicester's brother-
in-law, having married the widow of Sir Henry Dudley, Leicester's younger
brother.

[2] Zayas, the King of Spain's Secretary, to whom the letter was addressed.

12

and has requested permission to go and serve His Highness, which the Queen refused, and asked him why he did not go and serve the Archduke Mathias, to which he replied that he would not go and serve another Sovereign than his own, unless it were a very great one, such as the King of Spain.[1]

" His Highness " was Don John of Austria, the half-brother of the King of Spain. He is chiefly remembered for his celebrated sea victory over the Turks at Lepanto in 1571. The memory of Lepanto and Don John would have been very fresh in Venice when Oxford was there in 1575. Venice was the great Naval Base of the Christian fleets in the Mediterranean, and the Republic had provided the majority of the ships comprising the Allied Navy at the battle. Don John had afterwards been sent by King Philip to the Netherlands as Governor-General on the death of Requesens in 1576. But his conciliatory policy was a failure, and he was obliged to leave Brussels and retire to Namur in the following year. After his departure the Prince of Orange was induced to enter Brussels, but he was equally unsuccessful in reconciling the religious factions. In October 1577 the Archduke Mathias, the twenty-two-year-old brother of the Habsburg Emperor, arrived in Brussels to take over the sovereignty of the Netherlands at the invitation of the Dutch Catholic Nobles. Orange announced that he was willing to co-operate with him in the Government ; but in January 1578 Don John, who had been reinforced by the Duke of Parma with troops from Spain, inflicted a crushing defeat on the Protestants at Gemblours.

Mendoza's story that Lord Oxford had asked for per-mission to serve under Don John must be taken with considerable reservation. In the previous year Elizabeth had written a letter to the King of Spain in which she had referred to Don John as her " most mortal enemy." [2] It is out of the question that Oxford would have been able to maintain his favoured position with the Queen if he

[1] Cal. S.P. Spanish (1568–79), p. 607.   [2] Camden, *Queen Elizabeth*, p. 222.

THOMAS RADCLIFFE
3RD *EARL OF SUSSEX, K.G.*

Artist unknown

had expressed a genuine desire to serve under her most mortal enemy.   But it is by no means unlikely that, with his privileged position, he should have jokingly remarked to his Royal Mistress that he intended so to do—a remark that Mendoza, with true Spanish gravity, accepted at its face value.   Moreover, it would naturally be the Spanish Ambassador's policy to exaggerate any pro-Spanish sympathies, real or imagined, that he could detect among the English nobility.

However this may be, Lord Oxford's refusal to dance before the French Ambassador bears quite a different interpretation.   It had nothing to do with hostility towards Alençon, for we shall find him next year ardently supporting the proposed marriage between Elizabeth and the French Prince.   His disobedience of the Queen's command was simply his way of showing her what he thought of her childish behaviour to her Lord Steward over the episode of the supposedly insufficient display of plate on the dinner-table.   It affords another example of the great esteem in which Oxford held the Earl of Sussex.

Early next year Lord Oxford and some other courtiers presented a masque before the Queen.   They acted in it themselves, as the following letter shows :

It is but vain to trouble your Lordship [writes Gilbert Talbot to his father the Earl of Shrewsbury] with such shows as were showed before Her Majesty this Shrovetide at night.   The chiefest was a device presented by the persons of the Earl of Oxford, the Earl of Surrey, the Lords Thomas Howard and Windsor.[1]   The device was prettier

---

[1] Lord Thomas Howard was a half-brother of the Earl of Surrey. He was now eighteen years old, and was the son of the Duke of Norfolk—Oxford's first cousin—by his second wife Margaret, daughter of Lord Audley de Walden. He was created Lord Howard de Walden in 1597, and Earl of Suffolk by King James on his accession.

Frederick, 4th Baron Windsor (1559–85) was the eldest son of Lady Katharine Vere, Oxford's half-sister. He was a great " swordsman " (to use Naunton's expression) and won great distinction in Tournaments. He was a challenger, together with Oxford and Sidney, in the Tournament of 1580 described by Segar in his *Honour Military and Civil*.

than it happened to have been performed ; but the best of it, and I think the best liked, was two rich jewels which were presented to Her Majesty by the two Earls.[1]

No other details about this masque exist. But Gilbert Talbot's letter is important as being the first piece of definite information that Lord Oxford was inclining towards the drama as an outlet for his literary activities. We shall trace the development of this interest in a subsequent chapter.

§ IV. Philip Sidney

In the spring of 1579 an incident occurred that set the whole Court talking. This was the arrival in London of M. de Simier, who had been sent from France with a view to opening negotiations for a marriage between Queen Elizabeth and the Duc d'Anjou, the twenty-five-year-old brother of the King of France. This match was being eagerly sought by his mother, Catherine de Medicis.[2]

At the English Court opinions as to the proposal were sharply divided. The majority, which included Sussex, Burghley, Hunsdon, and Oxford, were in favour of it ; but the Earl of Leicester and his following, among whom was his nephew and prospective heir, Philip Sidney, were strongly opposed to it.

In August, however, the Leicester faction received a severe rebuff. Simier had discovered that Leicester was secretly married to Lettice, the daughter of Sir Francis Knollys, and the widow of Walter Devereux, Earl of Essex, who had died in 1576. He quickly realised that fate had played into his hands, and at once informed the Queen. She emptied the vials of her wrath on Leicester's head, and banished him from the Court. For the time being, there-

---

[1] Lodge, *Illustrations of British History*, p. 22.

[2] Catherine de Medicis, the " Florentine," had been Queen-Mother of France since 1559. She had had four sons : the eldest, François II., who was the first husband of Mary Queen of Scots, had reigned from 1559 to 1560 ; the second, Charles IX., had reigned from 1560 to 1574 ; the third, Henri III., was now on the throne, and it was to him that Lord Oxford had been introduced when in Paris in 1575 ; the fourth, Hercule-François, had recently been created Duc d'Anjou.

fore, Philip Sidney was left as the leader of the opposition
to the French match.

This was not the first time that Oxford and Sidney had
found themselves at cross purposes.   It will be remembered
that Anne Cecil, before her marriage to Oxford, had for
a time been engaged to Sidney. Moreover, another cleavage
had begun to appear over the question of poetry and
literature, matters as we know very dear to the hearts
of both the brilliant young Courtiers.   This important
question will be dealt with in detail elsewhere, and need
not therefore receive more than a passing mention here.

In an atmosphere already rendered electric an incident
soon occurred that set their rivalry ablaze.   This was the
famous Tennis Court quarrel.   As most people know
nothing of Lord Oxford except in connexion with this
episode, a few explanatory words will first be necessary.

Sir Philip Sidney has very properly been classed as one
of our national heroes.   His title to this position is beyond
dispute.   But it has had an unfortunate result from the
point of view of the relating of true history.   For every
historian who has devoted an hour to reading about Lord
Oxford there are hundreds who have devoted years to
studying Sidney's life.   And it is perhaps inevitable that
when they constitute themselves Sidney's biographers they
should start with the preconceived idea, regardless of any
evidence that may exist to the contrary, that anybody
who dared to quarrel with Sidney must *ipso facto* be a
" brute " and a " scoundrel " and entirely to blame.

But if we can forgive Sidney's biographers for painting
Lord Oxford black in order to show up the virtues of their
hero in greater relief, we can less readily forgive them for
suppressing the truth.   I do not assert that this has been
done deliberately ; but in any case it is a serious charge
and one which requires to be fully substantiated.

The sources of our knowledge of the Tennis Court
quarrel are two, and two only.   I will deal with each in
turn :

1. The first occurs in *The Life of the Renowned Sir Philip*

Sidney, written by his intimate friend Fulke Greville, Lord Brooke. It was written, as the author himself tells us, a long time after Sidney's death, and was first published in 1652. Mr. Nowell Smith, who edited it for the Clarendon Press in 1907, makes the following remark in his Introduction :

The treatise is indeed our first authority for some of the well-known stories of Sidney, notably that of the cup of water at Zutphen, and that of the quarrel with the Earl of Oxford [1] in the tennis-court (Greville, however, does not give the Earl's name) ; but it is at once much less and much more than a regular biography of Sidney. There are no dates, no details of personal appearance, place of abode, habits, friends, and acquaintances ; nothing of marriage ; scarcely anything of life at Court ; nothing even of Sidney's literary pursuits, except an interesting criticism of the *Arcadia* solely from the point of view of the political philosopher.[2]

In other words Greville's *Life* is really an essay written from memory, and descriptive of events that had taken place many years before. This should be remembered when we come to consider the second source from which we derive our knowledge of the quarrel.

2. This second source is of far greater importance historically because it is absolutely contemporary with the event. The information that it provides occurs in a letter written to Sidney from Antwerp in October 1579 by his friend Hubert Languet.[3] Languet and Sidney had

---

[1] Mr. Smith is mistaken here. There is a contemporary account of the quarrel, which we shall examine presently, written many years before Greville's *Life*.

[2] pp. v, vi.

[3] Hubert Languet (1518–81) was a French Huguenot writer and diplomat. As the Elector of Saxony's Ambassador at the French Court he had narrowly escaped assassination during the massacre of St. Bartholomew. Sidney was also in Paris at this time (1572), and it was probably from about then that their friendship dated. Languet left Paris shortly afterwards and settled in Antwerp, where he became the valued adviser of the Prince of Orange.

first met when the latter was travelling on the Continent.
They kept up a regular correspondence between November
1573 and October 1580. Altogether ninety-six letters
from Languet to Sidney have been preserved. Unfortunately, only seventeen of Sidney's letters to Languet have
survived, the last being dated March 10th, 1578 ; and
the one in which Sidney described the tennis-court
quarrel to Languet has been lost. But Languet's reply,
and his significant comments, give us all the information
that is necessary.

Their correspondence was conducted in Latin. Languet's
letters, with which we are here concerned, were first
collected and published by the Elzevirs at Leyden in
1646, under the title *Huberti Langueti Epistolæ Politicæ
et Historicæ ad Philippum Sidnæum.* They were printed
in the original Latin and *in extenso.* The first English
translation was made in 1845 by Steuart A. Pears, and
published in a book entitled *The Correspondence of Sir
Philip Sidney and Hubert Languet.* But these translations were not made *in extenso.* Pears distinctly explains
this in his Preface, where he says that he has only made
selections from the volume.[1]

In spite of this warning all Pears's successors appear to
have been satisfied with his excerpts. As a matter of
fact, in the very letter dealing with the quarrel a long
paragraph has been omitted. In this paragraph Languet
administers a rebuke to Sidney. He says quite bluntly,
" you have gone further than you ought to have done,"
and that " carried away by your quick temper you have
sent him [i.e. Lord Oxford] a challenge, and thus you have
deprived yourself of the choice of weapons." But this
plain speaking on the part of Languet has been too much
for Sir Philip's biographers. It was no doubt unbearable
for them to think that their hero could in any way have
been responsible for the quarrel. They have therefore
quietly ignored Languet's trenchant remarks.

Another thing we should remember is that Languet

---

[1] p. vii. All the omissions are marked quite plainly by asterisks.

was a very real and genuine friend to Sidney. This enhances the importance of his censure a thousandfold. Had he been Sidney's enemy, or even a neutral, it might with justice be argued that his rebuke was tinged with bias. But he was quite definitely one of Sidney's closest friends. He says, and there is no reason to doubt him, that he is much distressed about the whole affair. If Sidney had been absolutely blameless, and had come off with the flying colours that his modern biographers would have us believe, it is difficult to see why Languet should have been so disturbed about it. But when we read the letter in full we shall realise that his anxiety arises because he perceives that Sidney's hasty temper has placed him in an awkward predicament.

I have dwelt somewhat at length on these points, not because I wish to disparage the work of Sidney's biographers, but because I wish to make it clear that I am now publishing for the first time *in full* the English version of Languet's comments on the tennis-court quarrel. If the reader should conclude therefrom, as I think he must, that it is impossible to clear Sidney of all blame, I would remind him that the story has not been conjured up out of my imagination, but has been told exactly as Languet told it within a month of the event. But there is yet another reason why this preliminary investigation has been rendered necessary. I have already said that most people only know of Lord Oxford as the ill-mannered blackguard who deliberately provoked a quarrel with the " renowned Sir Philip Sidney." This, more than anything else, has led to the assumption that Oxford's character was " ill-tempered " and " churlish." But what value are we to place on this assumption when we know it to be based on false data ? I think most people will agree that the answer is emphatically none. Let us then, with our minds freed from the vapourings of our modern historians, listen to the story of the tennis-court quarrel as told first by Fulke Greville and then by Hubert Languet.

Greville tells us that Sidney :

being one day at Tennis, a peer of this Realm, born great,
greater by alliance, and superlative in the Prince's favour,[1]
abruptly came into the Tennis Court ; and speaking out
of these three paramount authorities he forgot to entreat
that which he could not legally command. When by the
encounter of a steady object, finding unrespectiveness in
himself (though a great Lord) not respected by this
Princely spirit, he grew to expostulate more roughly.
The returns of which style coming, still from an understanding heart, that knew what was due to itself and what
it ought to others, seemed (through the mists of my
Lord's passions swollen with the wind of his factions then
reigning [2]) to provoke in yielding. Whereby, the less
amazement or confusion of thoughts he stirred up in Sir
Philip, the more shadows this great Lord's own mind was
possessed with, till at last with rage (which is ever ill-
disciplined) he demands them to depart the court.   To this
Sir Philip temperately answers that if his lordship had been
pleased to express desire in milder characters perchance
he might have led out those that he should now find would
not be driven out with any scourge of fury.   This answer
(like a bellows) blowing up the sparks of excess already
kindled, made my Lord scornfully call Sir Philip by the
name of Puppy.   In which progress of heat, as the tempest
grew more and more vehement within, so did their hearts
breathe out their perturbations in a more loud and shrill
accent.   The French Commissioners, unfortunately, had
that day audience in those private galleries whose windows
looked into the Tennis Court.   They instantly drew all
to this tumult, every sort of quarrels sorting well with
their humours, especially this.   Which Sir Philip perceiving, and rising with inward strength, by the prospect
of a mighty faction against him, asked my Lord with a
loud voice that which he heard clearly enough before.
Who (like an echo that still multiplies by reflections)
repeated this epithet of " Puppy " the second time.   Sir
Philip, resolving in one answer to conclude both the atten-

---

[1] The " peer of this Realm " is Lord Oxford ; the " Prince " is Queen
Elizabeth.

[2] The " faction " favouring the French match, of which Oxford was a
leader.

tive hearers and passionate actor, gave my Lord a lie,
impossible (as he averred) to be retorted ; in respect all
the world knows, Puppies are gotten by Dogs, and Children
by Men.   Hereupon those glorious inequalities of fortune
in his Lordship were put to a kind of pause by a precious
inequality of nature in this gentleman.   So that they both
stood silent awhile like a dumb show in a tragedy ; till
Sir Philip, sensible of his own wrong, the foreign and
factious spirits that attended, and yet even in this question
between him and his superior tender to his Country's
honour, with some words of sharp accent led the way
abruptly out of the Tennis Court ; as if so unexpected an
accident were not fit to be decided farther in that place.
Whereof the great Lord, making another sense, continues
his play, without any advantage of reputation, as by the
standard of humours in those times it was conceived.

A day Sir Philip remains in suspense, when hearing
nothing of, he sends a gentleman of worth to awake him
out of his trance ; wherein the French would assuredly
think any pause, if not death, yet a lethargy of true honour
in both.   This stirred a resolution in his Lordship to send
Sir Philip a challenge.   Notwithstanding, these thoughts
in the great Lord wandered so long between glory, anger,
and inequality of state, as the Lords of Her Majesty's
Council took notice of the differences, commanded peace,
and laboured a reconciliation between them.   But needlessly in one respect, and bootlessly in another.   The great
Lord being (as it should seem) either not hasty to adventure
many inequalities against one, or inwardly satisfied with
the progress of his own acts ; Sir Philip on the other side
confident he neither had nor would lose, or let anything
fall out of his right.   Which Her Majesty's Council
quickly perceiving, recommended this work to herself.

The Queen, who saw that by the loss or disgrace of either
could gain nothing, presently undertakes Sir Philip, and
(like an excellent Monarch) lays before him the difference
in degree between Earls and Gentlemen, the respect
inferiors ought to their superiors, and the necessity in
Princes to maintain their own creations, as degrees descend-
ing between the people's licentiousness and the anointed
sovereignty of Crowns ; how the Gentleman's neglect of
the Nobility taught the peasant to insult both.

Whereunto Sir Philip, with such reverence as became

him, replied : first, that place was never intended for
privilege to wrong ; witness herself, for how sovereign
soever she were by Throne, birth, education, and nature,
yet was she content to cast her own affections into the same
moulds her subjects did, and govern all her rights by their
laws.   Again, he besought Her Majesty to consider that
although he were a great Lord by birth, alliance, and
grace, yet he was no Lord over him : and therefore the
difference of degrees between free men could not challenge
any other homage than precedency.   And by her father's
act (to make a Princely wisdom become the more familiar)
he did instance the Government of King Henry the
Eighth, who gave the gentry free and safe appeal to his
feet against the oppression of the Grandees, and found
it wisdom by the stronger corporation in number to keep
down the greater in power, inferring else that if they
should unite the overgrown might be tempted, by still
coveting more, to fall (as the Angels did) by affecting
equality with their Maker.[1]

The other account of the quarrel occurs, as has been
said, in Languet's letter to Sidney written from Antwerp
on October 14th, 1579.   The paragraph omitted by Pears
has been put into italics :

On my arrival here [i.e. Antwerp] I found our friend
Clusius prepared for a journey, which I delayed for a day
or two that I might hear from him all about your affairs.
From your letter, as well as from his mouth, I was
informed of the dispute between you and the Earl of
Oxford, which gave me great pain.   I am aware that by
a habit inveterate in all Christendom, a nobleman is disgraced if he does not resent such an insult : still, I think
you were unfortunate to be drawn into this contention,
although I see that no blame is to be attached to you for
it.   You can derive no true honour from it, even if it gave
you occasion to display to the world your constancy and
courage.   You want another stage for your character,
and I wish you had chosen it in this part of the world.
*On the other hand be careful lest under the influence of swash-
bucklers you should overstep the bounds of your native modesty.*

[1] Sir Fulke Greville, *The Life of the Renowned Sir Philip Sidney*, ed.
Nowell Smith (1907), p. 63.

*In this very quarrel, sound as your position was, you have
gone further than you ought to have done, for when you
had flung back the insult thrown at you, you ought to have
said no more ; as a matter of fact, carried away by your quick
temper, you sent him a challenge, and thus you have deprived
yourself of the choice of weapons if at any time this controversy should have to be decided by a duel ; for it is the
people who want to teach us how we should go mad by rule
who have applied their own laws to duels, which of all things
are the most unjust.   If you had stood fast after you had
given your adversary the lie, it would have been his business
to challenge you.   In our time not a few jurists have written
about duelling.   William of Neuburg, an English writer,
quotes the decrees of a certain Synod by which duels are
altogether condemned, and Christians forbidden to take part
in them.*

Since your adversary has attached himself to Anjou's
party, if your wooer [1] shall return to you with a crowd
of French Noblemen about him you must be on your
guard, for you know the fiery nature of my countrymen.[2]

We can now examine the whole affair.   In the first place,
taking Greville's account, we notice one definite incon-
sistency.   He contradicts himself over the important point
as to who was in occupation of the tennis-court when the
quarrel broke out.   He says in his opening sentence that
Sidney was playing when Oxford came in and " abruptly "
ordered him out.   But a little further on we read that
after Sidney had retired with " some words of sharp
accent " Lord Oxford " continues his play."   It would
be idle to speculate which of these two contradictory statements is correct ; but it is well to remember that any
blame in the matter depends to a considerable extent upon
who was playing at the time.

In another respect, however, Sir Fulke has clearly
made an incorrect statement.   He says that it was Oxford
who sent Sidney the challenge.   But Languet, in that part
of his letter that now appears for the first time, tells us

---

[1] Anjou.

[2] *Huberti Langueti Epistolæ* . . . Ed. Hailes (1776), p. 239 ; cf. Pears,
op. cit., p. 165.

exactly the opposite ; and Languet we know was writing
with Sidney's own account in front of him.   In fact, he
does more than this.   He rebukes Sidney for having gone
too far, and for having shown an over-hasty temper.
But when all is said and done these are comparatively
trivial details.   The whole incident has been magnified
by modern historians into an importance far greater than
it really deserves.   It would be absurd to suppose that
two members of Parliament who had spent the afternoon
hurling epithets at one another across the floor of the
House must inevitably become lifelong enemies.   After
all, Oxford and Sidney were ordinary quick-tempered
human beings like ourselves, and there is no reason to
suppose that they thought or acted differently from the
rest of humanity.   Nor is proof of this lacking.   In the
Tournament held on January 22nd, 1581, we find them
jousting side by side as " defendants " against the " challengers " Lord Arundel and Sir William Drury.   And yet
Sidney's modern biographers would lead us to imagine
that they were irreconcilable enemies !   Two high-spirited
young men are always as generous to forgive as they
are quick to quarrel ; and this seems, to the present writer
at least, a much more sensible way of viewing the so-called
tennis-court quarrel than the time-honoured one of
rigidly isolating it from its historical context, and then
exaggerating it into an event with lasting consequences.

No one would surely deny that rivalry and healthy com-
petition are the very essence of human activity and
progress.   The chief thing any Government really dreads
is being confronted by a weak and flabby Opposition.
What would Disraeli have achieved had it not been for
Gladstone ?   Was it not Lord Byron's " quarrel " with
Bob Southey that stimulated him into writing *Don Juan* ?
Olivia's Clown in *Twelfth Night* sums the whole matter
up for us in the following piece of wise foolery administered
to Duke Orsino who was arguing on the other side :
" Marry, sir, my friends praise me and make an ass of
me ; now my foes tell me plainly I am an ass : so that

by my foes, sir, I profit in the knowledge of myself, and by my friends I am abused." A hundred volumes could be filled with such examples, and still only the fringe of the subject be touched.

Oxford and Sidney mutually provided each other with the necessary stimulus without which no human achieve-ment can be attained. Languet, who was no flaccid weakling, recognised this and told Sidney so quite plainly :

If the arrogance and insolence of Oxford has roused you from your trance, he has done you less wrong than they who have hitherto been more indulgent to you.[1]

These words are a far finer tonic than the sentimental sympathy with which Sidney has been overwhelmed by his modern biographers.

Oxford and Sidney, as Courthope tells us, were the leaders of the two great literary factions at Court. Oxford headed the newly arisen Euphuist movement, which aimed at refining and enriching the English language. It was the magic of words and the imagery of sentences that appealed to him and to his lieutenants, John Lyly and Antony Munday. Sidney was the leader of the Romanticists. Their object was to reclothe the old stories of knighthood and chivalry so as to render them more vivid and applicable to their own times. It was, in particular, the novel with a love plot that Sidney and his associates, chief of whom was Spenser, developed.[2] In a word, Oxford was interested primarily in the language, while Sidney was occupied more with the story.

There is nothing essentially antagonistic in these two points of view. Neither can live without the other. Oxford

---

[1] Pears, op. cit., p. 168. Languet to Sidney, Nov. 14th, 1579. Languet, when he wrote this, was evidently thinking of a sentence in one of Sidney's recent letters : " The use of the pen has plainly gone from me, and my mind, if ever it was active about anything, is now, by reason of indolent sloth, beginning imperceptibly to lose its strength, and to lose it without any reluctance." (Cf. Courthope, *A History of English Poetry*, vol. ii, p. 208.)

[2] Cf. Courthope, op. cit., vol. ii, pp. 224, 234, etc.

and Lyly on the one hand, Sidney and Spenser on the other, were pioneers. English literature, as we who are living in the twentieth century understand it, was still unwritten, and good-humoured rivalry between the two leaders of literary thought was the best stimulus to progress. The following episode will illustrate my meaning :

[Lord Oxford] was not only witty in himself, but the cause of wit in others. Several of the courtiers set themselves to solve the problem proposed in his well-known epigram—

> Were I a King, I might command content,
> Were I obscure, unknown should be my cares,
> And were I dead, no thoughts should me torment,
> Nor words, nor wrongs, nor love, nor hate, nor fears.
> A doubtful choice of these three which to crave,
> A kingdom, or a cottage, or a grave.

Sir Philip Sidney declared that there could be no doubt as to the answer :

> Wert thou a King, yet not command content,
> Sith empire none thy mind could yet suffice.
> Wert thou obscure, still cares would thee torment,
> But wert thou dead all care and sorrow dies.
> An easy choice of these three which to crave,
> No kingdom, nor a cottage, but a grave.[1]

Here is another example. The poet Spenser, in a letter written to Gabriel Harvey and dated from Leicester House in October 1579—just a month after the quarrel—says that Sidney and Dyer—

have proclaimed in their Areopagos [2] a general surceasing and silence of bald rhymers, and also of the very best too ; instead whereof they have, by authority of their whole Senate, prescribed certain laws and rules of quantities of English syllables for English verse ; having had thereof already great practice, and drawn me to their faction.[3]

---

[1] Courthope, op. cit., vol. ii, p. 313.

[2] The Areopagos was a literary club founded by Sidney and the Romanticists.

[3] *The Works of Spenser*, ed. R. Morris (1890), p. 706.

Very little is known of the Areopagos, except that it fired
Harvey to write a fantastic hexameter poem in which
he poked fun at Lord Oxford.   It appears then to have
died the natural death it deserved.   But it is obvious that
it came into being as a counterblast to the Euphuists and
their leader.[1] These, and no doubt scores of similar
incidents, formed the predisposing causes of which the
tennis-court quarrel was the outward and visible sign.
In the following Interlude an endeavour will be made to
trace in outline the historical development of the Tudor
court poets, particularly in relation to Lord Oxford and
his Euphuists.

Before we pass on a word may be added as to the sequel
of the quarrel.   When the Queen had rightly forbidden the
duel the Court became too small a place to hold both
proud young courtiers.   And it was Sidney who had to
give way.   He retired (the exact date is not known)
to his sister's house at Wilton.[2]   Here he found the leisure
to write, for the entertainment of his hostess, *The Countess
of Pembroke's Arcadia*.   Thus we see that Languet's hope
that the quarrel might bring Sidney out of his " trance "
was fulfilled, for English literature has been permanently
enriched as a direct result of it.

It was probably from Wilton early in 1580 that Sidney
sent his famous letter to the Queen urging her not to marry
Anjou.[3]   It seems to have been at Leicester's instigation
that he took this step.[4]   Although his advice was un-
popular with the Queen at the time, Sidney's views prevailed in the end.   He returned to court favour about

[1] Fox Bourne, in his *Life of Sidney* (p. 201), rightly recognises that the
Areopagos must not be taken too seriously ; " There was evidently more
frolic than seriousness in it, and there was a serious purpose in the frolic."

[2] Mary Sidney, who had married Henry Herbert, 2nd Earl of Pembroke,
in 1577.   She is famous as a poetess and a patron of men of letters.

[3] This letter, which is undated, has been printed in the *Sidney Papers*,
vol. i.

[4] Cf. Languet to Sidney, October 1580: " Since, however, you were
ordered to write as you did by those whom you were bound to obey, no
fair-judging man can blame you for putting forward freely what you
thought good for your country " (Pears, op. cit., p. 187).

October 1580, for on the 22nd of that month Languet writes :

Your letter was on many accounts most delightful to me, but especially because I learn from it that you have come forth from that hiding-place of yours into the light of the Court.[1]

It is not unlikely that his return coincided with a secret change in the Queen's disposition towards Anjou. At any rate he had the supreme satisfaction in February 1582 of helping to convey the rejected royal suitor back to his native land across the Channel.

[1] *Huberti Langueti Epistolæ* . . . (cit.), p. 284. Pears in his translation (p. 187) says, "into open *day* "; but the Latin version reads, " in lucem *aulæ*."

INTERLUDE: LORD OXFORD'S EUPHUISTS
1579–1588

This Pamphlet,[1] Right Honourable, containing the estate of England, I know none more fit to defend it than one of the Nobility of England, nor any of the Nobility more ancient or more honourable than your Lordship; besides that describing the condition of the English Court, and the Majesty of our dread Sovereign, I could not find one more noble in Court than your Honour, who is or should be under Her Majesty chiefest in Court, by birth born to the greatest office, and therefore, methought, by right to be placed in great authority; for whoso compareth the honour of your Lordship's noble house with the fidelity of your ancestors may well say, which no other can truly gainsay, *Vero nihil verius.* . . . Now *Euphues* is shadowed, only I appeal to your Honour, not meaning thereby to be careless what others think, but knowing that if your Lordship allow it there is none but will like it, and if there be any so nice whom nothing can please, if he will not commend it let him amend it.

John Lyly to the Earl of Oxford, 1580.

Since the world hath understood—I know not how—that your Honour had willingly vouchsafed the acceptance of this work, and at convenient leisures favourably perused it, being as yet but in written hand, many have oftentimes and earnestly called upon me to put it to the press, that for their money they might but see what your Lordship, with some liking, had already perused.

Thomas Watson to the Earl of Oxford, 1582.

Your Honour being a worthy favourer and fosterer of learning hath forced many through your excellent virtue to offer the first-fruits of their study at the shrine of your Lordship's courtesy.

Robert Greene to the Earl of Oxford, 1584.

Your Lordship, whose infancy from the beginning was ever sacred to the Muses.

Angel Day to the Earl of Oxford, 1586.

A POINT has now been reached in the story of Lord Oxford's life when we must pause for a while and examine the literary environment in which he was living. We have seen in the foregoing pages that before he attained his thirtieth birthday his contemporaries accounted him a

[1] *Euphues and his England.*

178

renowned poet, a pioneer in literature, and a keen patron
of men of letters.   Let us now frame this picture of the
Earl so that we may the better judge how and where he
stood in relation to his predecessors and contemporaries,
and to the literary thought that was at this time finding
expression.

The wave of the Renaissance that flowed westward over
Europe after the capture of Constantinople by the Turks
in 1453 culminated in England in the latter years of King
Henry VIII.   It found an outlet in the lyrics and sonnets
written by a group of courtier poets.   The chief of these
were Sir Thomas Wyat (born about 1503) ; Thomas,
second Lord Vaux (born 1510) ; Henry Howard, Earl of
Surrey (born 1517) ; and Edmund, first Lord Sheffield (born
1521).[1]   Two of them, Surrey and Sheffield, married sisters
of the sixteenth Earl of Oxford ; and both died violent
deaths.   Lord Surrey, when he was thirty, fell under the
headsman's axe as a victim of King Henry's homicidal
mania : Lord Sheffield, when he was twenty-eight, was
killed while helping to suppress Ket's rebellion.   During
the troublous times of the minority reign of King Edward
VI and the Catholic reaction of Queen Mary there was little
scope or opportunity for the pursuit of poetry ; and the last
survivor of this group, Lord Vaux, died in 1556.

The following year a book was published which proved
to be the progenitor of Elizabethan poetry.   It was an
anthology, and bore the title—*Songs and Sonnets of the
Right Honourable the late Earl of Surrey and other*.   How
this book came to be published is not altogether clear.
It is popularly supposed that the poems were " collected "
by the printer, Richard Tottel.   But how he obtained the
manuscripts, and who gave him permission to print them,
is left to our imagination.   It seems most likely that
behind Tottel stood some unknown figure who moved

---

[1] None of Lord Sheffield's poems survive, but we know that he was
a poet because Fuller says of him : " Great his skill in music, who wrote
a book of sonnets according to the Italian fashion." (Cf. *Dict. Nat.
Biog.*)

in court circles and was acquainted with the aristocratic poets and their descendants. Who this may have been we do not know, but, judging from the title, we may hazard the guess that he had been a personal friend of Lord Surrey whose memory he wished to perpetuate.

With the accession of Queen Elizabeth English men of letters found their greatest ally and supporter. Not only did she bring to the realm peace and tranquillity, but she proved throughout her long reign to be an active promoter of all literary interests. " The following description (quoted from Roger Ascham) of her accomplishments," writes Courthope, " whatever deduction may be made from it in consideration of partiality or flattery, must be accepted as the testimony of the highest possible authority :

Among the learned daughters of Sir Thomas More, the Princess Elizabeth shines like a star of distinguished lustre ; deriving greater glory from her virtuous disposition and literary accomplishments than from the dignity of her exalted birth. I was her preceptor in Latin and Greek for two years. She was but little more than sixteen when she could speak French and Italian with as much fluency and propriety as her native English. She speaks Latin readily, justly, and even critically. She has often conversed with me in Greek, and with tolerable facility. When she transcribes Greek or Latin nothing can be more beautiful than her handwriting.[1] She is excellently skilled in music, though not very fond of it. She has read with me all Cicero, and a great part of Livy. It is chiefly from these two authors alone that she has acquired her knowledge of the Latin language. She begins the day with reading a portion of the Greek Testament, and then studies some select orations of Isocrates and the tragedies of Sophocles. . . . In every composition she is very quick in pointing out a far-fetched word or an affected phrase. She cannot endure those absurd imitators of Erasmus who mince the whole Latin language into proverbial maxims. She is much pleased with a Latin oration naturally arising from

---

[1] This is no exaggeration. Frederick Chamberlin, in his *Private Character of Queen Elizabeth*, gives four facsimiles of the Queen's exquisite calligraphy.

its subject, and written both chastely and perspicuously. She is most fond of translations not too free, and with that agreeable clash of sentiment which results from a judicious comparison of opposite or contradictory passages. By a diligent attention to these things her taste is become so refined, and her judgment so penetrating, that there is nothing in Greek, Latin, and English composition, either extravagant or exact, careless or correct, which she does not in the course of reading accurately discern ; immediately rejecting the one with disgust, and receiving the other with the highest degree of pleasure."[1]

With such a Sovereign at their head it is not surprising to find the courtiers conforming to the fashion she set. When, for example, she paid her first visit to Cambridge University in 1564, we cannot help being struck by the list of courtiers who were given degrees. Seven of them were over thirty years of age, and two over fifty.[2] It is difficult to believe that all these comparatively elderly statesmen were suddenly seized with the idea that their lives were incomplete until they could affix the letters M.A. to their names. Such a thought does not seem to have occurred to them during the two previous reigns. But now that culture and learning were a *sine qua non* at Court, they were quick to follow the lead of their Royal Mistress.

Stimulated and encouraged by the Queen, Lord Surrey's work, so cruelly terminated on Tower Hill in 1547, began to take fresh root. It is impossible here to follow in detail the part played in this revival by men like Lord Buckhurst, Thomas Churchyard, George Ferrers, and George Gascoigne. Churchyard, it may be mentioned, provides a direct link between the " Surrey tradition " and Lord Oxford's Euphuists of the fifteen seventies. He had been a page, while still a boy, in Surrey's household ; and after spending his early manhood at the wars, he settled down to pursue his writing in Lord Oxford's household about 1569.

The first anthology published in Elizabeth's reign, and the

---

[1] Courthope" *A History of English Poetry*, vol. ii, p. 129.
[2] Cf. Nichols, *Progresses*, vol. i.

direct successor to the *Songs and Sonnets*, was *A Hundreth Sundrie Flowres*. Lord Oxford's probable connexion with its publication, and the bold innovation he introduced by publishing not only his own but other courtiers' poems while they were still alive, has been fully investigated in a previous Interlude.[1]

The title of the book [writes Courthope] is very interesting as marking the approach of Euphuism.
A Hundreth Sundrie Flowres bound up in one small Poesy, gathered partly by translation in the fine outlandish gardens of Euripides, Ovid, Petrarch, Ariosto, and others ; and partly by invention out of our own fruitful orchards in England. Yielding sundry sweet savours of Tragical, Comical, and Moral Discourses, both pleasant and profitable to the well-smelling noses of learned readers.[2]

Although English literature was making rapid strides it was still far behind that of continental countries, particularly Italy. It was towards the native land of Petrarch and Ariosto that enthusiastic men of letters like Oxford and Sidney continually turned. Sidney was the first to have his wish to see the home of poetry gratified. From 1572 to 1575 he was travelling in France, Italy, Germany, and Poland. And during this time Lord Oxford, as we have seen, was eating his heart out in London. His turn came, however, in 1575 ; and he then spent sixteen months in France, Italy, and Germany. The story of the rivalry between the two returned travellers, culminating in 1579, has already been touched on.

Let us pause here for a moment and consider *The Shepherd's Calendar*, which was written by Spenser—who was then living in Leicester House with Sidney—under the pseudonym " Immerito " in 1579. One of the eclogues in this remarkable piece of work, entitled *August*, gives us a glimpse of Sidney, and perhaps Oxford, before their quarrel on the tennis-court. In it we read of the meeting between two poetical " shepherds "—Willye and Perigot. They agree to pass the time of day in a rhyming match ;

---

[1] See p. 130, *ante*.   [2] Courthope, op. cit., vol. ii, p. 169.

and having laid down their wagers, they call on a third
" shepherd "—Cuddie—to act as judge.   Says Cuddie:

> Gynne when ye lyst, ye jolly shepheards twayne :
> Sike a judge as Cuddie were for a king.

The two competitors accordingly start off, Perigot leading :

> PER. : It fell upon a holy eve,
> WIL. :   Hey, ho, hollidaye !
> PER. : When holy fathers wont to shrieve ;
> WIL. :   Now gynneth this roundelay.
> PER. : Sitting upon a hill so hye,
> WIL. :   Hey, ho, the high hyll !
> PER. : The while my flocke did feede thereby ;
> WIL. :   The while the shepheard selfe did spill.
> PER. : I saw the bouncing Bellibone,
> WIL. :   Hey, ho, Bonibell !
> PER. : Tripping over the dale alone,
> WIL. :   She can trippe it very well.
> PER. : Well decked in a frocke of gray,
> WIL. :   Hey, ho, gray is greete !
> PER. : And in a kirtle of greene saye,
> WIL. :   The greene is for maydens meete.
> PER. : A chapelet on her head she wore,
> WIL. :   Hey, ho, chapelet !
> PER. : Of sweete Violets therein was store,
> WIL. :   She sweeter than the Violet.

And so on.

Now, " Willy " was the name given to Sidney.[1]   Who
then is most likely to be Perigot who matches his skill
against Sidney in a rhyming match ?   The most plausible
suggestion I can offer is that Perigot is Lord Oxford, whose
epigram " Were I a King " was answered, as we have seen,
by Sidney.   Indeed, may not Cuddie's words to the two
competitors :

> Gynne when ye lyst, ye jolly shepheards twayne :
> Sike a judge as Cuddie *were for a king,*

contain a direct reference to this incident ?

But whether or no Perigot, or perhaps Cuddie, is to be
identified as Lord Oxford, is of little moment here.   It
is sufficient that the incident of the rhyming match,
described by Spenser, must have been characteristic of the

---

[1] He was called Willy—possibly a corruption of Philip or Phil—in an
eclogue lamenting his death ; see Appendix D.

friendly rivalry that existed between the Euphuists and the Romanticists.

Early in 1579 John Lyly published *Euphues, the Anatomy of Wit*, which he dedicated to Lord de la Warr.[1] It is generally taken to have been the first English novel, but this is not strictly correct, because *The Adventures of Master F. I.* preceded it by six years.[2]

The story of *Euphues* is its least important part. It was the wealth of metaphor and rhetoric, the interminable juggling with words and sentences, that appealed so much to the Elizabethans and made Lyly's novel in a single day the most widely read book in the country.

Euphuism [as Courthope says] was the form assumed in England by a linguistic movement which, at some particular stage of development, affected every literature in modern Europe. The process in all countries was the same, namely, to refine the vocabulary and syntax of the language by adapting the practice of early writers to the usage of modern conversation. . . . Edward de Vere, seventeenth Earl of Oxford, is unfortunate in being chiefly known to posterity as the antagonist of Sidney in the quarrel already alluded to ; beyond this little is recorded of him. We see, however, that he was a great patron of literature, and headed the literary party at Court which promoted the Euphuistic movement.[3]

Anthony Munday, and later Thomas Lodge, rallied under Lord Oxford's banner that had been unfurled by the publication of *Euphues*. In this same year (1579) Munday dedicated *The Mirror of Mutability* to Lord Oxford. The

[1] William West, 1st or 11th Baron de la Warr, was born before 1538 and died in 1596. He was brought up by his uncle Thomas, 10th Lord de la Warr, with a view to his succeeding him in the Barony. He rewarded his uncle's generosity, however, by attempting to poison him in 1551 ; for which act Parliament very properly disabled him from the succession. In 1556 he was imprisoned in the Tower and sentenced to death for complicity in the same anti-Catholic plot that Lord Oxford's father had been suspected of helping to promote. Six months later he was pardoned, and in 1569 he was restored to the Barony. Very little is known about him, and he does not receive a notice in the *Dictionary of National Biography*.

[2] See p. 133, *ante*.

[3] Courthope, op. cit., vol. ii, pp. 179, 312.

opening sentences of the dedication show us how the cult of Euphuism was beginning to spread :

To the Right Honourable and his singular good Lord and Patron Edward de Vere, Earl of Oxenford, Lord of Escales and Badlesmere, and Lord Great Chamberlain of England, Antony Munday wisheth in this world a triumphant tranquillity, with continual increase of honourable dignity, and after this life a crown of everlasting felicity in the eternal hierarchy.

After that I had delivered (Right Honourable) unto your courteous and gentle perusing my book entitled *Galien of France*,[1] wherein, having not so fully comprised such pithiness of style as one of a more riper invention could cunningly have carved, I rest, Right Honourable, on your clemency, to amend my errors committed so unskilfully. But at that time being very desirous to attain to some understanding in the languages, considering in time to come I might reap thereby some commodity, since as yet my web of youthful time was not fully woven, and my wild oats required to be furrowed in a foreign ground, to satisfy the trifling toys that daily more and more frequented my busied brain yielded myself to God and good fortune, taking on the habit of a traveller.

The rest of the dedication is occupied with a long account of Munday's travels in France and Italy, which need not concern us here. But his reference to Lord Oxford's " courteous and gentle perusing " of his (now lost) book *Galien of France* is interesting. Munday was finding, in just the same way that Bedingfield had done in 1572, that Lord Oxford was no ordinary patron. He was evidently willing to give both his time and attention to manuscripts submitted to him, and could be relied on to make suggestions and offer advice. But in some ways the most interesting part of *The Mirror of Mutability* lies in the last four lines of a Latin poem [2] which Munday addresses at the end of his

---

[1] This book no longer exists.
[2] Mi formose vale, valeat tua grata voluntas,
   Deprecor optata tutus potiaris arena.
   Te, cunctosque tuos CHRISTO committo tuendos,
   Donec præstentes sermone fruamur amico.

book " Ad preclarum et nobilissimum virum E. O." [1]   The translation of these lines is as follows :

My noble master, farewell.   May your desires which are dear to us all prevail.   Earnestly do I pray for your welfare and success in the struggle.   To the guardianship of Christ I commit you and yours, till the day when as conquerors we may peacefully resume our delightful literary discussions.

The unmistakeable reference to the rivalry between the Euphuists and the Romanticists shows how Munday and his fellows were all looking to their leader in this literary warfare.

The following year (1580) Lyly brought out the second part of *Euphues*.   It was called *Euphues and his England*, and was dedicated to " the Right Honourable my very good Lord and Master Edward de Vere, Earl of Oxenford " :

This Pamphlet (Right Honourable) containing the estate of England, I know none more fit to defend it than one of the Nobility of England, nor any of the Nobility more ancient or more honourable than your Lordship ; besides that describing the condition of the English Court and the Majesty of our dread Sovereign, I could not find one more noble in Court than your Honour, who is or should be under Her Majesty chiefest in Court, by birth born to the greatest office, and therefore, methought, by right to be placed in great authority ; for whoso compareth the honour of your Lordship's noble house with the fidelity of your ancestors may well say, which no other can truly gainsay, *Vero nihil verius*.

He goes on to make a curious reference as to the circumstances of the publication of his two volumes :

I have brought into the world two children ; of the first I was delivered before my friends thought me conceived ; of the second I went a whole year big, and yet when everyone thought me ready to lie down I did then quicken. . . . My first burthen coming before his time must needs be a blind whelp, the second brought forth after his time must

---

[1] " E. O." (i.e. Edward Oxford) was the signature Oxford used in signing his poems which appeared in *The Paradise of Dainty Devices* (1576).

needs be a monster; the one I sent to a Nobleman to nurse, who with great love brought him up for a year, so that wheresoever he wander he hath his Nurse's name in his forehead, where sucking his first milk he cannot forget his master.   The other (Right Honourable) being but yet in his swathe cloutes I commit most humbly to your Lordship's protection, that in his infancy he may be kept by your good care from falls, and in his age by your gracious continuance defended from contempt.

There has been much conjecture as to the identity of the "nobleman" who "nursed" *Euphues, the Anatomy of Wit*. It has been thought that he may have been Lord de la Warr, to whom it was dedicated.   But it is curious that in the dedication Lyly makes no mention of his having interested himself in the manuscript.   May not this "nobleman" have been Lord Oxford, who, as the leader of the Euphuists, would surely be the most natural "nurse" for his private secretary, John Lyly, to choose ?   The connexion between the two men did not necessarily begin with *Euphues and his England*, and Munday had just spoken of his "courteous and gentle perusing" of *Galien of France* in this very year.   There is, of course, no proof of this, but the suggestion may be worth considering.

In the same year (1580) Anthony Munday produced yet another book.   From the dedication we see that he has now become the "servant" of Lord Oxford, which means presumably that, like Lyly, he was attached to the Earl's household, whence he was helping in the Euphuist campaign to enrich the English language.   The book was entitled :

Zelauto, the Fountain of Fame, . . . given for a friendly entertainment to Euphues, at his late arrival into England. By A. M. Servant to the Right Honourable the Earl of Oxenford . . . 1580.

A few extracts from the dedication may here be given :

. . . So my simple self (Right Honourable) having sufficiently seen the rare virtues of your noble mind, the heroical qualities of your prudent person, thought, though ability were inferior to gratify with some gift, yet good will was ample to bestow with the best. . . . And lo, Right

Honourable, among such expert heads, such pregnant inventions, and such commendable writers, as prefer to your seemly self works worthy of eternal memory ; a simple soul (more emboldened on your clemency than any action whatsoever he is able to make manifest) presumeth to present you with such unpolished practices as his simple skill is able to comprehend. Yet thus much I am to assure your Honour, that among all them which owe you dutiful service, and among all the brave books which have been bestowed, these my little labours contain so much faithful zeal to your welfare as others whatsoever, I speak without any exception. But lest that your Honour should deem I forge my tale on flattery, and that I utter with my mouth my heart thinketh not, I wish for the trial of my trustiness what reasonable affairs your Honour can best devise, so shall your mind be delivered from doubt, and myself rid of any such reproach. But as the puissantest Prince is not void of enemies, the gallantest champion free from foes, and the most honest liver without some backbiters, even so the bravest books hath many malicious judgments, and the wisest writers not without rash reports. If then (Right Honourable) the most famous are found fault withal, the cunningest controlled, and the promptest wits reproached by spiteful speeches, how dare so rude a writer as I seem to set forth so mean a matter, so weak a work, and so skill-less a style ?

We must now leave the Euphuists at their labours in Vere House and enter Leicester House, the domicile of the Romanticists, so as to see how Sidney and Spenser were taking this bombardment of Euphuistic literature.

In October 1579, as we have seen, they had started, under Sidney's leadership, a literary club called the Areopagos. In a letter dated October 5th to his old College friend and tutor, Gabriel Harvey, Spenser observes that they have decided to discontinue the use of rhyme, and have laid down certain rules for the construction of English hexameters. Harvey apparently replied with some hexameters of his own composition, for in April 1580 Spenser wrote to him again :

Good Master Harvey, I doubt not but you have some

great important matter in hand, which all this while restraineth your pen and wonted readiness, in provoking me unto that wherein yourself now fault.   If there be any such thing in hatching I pray you heartily let us know, before all the world see it. . . .   I think the earthquake was also there with you (which I would gladly learn) as it was here with us [1]; overthrowing divers old buildings and pieces of churches. . . .   I like your late English hexameters so exceedingly well that I also enure my pen sometime in that kind, which I find indeed, as I have heard you often defend in word, neither so hard nor so harsh, that it will easily and fairly yield itself to our Mother Tongue.[2]

To this Harvey made answer in a " short but sharp and learned judgment of earthquakes," at the end of which he added some more of his hexameter poems.   One of these, called *Speculum Tuscanismi,* was an obvious caricature of Lord Oxford :

Since Galatea came in, and Tuscanism gan usurp,
Vanity above all : villainy next her, stateliness Empress.
No man but minion, stout, lout, plain, swain, quoth a Lording :
No words but valorous, no works but womanish only.
For life Magnificoes, not a beck but glorious in show,
In deed most frivolous, not a look but Tuscanish always.
His cringing side neck, eyes glancing, fisnamie smirking,
With forefinger kiss, and brave embrace to the footward.
Large bellied Kodpeasd doublet, unkodpeasd half hose,
Straight to the dock like a shirt, and close to the britch like a diveling.
A little Apish flat couched fast to the pate like an oyster,
French Camarick ruffs, deep with a whiteness starched to the purpose.
Every one A per se A, his terms and braveries in print,
Delicate in speech, quaint in array : conceited in all points,
In Courtly guiles a passing singular odd man,
For Gallants a brave Mirror, a Primrose of Honour,
A Diamond for nonce, a fellow peerless in England.
Not the like discourser for Tongue, and head to be found out,
Not the like resolute man for great and serious affairs,
Not the like Lynx to spy out secrets and privities of States,

---

[1] Stow, in his *Annals* under date 1580, relates that : " The 6th of April, being Wednesday in Easter week, about six of the clock towards evening, a sudden earthquake happening in London and almost generally throughout England, caused such amazedness of the people as was wonderful for that time, and caused them to make their earnest prayers unto Almighty God " (ed. 1631, p. 689).

[2] *The Works of Spenser,* ed. R. Morris, p. 611.

Eyed like to Argus, eared like to Midas, nos'd like to Naso,
Wing'd like to Mercury, fittst of a thousand for to be employ'd ;
This, nay more than this, doth practise of Italy in one year.
None do I name, but some do I know, that a piece of a twel ve month
Hath so perfited outly and inly both body, both soul,
That none for sense and senses half matchable with them.
A vulture's smelling, Ape's tasting, sight of an Eagle,
A Spider's touching, Hart's hearing, might of a Lion.
Compounds of wisdom, wit, prowess, bounty, behaviour,
All gallant virtues, all qualities of body and soul :
O thrice ten hundred thousand times blessed and happy,
Blessed and happy travail, Travailer most blessed and happy. . . .

Tell me in good sooth, doth it not too evidently appear that this English
Poet wanted but a good pattern before his eyes, as it might be some delicate
and choice elegant Poesy of good Master Sidney's or Master Dyer's (our
very Castor and Pollux for such and many greater matters) when this trim
gear was in the hatching ? [1]

It would be difficult in the whole of English literature to
find a parallel to these execrable hexameters by Gabriel
Harvey. And yet certain writers have imagined that
they were written *au grand sérieux* ! This certainly was not
Harvey's own view, for he indignantly denied that his
verses had any malicious intent towards the Earl, " whose
noble Lordship I protest I never meant to dishonour with
the least prejudicial word of my tongue or pen, but ever
kept a mindful reckoning of many bounden duties toward
the same " ; adding that " the noble Earl, not disposed to
trouble his Jovial mind with such Saturnine paltry, still
continued like his magnificent self." [2]

The truth probably is that Harvey had no idea Spenser
meant to print his letters,[3] and he must have been much
relieved to find that Lord Oxford took his foolish lampoon
in such good part. On the other hand Thomas Nashe, who
in after years was engaged in a violent paper quarrel with
Harvey, tells us a very different story. Harvey, he says—
came very short but yet sharp upon my Lord of Oxford

[1] *The Works of Gabriel Harvey*, *D.C.L.*, ed. Dr. A. B. Grosart (1884),
vol. i, pp. 83–6.

[2] Grosart, op. cit., vol. i, p. 184.

[3] Altogether five letters passed between Spenser and Harvey. They
were published in the form of two pamphlets : first, *Three proper and witty,
familiar letters* . . . dated June 19th, 1580 ; and second, *Two other very
commendable letters* . . . (no month) 1580.

in a rattling bunch of English hexameters. . . . I had forgot
to observe unto you, out of his first *Four Familiar Epistles*,
his ambitious stratagem to aspire : that whereas two great
Peers being at jar,[1] and their quarrel continued to blood-
shed, he would needs, uncalled and when it lay not in his
way, step in on the one side, which indeed was the safer
side (as the fool is crafty enough to sleep in a whole skin)
and hew and slash with his hexameters ; but hewed and
slashed he had been as small as chippings, if he had not
played Duck Fryer and hid himself eight weeks in that
nobleman's house for whom with his pen he thus bladed.[2]

Even if this is an exaggeration we may perhaps permit
ourselves a smile at the picture of the worthy Dr. Gabriel
Harvey, D.C.L., taking refuge in Leicester House to escape
from Lord Oxford's wrath. But Tom Nashe, having
discovered an excellent stick to beat the Doctor with,
continued to use it unmercifully. In another of his
satirical pamphlets he calls to mind the time when Harvey
" cast up certain crude humours of English hexameter
verses that lay upon his stomach ; a Nobleman stood in his
way as he was vomiting, and from top to toe he was all
to bewrayed him with Tuscanism." He goes on to say
that Lyly, in *Pap with a Hatchet*, had spoken up for
Harvey, although Harvey had accused Lyly of trying to
inflame Lord Oxford against him :

He [Lyly] that threatened to conjure up Martin's [Martin
Marprelate] wit, hath written something too in your [Har-
vey] praise, in Pap-hatchet, for all you accuse him to have
courtly [greatly ?] incensed the Earl of Oxford against you.
Mark him well ; he is but a little fellow, but he hath one
of the best wits in England. Should he take thee in hand
again (as he flieth from such inferior concertation) I
prophesy there would more gentle readers die of a merry
mortality engendered by the eternal jests he would maul
thee with, than there have done of this last infection. I
myself, that enjoy but a mite of wit in comparison of his
talent, in pure affection to my native country, make my
style carry a press [of] sail, am fain to cut off half the stream

[1] A reference to the tennis-court quarrel.
[2] *Works of Thomas Nashe*, ed. McKerrow, vol. iii, p. 78.

of thy sport breeding confusion, for fear it should cause a general hicket [hiccup] throughout England.[1]

This paragraph about the " little fellow " who had one of " the best wits in England " has always been assumed to refer to John Lyly. Lyly's biographers and critics, however, are always careful to omit the first sentence in which the Earl of Oxford's name occurs. But if the paragraph is read in its entirety it seems perfectly clear that Nashe is really referring to Lord Oxford. Lyly had never " taken Harvey in hand " ; but we have it on Nashe's own showing that Oxford had done so with such effect that Gabriel had been obliged to spend eight weeks in concealment in Leicester House. Moreover, Harvey, who was a D.C.L. and a fellow of Pembroke College, could not possibly be described as being of " inferior concertation " to Lord Oxford's private secretary. On the other hand, it may perhaps be argued that Nashe would not dare to refer to a nobleman as " a little fellow." But we should remember that Harvey, in the very lampoon Nashe is discussing, calls Lord Oxford " a fellow peerless in England " ; and it seems to me highly likely that Nashe had this actual phrase in mind when he spoke of the " little fellow " who " hath one of the best wits in England." [2]

In February 1581 another lampoon was directed against Lord Oxford.[3] This time the author was Barnabe Riche,[4] and the book *Farewell to Military Profession*. Riche, having returned from the wars in the Low Countries, had adopted Sir Christopher Hatton as his patron and

My very good Lord and upholder, who having builded a house in Northamptonshire called by the name of Holdenby, which house for the bravery of the buildings, for the stateliness of the chambers, for the rich furniture of the

---

[1] McKerrow, op. cit., vol. i, p. 300.

[2] See Appendix K.

[3] Although the remainder of this Interlude is anticipating the story of Lord Oxford's life, I have thought it best for the sake of continuity to complete this survey of his literary environment.

[4] Barnabe Riche (1540 ?–1620 ?) was, like Gascoigne and Churchyard, a soldier first and a writer second. He had fought in France and the Low Countries, and had finished his military career as a Captain.

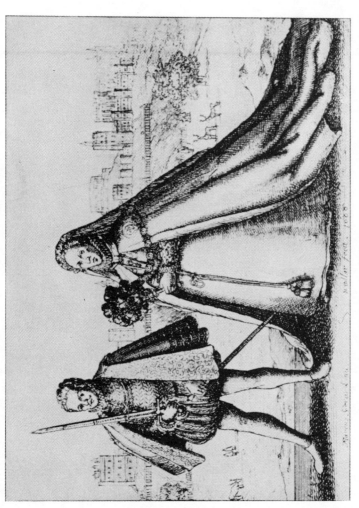

*THE EARL OF OXFORD BEARING THE SWORD OF STATE BEFORE QUEEN ELIZABETH
AT WINDSOR CASTLE ON JUNE 18th, 1572.*

lodgings, . . . is thought by those that have judgment to
be incomparable, and to have no fellow in England that
is out of Her Majesty's hands.[1]

Hatton, as we know, was no friend of Lord Oxford,
and although he does not appear to have taken part in
the Areopagos controversy, we may be sure that he
would lose no chance of ridiculing the man he secretly
detested. Such an opportunity occurred when Lord
Oxford fell temporarily from the Queen's high favour in
January 1581, and there can be no doubt that Riche's
lampoon, so obviously directed at Oxford a month after his
disgrace, was instigated by the Vice-Chamberlain. Moreover, Hatton belonged to Leicester's faction in opposing
the French match, and Riche's description of a man in
a French ruff, a French cloak, and a French hose makes
it practically certain that he is caricaturing Lord Oxford :

It was my fortune at my last being at London to walk
through the Strand towards Westminster, where I met one
came riding towards me on a footcloth nag, apparelled
in a French ruff, a French cloak, a French hose, and in his
hand a great fan of feathers, bearing them up (very
womanly) against the side of his face. And for that I
had never seen any man wear them before that day, I
began to think it impossible that there might a man be
found so foolish as to make himself a scorn to the world
to wear so womanish a toy ; but rather thought it had
been some shameless woman that had disguised herself
like a man in our hose and our cloaks ; for our doublets,
gowns, caps, and hats, they had gone long ago.
But by this time he was come something nigher me and
I might see he had a beard, whereby I was assured that he
should have been a man. . . . And as he passed by me
I saw three following that were his men, and taking the
hindermost by the arm I asked him what gentlewoman
his master was. But the fellow, not understanding my
meaning, told me his master's name and so departed.
I began then to muse with myself to what end that fan
of feathers served, for it could not be to defend the sun

[1] *Eight Novels* . . . by Barnabe Riche, 1581. (Shakespeare Society,
1846.)

14

from the burning of his beauty, for it was in the beginning of February, when the heat of the sun may be very well endured.

Now, if it were to defend the wind or the coldness of the air, methinks a French hood had been a great deal better, for that had been both gentlewomanlike, and being close pinned down about his ears would have kept his head a great deal warmer ; and then a French hood on his head, a French ruff about his neck, and a pair of French hose on his legs, had been right—à la mode de France ; and this had been something suitable to his wit.

There can surely be little doubt that the Elizabethan reader would see in Riche's lampoon a picture of the chief supporter of the Anjou match.

These fleeting vignettes, sketched by the literary underworld of London, give us a vivid glimpse of Lord Oxford and his Bohemian friends and foes. We may perhaps be surprised at the familiar tone in which men like Harvey, Nashe, and Riche spoke of the Lord Great Chamberlain ; but the fraternity of letters has always broken down the artificial barriers of caste, and we shall undoubtedly miss the light-hearted buffoonery of these quips if we attempt to analyse them without a sense of humour. The Elizabethans were not grave, solemn scholars who issued learned treatises from the seclusion of their studies. They were first and foremost men of action, full of *joie de vivre*, and bubbling over with the irrepressible spirits of over-grown schoolboys. They had nearly all, at one time or another, trailed a pike as volunteers in the Protestant armies on the Continent, and they revelled in such escapades as Drake's mad pranks in his "private war" with the King of Spain. To them life, literature, and war were indissolubly mixed, and could only be enjoyed to the full after a liberal admixture of fun and adventure. No one who fails to appreciate this can catch the true spirit of Elizabethan England.

But it is time now to return once more to Vere House. In 1582 a new recruit joined the Euphuists. This was Thomas Watson, who dedicated his collection of poems

called *Hekatompathia, the Passionate Century of Love,* to
Lord Oxford on March 31st :

Alexander the Great [he writes] passing on a time
by the workshop of Apelles, curiously surveyed some of
his doings ; whose long stay in viewing them brought all
the people into so great a liking of the painter's workman-
ship that immediately after they bought up all his pictures,
what price soever he set them at.

And the like good hap (Right Honourable) befel unto
me lately concerning these my Love Passions, which then
chanced Apelles for his portraits.   For since the world
hath understood (I know not how) that your Honour had
willingly vouchsafed the acceptance of this work, and at
convenient leisures favourably perused it, being as yet
but in written hand, many have oftentimes and earnestly
called upon me to put it to the press, that for their money
they might but see what your Lordship with some liking
had already perused.   And thus at this moment I humbly
take my leave ; but first wishing the continual increase
of your Lordship's honour, with abundance of good friends,
reconciliation of all foes, and what good soever tendeth
unto perfect happiness.

Your Lordship's humbly at command,

THOMAS WATSON.

In wishing his patron " reconciliation of all foes " Watson
gives us a glimpse of the unhappy and troubled life that
Lord Oxford was leading during his years of disgrace.[1]
The Earl no doubt was turning more and more from the
interminable intrigues of the Court to his literary associates.

While on the subject of the *Hekatompathia* it is perhaps
worth quoting what that profound Elizabethan critic,
Edward Arber, has to say about it in the Introduction to
his reprint of Watson's poems :

Whoever reads this remarkable work will wonder how
it can have fallen into such oblivion.   On the poems
themselves we shall say nothing.   They reveal themselves.
Each of them is headed with " an annotation."   To these
short introductions we would call attention.   They are most
skilfully written.   Who wrote them ? May he have been the

---

[1] Oxford was out of favour with the Queen from January 1581 to
June 1583.

Earl of Oxford ? Was he the friend whom Watson addresses in Number 71 as " dear Titus mine, my ancient friend " ?

The answer to this suggestion—that Lord Oxford supplied the introductory annotations when he read the poems in manuscript—can be found, I think, in the annotation to the 67th poem. Here Watson says that someone who—

for some good he had conceived of the works vouchsafed with his own hand certain poesies [i.e. " posies," or annotations] concerning the same ; amongst which was this one : " Love hath no leaden heels."

Surely this anonymous individual must have been the same as he who " at convenient leisures " had perused the manuscript " being as yet but in written hand " ?

Still more striking is the fact that in another of Watson's books of verse—the posthumous *Tears of Fancy* (1593)— the last sonnet of the series beginning " Who taught thee first to sigh, alas, my heart ? " has been definitely ascribed to Lord Oxford himself in the Rawlinson manuscript. I give the poem in full :

> Who taught thee first to sigh, alas, my heart ?
>> Who taught thy tongue the woeful words of plaint ?
>> Who filled thine eyes with tears of bitter smart ?
>> Who gave thee grief and made thy joys to faint ?
> Who first did paint with colours pale thy face ?
>> Who first did break thy sleeps of quiet rest ?
>> Above the rest in Court, who gave thee grace ?
>> Who made thee strive in honour to be best ?
> In constant truth to bide so firm and sure,
>> To scorn the world, regarding but thy friends ?
>> With patient mind each passion to endure,
>> In one desire to settle to the end ?
> Love then thy choice, wherein such choice thou bind,
> As nought but death may ever change thy mind.
>   Finis.   Earl of Oxenforde.[1]

Whatever may be the true facts of the case, it is evident that an exceedingly close link exists between the Earl of Oxford and the poems of Thomas Watson. The poems themselves are not all of the highest standard, but they certainly do not deserve the scorn that is heaped on them

[1] Bodleian Library, Rawlinson Poetical MSS. 85. 16. There are slight variations in the version published in the *Tears of Fancy*.

by Professor Courthope. As Watson was one of the
Euphuists, and as, like Bedingfield, Lyly, and Munday, he
had submitted his manuscript to his patron for help and
advice, it seems quite likely that some of the poems
published by him were really the work of the Earl. But
this is mere conjecture which may, some day, be proved
or disproved.

Two years after Watson had enrolled himself as a
Euphuist under Lord Oxford he was followed by one of
the most interesting personalities in Elizabethan literature,
Robert Greene. Says Courthope :

Lyly's most brilliant disciple, Greene, was ready to avail
himself of any subject which offered opportunities of
treatment in the Euphuistic manner. When he began to
write he naturally turned, like his master, to the theme of
Love, and for several years poured forth a succession of
amorous pamphlets and romances which were read with
eagerness by all sorts and conditions of men, to whose
barbarous taste the tricks of Euphuism seemed miracles
of art. . . . What is best and most characteristic in the
plays of Greene is the poetry of his pastoral landscape, and
his representation of the characters of women ; in both
of these respects he exercised an unmistakeable influence
on the genius of Shakespeare. His pastoral vein is displayed rather in his novels than in his dramas ; it runs very
happily through *Menaphon*, and even more so through
Pandosto, a story which furnished Shakespeare with the
outline of his *Winter's Tale*.[1]

One of Greene's earliest books, published in 1584, was
dedicated to Lord Oxford. It bore the title *Greene's
Card of Fancy, wherein the folly of those Carpet Knights is
deciphered, which guiding their course by the compass of
Cupid, either dash their ship against most dangerous rocks,
or else attain the haven with pain and peril . . . by Robert
Greene, Master of Art in Cambridge.* The dedication
runs as follows :

To the Right Honourable Edward de Vere, Earl of
Oxenford, Viscount Bulbeck, Lord of Escales and Badles-

[1] *A History of English Poetry*, vol. ii, pp. 388, 395.

mire, and Lord Great Chamberlain of England : Robert Greene wisheth long life with increase of honour.

That poor Castilian Erontino (Right Honourable) being a very unskilful painter, presented Alphonsus, the Prince of Aragon, with a most imperfect picture, which the King thankfully accepted ; not that he liked the work, but that he loved the art. The paltering poet Cherillus dedicated his dancing poems to that mighty monarch Alexander, saying that he knew assuredly if Alexander would not accept them that they were not pithy, yet he would not utterly reject them in that they had a show of poetry. Cæsar ofttimes praised his soldiers for their will, although they wanted skill ; and Cicero as well commended stammering Lentulus for his painful industry as learned Lælius for his passing eloquence. Which considered (although wisdom did will me not to strain further than my sleeve would stretch) I thought good to present this imperfect pamphlet to your Honour's protection, hoping your Lordship will deign to accept the matter in that it seemeth to be prose, though something unsavoury for want of skill, and take my well meaning for an excuse of my boldness, in that my poor want. The Emperor Trajan was never without suitors, because courteously he would hear every complaint. The Lapidaries frequented the Court of Adobrandinus, because it was his chief study to search out the nature of stones. All that courted Atlanta were hunters, and none sued to Sapho but poets. Wheresoever Mæcenas lodgeth, thither no doubt will scholars flock. And your Honour being a worthy favourer and fosterer of learning hath forced many through your excellent virtue to offer the first-fruits of their study at the shrine of your Lordship's courtesy. But though they have waded far and found mines, and I gadded abroad to get nothing but mites, yet this I assure myself, that they never presented unto your Honour their treasure with a more willing mind than I do this simple trash, which I hope your Lordship will so accept. Resting therefore upon your Honour's wonted clemency, I commit your Lordship to the Almighty.

Your Lordship's most dutifully to command,
ROBERT GREENE.[1]

---

[1] From the 1603 edition in the British Museum ; but the first edition was 1584. (Cf. Courthope, op. cit., vol. ii, p. 388.)

In 1586 Angel Day [1] dedicated his first book—*The English Secretorie, wherein is contained a perfect method for the vindicating of all manner of epistles and familiar letters* —to Lord Oxford.   He was evidently another disciple of Euphuism as the dedication shows :

To the Right Honourable Lord Edward de Vere, Earl of Oxenford, Viscount Bulbeck, Lord Sandford and of Badlesmere, and Lord Great Chamberlain of England : all honour and happiness correspondent to his noble desires, and in the commutation of this earthly being endless joys and an everlasting habitation.

. . . My honourable Lord, the exceeding bounty where-with your good Lordship hath ever wonted to entertain the deserts of all men, and very appearance of nobility herself, well known to have reposed her delights in the worthiness of your stately mind, warrenteth me almost that I need not blush to recommend unto your courteous view the first-fruits of these my foremost labours, and to honour this present discourse with the memory of your everlasting worthiness.   And albeit by the learned view and insight of your Lordship, whose infancy from the beginning was ever sacred to the Muses, the whole course hereof may be found nothing such, as the lowest part of the same may appear in any sort answerable to so great and forward excellence. . . .

Your Lordship's most devoted and loyally affected
ANGEL DAIE.

It was in the same year that Lord Oxford received the highest possible tribute to his skill in poetry :

I may not omit the deserved commendations of many honourable and noble Lords and Gentlemen in Her Majesty's Court, which, in the rare devices of poetry, have been and yet are most skilful ; among whom the Right Honourable Earl of Oxford may challenge to himself the title of the most excellent among the rest.[2]

[1] Angel Day was the son of Thomas Day, a parish clerk of London. He was apprenticed to Thomas Duxsell, a London stationer, for twelve years from 1563.   His first work—*The English Secretary*—was reprinted six times before 1614.   He published three other works, including a poem " upon the life and death . . . of Sir Philip Sidney."

[2] William Webbe, *A Discourse of English Poetry*.   (See Haslewood's *Ancient Critical Essays*, vol. ii, p. 34.)

Three years later the same high praise was meted out to him by the author of *The Arte of English Poesy.* I shall deal with this evidence more in detail elsewhere.

During the eighties Anthony Munday had been hard at work translating from French, Italian, and Spanish a cycle of books which have come to be known as the " Romances of Chivalry." There were originally at least fifteen volumes, and they were published by Munday at intervals between 1583 and 1618.[1] Unfortunately five of them have been lost altogether, and only a few first editions of the remainder exist. Probably the lost *Galien of France,* which Lord Oxford had read evidently with appreciation while it was still in manuscript in 1579, was the first of these translations which Munday undertook. Moreover, at least five of the first editions of the cycle— viz. *Palmerin d'Oliva,* Parts I and II, and *Primaleon of Greece,* Parts I, II, and III—are known to have been dedicated to Lord Oxford.[2] This certainly looks as if the Earl had been responsible in encouraging Munday in this particular line.

Of these five dedications, however, only one—*Palmerin,* Part I—now exists. The title runs :

Palmerin d'Oliva : the Mirror of Nobility, Map of Honour, Anatomy of rare fortunes, Heroical president of Love, Wonder for Chivalry, and most accomplished Knight in all perfections. Written in the Spanish, Italian, and French, and from them turned into English by A. M. one of the Messengers of Her Majesty's Chamber. . . . 1588.

The dedication is as follows :

To the right noble, learned, and worthy minded Lord Edward de Vere, Earl of Oxenford, . . . A. M. wisheth continual happiness in this life and in the world to come.

Among the Spartans, right noble Lord and sometime my honourable master, nothing was accounted more

[1] There is an interesting account of this cycle in an article by Gerald R. Hayes in *The Library,* 4th Series, vol. vi, p. 57 (1926).

[2] It is probable that eight, and possibly more, were dedicated to him, but this cannot be definitely proved.

odious than the forgetfulness of the servant towards the master. . . .

Though this example (my good Lord) be unfit for me, in what respect beseems me not to speak, yet that excellent opinion of the Spartans I count it religion for me to imitate. For if this vice was so despised among such famous persons, what reproach would it be to so poor an abject as myself, being once so happy as to serve a master so noble, to forget his precious virtues, which makes him generally beloved, but chiefly mine own duty, which nothing but death can discharge. . . . If Palmerin hath sustained any wrong by my bad translation, being so worthily set down in other languages, your Honour having such special knowledge in them I hope will let slip any faults escaped, in respect I have done my good will, the largest talent I have to bestow.

And seeing the time affords me such opportunity that with ending this first part the old year is expired, I present it to my noble Lord as your servant's New Year's gift, and therewithal deliver my most affectionate duty, evermore ready at your Honour's commandment.

Needless were it by tediousness to grow troublesome when a word sufficeth to so sound judgment. I submit myself and my book to your gracious conceit, and the second part, now on the press, and well near finished, I will shortly present to my worthy patron.

In meanwhile I wish your Honour so many New Years of happiness as may stand with the heavenly appointment, and my modesty to desire.

Sometime your Honour's servant yet continuing in all humble duty,

ANTHONIE MONDAY.

It may be mentioned in passing that in 1619 Munday brought out a second edition in three parts of *Primaleon of Greece*, all of which were dedicated to Henry, the eighteenth Earl of Oxford. The following extract is of interest, not only because we see that it was originally dedicated to the seventeenth Earl, but also because it shows that Munday maintained a close friendship with both father and son for at least forty years :

Sir, having sometime served that most noble Earl your

father of famous and desertful memory ; and translating divers honourable histories into English out of French, Italian, and other languages, which he graciously pleased to countenance with his noble acceptance ; among the embrions of my then younger brain these three several parts of *Primaleon of Greece* were the tribute of my duty and service to him, which books, having long time slept in oblivion and (in a manner) quite out of memory, by favour of these more friendly times coming once more to be seen on the world's public theatre, in all duty they offer themselves to your noble patronage ; for you being the true heir of your honourable father's matchless virtues, and succeeding him in place of degree and eminency, who should inherit the father's trophies, monuments, and ancient memories but his truly noble, hopeful, and virtuous son ? In whom old Lord Edward is still living and cannot die so long as you breathe.

For his sake then, most honourable Earl, accept of poor *Primaleon*, newly revived, and rising from off your father's hearse in all humility cometh to kiss your noble hand ; with what further dutiful service wherein you shall please to employ me.

Your Honour's ever to be commanded,
A. M.

Lord Oxford's position as the principal patron of these Continental Romances of Chivalry is a clear indication of the extent of his literary interests. From 1564 to 1571 we have seen him extending his patronage to the early translators of the classics like Arthur Golding and Thomas Underdoune. After his return from Italy he constituted himself the leader of the new Euphuist movement, the chief exponent of which, John Lyly, was for many years a member of his household. During the eighties we find him encouraging another of his " servants " —Anthony Munday—to undertake the task of translating a great cycle of Continental Romances. His skill and supremacy in poetry were universally acknowledged ; and, as we shall see later, from 1580 onwards he was organising and writing plays for a company of actors he had taken under his patronage. But even so wide a range of interests as is comprised in the Classics, Poetry, Euphuism, the Drama, and Romantic literature failed to satisfy the Earl's craving for culture and the arts. In 1591 John Farmer [1] dedicated his first song-book—*Forty several ways of two parts in one made upon a plain song*—to Lord Oxford. The wording of the dedication leaves no doubt as to why he chose the Earl as his patron :

. . . This poor conceit I have presumed of your honourable favour to present unto your Lordship, under coverture of whom to the view of the world ; not but that I knew it unworthy of so high a personage, the less is in it to recommend itself, which, how little it is, I am greatly in fear. Hereunto, my good Lord, I was the rather emboldened for your Lordship's great affection to this noble science [i.e. music], hoping for the one you might pardon the other, and desirous to make known your inclination this way. . . . Besides this, my good Lord, I bear this conceit, that not only myself am vowed to your commandment, but all that is in me is dedicated to your Lordship's service.

Farmer's second book—*The First Set of English Madrigals*—was published in 1599. Once again in the dedication he pays tribute to Lord Oxford's skill as a musician :

Most honourable Lord, it cometh not within the compass of my power to express all the duty I owe, nor to pay the least part ; so far have your honourable favours outstripped all means to manifest my humble affection that there is nothing left but praying and wondering. There is a canker worm that breedeth in many minds, feeding only upon forgetfulness and bringing forth to birth but ingratitude. To show that I have not been bitten with that monster, for worms prove monsters in this age, which yet never any painter could counterfeit to express the ugliness, nor any poet describe to decipher the height of their

---

[1] Nothing appears to be known of John Farmer except that he was a musical composer who dedicated his only two song-books to Lord Oxford. It seems probable that at any rate between the dates of their publication (1591-9) he was in Oxford's household.

illness, I have presumed to tender these Madrigals only as
remembrances of my service and witnesses of your Lordship's liberal hand, by which I have so long lived, and from
your honourable mind that so much have all liberal
sciences.   In this I shall be most encouraged if your
Lordship vouchsafe the protection of my first-fruits, for
that both of your greatness you best can, and for your
judgment in music best may.   For without flattery be it
spoke, those that know your Lordship know this, that
using this science as a recreation, your Lordship have
overgone most of them that make it a profession.   Right
Honourable Lord, I hope it shall not be distasteful to
number you here amongst the favourers of music, and the
practisers, no more than Kings and Emperors that have
been desirous to be in the roll of astronomers, that being
but a star fair, the other an angel's choir.

Thus most humbly submitting myself and my labours
and whatever is or may be in me to your Lordship's censure
and protection, I humbly end, wishing your Lordship as
continual an increasing of health and honour as there is a
daily increase of virtue to come to happiness.

Your Lordship's most dutiful servant to command,

JOHN FARMER.

We do not know for certain whether Lord Oxford was
himself a composer, but it is probable that he was so.   In
1588 Antony Munday, who had once been in the Earl's
employ but was then a " servant of the Queen's Majesty,"
published *A Banquet of Dainty Conceits*.   This was a book
containing twenty-two poems of his own, and in it he
gives to each a musical setting.   One of them, we read,
can be sung to the " Earl of Oxford's march," and another
to the " Earl of Oxford's galliard."   These tunes have now
been lost.

In 1599 George Baker, who had once been Lady Oxford's
personal doctor, but, presumably at her death in 1588,
had been appointed " one of the Queen's Majesty's chief
chirurgiens in ordinary," dedicated his *Practise of the New
and Old Physic* to Lord Oxford.   It was a reprint, having
first appeared in 1576 under the title of the *New Jewel of
Health*, with a dedication to the Countess his mistress.

The new dedication, which was only slightly altered to suit his new patron, concludes as follows :

Wherefore I at this time, to pleasure my country and friends have published this work under your honourable protection, that it may more easily be defended against sycophants and fault finders, because your wit, learning, and authority hath great force and strength in repressing the curious crakes of the envious and bleating babes of Momus' charm.

Your Honour's for ever to command,

G. BAKER.

But it is time now to retrace our steps and return once more to the point where we last left Lord Oxford at the height of his power and prominence after the tennis-court quarrel with Philip Sidney. His contemporaries at this time must have discerned in him the man who was almost certain to supplant the Earl of Leicester as Her Majesty's chief favourite. This, indeed, had already been more than half accomplished; for with Leicester's disgrace in 1578 the field seemed to be clear, and Lord Oxford's goal assured. His only possible rival was Sir Christopher Hatton, the recently appointed Vice-Chamberlain. Sir Walter Ralegh's meteoric career was still undreamed of ; and the Earl of Essex, who became so great a figure in the latter years of the reign, was a boy in his 'teens. Well might the Court in 1580 have felt that nothing could shake the secure foundations on which Lord Oxford's position rested.

But it was not to be. Within a brief year the whole fabric of the brilliant career that appeared almost within his reach had crumbled to the ground, and his life passed out of the sunshine of prominence into the sombre gloom of shadow.

CHAPTER V

1580–1586

> " My report was once
> First with the best of note. . . .
> And when a soldier was the theme, my name
> Was not far off : then was I as a tree
> Whose boughs did bend with fruit : but in one night,
> A storm, or robbery, call it what you will,
> Shook down my mellow hangings, nay, my leaves,
> And left me bare to weather. . . .
> My fault being nothing, as I have told you oft,
> But that two villains, whose false oaths prevailed
> Before my perfect honour . . ."
>
> *Cymbeline*, Act III, Sc. III, 57–68.

§ I. Lord Henry Howard

THE summer of 1580 may be said to mark the highest point attained by Lord Oxford as a courtier and Royal favourite. In 1579, at the time of the quarrel with Sidney, we have it on Fulke Greville's authority that he was " superlative in the Prince's favour " ; and indeed Sidney's banishment from the Court and retirement to Wilton until October 1580 sufficiently shows the attitude of the Queen at this period towards the Earl of Oxford.

But before the end of 1580 he took the first step in a course of action which—however patriotically intended—was destined to dethrone him from that position of prestige and authority which he had occupied at the Court since the time of his marriage to Anne Cecil on December 19th, 1571. In order to understand the motives that prompted his action this winter it is necessary to go back some four or five years to the time of his return from the Continent in April 1576.

This return to England marked, as we have already seen, a crisis in his affairs. It is difficult to say with certainty what the precise causes of this crisis were. He was probably angry and suspicious in matters that con-

cerned not only his wife, but also some of his old friends
and literary associates such as George Gascoigne and
Christopher Hatton, perhaps also Lord Burghley and the
Queen herself.   Whatever these causes may have been,
he and several friends, including Lord Henry Howard,
Francis Southwell, and Charles Arundel, joined together
soon after his arrival, and made a secret profession of their
adherence to the Catholic religion.[1]

That Oxford was partly influenced in taking this step
by other motives than purely religious ones is probable
from what we know of his affairs at the time, and also
from his own subsequent statements.   But he never
allowed his Catholic sympathies to interfere with his
patriotism, and when he found that the adoption of
Catholicism meant, in the case of some of his friends, a
secret leaning towards Spain, he began to regret his
precipitate action in having become reconciled to the
Church of Rome.   We have all this on the testimony of
Mauvissière de Castelnau, the French Ambassador, who
on January 11th, 1581, wrote as follows to the King of
France :

A few days before Christmas the Earl of Oxford (who
about four and a half years ago on his return from Italy
made profession of the Catholic faith together with some
of his relatives among the nobility and his best friends, and
had sworn, as he says, and signed with them a declaration
that they would do all they could for the advancement
of the Catholic religion) accused his former friends to
the Queen of England your good sister.   For his own part
he craved forgiveness for what he had done, saying that
he now recognised that he had done wrong.   He then
proceeded to accuse his best friends who had supported
him in his recent quarrels of having conspired against the
State by having made profession of the Catholic faith,
and he endeavoured to do them all the harm he could.
The Queen your good sister was very much upset about it,
for she was very fond of most of those accused by the Earl ;
among whom were Lord Henry Howard, a brother of the
late Duke of Norfolk, and Charles Arundel, who is very

[1] *Catholic Record Society*, vol. xxix, p. 29.

devoted to your Majesties and to Monseigneur your
brother, both of them being strong advocates of the
marriage. . . .

It was to her great regret, as the Queen herself told me,
that she was obliged to place them under restraint in the
custody of some of her Councillors : Lord Henry under the
charge of Sir Christopher Hatton, Captain of the Guard ;
and Francis Southwell under the charge of Sir Francis
Walsingham.

Having been questioned regarding the accusations
preferred against them by the Earl of Oxford, namely
that they had conspired against the State, they were able
to clear themselves very satisfactorily ; and as concerns
Catholicism, they are known to be well affected to it, as
indeed is the case with most of the nobility of this kingdom.
The Queen knew this perfectly well ; and Lord Henry
Howard, Arundel, and Southwell, although Catholics at
heart, are nevertheless much esteemed and favoured by
her, seeing that both they and their friends have always
been in favour of the marriage and of the French alliance.
The Earl of Oxford thus found himself alone in his evidence
and accusations.   He has lost credit and honour, and has
been abandoned by all his friends and by all the ladies of
the Court. . . .

Nevertheless, up to the present the Queen has been
endeavouring to find out all she can about the matter.
She has told me recently that they were madmen, but
that there were certainly plots being hatched, with their
roots abroad ; and that she very much regretted to find
her own subjects implicated in them, especially those who
were so well affected to France and so favourable to the
marriage.   She added that she would close her eyes to it
as far as possible in view of their attitude towards the
marriage. . . .

The Earl of Oxford, finding himself alone and unsupported,
threw himself on his knees several times before the Queen,
and begged her to hear from my lips whether it was not
true that I knew of a Jesuit who had celebrated the Mass
about four years ago at which they were reconciled to the
Roman Church.   The Queen earnestly begged me to tell
her the facts not so much to injure them in any way,
but to satisfy her as to the truth.   She said that I knew
quite well her favourable attitude towards Catholics who

did not place their consciences in antagonism to the State, and entreated me to let her know about it.

I denied all knowledge of the business ; saying that I not only knew nothing about it, but that I had never even heard it talked about.

On hearing this the Earl of Oxford once again threw himself on his knees before her, and implored her to urge me to tell her the truth. At the same time he begged me to do him the favour to recall a circumstance which touched him very closely. He reminded me that he had sent me a message begging me to assist the said Jesuit to return in safety to France and Italy, and that when I had done so he gave me his thanks. I replied clearly and unequivocally to the Queen that I had no recollection whatever of this incident. The effect of my reply was that the Earl was fairly put to confusion in the presence of his Mistress.[1]

The Ambassador goes on to say that Oxford then implored him to report what he did remember. " I bade him speak no more. He is evidently trying to sicken those who were earnest on the side of the match. Perhaps he is jealous of others, or is of the Spanish faction."

How wrongly de Castelnau judged of Oxford's action can be seen from the following letter written by the Spanish Ambassador Bernardino de Mendoza, on December 25th, 1580, to the King of Spain :

Milord Henry Howard, brother of the Duke of Norfolk, has for some years—as I know through some priests—been very Catholic. . . . He desired that the [French] match should take place ; believing, like many other Catholics, that by this means they would be allowed to exercise their religion in freedom.

On hearing that the Earl of Oxford had accused him, together with Charles [Arundel and Francis] Southwell of being reconciled to Rome, they did not dare to trust themselves to the French Ambassador ; but coming to my house at midnight, though I had never spoken to them, they told me the danger in which they found themselves of losing their lives, unless I would hide them. As they were

[1] *Catholic Record Society,* vol. xxi, pp. 29, 30.

15

Catholics I entertained them. . . . Milord Harry, in gratitude
. . . has informed and continues to inform me of everything
he hears. . . . To touch of the greatness of the affection with
which he occupies himself in the service of your Majesty
is impossible.[1]

These two letters of the French and Spanish Ambassadors
enable us to follow the sequence of events and to understand their political import.

Throughout the seventies a Court Catholic party
favouring the French match and the French alliance had
been in existence. The rising power of Spain during the
same period was, however, beginning to attract more and
more attention. Oxford had observed among his friends
the growth of this influence, and it would seem that in his
opinion it had by December 1580 reached a point of actual
disloyalty and treason. There is no reason to suppose
that he was influenced by other than patriotic motives
when he denounced his former friends to the Queen in
the presence of the French Ambassador. He evidently
expected to be supported by Mauvissière de Castelnau,
in the interests of whose country he was genuinely acting.
It must have been a serious shock to him to find himself
left in the lurch. On the other hand, if we place ourselves
in the position of the French Ambassador, it is easy to see
that he would naturally be suspicious of Oxford's motives,
and that a categorical denial would seem to be the only safe
line for him to take. There is no reason to doubt the veracity
of the statement made by Bernardino de Mendoza that he
had never spoken to Howard, Arundel, and Southwell
before they came to his house at midnight just before
Christmas. The inference to be drawn from the two letters
is that Oxford's action was the immediate cause of the
break-up of the Court Catholic party into two factions,
and that the disloyal Spanish faction was not formed until
Oxford, with what may seem to us now undue precipita-
tion, blurted out his accusation in the Presence Chamber.
The written charges and counter-charges that followed

---

[1] *Catholic Record Society*, vol. xxi, pp. 30, 31.

are voluminously recorded in the State Papers Domestic, volume cli, articles 42 to 57, and in State Papers Domestic, Addenda, volume xxvi, article 46, some of which have already been quoted.

It will be sufficient to say here that during the four months of wrangling on paper Lord Henry Howard was placed under close restraint in the charge of Sir Christopher Hatton, and Charles Arundel was similarly placed in a house (the owner of which I have been unable to discover) at Sutton. One of the latter's bitterest complaints, to which he gave vent in a letter to Hatton, was that while he himself had been virtually imprisoned his enemy was free and allowed to " graze in the pastures." At the same time there is a curious letter, signed by the Privy Council, which shows conclusively that Lord Oxford was *released* from the Tower on June 8th :

9th June 1581.

A letter to Sir William Gorges [1] that where their Lordships understand that the Earl of Oxford, being yesterday by Her Majesty's commandment released of his imprisonment in the Tower, at his Lordship's departure he [i.e. Gorges] did demand his upper garment and other things as fees due unto him by his office ; and hath thereupon caused certain of his Lordship's stuff to be stayed : [we therefore] giving him [i.e. Gorges] to understand *that for as much as his Lordship was not committed thither upon any cause of treason or any criminal cause,* it is thought that he cannot challenge any such fees ; and therefore do hereby require him to forebear to demand the same and to suffer the stuff stayed by him to pass ; whereof he is to have regard also for that the Earl supposeth he may not a little be touched in honour if he shall be brought to yield unto a custom only upon persons committed to that place for treason, and for that respect especially neither may the Earl well yield thereunto, nor he [i.e. Gorges] demand it.[2]

---

[1] The Yeoman Porter of the Tower. " Amongst the Yeoman Porter's perquisites we find it laid down in 1555 that ' the Porter shall have of every prisoner condemned by the King and Queen's Majesty to the said Tower for treason, his uppermost garment, or he agree with him for it ' " (Sir George Younghusband, *The Tower of London*, 1924, p. 88).

[2] *Acts of the Privy Council*, New Series, XIII. 74.

It was with the object of trying to discover how long Lord Oxford had been imprisoned in the Tower that I undertook a search among the lists of prisoners, whose names are recorded in the bills for their keep and custody rendered quarterly to the Privy Council by the Lieutenants of the Tower. The bills for this particular period—and indeed for the whole of Sir Owen Hopton's tenure of the Lieutenancy—are absolutely complete. But to my surprise there was no mention whatsoever of the Earl of Oxford in the lists for the two quarters beginning December 23rd, 1580, and ending June 24th, 1581. The Earl of Clanricarde, who was imprisoned on December 4th, 1580, is shown, and there are about a score of other prisoners, but Lord Oxford does not appear.

Now the object of these lists was solely to enable the Lieutenant of the Tower to obtain a refund of the expenses he had incurred in rationing the prisoners under his charge. It is therefore obvious that the Earl of Oxford cannot have had any meals in the Tower during his imprisonment. As the charges, which were absolutely baseless, brought against him by his former friends included an alleged attempt to murder them all three ; such " dangerous practices " as the attempted murder of Leicester, Walsingham, Sidney, Ralegh, and Sir Harry Knyvet ; treasonable correspondence with the Spanish Ambassador as well as with the English fugitives at Rome ; and lastly, " notable dishonesty of life " of a criminal nature, it is clear that his confinement must be referred to some other cause— because it is obvious that if he had been found guilty of any of these charges he would have spent months, and perhaps years, in the gloomy fortress.

On the other hand, there were a host of minor charges preferred against him, and the following statements that he was alleged to have made are significant :

That the Catholics were great Ave Maria coxcombs that they would not rebel against the Queen ;
My Lord of Norfolk worthy to lose his head for not following his [i.e. Oxford's] counsel at Lichfield to take arms ;

Railing at my Lord of Arundel for putting his trust in
the Queen ;

Railing at Francis Southwell for commending the Queen's
singing one night at Hampton Court, and protesting by
the blood of God that she had the worst voice and did
everything with the worst grace that ever woman did,
and that he was never [so] nonplussed but when he came
to speak of her ;

Daily railing at the Queen, and falling out with Charles
Arundel, Francis Southwell, and myself [i.e. Lord Henry
Howard] in defence of her.

It would seem that Lord Henry Howard took the
precaution of sending these written charges to his fellow-
conspirators in order to see how far they would be prepared
to support him in confirmation of his statements. Opposite
the last two charges referring to the Queen occur the following words, written in another hand : " Audibi, sed in
poculis." [1] The handwriting of the marginal remark does
not seem to be that of Charles Arundel, and we may therefore surmise that it was written by Francis Southwell,
who does not appear to have originated any charges himself.

If this file of correspondence was ever submitted to
the Queen we may well imagine how angry she must have
been. Sir Christopher Hatton was Vice-Chamberlain at
the time, and it is unlikely that he would have failed to take
advantage of such a golden opportunity to damage his
most formidable rival in the eyes of the Queen. Although
she evidently declined to allow the random accusations of
Lord Henry Howard and Charles Arundel to be made the
basis of a legal process, it is not unreasonable to suppose
that she may have ordered Lord Oxford to be sent to the
Tower for a night as a disciplinary measure.[2]

This would also explain why the Privy Council, in their

---

[1] " Yes, I heard him say so, but he was intoxicated at the time."

[2] It may be recalled that a similar sort of incident occurred during
Essex's campaign in Ireland in 1599. Lord Grey de Wilton, who commanded a regiment of cavalry, had disobeyed a command given him by
the Earl of Southampton, General of the Horse. The episode was
not sufficiently serious to warrant deprivation of command ; but
Southampton, as a disciplinary measure, ordered Grey to sleep one night
in the custody of the Provost-Marshal.

letter to Sir William Gorges, not only forbade him to take
his legal perquisite of the Earl's " upper garment," but
expressly stated that he was not committed " upon any
cause of treason or any criminal cause."

Whatever the Queen may have thought about these
personal affronts, she had no illusions whatsoever concerning the revelations Lord Oxford had made in showing up
the Catholic conspirators and their Jesuit accomplices.
We are told that—

.about the 12th of January (1581) Proclamation was published at London for the revocation of sundry of the
Queen's Majesty's subjects remaining beyond the seas
under the colour of study, and living contrary to the laws
of God and of the Realm.   And also against the retaining
of Jesuits and Massing Priests, sowers of sedition and other
treasonable attempts, etc.[1]

This Proclamation marks the turning-point of Elizabeth's
policy towards her Catholic subjects.   For twenty-three
years she had striven to win their loyalty by leniency and
tolerance.   But Lord Oxford had opened her eyes.   From
this time forward Jesuits who ventured into England were
remorselessly hunted down, persecuted, and executed ;
and the law imposing fines on Catholics for non-attendance
at Protestant services, which had remained practically a
dead-letter since it received the royal assent at the beginning of Elizabeth's reign, was resuscitated and put into
rigorous execution.   It is worth remarking that this change
of policy is frequently attributed to the well-known mission
to England of the Jesuits Campion and Parsons.   But they
landed in England as far back as April 1580 ; and it was
not till after Lord Oxford's disclosures in December and
the Proclamation in January, that Campion was appre-
hended and sentenced to death.   These dates make it
clear that it must have been Lord Oxford's dramatic
interview that induced the Queen to take the first decided
step against her Catholic subjects—a step that Burghley,
Walsingham, and the House of Commons had vainly urged
upon her over and over again in the past.

[1] Stow, *Annals*, p. 688.

§ II.   CHARLES ARUNDEL

In order to assist us in our appreciation of the utter worthlessness of the evidence given by Charles Arundel against Lord Oxford it will be necessary to follow the former's subsequent career with as much detail as the records permit.

On January 9th, 1581, Bernardino de Mendoza, the Spanish Ambassador, wrote as follows to the King of Spain :

The Queen has recently ordered the arrest of Lord Howard, brother of the Duke of Norfolk, and two other gentlemen, Charles Arundel and Southwell, who were formerly great favourites at the Court. The reason for this is partly religious . . . but it is suspected also that it may be attributed to their having been very intimate with the French Ambassador, with the apparent object of forwarding the Alençon match, together with some Court ladies of the same party who were favourites of the Queen. What adds to the mystery of the matter is their having been taken to the Tower, and Leicester's having spread the rumour that they were plotting a massacre of the Protestants, beginning with the Queen. His object in this is to inflame the people against them and against the French, as well as against the Earl of Sussex who was their close friend.

In view of the subsequent scurrilous libel published abroad in 1584 entitled *La Vie Abominable . . . du Comte de Leycester*, it is interesting to note that Leicester's name occurs as early as 1581 in connexion with a rumour implicating Charles Arundel.

There is no definite information as to the length of time that Charles Arundel was kept imprisoned in the Tower ; but there are copies of some half-dozen letters of his in a Letter Book of Sir Christopher Hatton, and from internal evidence they undoubtedly belong to this period. These letters have all been reprinted by Sir Harris Nicolas in his *Life of Hatton*, from the original Letter Book in the British Museum.

None of the letters are dated, and Arundel refers in veiled terms only to the Earl of Oxford, whom he never

mentions by name. He complains of his long imprisonment without trial, and evidently counts on Hatton's
sympathy. We may readily believe that this was forthcoming, for we know Oxford and Hatton were old rivals
for the Queen's favour.

It is probable that Arundel was released some time in
1583, and as Oxford was restored to court favour in the
summer of that year it is reasonable to suppose that he
was able to make things very unpleasant for his accuser.
Nor is this only a matter of surmise, because on
January 19th, 1585, we find a certain Thomas Vavasour,
who had been quoted by Arundel as a witness against
Oxford, inditing what is endorsed " a lewd letter " to the
Earl, in which he uses this expression : " Is not the
revenge taken of thy victims sufficient ? " [1]

At all events, shortly after Oxford's restoration to
favour, we hear that Charles Arundel has fled from England,
our informant being Sir Edward Stafford, the Ambassador
in Paris, who writes as follows to Sir Francis Walsingham
on December 2nd, 1583 :

Lord Paget, with Charles Paget and Charles Arundel,
suddenly entered my dining chamber before anyone was
aware of it, and Lord Paget says " they came away for
their consciences, and for fear, having enemies " ; adding
that " for all things but their consciences they would live
as dutifully as any in the world." [2]

Charles Paget was probably well known to the English
Ambassador, for he had been living in Paris for the last
eleven years or so as joint secretary with Thomas Morgan
to James Beaton, Archbishop of Glasgow, and Ambassador
of Mary Queen of Scots at the French Court.[3] His elder
brother Thomas, Lord Paget, although a zealous Roman
Catholic, did not altogether approve of his brother's openly
treasonable attitude, and had written to him six weeks

---

[1] Lansdowne MSS., 99. 93.   [2] Cal. S.P. Foreign.
[3] *Dict. Nat. Biog.*, vol. xliii, p. 46.

before that he was sorry to hear by some good friends
that he had carried himself not so dutifully as he ought to
do, and that he would disown him as a brother if he forgot
the duty that he owed to England.

However, shortly after the detection of Francis Throckmorton's conspiracy in November 1583, Lord Paget
followed his brother's example by taking refuge in Paris ;
and on the same day on which his sudden irruption into
Sir Edward Stafford's dining-room was reported to Walsingham he wrote to his mother, Lady Paget, trusting
that she would not mislike the step he had now taken, that
he might enjoy liberty of conscience and the free exercise
of his religion.   He also wrote to Lord Burghley explaining
that he had been long minded to travel for two reasons :
one, to cure his gout ; the other, of more moment, for the
satisfying of his conscience, about which he had been with
himself at marvellous conflict almost three years.[1]   The
estates and goods of Lord Paget were seized immediately
after his flight from England, and a Proclamation was
issued by the Queen commanding his return.   He never
did return to England, and died at Brussels in 1590.

In June 1584 Sir Edward Stafford made a formal demand,
in the name of Queen Elizabeth, for the surrender of
Lord Paget, Charles Arundel, Thomas Throckmorton (a
brother of Francis the conspirator) and Thomas Morgan,
on the ground that they had conspired against the life of
the English Queen.   The King of France refused to deliver
them up, although he shortly afterwards imprisoned
Morgan and forwarded his papers to Queen Elizabeth.

Charles Paget had had longer experience as a conspirator than any of the others, and he was not uniformly
consistent in his fidelity to his foreign employers.   For
instance, on January 8th, 1582, we find him writing to
Walsingham from Paris :

God made me known to you in this town, and led me
to offer you affection ; nothing can so comfort me as Her
Majesty's and your favour.

[1] *Dict. Nat. Biog.*, vol. xliii, p. 59.

Again on September 28th, 1582, he wrote :

In my answer to Her Majesty's command for my return
to England, assist me that she may yield me her favour
and liberty of conscience in religion. . . . If this cannot be
done, then solicit her for my enjoying my small living on
this side of the sea, whereby I may be kept from necessity,
which otherwise will force me to seek relief of some foreign
Prince.

On October 23rd he informed Walsingham that he
intended to go to Rouen for his health, and to drink
English beer.   He professed dutiful allegiance to Elizabeth,
and his readiness to be employed in any service, matter of
conscience in religion only excepted.

Charles Arundel seems to have modelled his behaviour
on that of Charles Paget, and to have acted the part of a
double spy during the last four years of his life.   He seems
to have lost no time in placing his services at the disposal
of the King of Spain, for within three weeks of his escape
from England we find the following reference to him in a
letter from Juan Baptista de Tassis to King Philip, dated
from Paris, December 22nd, 1583 :

Lord Paget and Charles Arundel have taken refuge here
on account of this affair,[1] they being Catholics and fearing
arrest.   Paget is the son of the Paget whom your Majesty
will probably recollect.   They have both secretly intimated
their arrival to me, and ask me to convey their humble
duty to your Majesty.[2]

It was not long before the English fugitives were
rewarded for their treachery, as may be seen from the
following letter from the King of Spain to Bernardino de
Mendoza, who had now been transferred to Paris :

You are already aware that, having regard to the rank
and parts of Lord Paget and his brother Charles, and
considering that they are fugitives from their home and
country for the sake of religion, I ordered Juan Baptista
de Tassis in September last (1584) to continue to pay these
allowances, namely, to Lord Paget 100 crowns a month,

[1] The Throckmorton Plot.   [2] Cal. S.P. Spanish (1580–86), p. 511.

and 50 to his brother Charles. I understand that this has not been done, and they petition me to have the allowances duly paid. I have granted this, and now order you to have them paid from the day the grant was made, and that in future the same allowances are to be paid regularly until contrary orders come from me, and the sums should be included in your account of extraordinary expenditure, which with their receipts shall be a good discharge for you. I have given strict orders to this effect, and no difficulty shall be raised about crediting you with the amounts.

In the margin of the letter the following note is written :

For Lord Paget and his brother Charles 150 crowns ; idem for Charles Arundel 80 crowns ; Thomas Throckmorton 40 crowns.[1]

Not long afterwards the Spanish Ambassador in Paris became suspicious of Charles Arundel, as is seen in the following letter from Bernardino de Mendoza to the King dated May 11th, 1586 :

Charles Arundel, an English gentleman, to whom your Majesty granted a pension of 80 crowns a month, in respect of the Queen of Scotland, was constantly in the house of the English Ambassador here when he was in Paris ; which Muzio[2] assures me was at his instructions, as the English Ambassador was needy, and he [Muzio] had given him 3000 crowns. In return for this the Ambassador gave him certain information through this Charles Arundel, to whom I gave letters for your Majesty when he went to Spain. I did this at the request of Muzio, and as he took with him very much more money than he stated, I have some suspicion that he may have gone at the instance of the English Ambassador, in order to discover something in your Majesty's Court, by which means he would be sure of obtaining the favour of the Queen of England. This may be concluded from the extreme care with which she obtains intelligence by every possible means of your Majesty's designs ; and although I have found nothing at all to inculpate Arundel, it will be advisable for your Majesty to send him and the rest of them away from the Court.

---

[1] Cal. S.P. Spanish (1580–86), p. 540.　　　[2] The Duc de Guise.

In a note written later in the same letter Mendoza says :

An English priest . . . feels himself bound to say that Charles Arundel had gone to Spain by orders of the Queen of England, in order to discover what was being done there, she having supplied him with money for the purpose. This confirms my suspicion, and your Majesty should order him to return.[1]

Arundel, however, continued to serve Spain, as the following account[2] drawn up by Mendoza in December 1586 shows :

Lord Paget, Baron Beaudesert, from March 24th, 1586, to the end of December, at 100 crowns a month	925	46	9
Charles Paget, 8 months and 8 days, at 50 crowns a month	412	52	4
Charles Arundel, 8 months and 23 days, at 80 crowns a month	699	23	7
Thomas Throckmorton, 8 months and 8 days, at 40 crowns a month	442	28	8
Thomas Morgan, 1 month, at 40 crowns a month	40	0	0
Earl of Westmoreland, 26 days, at 100 crowns a month	83	50	7
Charles Arundel has also to receive as a grant-in-aid from His Majesty	500	0	0
Total crowns	3,154	21	11

It is interesting to note in the foregoing list that Charles Arundel is the only pensioner to receive a special grant-in-aid in addition to his regular pension. What was the special service which earned him this large sum—more than Thomas Morgan's pension for a whole year ?

We have already seen that Morgan was imprisoned in the Bastille in 1584, where he remained for the next six years. In a letter of protest on the subject Mary Queen of Scots asserted that his imprisonment was really due to the Earl of Leicester, who suspected that the libel originally published in French in 1584 called *La Vie Abominable du Comte de Leycester*, and brought out in the following

---

[1] Cal. S.P. Spanish (1580–86), pp. 575–7.   [2] Ibid., p. 690.

year in English as *A Copy of a letter . . . from a Master of
Art of Cambridge*, was written by Morgan. If this particularly foul and scurrilous libel, subsequently known as
Leicester's Commonwealth, was really the work of the Queen
of Scots' Secretary, it is hardly likely that she would have
coupled his name with the work even in protest. The
libel, which shows an intimate knowledge of English
affairs and the doings of the nobility, was translated into
French and published in France in 1584 ; and Charles
Arundel, who was then a new arrival from England,
would have been well up in all the information it provides.
Moreover, his successful experience three years before in
defaming Lord Oxford would have strengthened his
confidence in this particular mode of attack.

But there is another curious piece of evidence connecting
Arundel with the *Vie Abominable*. Thomas Rogers, an
English spy, wrote on August 11th, 1585, to Walsingham
to say that he had been offered a bed in the house of a
certain Thomas Fitzherbert in Paris. Fitzherbert seems
to have been playing the dangerous game of taking money
from both sides, for Rogers explains that he—

gives and receives intelligence to and from all places,
and his house is the place of common conference, and the
lodging of Charles Arundel when in Paris ; but if I lodge
there I must do so amongst a great number of the libels
in French that were written against the Earl of Leicester.[1]

The evidence therefore points to Arundel as the most
likely author of this famous work. He seems to have been
endowed with literary ability as well as with force of
character, and the ability displayed in the libel is no less
conspicuous than its filthiness and scurrility. This is confirmed by the researches of the Catholic Record Society :

(*Leicester's Commonwealth*) appeared anonymously at
Paris or Rouen in September 1584. With our present
fairly full information we can say with some certainty
that the editor was Charles Arundel, with assistance of
other exiled followers of Mary Stuart.[2]

[1] Cal. S.P. Dom., Addenda, 29. 39.   [2] Vol. xxi, p. 58.

Arundel's death is referred to in a letter from the King
of Spain to Bernardino de Mendoza :

I learn by a letter of December 27th [1587] that Charles
Arundel had died of lethargy [*modorra*] and that you had
been obliged to assist him with money for his maintenance
during his last illness.   It was well you did this, for it was
an act of true piety ; and as the severity of his malady
prevented him from giving you a bill for the money so
provided, and you had also to find the money for his
funeral, he having left no property behind him, I approve
of the sum so expended being vouched for by your certificate only, receipts being furnished by the English doctor
who attended him, and by his servant, for the sums paid
to them through his confessor, the English Jesuit Father
Thomas.   You may therefore credit yourself in account
with these amounts, and this shall be your sufficient
warrant.   Madrid, January 1588.[1]

The story of a traitor is never pleasant, and Charles
Arundel's life and death is no exception to the rule.   But
it is, unfortunately, the case that many modern historians
have accepted at their face value the preposterous slanders
written by him about the Earls of Leicester and Oxford.
Whatever faults these two Earls may have had they were
never guilty of any unpatriotic action.

The King of Scots' opinion of *Leicester's Commonwealth*
is expressed very clearly in one of his Proclamations dated
at Holyrood, February 16th, 1584–5 :

For as much as we are credibly informed that there are
divers slanderous and infamous bruits readily brought in
and publicly dispersed in sundry hands within the Realm,
full of ignominies and reproachful calumnies devised and
set out by some seditious persons of purpose to obscure
with lewd lies the honour and reputation of our trusty
cousin the Earl of Leicester,—

Then follow the measures to be taken to suppress these
libellous books.[2]

It is to be hoped that in future all right-minded historians will follow the example of King James, and will

[1] Cal. S.P. Spanish (1587–1603), p. 187. [2] *Bibliotheca Lindesiana*, VI. 243.

never again advance the disgusting lies of the " suborned informer " Charles Arundel as reliable historical evidence.

§ III.   Her Majesty's Displeasure

Lord Oxford was released from the Tower on June 8th, 1581 ; but the Queen, irritated no doubt by the references to her in the Arundel accusations, still withheld from him full liberty.   In the following letter written in July to Lord Burghley the Earl complains both of this and other slanders with which he is assailed :

Robin Christmas [1] did yesterday tell me how honourably you had dealt with Her Majesty as touching my liberty, and that as this day she had made promises to your Lordship that it shall be.   Unless your Lordship shall make some [motion] to put Her Majesty in [mind] thereof, I fear, in these other causes of the two Lords, she will forget me.   For she is nothing of her own disposition, as I find, so ready to deliver as speedy to commit, and every little trifle gives her matter for a long delay.   I willed E. Hammond to report unto your Lordship Her Majesty's message unto me by Master Secretary Walsingham, which was to this effect : first, that she would have heard the matter again touching Henry Howard, Southwell, and Arundel ; then, that she understood that I meant to cut down all my woods especially about my house, which she did not so well like of as if I should sell some land else other- wise ; and last, that she heard that I had been hardly used by some of my servants during this time of my committal, wherein she promised her aid so far as she could, with justice to redress the loss I had sustained thereby.   To which I made answer as I willed Hammond to relate unto your Lordship.

Further, my Lord, whereof I am desirous something to write.   I have understood that certain of my men have reported unto your Lordship and sought by false reports of other of their fellows, both to abuse your Lordship and me ; but for that this bearer seems most nearly to be touched, I have sent him unto your Lordship as is his most earnest desire, that your Lordship might so know him, as your evil opinion being conceived amiss by these lewd fellows may be revoked.   And truly, my Lord, I hear of

[1] Robert Christmas and Roger Harlackenden were the Earl of Oxford's two principal estate agents.

these things wherewith he is charged, and I can assure you wrongfully and slanderously. But the world is so cunning as of a shadow they can make a substance, and of a likelihood a truth. And these fellows, if they be those —as I suppose—I do not doubt but so to decipher them to the world as easily as your Lordship shall look into their lewdness and unfaithfulness. Which, till my liberty, I mean to defer, as more mindful of that importing me at this time, than yet seeking to revenge myself of such perverse and impudent dealing of servants, which I know have not wanted encouragement and setting on.

But letting these things pass for a while, I must not forget to give your Lordship those thanks which are due to you for this your honourable dealing to Her Majesty on my behalf, which I hope shall not be without effect. The which, attending from the Court, I will take my leave of your Lordship, and rest at your commandment at my house this morning.

Your Lordship's assured,

EDWARD OXENFORD.[1]

But Her Majesty still continued to show her displeasure by forbidding him to come to Court, and by ordering him to keep to his house; and so Lord Burghley enlisted Walsingham on the Earl's behalf:

I dealt very earnestly with the Queen [wrote Walsingham in a letter to Burghley on July 14th] touching the Earl of Oxford's liberty, putting her in mind of her promise made both unto your Lordship and to the Lady his wife. The only stay groweth through the impertinent suit that is made for the delivery of the Lord Henry and Master Charles Arundel, whom, before their delivery, Her Majesty thinketh meet they should be confronted by the Earl, who hath made humble request to be set at liberty before he be brought to charge them, as he was at the time he first gave information against them. Her Majesty, notwithstanding the reasonableness of the request, and the promise made unto your Lordship that he should be first set at liberty before he be brought to confront them, cannot as yet be brought to yield. . . .[2]

In the same strain we find Burghley writing to Vice-

[1] Lansdowne MSS., 33. 6.   [2] Cal. S.P. Dom. (1581–90), p. 23.

Chamberlain Hatton, an important person to win over in any matter demanding the Queen's ear :

. . . yesterday, being advertised of your good and honourable dealing with Her Majesty in the case of my daughter of Oxford, I could not suffer my thanks to grow above one day old ; and therefore in these lines I do presently thank you, and do pray you in any proceeding therein not to have the Earl dealt withal strainably, but only by way of advice, as good for himself ; for otherwise he may suspect that I regard myself and my daughter more than he is regarded for his liberty.[1]

It is strange, on the face of it, to find Hatton apparently ready and willing to use his influence with the Queen in furthering Lord Oxford's cause. But there is little doubt that his assistance was more apparent than real, and that he continued to follow Dyer's sinister advice given nine years before. We have seen, moreover, that Hatton was, at this very time, secretly encouraging one of his literary protégés—Barnabe Riche—to write a thinly veiled satire designed to bring the Earl into ridicule. Nor is this all. Any lingering doubts as to Hatton's honesty of purpose must be finally dispelled when we find him receiving long letters from Oxford's worst enemy, Charles Arundel. These letters, like the rest of Arundel's effusions, are obscure and long-winded ; but the fact that he signs himself " your honour's fast and unfeigned friend " leaves little or no doubt as to where Hatton's true partisanship lay. In fact, the obviously genuine attempt by Burghley and Walsingham to get Lord Oxford restored to royal favour was very likely frustrated by the double-dealing of Master Vice-Chamberlain. It is evident that he must have had some powerful secret enemies standing between himself and the Queen, because with such strong allies as the Lord Treasurer and the Principal Secretary one would have imagined his release from the Tower would have coincided with his return to royal favour.

---

[1] Nicolas, *Life of Hatton*, p. 177.

16

On December 7th the Countess of Oxford made a fresh
appeal to her husband to bring their five-year-old separation
to an end :

My Lord, In what misery I may account myself to be,
that neither can see any end thereof nor yet any hope to
diminish it.　And now of late having had some hope in my
own conceit that your Lordship would have renewed some
part of your favour that you began to show me this summer,
when you made me assured of your good meaning, though
you seemed fearful how to show it by open address.　Now
after long silence of hearing anything from you, at the
length I am informed—but how truly I know not and yet
how uncomfortably I do not seek it—that your Lordship
is entered into for misliking of me without any cause in
deed or thought.　And therefore, my good Lord, I beseech
you in the name of that God, which knoweth all my
thoughts and love towards you, let me know the truth
of your meaning towards me ; upon what cause you are
moved to continue me in this misery, and what you would
have me do in my power to recover your constant favour,
so as your Lordship may not be led still to detain me in
calamity without some probable cause, whereof, I appeal
to God, I am utterly innocent.　From my father's house
at Westminster, the 7th December 1581.[1]

Her husband's reply is not recorded, but on the 12th
the Countess wrote again.　The original is lost, but a
transcript has been preserved which is endorsed : " A
copy of the Countess of Oxford's letter for answer to her
husband's letter."

My very good Lord, I most heartily thank you for your
letter, and am most sorry to perceive how you are un-
quieted with the uncertainty of the world, whereof I myself
am not without some taste.　But seeing you will me to
assure myself of anything that I may as your wife challenge of you, I will the more patient abide the adversity
which otherwise I fear, and—if God would so permit
it and that it might be good for you—I would leave the
greater part of your adverse fortune, and make it my
comfort to bear part with you.　As for my father, I do
assure you, whatsoever hath been reported of him, I know

---

[1] Lansdowne MSS., 104. 63.　A copy only.

no man can wish better to you than he doth, and yet the practices in Court I fear do make seek to make contrary shows.

For my Lady Drury [1] I deal as little with her as any can, and care no more for her than you would have me ; but I have been driven sometimes, for avoiding of malice and envy, to do that with both her and others which I would not with my will do.   Good my Lord, assure yourself it is you whom only I love and fear, and so am desirous above all the world to please you, wishing that I might hear oftener from you until better fortune will have us meet together. [2]

Early in March 1582 a fresh trouble overtook Lord Oxford. This was a quarrel with Thomas Knyvet, a Gentleman of the Privy Chamber.

In England of late [writes Faunt to Anthony Bacon on March 17th] there hath been a fray between my Lord of Oxford and Master Thomas Knyvet of the Privy Chamber, who are both hurt, but my Lord of Oxford more dangerously. You know Master Knyvet is not meanly beloved in Court, and therefore he is not likely to speed ill whatsoever the quarrel be. [3]

The only other detail about this quarrel is to be found in a note in the Diary of the Rev. Richard Madox, who had been appointed Chaplain to the proposed expedition for the discovery of the north-west passage under Captain Edward Fenton.   Writing on March 3rd he says that—

My Lord of Oxford fought with Master Knyvet about the quarrel of Bessie Bavisar, and was hurt, which grieved

---

[1] Lady Drury (*née* Elizabeth Stafford) had been a Maid of Honour, with Anne Cecil, before her marriage to Sir William Drury. He had left her a widow in 1579. He had been with Lord Sussex in the Scottish campaign of 1570. He was a distinguished soldier, his greatest feat being the storming of Edinburgh Castle in 1573, which was then held by Maitland and Grange on behalf of the Queen of Scots.

[2] Lansdowne MSS., 104. 64.

[3] Birch, *Memoirs of the Reign of Queen Elizabeth*, vol. i, p. 22. Thomas Knyvet (*d.* 1618) was probably one of the Knyvets of Buckenham Castle, Norfolk, and connected by marriage with the Earls of Derby. On Jan. 21st, 1582—just two months before the quarrel—he had been appointed Keeper of Westminster Palace. He was knighted some time before 1601, and seems to have held the Keepership until his death.

the Lord Treasurer so much the more for that the Earl hath company with his wife since Christmas. But through this mishap, and through the pains he took at the marriage of another daughter to my Lord Wentworth on Shroveday, my Lord Treasurer was sick.[1]

It is possible, to a certain extent, to reconstruct the story of this quarrel if we may assume that Madox really meant "Anne Vavasour" when he wrote "Bessie Bavisar." Anne Vavasour was one of the Maids of Honour.[2] She had evidently fallen in love with Lord Oxford, as the following verses, preserved in a manuscript in the Bodleian Library, show :

VERSES MADE BY THE EARLE OF OXFORDE

Sittinge alone upon my thoughte, in melancholy moode,
In sighte of sea, and at my back an ancyente hoarye woode,
I sawe a faire young lady come, her secret feares to wayle,
Cladd all in coulor of a Nun and covered with a vaylle :
Yet (for the day was callme and cleere) I myghte discerne her face,
As one myghte see a damaske rose hid under christall glasse :
Three tymes with her softe hand full harde on her left syde she knocks,
And syghed so sore as myghte have movde som pittye in the rockes :
From syghes, and sheddinge amber teares, into sweete songe she brake,
When thus the Echo answered her to everye word she spake :

ANN VAVESOR'S ECCHO

O heavens, who was ye first that bredd in me this feavere ?   *Vere.*
Whoe was the firste that gave ye wounde whose fearre I ware for evere ?
    Vere.
What tyrant, Cupid, to mye harme usurpes thy golden quivere ?   *Vere.*
What wighte first caughte this harte, and can from bondage it deliver ?
    Vere.
Yet who doth most adore this wighte, oh hollowe caves tell true ?   *You.*
What nymphe deservs his lykinge best, yet doth in sorrowe rue ?   *You.*
What makes him not rewarde good will with some rewarde or ruthe ?
    Youth.
May I his favour matche with love, if he my love will trye ?   *I.*
May I requite his birthe with faythe ? than faithfull will I dy ?   *I.*

          And I that knew this ladye well,
          Said Lord how great a mirakle
          To he[a]r how eccho toulde the truthe
          As true as Phoebus orakle.[3]

---

[1] Cotton MSS., Appendix 47.

[2] She was the daughter of Henry Vavasour of Coppenthorpe, and had a sister, Frances, also a Maid of Honour. There is no trace of any Vavasour of the name "Elizabeth," or "Bess," at the Court at this time.

[3] Bodleian, Rawlinson Poetical MS., 85. 11.

History does not relate how Thomas Knyvet came to be concerned in the matter. It seems probable that he was another of Anne's lovers. He was not her future husband, because she ultimately married Sir Henry Lee, Queen Elizabeth's Champion-at-Arms. But three years later, on January 19th, 1585, a certain Thomas Vavasour, who had been connected in a minor way with the Arundel accusations, sent Lord Oxford a challenge. This curious document is endorsed : " A lewd letter from Vavasour to the Earl of Oxford " :

If thy body had been as deformed as thy mind is dishonourable, my house had been yet unspotted, and thyself remained with thy cowardice unknown. I speak this that I fear thou art so much wedded to that shadow of thine, that nothing can have force to awake thy base and sleepy spirits. Is not the revenge taken of thy victims sufficient,[1] but wilt thou yet use unworthy instruments to provoke my unwilling mind ? Or dost thou fear thyself, and therefore hast sent thy forlorn kindred, whom as thou hast left nothing to inherit so thou dost thrust them violently into thy shameful quarrels ? If it be so (as I too much doubt) then stay at home thyself and send my abuses ; but if there be yet any spark of honour left in thee, or iota of regard of thy decayed reputation, use not thy birth for an excuse, for I am a gentleman, but meet me thyself alone and thy lackey to hold thy horse. For the weapons I leave them to thy choice for that I challenge, and the place to be appointed by us both at our meeting, which I think may conveniently be at Nunnington or elsewhere. Thyself shall send me word by this bearer, by whom I expect an answer.

THO. VAVASOR.[2]

Nothing more is definitely known about the Knyvet affair or its sequel. There is, however, preserved at the British Museum a long " declaration " by Roger Townsend,.

---

[1] This is evidently a reference to the just revenge Lord Oxford took on Lord Henry Howard and Charles Arundel in December 1583.

[2] Lansdowne MSS., 99. 93. I can find no other trace of Thomas Vavasour, or the sequel to his bombastic outburst. I daresay he was " dealt " with in the same way as his friend Charles Arundel had been.

Lord Arundel's private secretary, " touching the bruit
given out that the Earl of Oxford should have attempted
somewhat against Master Tho. Knevet." [1] This document,
unfortunately, gives us no details of the duel in March,
although it is dated June 18th.   But one interesting piece
of side-evidence comes out of it.   This is that Lord Oxford
was supping with his brother-in-law Lord Willoughby de
Eresby at Willoughby House, and that the two men were
obviously on friendly terms.

In the absence of any other documents on the subject
it is difficult to follow the exact meaning of this " declaration."   It appears that Knyvet and Townsend were dining
with Lord Arundel at Arundel House when word was
brought that the Earl of Oxford and Lord Willoughby were
planning to lie in wait for Knyvet and to attack him.
Townsend went round to Willoughby House, where he
found Oxford and Willoughby, having supped together,
walking in the garden.   After an interview with them
Townsend asserts that—

truly I did think in my conscience there was nothing
intent, for there was none in the company prepared [i.e.
armed] to any purpose.

It has been supposed that the duel between Oxford and
Knyvet took place *after* the events described in this
" declaration."   This is manifestly wrong, because the
duel took place before March 3rd, while the " declaration "
is dated June 18th.

It will be remembered that in 1577 Lord Willoughby,
then Peregrine Bertie, became engaged to Lady Mary
Vere, Oxford's only sister.   The Earl's opposition to the
marriage was so violent that, in Bertie's own words, " he
bandeth against me and sweareth my death."   It seems
likely that Oxford's secret reconciliation to the Roman
Church, which dated from 1576, may have led to his anger
at finding his sister engaged to an out-and-out Protestant.
At all events, they were on very friendly terms in June

---

[1] Lansdowne MSS., 154. 13. Printed in *Catholic Record Society*, xxi.

1582, by which time Lord Oxford had publicly recanted
his profession of the Catholic faith.

The quarrel with Knyvet, now a year old, seems to
have broken out afresh among their retainers in February
1583, for on the 21st of that month the Parish Registers
of St. Botolph's near Bishopsgate record the burial of
" Robart Brenings, ye L. Oxford's man, slayne 21 Febr."
And in March 1583 Lord Burghley was once more endeavouring to interest Hatton on Oxford's behalf.   The tenor of
his letter shows clearly how difficult it was for a courtier
who was out of favour to obtain justice, particularly when
he was embarrassed by enemies, both secret and open :

Good Master Vice Chamberlain, . . . I perceive yesterday,
by my Lord of Leicester, that you had very friendly
delivered speeches to Her Majesty tending to bring some
good end to these troublesome matters betwixt my Lord
of Oxford and Master Knevet. . . . And now perceiving by
my Lord of Leicester some increase of Her Majesty's
offence towards my Lord of Oxford,[1] and finding by
Master Thomas Knyvet that he only being called and
demanded of Her Majesty what he would say herein, he
did, as served his turn, declare to Her Majesty that his
men were evil used by Lord Oxford's men, and no redress
had.   I cannot but think that Her Majesty had just
occasion given by such an information to be offended
towards my Lord of Oxford or his men ; and did therefore,
like a Prince of justice and God's minister, command the
matter to be examined, which was done yesterday at
great length by my Lord of Leicester to his trouble and
my grief.   And I doubt not but my Lord of Leicester
will honourably declare to Her Majesty how my Lord of
Oxford resteth untouched, or at least unblotted, in any
kind of matter objected by Master Knyvet, whom we
heard at great length, and his men also . . . so as, where
Her Majesty had just cause to conceive somewhat hardly
of my Lord of Oxford, I doubt not but when Her Majesty
shall be informed by my Lord of Leicester of the truth
which he hath seen and not disproved, Her Majesty will
diminish her offensive opinion.

[1] It is not surprising to find Hatton's " friendly " speeches merely
increasing Her Majesty's " offence " towards Lord Oxford.

Good Master Vice Chamberlain, these things are hardly carried, and these advantages are easily gotten where some may say what they will against my Lord of Oxford, and have presence to utter their humours, and my Lord of Oxford is neither heard nor hath presence either to complain or defend himself.   And so long as he shall be subject to the disgrace of Her Majesty (from which God deliver him) I see it apparently that, innocent soever he shall be, the advantages will fall out with his adversaries ; and so, I hear, they do prognosticate.

Lord Burghley goes on to complain that the Queen has been told that the Earl is going about with a retinue of " fifteen or sixteen pages in a livery " ; but so far from this being the case, Lord Burghley asserts that his household consists of only four :

One of them waiteth upon his wife my daughter, another is in my house upon his daughter Bess, a third is a kind of tumbling boy, and the fourth is a son of a brother of Sir John Cutts. . . . When our son-in-law was in prosperity he was the cause of our adversity by his unkind usage of us and ours ; and now that he is ruined and in adversity we are only made partakers thereof, and by no means, no, not by bitter tears of my wife, can obtain a spark of favour for him, that hath satisfied his offence with punishment, and seeketh mercy by submission ; but contrariwise whilst we seek for favour all crosses are laid against him, and by untruths sought to be kept in disgrace.[1]

But Lord Oxford's term of disgrace and long separation from his wife was now drawing to a close.   The first indication of this is to be found in a letter written in May, where we read that " the Earl of Oxford . . . had a son born, who died soon after his birth." [2]   His burial is recorded in the Parish Register of the Church at Castle Hedingham : " 1583. May 9th. The Earl of Oxenford's first son."   This entry is interesting because it shows that the Earl and his Countess were evidently then living at the Castle.   This definitely gives the lie

---

[1] Nicolas, op. cit., p. 321.
[2] Birch, *Memoirs of the Reign of Queen Elizabeth*, vol. i, p. 31.

to one of those foolish and persistent legends that have grown up round Lord Oxford's life. All historians assert with confidence that when Lord Oxford had failed to obtain Burghley's assistance in saving the life of the Duke of Norfolk—

he swore he would ruin his estate at Hedingham, because it was the jointure of his first wife Anne, Lord Burghley's daughter. According to this insane resolution, he not only forsook his Lady's bed, but sold and wasted the best part of his inheritance ; he began to deface the Castle, pulled down the outhouses, destroyed all the pales of the three parks, wasted the standing timber and pulled down the walls that enclosed the Castle.[1]

This absurd story, for which it need hardly be said there is not a shred of evidence, can now be relegated to the limbo it deserves.

We are not told when or how the reconciliation between the Earl and his Countess took place, but we may be sure that it must have been a great relief to the Queen and Lord Burghley. Ever since the disastrous quarrel nearly six years before, Lord and Lady Oxford had lived apart. Now, with the healing of the breach, tempered as it was with sadness at the young Lord Bulbeck's death, brighter times seemed in store.

And the Queen, who was always solicitous for the happiness of the young couple whose marriage she had graced, was not slow to forgive her old favourite. On June 2nd Roger Manners wrote thus to the Earl of Rutland :

Her Majesty came yesterday to Greenwich from the Lord Treasurer's. . . . The day she came away, which was yesterday, the Earl of Oxford came to her presence, and after some bitter words and speeches, in the end all sins are forgiven, and he may repair to the Court at his pleasure. Master Ralegh was a great mean herein, whereat Pondus is angry for that he could not do so much.[2]

The two years' disgrace was over at last, and Lord

[1] See p. 387, *post*.
[2] Cal. Rutland MSS. " Pondus " I take to be a nickname for Lord Burghley.

Oxford, now aged thirty-three, once more took his place
in Gloriana's Court.

§ IV. ELSINORE

In July 1583 Lord Willoughby de Eresby was entrusted
with an important diplomatic mission by the Queen.
He was ordered to go to Elsinore, and there to invest
King Frederick II. with the Order of the Garter. Under
King Frederick's rule Denmark had risen to be one of
the Great Powers on the Continent. He had achieved
this by means of his sea power in the Baltic ; and " before
he died he was able to enforce the rule that all foreign ships
should strike their top-sails to Danish men-of-war as a
token of his right to rule the Northern seas." [1]

In consequence of their command of the Baltic the Danes
had claimed the right to levy dues on all foreign merchant
ships passing through the Sound. This had at first been
a severe blow to the English " Muscovy Company," which
since 1553 had been engaged in a profitable trade with
Russia. The merchants, however, hit upon a way out of
the difficulty by altering their base of operations to the
White Sea, and the trade was continued by way of the
North Cape. King Frederick, who found himself losing
his dues, wrote rather unreasonably to Elizabeth in 1576
protesting against this northern traffic route, and cited
certain old treaties by which merchant ships were bound to
trade with Russia via the Baltic.[2] Elizabeth brought all
her diplomatic powers into play, and nothing seems to have
happened beyond an exchange of notes. But her decision
to confer the Garter on the Danish King was not un-
connected with the diplomatic manœuvres she was engaged
in on behalf of her merchants.

The account of this mission is told in a " Relation of
my Lord Willoughby's embassy into Denmark, in his own
hand." [3] He sailed from Hull on July 14th, and landed at

---

[1] *Encyc. Brit.* (11th ed.), vol. viii, p. 32.
[2] Cf. E. P. Cheyney, *History of England,* vol. i, p. 329.
[3] Cotton MSS., Titus., CVII. 226.

Elsinore on the 22nd [1]; and on August 12th the Danish Chancellor came to his ship—

to know of me what points I had to treat with him, and in what order I meant to present them ; whom I answered my chief negotiation was to present Her Majesty's loving commendation, and for witness of her honourable opinion of him [i.e. the King] she had sent to honour him with the most famous and ancient Order of the Garter ; likewise I had to present certain grievances of some English merchants unto them, who thought themselves somewhat hardly dealt withal generally for great exactions and tolls meanly imposed upon them.

Two days later the ceremony took place to the accompaniment of a characteristically Danish custom :

The King, very royally prepared, received the robes with his own hands, and with great contentment accepted and wore the Garter, the Collar, and the George. . . . This being done we royally feasted, and the King all the ordnance of the Castle given us.[2] And we, demanding again the oath and protestation to be answerable to that favour and honour he had received from Her Majesty, he promised this instrument [i.e. document] which we have delivered, accompanied with many affectionate and loving speeches to Her Majesty and all of the Order. All of which performed after a whole volley of all the great shot of the Castle discharged, a royal feast, and a most artificial and cunning fireworks.

During the next few days Lord Willoughby and his retinue were entertained at the Castle and were taken hunting. The negotiations with regard to the Muscovy Company and the Russia trade were continued, it would seem, without any very definite result ; and the " Lord Ambassador, returning with his train, arrived at Broome-holme in Norfolk on September 20th." [3]

---

[1] The MS. reads " June," which is a slip of the pen. (Cf. Stow, *Annals*, p. 695.)

[2] The last sentence has been lightly scratched out in the MS.

[3] Stow, *Annals*, p. 695.

§ V. The North-west Passage

Before we go on to follow up Lord Oxford's return to
Court in June 1583, we must for a moment retrace our
steps and consider another interest that had been occupying
his mind during the past five years. This was Martin
Frobisher's famous attempts to discover a north-west
passage to China. But if Frobisher's story is to be fully
understood it must be framed in its historical context ;
and the construction of this frame first began when
Columbus discovered America in 1492.

The immense influence that this had upon the development of England cannot be too strongly emphasised.
From being situated in the " uttermost parts of the earth "
she gradually began to find herself in the centre—stationed
midway, as it were, between Europe and America. Unless
the psychological effect that this material cause had upon
the national character is recognised, the sea-faring exploits
of England under the last of the Tudors cannot be fully
understood.

Another factor, which is so well known that it scarcely
needs repeating, is that the English were a sea-faring
nation. They had to be, for England is an island, and all
foreign intercourse had to be conducted by means of ships.

At first there were not many signs of Englishmen seizing
the opportunities thus thrown open. True, the necessity
for sea-power was being felt, for it was in the reign of
King Henry VII. that the Royal Navy came into being.
But during the next three reigns the religious question
largely eclipsed everything else, including overseas exploration and enterprise.

With the accession of Elizabeth, however, a host of
adventurers came into the field.[1] The personal interest she
displayed in her seamen, and the money she subscribed
towards their overseas trading ventures (often indistinguish-
able from sheer piracy !) were not the least important
factors in the rise of English sea-power.

[1] Cal. S.P. Colonial, East Indies (1513–1616), Preface.

It was in 1565 that Anthony Jenckynson first urged the Queen to attempt the discovery of a shorter route to the " renowned Cathay," asserting that if this were done she would become the richest and most famous Princess in Christendom.   Next year, however, Jenckynson was sent on a voyage to Russia ; and it devolved mainly upon three other men, Humphrey Gilbert, Michael Lok, and Dr. Dee, to follow up his suggestion.

Lok and Gilbert were both experienced sailors, and Dee was the most famous mathematician and astronomer of his time.   About Easter 1575 the three men met, and their meeting resulted in the publication, a year later, of a pamphlet written by Gilbert called *A Discourse of a Discovery for a new passage to Cataia*.   It is not without interest that Lord Oxford's old acquaintance George Gascoigne, himself a " kinsman " of Martin Frobisher, was instrumental in procuring its publication.[1]

Lack of money prevented the enterprise from materialising that year ; but on June 12th, 1576, two barks of 25 tons and a pinnace of 10 tons under the command of Captain Martin Frobisher left Gravesend.

On October 2nd the expedition was back at Harwich, and although there was much rejoicing at their safe return, it had been a financial failure.   The total cost had been £1,600, of which Lok himself had subscribed nearly half ; but the profits, including the sale of the ships, only realised about £800.   Among the other " adventurers " who had invested sums of money varying from £25 to £50 were the Earl of Sussex, the Earl of Leicester, Lord Burghley, the Lord Admiral, Francis Walsingham, and Philip Sidney.

Nothing daunted by this preliminary failure, a second and much greater expedition was decided on for the following year.   The total cost this time was estimated at £4,500, the Queen giving a lead by subscribing £1,000.

---

[1] *Encyc. Brit.* art. *Gascoigne* : " Sir Humphrey Gilbert's *Discourse of a Discovery for a new passage to Cataia* has led to the assertion that Gascoigne printed the tract against its author's wishes ; but it is likely that he was really serving Gilbert, who desired the publication but dared not avow it."

Many new names, as well as those who had contributed to the first voyage, appear in the list of adventurers.[1]

Frobisher's second voyage lasted from May till September 1577. The most noticeable feature it presents is that the original intention to discover a north-west passage to China has been quite lost sight of, for we find the expedition returning with a large quantity of what they claimed to be " gold ore." The greatest excitement prevailed. Samples of the " ore " were sent to the mint to be tested ; and Lok asserted that in his opinion they would realise a profit of £40 a ton.

During the winter many contradictory statements as to the value of the " ore " were issued. One of the analysts estimated that each ton would yield 10 ounces of gold ; another declared that he could find no trace of any precious metal ; while Dee himself signed a statement in which he claimed to have obtained 7 ounces of silver from 2 cwt. of the ore. Optimism ran high, and encouraged no doubt by Dee's report, a new and still greater expedition was decided on. This time the cost was to be £15,000. Eleven ships were acquired, and Frobisher was instructed to bring back 500 tons of the ore.

Four days before the ships sailed Lord Oxford, who was an old friend of Dee, sent the following letter to the Commissioners who were organising the venture :

To my very loving friends William Pelham and Thomas Randolph Esquires : Master Yongem, Master Hogan, Master Field ; and others the Commissioners for the voyage to *Meta Incognita*.

After my very hearty commendations : Understanding of the wise proceeding and orderly dealing for the continuing of the voyage for the discovery of Cathay by the north west (which this bearer, my friend Master Frobisher, hath already very honourably attempted and is now eftsoons to be employed for the better achieving thereof) ; and the rather induced, as well for the great liking Her Majesty hath to have the same passage discovered, as also for the special good favour I bear to Master Frobisher,

---

[1] Cal. S.P. Colonial, 17.

to offer unto you to be an adventurer therein for the sum of £1,000 or more, if you like to admit thereof; which sum or sums, upon your certificate of admittance, I will enter into bond, shall be paid for that use unto you upon Michaelmas day next coming. Requesting your answers therein, I bid you heartily farewell. From the Court, the 21st of May 1578.

Your loving friend,

EDWARD OXENFORD.[1]

Not content with this, the Earl bought in addition £2,000 worth of stock from Michael Lok, whose share had by this time risen to £5,000.[2] Lord Oxford's venture was now £3,000, which made him the biggest single investor in the enterprise.

On September 25th the convoy returned and anchored off the Cornish coast. Frobisher immediately repaired to the Court at Richmond, and samples of the ore were brought to London to be tested. But the high hopes of the adventurers were destined to be utterly dashed to the ground. The ore was found to be absolutely worthless, and not a particle of gold or silver was forthcoming.

As soon as the bubble was pricked everybody started looking for a scapegoat, and the unfortunate Lok was attacked on all sides. On November 20th Frobisher, with forty men, came to his house in a fury, and accused him not only of falsifying the accounts, but also of having " cozened " Lord Oxford of £1,000 because he knew, asserted Frobisher, that the ore was worthless when he sold his shares.[2] In vain Lok protested his innocence, and he was imprisoned in the Fleet.

This disaster damped the spirits of the adventurers, but two years later a fresh development occurred. This was the return to Plymouth of the *Golden Hind*, in which Drake had successfully completed his famous circumnavigation voyage. Her cargo, however, was not mere worthless earth, but solid ingots of pure gold and silver captured from the Spanish treasure-ships off the coast of Peru. For a time the fate of Drake's capture hung in the balance, some

---

[1] S.P. Dom., 149. 42.   [2] Cal. S.P. Colonial, 50. 64.

of the Council holding that his seizure of the Spanish
ships was an act of piracy. But ultimately the Queen
decided that he had acted within his rights, and the
treasure was divided up among the adventurers.

Those who held shares in Drake's voyage immediately
became enormously wealthy. The exact amounts they
received are not known, but one authority states that a
dividend of 4,700 per cent. was paid. Working on this
basis Sir Julian Corbett estimates that " the Queen's
private share on her investment of a thousand crowns
would be £11,750 ; which, being equal to nearly £90,000
of our money, goes far to account for the favour she showed
Drake." [1] A Royal Warrant gives Leicester a share of
£4,000 and Hatton £2,300. But it is probable that these
figures, for diplomatic reasons, fall far short of the real
figures. Another estimate puts the Queen's share at over
£150,000 sterling, so we may perhaps guess that Hatton's
share was really more like £30,000. [2]

The remarkable success which had attended Drake
heartened the adventurers, and in September 1581 a
fresh project was mooted. Once again Frobisher was to
have command, but this time the course was to be south-
west instead of north-west. The prime mover seems to
have been the Earl of Leicester, who was flushed no doubt
by his recent success. For £2,000 he acquired a two-thirds
share in the flag-ship, a galleon of 400 tons, which was
renamed the *Leicester*. [3] He also induced Lord Shrewsbury
to come in for £800, which included a part share in
the bark *Talbot*. But Frobisher's previous ill success
had aroused distrust among courtiers who had money
to invest ; and on October 1st he wrote rather dole-
fully to Leicester that " he has not moved Sir Francis
Walsingham nor any of the rest but my Lord of Oxford,
who bears me in hand, and would buy the *Edward*

---

[1] Corbett, *Drake and the Tudor Navy*, vol. i, p. 410.

[2] E. F. Benson, *Sir Francis Drake*, p. 174. As Drake had rechristened
his ship the *Golden Hind*, after Sir Christopher Hatton's crest, we may
surmise that he was not the least of the adventurers in the voyage.

[3] Cal. S.P. Colonial, 72. 76.

Bonaventure " ; adding that he has offered £1,500 for
her, but the owners are holding out for £1,800.[1] As
the *Edward Bonaventure* ultimately sailed we must conclude that Lord Oxford was successful in buying her, but
no record of the sale exists.

In the list of adventurers [2] many names that had
appeared in Frobisher's previous voyages, notably that
of the Queen, are missing. There were three ships : the
galleon *Ughtrede* (renamed the *Leicester*), the *Edward
Bonaventure*, and the bark *Talbot*, their total value being
entered as £6,400. In addition, about £8,000 was subscribed, the principal adventurers being the Earl of
Leicester and Mr. Ughtrede, £3,000 [3] ; Sir Francis Drake,
£700 ; the Earl of Oxford, £500 ; Martin Frobisher, £300 ;
and Edward Fenton, £300. Among the other investors
who came in with smaller sums we find Sir Francis Walsingham, Sir Christopher Hatton, and Lord Burghley.

In February Frobisher's instructions were drawn up by
Burghley and Leicester. In them he is told that trade is
the main object of the voyage ; but, provided it does not
interfere with trading, exploration and discovery may be
carried out as well.[4] Both Frobisher and Drake knew
this to be quite impossible. Frobisher, who was interested
chiefly in the exploration side of the undertaking, did not
wish his hands tied with such restrictions. He accordingly
resigned the command, and Edward Fenton was appointed
in his place.[5]

Fenton's instructions were signed on April 9th by
Leicester, Burghley, and Walsingham.[6] They were in
substance the same as those that had been drafted for
Frobisher, though, if anything, more stringent. This

---

[1] Cal. S.P. Colonial, 67.   [2] Ibid., 73.
[3] Henry Ughtrede was a shipbuilder of Netley in Hampshire. He
owned the *Edward Bonaventure* and had just completed building the
Ughtrede. On July 2nd, 1581, he was given the usual ship subsidy of 5s.
per ton for " his new ship the galleon *Ughtrede* of 500 tons " (Privy Seal
Warrants, E. 403–2559). This subsidy had been granted by the Queen in
order to encourage ship construction in the country.
[4] Cal. S.P. Colonial, 75.   [5] Ibid., p. xxiv.   [6] Ibid., 77

interference by landsmen in purely sea matters was bound
to end disastrously. All Drake's marvellous successes had
been gained because his genius had been allowed free rein,
and he had been able, untrammelled by orders and restrictions, to draw up his plans of campaign according to the
requirements of the ever-changing situations.

Various delays occurred, and during the spring the ships
lay moored in the Thames, where they were visited by the
Queen—who " passed by us in a barge "—and by Leicester,
Walsingham, and Gilbert. At length, towards the end
of May, they weighed anchor, and by 11 p.m. on June 1st
were " athwart the Lizard sailing west-south-west." [1]

The following May, after nearly a year's absence, the
expedition returned to England. But it was a sorry report
that Captain Edward Fenton had to deliver to the Lord
Treasurer. The object of the voyage—honest and peaceable trading—had been totally defeated by the King of
Spain's edict. Wherever they touched the inhabitants
refused to have anything to do with them, for they had
express orders from Madrid " to deny the French, and
especially the English, any relief, in respect of the spoils
and robberies committed by Sir Francis Drake in the
South Seas." Fenton goes on to give an account of how
they were attacked by three Spanish ships, and their
flagship sunk. We may sympathise with him when he
exclaims that such wrongs are not to be put up with,
although Drake had shown quite clearly how to turn
Spanish wrongs to a most profitable account.

Once more Lord Oxford's venture had turned out to be
a complete failure ; and one cannot help remarking on the
strange caprice of fortune that had almost ruined Oxford
and at the same time had enriched his bitter rival Sir
Christopher Hatton beyond the dreams of avarice. It is
interesting, in this connexion, to recall Barnabe Riche's
Farewell to Military Profession, which he had dedicated
to Hatton in 1581. In it he gives a glowing account of
his patron's generosity and munificence which can un-

[1] Cal. S.P. Colonial, 85–7.

questionably be traced to Drake's windfall in 1580. The tables had been completely turned. Lord Oxford, who at the height of his power had poked fun in *The Adventures of Master F. I.* at the indigent Gentleman Pensioner Christopher Hatton, now found himself in turn lampooned by the protégé of the wealthy and powerful Vice Chamberlain.

Fenton's unfortunate voyage did not check Lord Oxford's interest in maritime exploration. In 1584 we find that in company with the Earls of Leicester and Bedford he was a shareholder in the new company known as " The Colleagues of the Fellowship for the Discovery of the North West Passage." The moving spirits of this company were Adrian Gilbert, Dr. Dee, and Walter Ralegh. In the following year they fitted out under the command of Captain John Davis an expedition which penetrated farther than Frobisher had done into the ice-bound waters. The fact that the name of Davis Straits continues to the present day is in itself sufficient evidence of the importance of the voyage. Soon afterwards relations with Spain became so strained that little or no " adventuring " for trade was done for some time. For the moment our seamen's attention was wholly diverted to that entertaining pastime which Drake called " singeing the King of Spain's beard." And it was not till 1600, when the Spaniards had practically shot their bolt, that English trade began its rapid development and expansion under the East India Company.

§ VI. THE WAR WITH SPAIN : THE LOW COUNTRIES

Although Ralegh had been " a great mean " in getting the Earl of Oxford restored to royal favour, he evidently thought that he was more likely to lose than gain by having helped to rehabilitate the Earl in the Queen's good graces. On May 12th, 1583, he had written thus to Lord Burghley :

The evening after the receipt of your Lordship's letter I spake with Her Majesty ; and ministering some occasion

touching the Earl of Oxford I told Her Majesty how
grievously your Lordship received her late discomfortable
answer. Her Majesty, as your Lordship had written—I
know not by whom lately and strangely persuaded—purposed to have a new repartition between the Lord Howard,
Arundel and others, and the Earl ; and said it was a
matter not so slightly to be passed over. I answered that
being assured Her Majesty would never permit anything
to be prosecuted to the Earl's danger—if any such possibility were—and that therefore it were to small purpose,
after so long absence and so many disgraces, to call his
honour and name again in question, whereby he might
appear the less fit either for her presence or favour.

In conclusion Her Majesty confessed that she meant it
only thereby to give the Earl warning ; and that, as it
seemed to me, being acquainted with his offences her grace
might seem the more in remitting the revenge or punishment of the same. I delivered her your Ladyship's
letter ; and what I said further how honourable and
profitable it were for [Her] Majesty to have regard to your
Lordship's health and quiet, I leave to the witness of God
and good report of Her Highness. And the more to
witness how desirous I am of your Lordship's favour and
good opinion, I am content, for your sake, to lay the
serpent before the fire as much as in me lieth ; that,
having recovered strength, myself may be most in danger
of his poison and sting. . . .[1]

The reason for Ralegh's apprehension—which proved
quite groundless—was no doubt Oxford's well-known
intolerance towards upstart courtiers who, though lacking
in birth, were nevertheless becoming daily more and more
powerful.[2] Naunton relates that when the Earl of Essex
was executed in 1601, Lord Oxford, apropos of Ralegh's
share in bringing about his downfall, remarked, " When
Jacks start up, heads go down." In justice to Ralegh,

---

[1] Lansdowne MSS., 39. 22.

[2] Peck, in his *Desiderata Curiosa*, said that he proposed to publish a
manuscript called " A pleasant conceit of Vere, Earl of Oxford, discontented
at the rising of a mean gentleman in the English Court, *circa* 1580." I
have been unable to trace this manuscript, which does not seem to have
been published ; but the date makes it probable that Ralegh was the
" mean gentleman " referred to.

who though not of the nobility was of good family,
Naunton adds that this " savours more of his Lordship's
humour than of the truth."

The Earl of Oxford's first act on being restored to favour
was to ask his father-in-law to intervene on behalf of his
friend and cousin Lord Lumley. Lumley, once a member
of the Privy Council, had been utterly ruined, and indeed
had nearly lost his life, owing to the part he had played
in the Ridolphi Plot in 1571. His political downfall had
led him to devote the remainder of his life to scholarship
and literature. For fifty years he was the High Steward
of Oxford University ; and he collected what must then
have been the finest library of books and manuscripts
in England. This library was afterwards bought by
King James I. for his son Prince Henry ; and now forms
the collection known as the " Royal Library " in the
British Museum. His friendship with Lord Oxford is
not only evidenced by the following letter, but by the
fact that at his death Lumley was in possession of a
" statuary," or full-length portrait of the Earl. This
is interesting because it shows us that Lord Oxford, even
after his restoration to royal favour, was still seeking his
friends among men of letters rather than among politicians
and courtiers.

I have been an earnest suitor [he writes to Lord Burghley
on June 20th] unto your Lordship for my Lord Lumley,
that it would please you for my sake to stand his good Lord
and friend, which as I perceive your Lordship hath already
very honourably performed ; the which I am in a number
of things more than I can reckon bound unto your Lordship, so am I in this likewise especially. For he hath
matched with a near kinswoman of mine, to whose father
I was always beholden unto for his assured and kind
disposition unto me. Further, among all the rest of my
blood, this only remains in account either of me or else
of them, as your Lordship doth know very well, the rest
having embraced further alliances to leave their nearer
consanguinity.

And as I hope your Lordship doth account me now—on whom you have so much bound—as I am ; so be you before any else in the world, both through match—whereby I count my greatest stay,—and by your Lordship's friendly usage and sticking by me in this time wherein I am hedged in with so many enemies. So likewise I hope your Lordship will take all them for your followers and most at command which are inclined and affected to me. Wherefore I say once again—being thus bound with your Lordship—to be so importunate in this matter, I crave your Lordship's favour in easing my Lord Lumley's payment to Her Majesty, wherein we will all give your Lordship thanks, and you shall do me as great an honour therein as a profit of it had been to myself. In this, through your Lordship's favour, I shall be able to pleasure my friend and stand needless of others who have forsaken me. Thus, for that your Lordship is troubled with many matters where you are, I crave pardon for troubling you.

Your Lordship's to command,

EDWARD OXEFORD.[1]

Lord Lumley had married secondly Elizabeth Darcy, daughter of John, second Lord Darcy of Chiche (1525–82). Her grandmother was Elizabeth de Vere, Lord Oxford's aunt. The Darcys lived at St. Osyth's Priory in Essex, which had been granted to Thomas, first Lord Darcy (1506–58) on the dissolution of the monasteries. The parish of St. Osyth borders that of Wivenhoe, and Lord Oxford's friendship with John, Lord Darcy, dates no doubt from the time that he was living in " his new country Muses of Wivenhoe." In the chancel of St. Osyth's Church are the recumbent effigies of Thomas and his wife Elizabeth de Vere, and John and his wife Frances, sister of Richard, Lord Rich. It is fair to conjecture that John Lord Darcy stood by the Earl of Oxford during the troubles of 1581, which would account for Oxford's speaking of " his assured and kind disposition unto me " in the letter just quoted.

Having thus done what he could to help his friend, Lord

---

[1] Lansdowne MSS., 38. 62.

Oxford turned relentlessly on his enemies, who soon felt the full fury of his revenge. Before November Lord Henry Howard was once more placed under restraint.[1] In December, as we have seen, Charles Arundel, accompanied by Lord Paget and other Catholic refugees, appeared suddenly in Paris without the Queen's licence to leave England, saying that " they came away from England for their consciences, and for fear, having enemies." In the following year Thomas Vavasour, who had been associated in a small way with the Arundel slanders, wrote in a letter to Lord Oxford : " Is not the revenge already taken of thy victims sufficient ? " We may judge therefore that the perpetrators of the scurrilous attacks on the Earl of Oxford's honour in 1581 received their just deserts.

Financial crises were never long absent in Lord Oxford's life, and in the previous October he had written to Lord Burghley begging his assistance in a " suit," which was probably an endeavour to stave off his creditors who were gathering round him. In a postscript he shows that he takes exception to Lord Burghley's attempts to control him, the phrase " I am that I am " being typical of his independent spirit :

My Lord, This other day your man, Stainner, told me that you sent for Amis, my man, and if he were absent that Lyly should come unto you. I sent Amis, for he was in the way. And I think [it] very strange that your Lordship should enter into that course towards me ; whereby I must learn that [which] I knew not before, both of your opinion and good will towards me. But I pray, my Lord, leave that course, for I mean not to be your ward nor your child. I serve Her Majesty, and I am that I am ; and by alliance near to your Lordship, but free ; and scorn to be offered that injury to think I am so weak of government as to be ruled by servants, or not able to govern myself. If your Lordship take and

---

[1] *Catholic Record Society*, vol. xxi, p. 338: " To John Dannetts, upon a Privy Council Warrant, dated 5th May, 1584, for his charges in safe keeping of Lord Henry Howard in the house of Sir Ralph Sadler for six months, the sum of £26."

follow this course you deceive yourself, and make me take another course that I have not yet thought of.

Wherefore these shall be to desire your Lordship, if that I may make account of your friendship, that you will leave that course as hurtful to us both.[1]

The expression " I serve Her Majesty " has more behind it than might appear. In 1586 Lord Oxford received a large annuity from the Queen " for services rendered." The nature of these services will be fully traced in a subsequent chapter. In brief, Lord Oxford at this time was a lessee of the Blackfriars Theatre, where his private secretary and actor manager, John Lyly, was producing his Court Comedies. In the winter these comedies were presented before the Queen by the Earl's company of boy actors. It was no doubt galling to Lord Burghley to find his son-in-law busied with such " lewd persons " as common actors. But when he protested Lord Oxford replied sharply that he was engaged on Her Majesty's service.

Foreign affairs were now rapidly heading towards a crisis. Open war between England and Spain was imminent. But as this *dénouement* had been gradually coming to a head over a long period of years, it will be well to follow the relations between Queen Elizabeth and " His Most Catholic Majesty " step by step.

The first landmark in the story occurred in 1567, when King Philip II. sent the Duke of Alva to the Netherlands, then a vassal State of Spain, with orders to suppress Protestantism and reintroduce the Catholic religion. English sympathy with the heroic defence put up by the Dutch burghers and their untiring leader William the Silent led in 1572 to a band of volunteers under Sir Roger Williams going to their assistance. They were not, of course, recognised diplomatically, but their action showed the temper of the English people.

Nor were our sailors behindhand in taking up the " Common Cause." Early in the seventies Captain Francis

[1] Lansdowne MSS., 42. 39.   October 30th, 1584.

Drake took the *Swan*, a 25-ton bark, across to the Spanish Main, and declared a " private war " on King Philip and the Holy Inquisition. His amazing exploits are unparalleled in history. The Spaniards firmly believed that the terrible " El Draque " was in league with the devil. It was in vain that the King of Spain issued bombastic edicts forbidding his colonists to trade with any foreigners. Drake's method of dealing with this difficulty was simplicity itself. He would arrive outside a Spanish seaport and politely ask the Governor for permission to trade. The Governor would equally politely draw his attention to the King's edicts. These formalities over, Drake and his Devon boys would land and take what they wanted—and if there was any trouble they burnt the town into the bargain.

All this time, of course, the " Jezebel of the North "—as the Spaniards called Queen Elizabeth—was by way of being on the best possible terms with her " good brother King Philip." When an indignant Spanish Ambassador came to her presence and drew her attention to Drake's latest outrage she would swear with great gusto that she knew nothing whatever about it, and would investigate the matter at once. Directly the Ambassador's back was turned she would send for Drake—and lend him ships of the Royal Navy to continue his peaceable trading ! Well might the Spanish Ambassador exclaim that " she must have a hundred thousand devils in her body ! "

The year 1580 brought two important developments. The first was the seizure by King Philip of the crown of Portugal, which not only added enormously to his possessions in the New World, but practically doubled his sea-power. The second was the return of Drake from his great circumnavigation voyage, which has already been touched on.

The political situation created when the *Golden Hind* anchored in Plymouth harbour was extremely critical. During the voyage Drake had captured the largest Spanish treasure-ship—the *San Felipe*—off the Chile coast. The treasure, which was worth over £300,000 according to some authorities, was now in the *Golden Hind.*

King Philip demanded not only the return of the treasure, but the execution of Drake as a pirate. The majority of the Privy Council, many of whom stood to gain enormously by Drake's plunder, held that he had acted legally. Others, among them Lord Burghley, counselled prudence, and advocated its return. For some months the Queen hesitated before coming to a decision ; but when she finally did so, she showed how accurately she had gauged the popular feeling in England. Amidst scenes of indescribable enthusiasm she knighted Drake on the quarter-deck of the *Golden Hind.*

From that moment the die was cast. Philip set to work with his customary thoroughness to build a fleet with which to invade England. But Elizabeth, dreading the cost of a war, used all her ingenuity towards putting off the final step.

In 1584, however, her hand was forced, for in that year William the Silent was assassinated. With his death it looked as if the Dutch defence would crumple up. Once the Netherlands were subdued Spain would be able to turn her whole power against heretic England. Sturmius, then in the last year of his life, saw the only course open to England. For a dozen years or more this great leader of Protestant thought in the Rhineland had been in receipt of a salary of £40 a year from the English Exchequer for acting as the Queen's Agent " in partibus Germaniæ." [1] On March 15th, 1584, he wrote to Elizabeth urging her to send " some faithful and zealous personage such as the Earl of Oxford, the Earl of Leicester, or Philip Sidney " in command of an expedition into the Low Countries.[2]

But England was not a rich country, and although Elizabeth was not averse to war, she did not want to have to pay for it. For a year negotiations between the Privy Council and the Dutch Deputies dragged on. Finally, on

[1] E. 403–2264 (Exchequer Roll of Issue, 1576–1577) in the Public Record Office.

[2] Cal. S.P. Foreign (1583–1584), p. 406.

May 29th, 1585, the States-General issued a " Resolution " to the effect that " 2,000 English footmen be enlisted for the relief of Antwerp." [1]

In the same month Colonel John Norris handed over the Presidency of Munster to his brother Thomas and hurried to London ; and on June 17th Alexander Witschayt was ordered to enlist 1,500 men in England.

On June 25th Lord Oxford wrote to Lord Burghley. The " suit " he refers to, in which he says that he is supported by Walsingham, was a request to be given a command in the impending war :

My very good Lord, As I have been beholden unto you divers times, and of late by my brother R. Cecil whereby I have been able the better to follow my suit, wherein I have some comfort at this time from Master Secretary Walsingham, so am I now bold to crave your Lordship's help at this present. For, being now almost at a point to taste that good which Her Majesty shall determine, yet am I as one that hath long besieged a fort and not able to compass the end or reap the fruit of his travail, being forced to levy his siege for want of munition. Being thus disfurnished and unprovided to follow Her Majesty, as I perceive she will look for, I most earnestly desire your Lordship you will lend me £200 till Her Majesty performeth her promise, out of which I shall make payment, if it please you, with the rest that your Lordship hath at sundry times, to my great furtherance and help in my causes, sent me by your servant and steward Billet. I would be loth to trouble your Lordship with so much, if I were not kept here back with this tedious suit from London, where I would have found means to have taken up so much to have served my turn till Her Majesty had despatched me, but for that I dare not, having been here so long and the matter growing to some conclusion, be absent. I pray your Lordship bear with me, that at this time wherein I am to get myself in order I do become so troublesome. From the Court this morning.

Your Lordship's ever bounden,

EDWARD OXEFORD.[2]

---

[1] *Het Staatsche Leger*, by F. J. G. ten Raa and F. de Bas, I. 189.

[2] Lansdowne MSS., 50. 22.

Events now moved with headlong rapidity. On July 10th Norris was charged to enlist 8,000 Englishmen for the war. On August 1st, 1,000 English soldiers disembarked without officers or arms on the island of Walcheren. On August 10th a treaty was signed by Elizabeth and the States-General, and on August 24th Norris, who had been appointed to command the Field Army of 4,000 foot and 400 horse, sailed for Holland.[1]

The expedition was too late, however, to achieve its primary object, for on August 18th Antwerp was captured by Parma. Philip II. was overjoyed. " Antwerp is ours ! " he exclaimed over and over again when he received the news in Madrid.[2]

Nevertheless preparations for war continued uninterruptedly in England. On August 27th some English ships arrived outside Flushing, and next day the Guard of the Earl of Oxford landed.[3] On August 29th Bernardino de Mendoza informed King Philip that the Earl of Oxford had left that day for the Netherlands by the Queen's orders. On September 3rd instructions were issued regarding the inspection of the English troops at the Hague, and also for the victualling of the Earl of Oxford and his retinue, Colonel Norris, and the Captains and superior officers assembled there.[4]

Meanwhile a new arrival had landed in Holland in the person of William Davison, afterwards one of Her Majesty's principal secretaries. His commission, signed by the Queen on September 3rd, was explicit. He was to receive the delivery of the towns of Flushing and Brill from the Dutch as a surety, in return for which Elizabeth undertook to maintain 5,000 foot and 1,000 horse during the continuance of the war.[5]

On September 4th he reported his arrival, as well as an

---

[1] *Het Staatsche Leger* ; and *Dict. Nat. Biog.*, article Norris, Sir John.
[2] Davies, *History of England* (1842), II. 170.
[3] Resolution of the Council of State assembled at Middelbourg. Dutch State Archives.
[4] *Het Staatsche Leger*, I. 189.
[5] Harleian MSS., 36. 347.

interview he had had with Prince Maurice, on whom the mantle of William the Silent had fallen. It appears that Prince Maurice disliked the idea of handing over Flushing to a civilian; " but," Davison adds significantly, " Sir Philip Sidney is much commended here for his virtues ; if Her Majesty would send him there is no doubt Flushing would be delivered into his hands." [1] Walsingham duly laid this letter before the Queen ; but she was not at first disposed to accept the suggestion. And on September 13th Walsingham replied to Davison :

Sir Philip Sidney hath taken a very hard resolution to accompany Sir Francis Drake in this voyage [to the West Indies], moved thereto for that he saw Her Majesty disposed to commit the charge of Flushing unto some other, which he reporteth, would fall out greatly to his disgrace, to see another preferred before him, both for birth and judgment inferior to him.[2]

The story of Sidney's flight to Plymouth to join Drake, his recall to Court, and subsequent forgiveness by the Queen, is so well known that it need not be repeated here. It is only necessary to add that by the end of September Davison had received the keys of Flushing and Brill, with orders that they were to be handed over to Sir Philip Sidney and Sir Thomas Cecil respectively. And on September 24th he wrote as follows to the Earl of Leicester :

I find those of Holland as desirous of Sir Thomas Cecil for the government of Brill, as in Zeeland they have been for Sir Philip Sidney.[3]

Leicester's appearance at this point is interesting. It would seem that as soon as Oxford had left for Holland on August 29th a scheme had been set on foot by Leicester and his party to supersede him ; for on September 8th Walsingham had written to Davison that the Queen was talking of sending over " a nobleman " to advise the States.[4] This is curious in view of the fact that Lord

[1] Cotton MSS., Galba C., VIII. 113.   [3] Cotton MSS., cit.
[2] Motley, *United Netherlands*, I. 362.   [4] Ibid.

Oxford had only just gone; but once he had left the
Court there was nobody in London to take his part except
the Queen and Lord Burghley.

Early in October Norris, for excellent military reasons,
took the offensive, and although Davison had nothing
whatever to do with strategical matters, being there solely
in a civilian capacity, he expressed his disapproval in a
letter to Leicester :

Of the General his doing your Lordship shall best understand from himself. He is now gone to some enterprise he
hath upon a fort between Arnhem and Doesburgh upon the
Yser ; where it is feared he will spend both his time and
his people (which fall sick daily) to little purpose.[1]

This uncalled-for interference on the part of Davison
was really only part of an old court intrigue. A bitter
feud had always existed between the Norris and Knollys
families, and Leicester, through his marriage with Lettice
Knollys, had been drawn into this quarrel.

A week later Davison reported that Norris had captured
Arnhem. And it was no doubt Leicester's influence over
the Queen that led her, instead of thanking him for his
victory, to condemn his action, saying in a personal letter
that her meaning was " to defend and not to offend."

Meanwhile the Earl of Oxford had been ordered home :

The Earl of Oxford [writes Thomas Doyley to Leicester
on October 14th] sent his money, apparel, wine, and
venison by ship to England. The ship was captured off
Dunkirk by the Spaniards on that day, and a letter from
Lord Burghley to Lord Oxford found by them on board.
This letter appointed him to the command of the Horse.[2]

On October 21st, in a letter to Captain Henry Norris,
Davison says cryptically that " the Earl of Oxford has
returned this night into England, upon what humour I
know not." [3] And in November Sir Philip Sidney, with the
rank of General of the Horse, took over the Governorship
of Flushing.

---

[1] Cotton MSS., cit.   [2] Wright, *Queen Elizabeth*, vol. ii, p. 266.
[3] Cal. S.P. Foreign (1585–6), p. 104.

The day after Oxford left Holland for England the
Queen signed the Earl of Leicester's commission as Lieutenant-General of the English forces in the Low Countries.[1]
On December 8th he sailed from Harwich attended by the
" flower and chief gallants of England." [2] Two days
later he landed at Flushing, where he was received with
great ceremony by Prince Maurice and Sir Philip Sidney.
. Such was the abrupt termination of Lord Oxford's share
in an enterprise that had opened so auspiciously.   We may
conjecture his bitter disappointment at this supersession
by his old rivals Leicester and Sidney ; but as no despatches
either from or to him exist, the details remain a mystery.
No doubt court intrigue played a large part in his recall,
but there may have been other reasons of which no record
survives.

§ VII. HER MAJESTY'S PRIVY SEAL

When Lord Oxford returned to England after his
supersession in the Low Countries he turned, as was his
wont, once more to literature.   His position at this time
in the world of letters is stated in no uncertain language in
A Discourse of English Poetry, published by William Webbe
in 1586 :

I may not omit the deserved commendations of many
honourable and noble Lords and Gentlemen in Her Majesty's
Court, which, in the rare devices of poetry have been, and
yet are, most skilful ; among whom the Right Honourable
Earl of Oxford may challenge to himself the title of the
most excellent among the rest.[3]

It is, of course, out of the question that Webbe, any more
than Gabriel Harvey in his eulogy at Audley End, could
have based his judgment of Lord Oxford's supremacy
in poetry on the half-dozen poems that had appeared over
the signature " E. O." in the *Paradise of Dainty Devices*.
Like Harvey, he must have been privileged to ·see the
Earl's unpublished manuscripts ; but as little or nothing

---

[1] *Leicester Correspondence*, p. 11.   [2] Stow, *Annals*, p. 711.
[3] Haslewood, *Ancient Critical Essays*, vol. ii, p. 34.

appears to be known about him, we cannot now say how this came about.[1]

Meanwhile Lord Oxford's financial position had been steadily going from bad to worse. If we refer to the table in Appendix B we shall find that out of the fifty-six separate sales of land he effected during his lifetime no fewer than thirty-two, or more than half, were made during the preceding five years (1580-85). On the face of it there is little to show for such a high expenditure. It is true that his investments as an " adventurer " in Frobisher's voyages must have been partly responsible ; and to a lesser extent his employment for six weeks in the Low Countries, although in the public service, would have made demands on his private purse. On the other hand, his life during this period was remarkable for its lack of ostentation. In a letter, already quoted, Burghley tells us that in 1583 his household consisted only of four servants. Nor had he been called on to undertake any of those duties that so often impoverished Elizabethan courtiers. He had never held appointments such as Lord Deputy of Ireland, Custodian of the Queen of Scots, or Ambassador at Paris—appointments that had been so disastrous financially to Sir Henry Sidney, Lord Shrewsbury, and Francis Walsingham. In latter years, from all we know, he had taken little part in court life or the public service.

At any rate, whatever may have led to the extensive sales of land by Lord Oxford from 1580 to 1585, there can be no doubt that by 1586 he was financially in very low water. Historians have been unanimous in asserting that he had been reduced to this state of penury through his own wasteful and spendthrift habits. Nothing, apparently, could be more obvious. Let us see, however, if this view is upheld by contemporary evidence.

---

[1] I use the expression " unpublished manuscripts," but this may not be altogether correct. The author of *The Arte of English Poesy* (1589) said that he knew " very many notable gentlemen in the Court that have written commendably and suppressed it again, *or else suffered it to be published without their own names to it* : as [if] it were a discredit for a gentleman to seem learned, and to show himself amorous of any good art."

On June 26th, 1586, Queen Elizabeth signed a Privy Seal Warrant. The wording of this document runs as follows :

Elizabeth, etc., to the Treasurer and Chamberlains of our Exchequer, Greeting. We will and command you of Our treasure being and remaining from time to time within the receipt of Our Exchequer, to deliver and pay, or cause to be delivered and paid, unto Our right trusty and well beloved Cousin the Earl of Oxford, or to his assigns sufficiently authorised by him, the sum of One Thousand Pounds good and lawful money of England. The same to be yearly delivered and paid unto Our said Cousin at four terms of the year by even portions : and so to be continued unto him during Our pleasure, or until such time as he shall be by Us otherwise provided for to be in some manner relieved ; at what time Our pleasure is that this payment of One Thousand Pounds yearly to Our said Cousin in manner above specified shall cease. And for the same or any part thereof, Our further will and commandment is that neither the said Earl nor his assigns nor his or their executors nor any of them shall by way of account, imprest, or any other way whatsover be charged towards Us, Our heirs or successors. And these Our letters shall be your sufficient warrant and discharge in that behalf. Given under Our Privy Seal at Our Manor of Greenwich, the six and twentieth day of June in the eight and twentieth year of Our reign.[1]

Before we attempt to discover the reason which led the Queen to grant this annuity to the Earl of Oxford, a few preliminary remarks may be made. In the first place, we cannot but be struck by its size. It would be idle to speculate what £1,000 a year represents in terms of modern money, but we may compare it with some contemporary salaries and incomes.

I have been able to trace only three instances where this specific sum has been mentioned :

1. The Earl of Huntingdon was appointed Lord President of the North in October 1572. This was a post of great responsibility and trust ; and he was paid £1,000

---

[1] An analysis of the Book of Privy Seal Warrants in which this entry occurs will be found in Appendix C.

a year, which was to cover the " diets and stipends " of himself and his Council.[1]

2. When William Stanley, sixth Earl of Derby, married Lord Oxford's daughter, Elizabeth Vere, in 1595, he offered to settle £1,000 a year on her. The enormous size of this jointure is accounted for by the fact that Lord Derby was the richest man in England. This is proved by a letter from Queen Elizabeth to the Emperor of Russia, written on September 11th, 1601 : " There might have been a convenient marriage between the Prince, your son, and one of the daughters and heirs of our Cousin the Earl of Derby, being of our Blood Royal and *of greater possessions than any subject within our Realm.*"[2]

3. The Rev. John Ward, who became Vicar of Stratford-on-Avon in 1662, tells us that Shakespeare in his last years " spent at the rate of £1,000 a year, as I have heard."[3]

There are a few, but not many, instances of salaries and incomes greater than £1,000 a year :

1. " The Office of the Lord Keeper is better worth than £3,000, of the Admiral more, of the Secretary little less."[4]

2. Stow tells us that Lord Burghley's expenditure at Cecil House was about £2,000 a year ; and that he maintained a household of eighty persons.[5]

3. In 1602 King James VI. of Scotland was granted an annuity of £2,500 by Elizabeth. This was raised next year to £5,000.[6]

[1] Cal. S.P. Dom., Addenda, XXI. 94.
[2] Hatfield MSS. (Cal. XI. 388).
[3] *The Diary of the Rev. John Ward.*
[4] Manningham's *Diary*, quoted by Cheyney, *A History of England,* vol. i, p. 50.   But the *salary* of Lord Admiral Buckingham in the reign of James I. was £133 6s. 8d. (*P.R.O.* E. 403–2371).   [5] See p. 18, *ante.*
[6] See Appendix C, p. 358.   I have included this item because it seems to be of unusual interest historically, and I do not remember having seen it referred to in any history of the time.   These two grants would seem to show that from 1602 onwards the Queen intended James to succeed her. But they cannot, of course, be compared in any way to a salary or annuity granted by the Queen to one of her subjects, because the motive was obviously political.   They come in the same category with Elizabeth's loans and grants to foreign Princes such as William of Orange and Henry of Navarre.

4. In 1601 Sir Thomas Parry was appointed Resident Ambassador at the Court of France. He was allowed £3 6s. 8d. a day (about £1,200 a year).[1]

5. In 1590 Sir John Stanhope, the Master of the Posts, was given £1,200 a year with which to maintain all ordinary postal services throughout England.[2]

The following are some of the many examples of incomes, salaries, and annuities under £1,000 a year :

1. The Earl of Southampton's total income from land was estimated at £1,145. Out of this £395 had to be devoted to annuities to various dependents. This left him a net income of £750, from which all charges arising out of the land had to be paid.[3]

2. Sir Nicholas Parker was allowed £560 a year to maintain fifty soldiers in the new fort at Falmouth in 1599.[4]

3. Lord Dunsany was allowed £200 a year to maintain " a company of horse " in Ireland in 1598.

4. In 1599 Lady Arabella Stuart, a niece of Mary Queen of Scots and in the direct succession to the English crown, was granted £200 a year " for her better maintenance." [5]

5. In 1599 Lord Henry Howard, then restored to favour through the offices of Sir Robert Cecil, was granted £200 yearly " so long as the lands of the late Earl of Arundel shall remain in the Queen's hands." [6]

---

[1] See Appendix C, p. 358. This, I imagine, included the upkeep of the Staff at the Embassy. Two of his predecessors, Dr. Dale and Francis Walsingham, had frequently drawn attention to the heavy expenses this post involved.

[2] See Appendix C, p. 357.

[3] Stopes, *Third Earl of Southampton*, p. 101.

[4] See Appendix C, p. 357.

[5] See Appendix C, p. 358. This was a case of destitution, the English estates belonging to the family having been sequestered by Elizabeth many years previously (cf. Camden, p. 229). Her father, the elder brother of the murdered Lord Darnley, had died in exile in England in 1576. Her grandmother, the Countess of Lennox, was another destitute exile in England who had received £400 a year from Elizabeth.

[6] See Appendix C, p. 357. Philip Howard, Earl of Arundel, died in the Tower in 1595. His uncle, Lord Henry, thus became heir to the family estates, which had been confiscated by the Crown on Arundel's attainder in 1589. There can be little doubt that the Exchequer did not lose by this compromise !

6. In 1601 an annuity of £100 a year was granted to James Crofts, a Gentleman Pensioner.[1]

7. "The Earl of Warwick was Master of the Buck Hounds with a fee of £50 a year, the Earl of Huntingdon of the Hart Hounds with a fee of £13 6s. 8d.[2]

8. In 1595 the four daughters of Francis Dacres, Esq., were given annuities of £50 each.[3]

9. In 1598 Joan and Elizabeth FitzGerald, daughters of the Countess of Desmond, were given an annuity of £33 6s. 8d. each " during pleasure." [4]

The foregoing salaries and annuities are typical of the period, and are sufficiently exhaustive to make it clear that £1,000 was a very large annuity indeed for a subject to receive from his Sovereign. Let us then examine the grant in rather more detail.

We observe, in the first place, that there is no hint as to the reason or purpose of the grant. All we are told is that it is " to be continued unto him during Our pleasure, or until such time as he shall be by Us otherwise provided for." This fact alone, to say nothing of its amount, puts it on quite a different footing from such allowances as those made to Lord Henry Howard and Lady Arabella Stuart.

The next point to notice is that the Queen expressly states that the Earl is not to be called on by the Exchequer to render any account as to its expenditure. This is the usual formula made use of in the case of secret service money. Thus Cheyney, in his *History of England*, 1914, vol. i, page 44, quoting *P.R.O. Doquet, Signet Office*,

[1] See Appendix C, p. 358. His father, Sir James Crofts, had been Comptroller of the Household for many years, and had died in 1590. Possibly £100 a year was the regular salary of a Gentleman Pensioner.

[2] Cheyney, vol. i, p. 51.

[3] See Appendix C, p. 357. This case is on a par with that of Lord Henry Howard, because the vast Dacres estates in Northumberland had been confiscated by the Crown after the rebellion and flight of Leonard Dacres, the head of the family, in 1570.

[4] See Appendix C, p. 357. Their father, Gerald FitzGerald, 15th Earl of Desmond, had been imprisoned, outlawed, and finally killed in 1583. This was presumably another case of destitution.

December 4th, 1589, states that considerable sums of
secret service money were put in the hands of Secretary
Walsingham, " to be by him employed in such causes of
Her Majesty's service as are appointed him, *without
charge or anie accompte to be laid uppon him for the
same.*" It would seem therefore that this annuity of a
thousand a year was to be paid on account of some secret
service.   But why should secret service money have been
paid to Lord Oxford ?   He did not hold, openly at least,
any official appointment [1] ; he was not a Privy Councillor ; and after 1585 he never left England on any foreign
diplomatic mission.   Moreover, if the £1,000 a year was
for some secret service in connexion with Home affairs
we should expect to find him constantly at Court, having
audience with the Queen or her confidential advisers.
But, in point of fact, absolutely the reverse is true. From
1586 until his death in 1604—a period of eighteen years,
during which he received the £1,000 a year regularly—his
absence from the Court is most remarkable.   He only
attended at the House of Lords on fourteen occasions—
mostly at the opening and proroguing of Parliament.
There is no record of his ever having an official audience
with the Queen, nor is there the slightest indication that
he corresponded or conferred with her Ministers, in spite
of the fact that most of this time he was living at Stoke
Newington and Hackney, a stone's-throw from Westminster.   This quite rules out the possibility that the
£1,000 a year was secret service money, at any rate in the
ordinarily accepted sense of the word.

This brings us to another line of argument. May it
not have been given in order to relieve him in his poverty ?
May it not, in other words, have been intended for the
maintenance of himself and his wife, and for the education
and upbringing of his children ? Assuming this as a

---

[1] His rank of Lord Great Chamberlain was not an appointment but an
hereditary honour. It only involved duties at Coronations. Moreover,
no preceding or subsequent Lord Great Chamberlain ever received an
official salary on that account ; and Lord Oxford himself had already been
Lord Great Chamberlain for twenty-four years without payment.

possible hypothesis, let us see how it fits in with the facts of the case.

In 1588 the Countess of Oxford died, but no reduction or alteration was made in the grant. Next year Lady Burghley, Lord Oxford's mother-in-law, died ; and the following remarkable sentences concerning her grand-daughters may be read to this day on the Burghley tomb in Westminster Abbey :

Lady Elizabeth Vere, daughter of the most noble Edward Earl of Oxford and Anne his wife, daughter of Lord Burghley, born 2nd July 1575. She is fourteen years old and grieves bitterly and not without cause for the loss of her grandmother and mother, but she feels happier because her most gracious Majesty has taken her into service as a Maid of Honour.

Lady Bridget, the second daughter of the said Earl of Oxford and Anne, was born on April 6th 1584, and al-though she was hardly more than four years old when she placed her mother's body in the grave, yet it was not without tears that she recognised that her mother had been taken away from her, and shortly afterwards her grand-mother as well. It is not true to say that she was left an orphan seeing that her father is living and a most affectionate grandfather *who acts as her painstaking guardian.*

Lady Susan the third daughter was born on May 26th 1587. On account of her age she was unable to recognise either her mother or her grand-mother ; indeed it is only now that she is beginning to recognise her most loving grand-father, *who has the care of all these children,* so that they may not be deprived either of a pious education or of a suitable up-bringing.[1]

So it was not Lord Oxford but Lord Burghley who was bringing up and educating the Earl's three children ! Need we doubt any longer that the £1,000 a year had nothing whatever to do with Lord Oxford's family ?

[1] From the west panel of the Burghley Memorial in Westminster Abbey, translated from the original Latin. The last sentence reads : " . . . qui omnium harum curam habet ita ut nec pia educatione nec congrua vivendi ratione destituantur."

But if this rules out the family as the intended bene-
ficiaries of the Queen's annuity it does not necessarily
rule out Lord Oxford himself.   Is it not possible that the
Queen intended it as a personal gift to help him out of
financial difficulties ?   There are three weighty arguments
against this.   In the first place, it would have been an
extraordinary act for a frugal Queen like Elizabeth to make
so munificent a reward to a man who had simply squandered
his patrimony.   In the second place, why should she
choose public funds from which to effect a purely personal
gift ?   Her customary method of rewarding men like
Leicester, Hatton, Ralegh, and Essex for their faithful
services was by gifts of land or monopolies.   Never, as
far as I have been able to trace, did she give them annuities
from the Exchequer.   In the third place, the grant was
continued as a matter of routine after the accession of
King James, until the payment was regularised by a new
Privy Seal Warrant issued by the King.

What, then, was it for ?   It must have been for *something*,
because we know that Elizabeth was the last person in the
world to scatter largesse around without expecting any
return.   But the records have not revealed the slightest
clue.   In view of this failure of direct evidence, due, it
would seem, to a deliberate desire for secrecy on the
Queen's part, we are compelled to fall back on indirect
evidence and inference.   I must therefore ask the reader
to bear with me in a digression to see how Lord Oxford
was occupied before and during 1586.

INTERLUDE : LORD OXFORD'S ACTORS
1580–1602

" For Tragedy Lord Buckhurst and Master Edward Ferrys do deserve the highest price : the Earl of Oxford and Master Edwards of Her Majesty's Chapel for Comedy and Enterlude."

Lord Lumley, in *The Arte of English Poesie*, 1589.

" The best for Comedy among us be Edward Earl of Oxford. . . ."

Francis Meres, in *Palladis Tamia*, 1598.

WE have seen in a previous interlude that about 1579 Lord Oxford had constituted himself the leader of the literary party known as the Euphuists, and that he had drawn to his side men like Lyly, Munday, and Greene. Against him were ranged the Romanticists, whose party, under the leadership of Philip Sidney, included Spenser, Dyer, Harvey, and others. And we have followed in some detail the paper warfare that raged between these two factions, in which Oxford received the adulations of his lieutenants and the ridicule of his opponents.

Whilst this battle was in progress the object of these eulogies and witticisms was finding a new outlet for his literary interests. In 1580 the Earl of Warwick's company of actors transferred to Lord Oxford's service ; and John Lyly, who was then his private secretary,[1] was probably appointed manager of the company.

The Earl of Oxford's acquaintance with the stage had begun in his earliest boyhood. We have already observed that his father had a company of actors who can be traced in various parts of England between the years 1555 and 1563.[2] It is not unlikely that when the Queen visited Castle Hedingham in 1561 a play by the Earl's men formed

---

[1] Cf. R. W. Bond, *Complete Works of John Lyly*, vol. i, p. 24. Lyly, as we shall see, remained in Lord Oxford's service until at least 1589, and probably till the early nineties.

[2] E. K. Chambers, *Elizabethan Stage*, vol. ii, p. 99.

part of the entertainment.　At any rate, we may be sure that as a boy Edward de Vere witnessed the dramatic performances of his father's company.　But when he succeeded to the Earldom at the age of twelve, and became a Royal Ward in Lord Burghley's household, the company was discontinued.

When Queen Elizabeth first came to the throne the privilege of entertaining Her Majesty with plays and masques was virtually a monopoly of the Choir Boys of the various Chapels.　From 1558 to 1572 numerous performances were given at the Court by the Children of Paul's, of Westminster, of Windsor, and of the Chapel Royal.　There were at the same time only four companies under the patronage of courtiers which appeared at Court, viz. the Earl of Warwick's, Lord Robert Dudley's, Lord Rich's, and Sir Robert Lane's.　They can hardly be called permanent institutions, however, for during the fourteen years mentioned Warwick's men only appeared twice (before 1564), Dudley's three times (before 1562), Rich's four times, and Lane's twice.

In 1573 the Earl of Sussex started a company, and Dudley (now Earl of Leicester) re-formed his.　From then onwards they appeared fairly regularly at Court during the " season " between Christmas and Lent.　In 1575 the Earl of Warwick's men appeared once more at Court after an absence of nine years, and in 1577 and 1580 respectively Lord Howard of Effingham and Lord Derby brought their companies to Court.

Oxford's friend, Lord Chamberlain Sussex, took a particular interest in the court dramatic performances. He not only personally selected the plays to be performed, but superintended the rehearsals, as the following entries in Revels Accounts for 1577 show :

Boat hire to and from the Court, to carry the stuff for the Children of the Chapel to recite before my Lord Chamberlain.

Boat hire to the Court to carry my Lord Chamberlain's patterns of the masque.

For a car the next day to carry two baskets of stuff to
    Barmesey [1] to show my Lord Chamberlain.
Mr. Blagrave's boat hire to and from the Court, being
    sent for by my Lord Chamberlain. [2]

An interesting point arises out of the appearance of
Sussex's and Leicester's men in 1573. The cost of the
office of the Revels had grown by this year to about £1,500.
From then onwards it fell rapidly, till by 1576 it was little
more than £300, at which figure it remained until the end
of Elizabeth's reign. [3] In commenting on this curious
phenomenon, which was accompanied not by decreased
but heightened splendour in the entertainments, [4] Sir
Edmund Chambers holds the view that the Office of Works
was called upon to bear the cost of buildings, scenery, and
other properties. This may be so ; but it seems also
probable that it was partly due to the shifting of the
burden of maintaining the actors on to the shoulders of
the various patrons.

There is, moreover, evidence to prove that actors could
not and were not expected to maintain themselves by
playing alone. This transpires incidentally in a letter
written by the Corporation of London to the Privy Council
in or about November 1584 :

It hath not been used nor thought meet heretofore that
players have or should make their living on the art of
playing, but men for their livings using other honest and
lawful arts, or retained in honest services, have by com-

1 One of Sussex's houses was situated near Bermondsey Cross on the
south bank of the river, nearly opposite the Tower and about a quarter
of a mile east of London Bridge. It was called Bermondsey House, and
had been built shortly after the dissolution of the monasteries by Sir
Thomas Pope on the site of the old Abbey. Sussex died here in 1583 ;
but prior to this, in 1562, he seems to have been living in a house in Cannon
Row, Westminster. Cf. Wheatley, *London Past and Present*, vol. i, p. 168.
    2 M. S. Steele, *Plays and Masques at Court*, p. 69. Thomas Blagrave
was Clerk in the office of the Revels from 1560 to 1603.
    3 E. K. Chambers, *The Tudor Revels*, p. 63.
    4 " Camden notes a growing tendency to luxury about 1574 ; others
trace the change to the coming of the Duke of Alencon in 1581 " (Chambers,
vol. i, p. 5).

panies learned some Enterludes for some increase to their profit by other men's pleasures in vacant times of recreation.[1]

Sir Sidney Lee would have us believe that Elizabethan companies of actors were under the " nominal " patronage of noblemen ; implying that as soon as a company had persuaded a nobleman to grant them the use of his name all connexion between patron and player ceased. So far from this being the case the document I have just quoted shows that the patron occupied the essential position of paymaster ; and that but for his financial support the company would have been quite unable to carry on.[2] In brief, it was the demand at Court for theatrical entertainments that brought the companies into existence, and so it was naturally the courtiers themselves who had to foot the bill for their maintenance by " retaining them in their services."

In 1580, as stated above, Lord Oxford took over Warwick's Company. We do not know the exact date, but it must have been after January 1st, 1580, because on that date the company performed *The Four Sons of Fabius* at Court and are shown as still under the patronage of Warwick. By April the transfer was complete, because on the 13th of that month " Robert Leveson and Larrance Dutton, servants of the Earl of Oxford," were committed to the Marshalsea for frays committed upon certain Gentlemen of the Inns of Court three days before at the Theatre. We know that these two men were actors because two brothers, Lawrence and John Dutton, had been transferred to Oxford's service with the rest of Warwick's Company.[3]

We next hear of Oxford's men on tour. On June 21st John Hatcher, Vice-Chancellor of Cambridge University, wrote to Lord Burghley :

My bounden duty remembered with most humble and

---

[1] Chambers, vol. iv, p. 300.

[2] It must be understood that I am talking of a time before the days of Henslowe and Burbage, when the position was considerably altered.

[3] Chambers, vol. ii, p. 99.

hearty recommendations. Where it hath pleased your Honour to commend unto me and the heads of the University my Lord of Oxford his players, that they might show their cunning in certain plays already practised by them before the Queen's Majesty : I did speedily counsel with the heads and others, viz., Dr. Styll, Dr. Howland, Dr. Binge, Dr. Legge, etc. And considering and pondering that the seed, the cause, and the fear of the pestilence is not yet vanished and gone this hot time of the year, this Midsummer Fair time having confluence out of all countries as well of infected as not : the commencement time at hand which requireth rather diligence in study than dissoluteness in plays : and also of late we denied the like to the Right Honourable the Lord of Leicester his servants : and specially for that all assemblies in open places be expressly forbidden in this University and town, or within five miles compass by Her Majesty's Council's letter 30th October 1575. Our trust is that your Honour, our most dear loving Chancellor, will take our answer made unto them in good part ; and being willing to impart something from the liberality of the University to them, I could not obtain sufficient assent thereto, and therefore I delivered them but twenty shillings toward their charges. Also they brought letters from the Right Honourable the Lord Chancellor and the Right Honourable the Lord of Sussex to the Vice Chancellors of Cambridge and Oxford. I trust their Honours will accept our answer. Thus leaving to trouble your Honour any longer with my rude writing, I take my leave. Cambridge, the 21st of June 1580.

Your Lordship's humble and unworthy deputy,

JOHN HATCHER, Vicar.[1]

In 1580 Richard Farrant (Master of the Children of Windsor) and William Hunnis (Master of the Children of the Chapel Royal) first conceived the idea of a theatre open to the public on payment where the Choir Boys could be rehearsed before appearing at Court. They selected a room in the old Blackfriars Convent, in which building the Office of the Revels had been established since 1550. Farrant died later in the year, but Hunnis

[1] S.P. Dom., 130. 26.

continued the experiment till 1583, when he sold his lease to Henry Evans. The latter shortly afterwards transferred it to Lord Oxford, who in turn passed it on to his secretary and actor manager John Lyly. Sir Edmund Chambers remarks that :

doubtless Hunnis, Lyly, and Evans were all working together under the Earl's patronage, for a company under Oxford's name was taken to Court by Lyly in the winter of 1583-4, and by Evans in the winter of 1584-5, and it seems pretty clear that in 1583-4 at any rate it was made up of boys from the Chapel and Paul's.[1]

Lyly subsequently sold the lease to Signor Roco Bonetti, the fashionable Italian fencing master. It was here that the latter established his famous school to which the Court gallants flocked to learn the " art of defence." It is curious that just about this time Lord Oxford seems to have had a quarrel with Bonetti, though its cause does not transpire.[2] Students of Shakespeare will remember that the Italian's fantastic fencing terms are ridiculed in *Romeo and Juliet* (Act II., Scene iv.) :

MER. Ah ! the immortal passado ! the punto reverso ! the hay !
BEN. The what ?
MER. The pox of such antick, lisping, affecting fantasticoes ! These new tuners of accents ![3]

Lord Oxford's Company of Choir Boys was quite distinct from the adult troupe that he had acquired from the Earl of Warwick, though it is possible that they may sometimes have worked together. But their tenancy at Blackfriars was a short one, for in 1584 Sir William More recovered possession of his property. It is interesting to find Lord Oxford so closely connected with the founding of the first theatre in England.

Lord Oxford's adult company can be traced in the provinces from 1581 to 1590, but after 1584 they do not appear by the records to have acted at Court. The reason

[1] Chambers, vol. iv, p. 497.
[2] Cal. S.P. Foreign, April 16th-26th, 1583.
[3] Cf. J. Q. Adams, *Shakespearean Playhouses*, p. 195.

for this, I suggest, can be found in the appearance of a new company, called the Queen's Men, in 1583.

This new company had been raised, no doubt at the Queen's instigation, by Edmund Tilney,[1] the Master of the Revels. On March 10th, 1583, he had been summoned to Court by a letter from Sir Francis Walsingham, the Principal Secretary, in order " to choose out a company of players for Her Majesty." [2] Stow, in his *Annals*, under date 1583, gives us the following information :

> Comedians and stage players of former times were very poor and ignorant, in respect of these of this time, but being now grown very skilful and exquisite actors for all matters, they were entertained into the service of diverse great Lords, out of which companies there were twelve of the best chosen, and at the request of Sir Francis Walsingham they were sworn to the Queen's servants, and were allowed wages and liveries as Grooms of the Chamber : and until this year 1583 the Queen had no players. Amongst these twelve players there were two rare men, viz., Thomas Wilton, for a quick, delicate, refined, extemporal wit : and Richard Tarleton, for a wondrous plentiful, pleasant, extemporal wit, he was the wonder of his time ; he lieth buried in Shoreditch Church.

This brief notice by Stow is perhaps more interesting than appears at first sight. The Queen, we know, took great delight in plays and masques, and it is natural to suppose that it was at her instigation that the company was started. It is probable that she was dissatisfied at the inferior standard of entertainment provided in the past, and was determined to raise the status of actors appearing at Court by ranking them with Grooms of the Chamber.

---

[1] Edmund Tilney (born before 1554 ; died 1610) was a second cousin of Charles Lord Howard of Effingham, both men having a common great-grandfather in Hugh Tilney, whose daughter, Agnes Tilney, was Lord Howard's grandmother. He was also connected with Lord Oxford, Lord Howard's aunt, Anne Howard (daughter of the 2nd Duke of Norfolk by Agnes Tilney) having married the 14th Earl of Oxford. Tilney was Master of the Revels from 1579 to 1610.

[2] Chambers, *Tudor Revels*, p. 62.

The twelve actors chosen for the Queen's company were Robert Wilson, John Dutton, Richard Tarleton, John Laneham, John Bentley, Thobye Mylles, John Towne, John Synger, Leonell Cooke, John Garland, John Adams, and Wyllyam Johnson. They were licensed on November 28th, 1583, by the City Authorities to play at the Bull in Bishopsgate Street and the Bell in Gratious Street.[1] Three of them—Wilson, Laneham, and Johnson—came from Leicester's company, and one — Adams — from Sussex's. John Dutton, as we have seen, was one of Oxford's men; and his brother, Lawrence, also one of Oxford's men, must have joined the Queen's Company later, because in 1591 " Lawrence Dutton and John Dutton " were payees for " Her Majesty's players and their company " after a performance at Court. It is quite possible that some of the remaining seven were also drafted in from Oxford's. If so, his company, denuded of their stars, may very well have been relegated to provincial status pure and simple, which would account for their ceasing to appear at Court after 1584.

The new Queen's Company made its first appearance at the beginning of the Court season on December 26th, 1583. On January 1st a performance was given by Oxford's men; and as John Lyly appears in the Chamber Accounts as payee for the company on that date there is every reason to believe, with Sir Edmund Chambers, that the play acted was Lyly's *Campaspe*. On March 3rd both Oxford's and the Queen's men performed; once again Lyly was payee for Oxford's, and Sir Edmund confidently conjectures that the play acted was *Sapho and Phao*.[2] Now, it seems unreasonable to suppose that two plays were presented on this day; the most likely solution, therefore, would be that the two companies were amalgamated and rehearsed by Lord Oxford's private secretary John Lyly, the author of the play. No other adult companies besides these two appeared at Court during this season.

[1] Chambers, vol. iv, p. 296.   [2] Chambers, vol. iii, pp. 414, 415.

Next season (1584–5) the Queen's was the only adult company that performed at Court. Two other entertainments only were provided : one by " the children of the Earl of Oxford," the payee being Henry Evans, and the play *Agamemnon and Ulysses* ; and the other by " John Symons and his fellows, servants of the Earl of Oxford," who gave a display of vaulting and other activities.[1] The fact that Lord Oxford's actors have by this time been reduced to " children " and " tumblers " looks to me as if the amalgamation in the preceding March had been made a permanency ; in other words that the Queen's had absorbed an important adult portion of his company, that Lyly was lent with them to act as coach, and that Henry Evans took over from Lyly the juvenile remnants of Oxford's players, and united them with boys from the Chapel Royal and Paul's.

But there is still stronger evidence connecting Lyly in some unofficial capacity with the Queen's company. It is to be found in three of his letters, written between 1597 and 1600, from which we elicit the following facts :

1. That in 1588, if not earlier, he was " entertained Her Majesty's servant."

2. That in 1585 the Queen had led him to hope for the reversion (on Tilney's death) of the Mastership of the Revels, or the Clerkship of the Tents and Toyles, which was closely connected with the Revels Office.

3. That he had quite definitely received neither of these posts by 1601.[2]

Now, we know that at least till 1589 Lyly was in Lord Oxford's service. He is quoted as " payee " for Oxford's Company in January and March 1584 ; he is spoken of as " servant to the Right Honourable the Earl of Oxford "

---

[1] Chambers, vol. iv, pp. 101, 160, 161.

[2] These letters are printed *in extenso* by Feuillerat, *John Lyly*, pp. 554–62 ; and by Bond, *Complete Works of John Lyly*, vol. i, pp. 64–71, 378, 390–395. Cf. Chambers, vol. iv, p. 412 : " Mr. R. W. Bond bases many conjectures about Lyly's career on a theory that he actually held the post of Clerk Comptroller in the Revels Office, but the known history of the post makes this impossible."

in a legal document dated May 10th, 1587, and in 1589
Gabriel Harvey calls him " the minion secretary." [1]   It
is not definitely known how much longer he remained with
Lord Oxford ; but I think we may detect a reference to
his discharge in an appeal he addressed to Sir Robert
Cecil, Oxford's brother-in-law, dated January 17th,
1594–5 :

> Among all the overthwartes of my poor fortunes this is
> the greatest, that where I most expected to show my
> dutiful affection I am cut off from the means.[2]

If this, as I think, refers to his discharge by Lord Oxford,
we may fairly confidently date that event as having taken
place in the early nineties.

Not one of Lyly's biographers has hitherto succeeded
in explaining how he could have been Her Majesty's servant and Lord Oxford's private secretary at one and the
same time. The simplest solution is surely the one I
have suggested, viz. that when the Queen's Company
absorbed some of Oxford's leading actors Lyly was lent
unofficially as stage manager and coach. If so it would
have been in 1584.

Now in 1585 Thomas Giles, the Master of the Children
of Paul's, was authorised to " take up " fresh Choir Boys.
This, as Mr. Bond says, " may safely be taken as implying
a renewal of their permission to act." If, then, Lyly was
at this time employed in coaching the Queen's men, what
could be more natural than to suppose that his duties were
extended in similar capacity to the Paul's Boys ? It is
clear that he was closely connected with these boys
because, as Mr. Bond says, " all his plays, except *The
Woman in the Moone*, are described on their title-pages as
presented by these children." This, moreover, would
completely explain what Gabriel Harvey meant when he
said in 1593 that—

[1] Chambers, vol. iv, p. 160 ; Feuillerat, p. 541 ; Bond, vol. i, p. 28.
[2] Feuillerat, p. 552 (*in extenso*).

19

[Lyly] hath not played the Vicemaster of Poules, and the Foolemaster of the Theater for naughtes.[1]

Considered in this light the vexed question of Lyly's employment by the Queen becomes perfectly clear and comprehensible.

This would bring both Lord Oxford and his private secretary into close touch with the Queen's Company, and brings me to another point in connexion with Lyly's eight Court Comedies. We may take it as certain that all his plays were written and acted while he was in Lord Oxford's employ.[2] And although he had probably left the Earl's service by 1594 at the latest, and lived for at least another twelve years, he never wrote another play. This is all the more curious because the whole of this time he was out of a job, and was applying to the Queen for the post of Master of the Revels ; so that it is evident that his ceasing to write plays cannot be attributed to a voluntary severance of his connexion with the stage.[3] Now, we have it on the

[1] Grosart, *Works of Gabriel Harvey*, vol. ii, p. 212. The word "played" and the expression "Foolemaster of the Theater" seem to me to imply unofficial rather than official duties. Harvey, of course, knew perfectly well that officially Lyly was in Lord Oxford's employ—"the minion secretary," as he himself called him in 1589.

[2] The dating of the composition and first performance of Lyly's plays, which bear little or no relation to the dates on which they were published in quarto, is a question upon which opinions differ slightly. The following table gives the dates assigned by Sir Edmund Chambers, M. Feuillerat, and Mr. Bond :

Play.	Date of composition or first performance.			Quarto.
	Chambers.	Feuillerat.	Bond.	
Campaspe . . .	1584	1581	1579–80	1584
Sapho and Phao . .	1584	1582	1581	1584
Galathea . . .	1584–5	before Ap. '85	1582–4	1592
Love's Metamorphosis .	1589–90	1588–90	1584–8	1601
Endimion . . .	1588	before Feb. '87	1585	1591
Midas . . .	1589–90	1589	1589	1592
Mother Bombie . .	1587–90	1589–90	1590	1594
Woman in the Moon .	1590–5	1593–4	1591–3	1595

[3] Mr. Bond (vol. i, p. 78) says : "It is not therefore surprising that between 1595 and 1606 we have practically no new work from Lyly's pen." Personally I think it *is* surprising—very surprising. Lyly was a professional playwright who was out of a job, and who was repeatedly applying for

authority of the author of *The Arte of English Poesie*
in 1589, and of Francis Meres in 1598, that Lord Oxford
was the best writer of comedy at that time. Is it not
possible that Lyly's Court Comedies were really a collaboration between the Earl and his private secretary ?

It may be argued that this is pure hypothesis, and that
no evidence exists to prove such a collaboration. But this
is not the case. There are six definite reasons for supposing that Lord Oxford had more than a sleeping partner's
interest in the Lyly comedies.

1. Mr. Bond makes the following comment in a note on
Act I. scene 1 of *Sapho and Phao* :

> *At the Ferry* : the ferry and the passage of Venus is
> from Aelian, *Var. Hist.* xii. 18. Lyly, in transferring it
> from Mitylene to Syracuse, may have had no thought of
> topography ; yet this mention of a river, a passage of some
> distance, the possibility of meeting with rough weather,
> and further the making Pandion send his boy " about by
> land," would all correspond accurately with a ferry con-
> ceived as running from somewhere near the mouth of the
> Anapus on the west side of the Great Harbour across to the
> promontory of Ortygia, on which the oldest part of Syra-
> cuse was built.[1]

We know, of course, that Lyly had never been to Sicily,
so we must assume that he received his information from
some returned traveller. May not this returned traveller
have been Lord Oxford, who can be definitely located at
Palermo in 1575 or 1576 ?[2] Since *Sapho and Phao* was
unquestionably written, acted, and printed while Lyly
was Lord Oxford's private secretary, this seems to me to
be the clearest possible indication that collaboration of
some kind did actually take place between the two men.

2. The well-known lyrics which are to be found in Lyly's

the Mastership of the Revels. I wonder what Mr. Bond's comment would
be if a new play by Lyly were unexpectedly discovered together with
proof that it was written in, say, 1600 ? Would he say it is very curious
to find Lyly writing plays in 1600 ?

[1] Bond, vol. ii, p. 555.

[2] See p. 111, *ante*.

plays provide an interesting problem. They are the only poems by him which have come down to us.[1] None of them were printed in the quarto editions of the plays,[2] and they were not published until Blount brought out the first collected edition called *Sixe Court Comedies* in 1632— that is to say, twenty-six and twenty-eight years after the deaths of Lyly and Oxford respectively. If Lyly had written them why did he refrain from publishing them during his lifetime ? They would surely have helped rather than have hindered his sales. Personally I think he did not publish them for the simple reason that they were not his to publish.[3] They are universally admitted to be of the highest standard ; and I suggest that the author was Lyly's employer, who, as Webbe said in 1586, " in the rare devices of poetry may challenge to himself the title of the best among the rest."

3. The allegorical character of many of Lyly's plays seems to me totally out of keeping with his social position. Critics tell us with a confidence that does not admit of argument that *Sapho and Phao* was a scarcely veiled allegory in which the two lovers—Sapho and Phao— represent Queen Elizabeth and the Duc d'Anjou. Mr. Bond, having traced the classical sources of the play, makes the following remarks :

This medley of classical suggestion is made to serve the author's main purpose of flattering the Queen by an allegorical representation of the relations between herself and her suitor the Duc d'Alençon [4] . . . . It is to this under-lying allegory, clearly alluded to in the Prologue at Court, and the Epilogue, especially in the words about " the necessitie of the hystorie " and the comparison of the whole inconclusive story to the mazes of a labyrinth, that the

[1] With the possible exception of the ballad quoted on page 291, post.

[2] Except two which appear, evidently unintentionally, as part of the dialogue in the *Woman in the Moon*.

[3] Dr. W. W. Greg, *Modern Language Review*, October 1905, argues against Lyly's authorship of these lyrics.

[4] The Duc d'Alençon had been created Duc d'Anjou in 1576, and it was therefore under the latter title that he came to England as Elizabeth's suitor in 1581.

changes made in the classical myth of *Sapho* are chiefly due. Hence the representation of her as Queen with a Court, and the suppression, surprisingly and needlessly thorough, of her poetic fame and functions : hence the striking beauty and majesty of person with which she is dowered, whereas Ovid represents her as of dark complexion and short stature : hence the initiation of Phao to her Court, her struggle against her passion and final conquest of it ; while her secure assumption at the close of the prerogatives of Venus and the person of Cupid are in the happiest vein of courtly flattery. The distress and perplexities of Phao, and his departure from Sicily at the call of other destinies, are quite in keeping with the facts of Alençon's courtship ; nor need the marked ugliness of the Duke disqualify him for the part. Elizabeth had declared in 1579 that " she had never seen a man who had pleased her so well, never one whom she could so willingly make her husband " (Froude, vol. xi, p. 155). And the courtly poet saw and seized his opportunity in the tale that Love herself had made Phao beautiful.[1]

Is it conceivable that a man in Lyly's position would have dared, on his own initiative and without any support, even to write, let alone present before Her Majesty, an allegorical play such as this ? M. Feuillerat is emphatically of opinion that it would have been impossible for him to have done such a thing :

Comment peut-on admettre qu'un dramatiste ait été assez audacieux pour mettre à la scène les sentiments les plus intimes les plus secrets de la reine ? [2]

This seems to me unanswerable. But what also seems unanswerable is that it is just the very thing that Lord Oxford might have done. We have seen how strongly he supported the French match ; and we know that his great friend Lord Sussex had addressed a letter on August 26th, 1578, to Her Majesty urging her to marry Anjou. Is it not highly probable that *Sapho and Phao*, which was acted (*vide* Chambers) by Oxford's own company,

---

[1] Bond, vol. ii, p. 366.   [2] Feuillerat, p. 148.

was his share in the campaign led by Sussex for promoting the Anjou marriage ? [1] This does not necessarily mean that Lord Oxford wrote the play himself ; a collaboration between him and Lyly seems most likely.

4. All the quartos of Lyly's plays were published anonymously. This is most odd if we are to understand that Lyly himself was the sole author, and had connived at the publication. It is well-nigh impossible to believe that a professional playwright, who was hoping to be appointed to the Mastership of the Revels, should have objected to having his name printed on the title-pages of his own plays. But if he could not claim them as entirely his own the matter becomes quite different. Equally incomprehensible is the hypothesis that the quartos were " pirated " and published against Lyly's wishes. As Lord Oxford's private secretary he would not lack the means of bringing influence to bear against the action of piratical publishers. Are we to understand that he calmly allowed his plays to be purloined one by one without so much as raising a protesting murmur ? This, anyhow, was not the case with *Sapho* as the following entry in the Stationers' Register proves :

6to Aprilis 1584. Thomas cadman Lyllye it is granted unto him yat yf he gett ye commedie of Sapho laufully alowed vnto him. Then none of this cumpanie shall Interrupt him to enjoye it.[2]

The mention of Lyly by name shows that this was not a piratical venture, and that Lyly himself was concerned in the publication. Surely these anonymous quartos only become comprehensible if we recognise that the plays were

---

[1] I am aware, of course, that Sir Edmund Chambers dates the perform- ance of *Sapho* two years after Anjou's departure from England, but this latter event by no means meant that a definite rupture in the marriage negotiations had taken place. As long as he remained alive—and he did not die till June 10th, 1584—there was always the chance that the Queen would once more change her mind. Bond and Feuillerat, moreover, date the composition of the play in 1581 and 1582 respectively.

[2] Arber, *Stationers' Register*, vol. ii, p. 430.

a collaboration, and that Lord Oxford, for personal reasons, preferred them to be brought out anonymously.

5. If we are to assume that Lyly, alone and unaided, wrote, produced, and printed allegories like *Sapho* and *Endimion*, what explanation can we offer for their passing the rigid censorship ? Tilney's commission to censor all plays was dated 1581. Does anyone imagine for a moment that if a professional playwright like Lyly had submitted a play like *Sapho* to Tilney, he would have authorised its acting and publication ? It is surely out of the question that any censor would have dared to pass any play containing obvious allusions to the Queen's love affairs. But if we substitute the Lord Great Chamberlain of England for the professional playwright all difficulties vanish.

6. In *Pierce's Supererogation* (1593) Gabriel Harvey makes the following enigmatic reference to Lyly :

Himself a mad lad as ever twang'd ; never troubled with any substance of wit, or circumstance of honesty ; sometime the fiddlestick of Oxford, now the very babble of London.

It is perhaps a moot point whether by " Oxford " Harvey meant the University or the Earl. But if, as I think, he intended the latter—he may even have had in mind a *double entendre*—its significance at once becomes apparent. Surely the interpretation is that Lyly was at one time the passive instrument employed by Lord Oxford to play his tunes.

Indeed, the more one thinks it over the more one is obliged to confess that Lyly recedes further into the background, and Lord Oxford appears in greater prominence. Nevertheless, in the article on Lyly, which occupies over two pages in the *Encyclopædia Britannica*, Lord Oxford is not mentioned ! Incredible as this may seem it is really scarcely more than typical of the treatment the Earl has received at the hands of historians and literary critics.

I do not propose for the moment to disentangle the ins and outs of Lord Oxford's actors from 1590 onwards ;

but a brief retrospect may be permitted. That he had an adult company which acted provincially throughout the eighties is certain. That they occupied the Black-friars Theatre in 1580 and again in 1583-4 is also certain. That he had another company consisting, according to Sir Edmund Chambers, of Choir Boys working at Court and at the Blackfriars Theatre under Lyly, Hunnis, and Evans may be taken as equally certain. Finally, there is little doubt that the Earl himself collaborated in the writing and production of Lyly's Court Comedies ; and that from 1585 onwards Lyly was lent by him to assist in staging the entertainments provided at Court by the Choir Boys, and, probably, by the Queen's Company as well.

Let us now return to the point from which this digression about the Earl of Oxford's actors started. Why did he receive £1,000 a year from the Queen in 1586 ?

In the first place, we must remember that in court social circles the majority would have deemed it a terrible disgrace for a great nobleman to write, produce, and pub-lish plays.[1] But there were two people at Court who quite emphatically did not belong to this unenlightened majority. The first was the Queen. Her attitude towards actors admits of no dispute. Had she despised them we should have had a very different story to tell. How many " noble-men's companies " should we have found springing up ? Is it likely that she herself would have ordered a company to be picked for her especial patronage, and have advanced her players socially to the rank of Grooms of the Chamber ? The other was Lord Oxford. From the very beginning his interests had centred round literature, poetry, and the drama. His " lewd friends " were the despair of Lord Burghley. Even a man like Gabriel Harvey thought he had overstepped the mark in allowing the " paltry pen " to become an obsession.

There can be no two opinions that in this matter he and the Queen saw eye to eye. Moreover, she would

---

[1] This, of course, does not apply to masques, which were really private theatricals ; or to translations, especially from the classics.

have had no illusions as to the financial aspect of what we,
in the twentieth century, might be inclined to think was
an inexpensive hobby.   She knew quite well that tenements in the Savoy or elsewhere for servants like Lyly,
Munday, and Evans cost money.   She knew, no doubt,
that in 1584 the Earl had granted Lyly land to the annual
value of £30 13s. 4d. " in consideration of the good and
faithful service that the said John Lyly hath heretofore
done unto the said Earl " [1] ; and that in the same year
Lord Oxford had given his lease of the Blackfriars Theatre
to his private secretary.   Nor need we suppose that
Henry Evans, Munday, Greene, and others were giving
their services and dedicating their books to him for nothing.
She was fully aware that companies of actors, no less than
companies of foot-soldiers, required food, clothes, shelter,
and pay.   We need not doubt that by some means she
would have been informed that by 1583 Lord Oxford's
financial position had become so straitened that he was
only maintaining a personal household of four servants.
And, most important of all, she knew far better than we
do now the why and the wherefore of his many sales of
land between 1580 and 1585.

This latter consideration receives remarkable confirmation in a letter Lord Oxford wrote many years afterwards
to his brother-in-law, Sir Robert Cecil.   He was appealing
for Cecil's help to obtain for him the post of President of
Wales, and advances the following reason in support of
the justness of his claim for the Queen's consideration :

But if Her Majesty, in regard of my youth, time, and
fortune spent in her Court, and her favours and promises
which drew me on *without any mistrust the more to presume
in mine own expenses,* confer so good a turn to me, that
then you may further it as you may.[2]

Surely the only possible interpretation of the sentence
I have italicised is that in some way Lord Oxford in his

[1] Feuillerat, p. 536.
[2] See p. 335, *post.*

courtier days had been spending his money on behalf of
the Queen rather than himself, and that she in return had
promised that he would not be the loser thereby.

What did he spend this money on ? and what did he
do in return for his £1,000 a year ?

He certainly did none of the things we might have
expected. He did not serve her as a Minister, as a Privy
Councillor, as an Ambassador, or as a Soldier. But in a
less obvious respect he undoubtedly did serve her. He
was instrumental, by means of his brain, his servants,
and his purse in providing the Court with dramatic
entertainment.

Elizabeth, we may be sure, was fully alive to the importance of masques and similar entertainments in promoting
the well-being of the Court. A well-organised recreation
department was as essential to herself and her courtiers as a
plentifully supplied supper-table. There can be no doubt
that a great part of the winter evening diversions during
the early eighties had emanated from Lord Oxford and Lyly.
She would very naturally be unwilling to allow so valuable
a courtier to go bankrupt and be compelled to leave the
Court just for lack of means to maintain his position.

I do not for a moment mean to suggest that the Earl of
Oxford had been selling land at the rate of something like
a dozen estates a year simply and solely in order to maintain
one or more companies of actors. Such an idea would be
absurd. He had beyond all doubt been a spendthrift.
His foreign tour had cost him about £5,000, and he must
have lost nearly as much in the Frobisher speculations.
But looked at from the Queen's point of view, the plain
fact was that by 1586 she was in imminent danger of losing
the services of one who, both directly and indirectly, had
been and still was the chief agent in providing the winter
entertainments. Had he been a person of no consequence
to her is it likely that she would have given him an annuity
of £1,000 a year ?

Anyway, I imagine she got her money's worth—she
usually did.

CHAPTER VI

1587–1588

" Were't aught to me I bore the canopy,
    With my extern the outward honouring ? "

Sonnet No. CXXV.

§ I. DEATH OF THE COUNTESS OF OXFORD

TOWARDS the close of 1586 two events overshadowed
everything else. On September 22nd Sir Philip Sidney
was mortally wounded at the battle of Zutphen ; and on
September 27th the Commissioners for the trial of Mary
Queen of Scots, among whom was Lord Oxford, were
assembled at Westminster.

Sidney's death was a national catastrophe. At the
early age of thirty-two one of the most promising lives in
England was abruptly cut short. His accomplishments
were as varied as they were graceful—soldier, scholar,
courtier, poet, diplomat ; whatever he turned his hand to
prospered, until he had become the admiration not only
of England but of the whole of Europe as well.

It is not easy to form an exact estimate of the relations
between Sidney and Oxford. No correspondence between
them exists ; indeed very little correspondence by either
of them, other than official or business communications,
has been handed down to us. But the fact that throughout
the seventies and eighties they were universally recognised
by their contemporaries as the two leading poets in the
country establishes between them a close and intimate
link.

Their lives, however, ran curiously at cross purposes.
We met them first in early youth—when Oxford was
twenty-one and Sidney seventeen—as rivals for the hand
of Anne Cecil. In the field of literature this rivalry was
continued, Oxford being the leader of the Euphuists,

283

while Sidney was head of the Romanticists. At Court their interests met and clashed over the Anjou marriage ; and on active service they appear as rivals for the last time, when Sidney and Leicester superseded the Earl in the Low Countries. It would be wrong, however, to exaggerate the importance of these incidents, and to argue therefrom that throughout their lives they were hostile to each other. Both were quick-tempered, proud, and inclined to be arrogant ; but it is usually the case that men whose tempers flare up suddenly under the slightest provocation are least inclined to sulk or bear ill-will.

Moreover, the mere fact of their long rivalry surely argues that fundamentally they held the same ideals. Both were endued with a patriotic desire to serve their country on the field of battle, and Her Majesty did not possess throughout the length and breadth of the land two more loyal or devoted subjects. Both had travelled to France, Germany, and Italy, and had come back to England exhilarated by the wonders of the Renaissance. Both were intensely keen on literature, poetry, and the kindred arts.

It has become an accepted rule among modern historians to paint Sidney white and Oxford black. This attitude, although not justified, is quite comprehensible when we recognise that most writers' knowledge of Lord Oxford is confined to the episode known as the Tennis-court Quarrel. But when we call on the Elizabethans to tell us the stories of these two men we hear a very different version. In the Great Queen's heart there was room for both the Earl of Oxford and Sir Philip Sidney ; surely, then, there should be room for them both in the pages of England's story ?

Within two days of Sidney's death Mary Queen of Scots was brought to trial before a court consisting of twenty-five English peers. She was condemned to death and was executed at Fotheringay on February 8th, 1587. Thus passed out of the page of history two famous figures : one, the idol of England and the hope of Protestant Europe ;

the other an exiled Catholic Queen, whose chief misfortune perhaps was the heritage of her birth.

Although the reconciliation between Lord Oxford and his wife had taken place some years before, the old fires of suspicion and mistrust were still smouldering and ready to break into flame at any moment. It was after one of these unhappy occasions that Lord Burghley opened his heart in the following tragic letter to Sir Francis Walsingham :

Sir, Although I am sure that you will not omit any convenient time to move Her Majesty to assent that Her Majesty's gift to my Lord of Oxford of Edward Jones' land and goods might be perfected ; yet I was so vexed yesternight very late by some grievous sight of my poor daughter's affliction whom her husband had in the after-noon so troubled with words of reproach of me to her— as though I had no care of him as I had to please others (naming Sir Walter Ralegh and my Lord of Cumberland whose books I had speedily solicited to pass)—as she spent all the evening in dolour and weeping. And though I did as much as I could comfort her with hope ; yet she, being as she is great with child, and continually afflicted to behold the misery of her husband and of his children, to whom he will not leave a farthing of land ; for this purpose I cannot forbear to renew this pitiful cause, praying you to take some time to have Her Majesty's resolute answer.

Then follow some business details which need not concern us here ; and the letter concludes :

No enemy I have can envy me this match ; for thereby neither honour nor land nor goods shall come to their children ; for whom, being three already to be kept and a fourth like to follow, I am only at charge even with sundry families in sundry places for their sustenance. But if their father was of that good nature as to be thankful for the same I would be less grieved with the burden. And so I will end this uncomfortable matter this 5th of May 1587.

Your most assured,
W. BURGHLEY.[1]

¹ S.P. Dom. Eliz., 201. 5.

Walsingham was successful in obtaining the Queen's consent,[1] and on May 13th Burghley acknowledges his letter :

I heartily thank you [he writes] for your care had of my Lord of Oxford's cause ; wishing his own case was the like to convert Her Majesty's goodness to his own benefit, and in some part for his children. . . . When the form is agreed to I must pray you that my Lord of Oxford may perceive that the making of the books may be directed from you, as by Her Majesty's order to Master Attorney. For anything directed by me is sure of his lewd friends, who still rule him by flatteries.[2]

The " lewd friends " were presumably the Earl's literary and dramatic associates, whose Bohemian manner of life was most distasteful to the Lord Treasurer.

A fortnight later, on May 26th, the Countess gave birth to a daughter, Susan Vere, who afterwards married Philip Herbert, Earl of Montgomery and Pembroke.

On September 12th Lady Frances Vere, one of their elder daughters, was buried at Edmonton.[3] She must have been quite a child, and nothing else is known of her.

Lord Oxford was evidently still holding Burghley responsible for his failure to obtain some preferment at Court. His father-in-law hotly denies this :

You seem to infer [he writes] that the lack of your preferment cometh of me, for that you could never hear of any way prepared for your preferment. My Lord, for a direct answer, I affirm for a truth—and it to be well proved—that your Lordship mistaketh my power. Howsoever, you say that I manage the affairs, the trouble whereof is laid upon me ; but I have no power to do myself or any kin or friend any good, but rather impeached, yea crossed ; which I am taught these many years patiently to endure, yea, to conceal.

---

[1] Lansdowne MSS., 53. 48.

[2] S.P. Dom. Eliz., 201. 16.

[3] All Saints' Parish Register.   In the *History of Edmonton* (Robinson) it is conjectured that she may have died at Pymmes, one of Lord Burghley's country residences.

Secondly, that there have been no ways prepared for your preferment I do utterly deny, and can particularly make it manifest, by testimony of Councillors, how often I have propounded ways to prefer your services. But why these could not take place, I must not particularly set them down in writing, lest either I discover the hinderers or offend yourself, in showing the allegations to impeach your Lordship from such preferments. . . .[1]

This last paragraph is interesting, for Lord Oxford had never been without enemies both open and secret. We could have wished Burghley had told us who these were ; but in the absence of direct information we may hazard the guess that they numbered among them Sir Christopher Hatton and Lord Henry Howard.

The Countess of Oxford did not long survive the birth of her youngest daughter ; for on June 5th, 1588, she died of a fever in the Royal Palace at Greenwich. The following notice of her funeral is taken from a manuscript by Sir William Dethicke, Garter King at Arms : [2]

She was interred in Westminster Abbey on June 25th, attended by many persons of great quality and honour. The chief mourner was the Countess of Lincoln, supported by the Lords Windsor and Darcy, and her train borne by the Lady Stafford ; and among other mourners at her funeral were the Ladies Russel, Elizabeth Vere, Willoughby, sister to the Earl of Oxford, Cobham, Lumley, Hunsdon, Cecil, wife to Sir Thomas Cecil. Six bannerets were borne by Michael Stanhope, Edward Wotton, Anthony Cooke, William Cecil, John Vere and Richard Cecil.

A sad note is struck in the foregoing account of Lady Oxford's funeral by the absence of any mention of her husband's name. The old suspicions sown by Lord Henry Howard's scandalous gossip in 1575 had never—it would seem—been thoroughly rooted out, although partial reconciliations between Oxford on the one hand and his father-in-law and wife on the other were continually taking place. The tragedy of estrangement is not the

---

[1] Lansdowne MSS., 103. 38 (December 15th, 1587).

[2] *Bibliographica Britannica*, vol. vi, part i, p. 4031.

less tragical, because it is so common ; and we feel that we are here in touch with one of those " old, unhappy, far-off things," which it were futile to discuss but none the less impossible to pass over without at least a momentary tribute of regret and sympathy.

It will be fitting to close this section by quoting a few lines from an elegy " written upon the death of the right honourable Lady Anne Countess of Oxford " by Wilfred Samonde :

> For modesty a chaste Penelope,
> Another Grissel for her patience,
> Such patience as few but she can use,
> Her Christian zeal unto the highest God,
> Her humble duty to her worthy Queen,
> Her reverence unto her aged Sire,
> Her faithful love unto her noble Lord,
> Her friendliness to those of equal state,
> Her readiness to help the needy soul,
> His worthy volume had been alterèd,
> And fillèd with the praises of our Anne,
> Who as she liv'd an Angel on the earth,
> So like an Angel she doth sit on high,
> On his right hand who gave her angel's shape.
> Thrice happy womb wherein such seed was bred,
> And happy father of so good a child,
> And happy husband of so true a wife,
> And happy earth for such a virtuous wight,
> But happy she thus happily to die.
> And now fair Dames cast off your mourning weeds,
> Lament no more as though that she were dead,
> For like a star she shineth in the skies,
> And lends you light to follow her in life.[1]

§ II. THE WAR WITH SPAIN : THE ARMADA

The story of His Most Catholic Majesty's Invincible Armada has been told so often and so well that only the briefest outline will be necessary here.

When Queen Elizabeth declared war on Spain in the autumn of 1585, and sent an expeditionary force under Lord Oxford and Colonel John Norris to the Netherlands, King Philip determined to undertake an invasion of England. His plan was to send a great fleet up Channel

[1] Hatfield MSS., 277. 8.

to Gravelines, where it was to join hands with the Spanish army in the Netherlands under the Duke of Parma ; and from here a landing was to be effected somewhere on the English coast. The fleet, which was to have sailed from Spain in 1587, was delayed for various reasons. But in July 1588 the Armada crossed the Bay of Biscay, and on August 23rd Sir Francis Drake, with the van of the English Fleet, was engaging the Spaniards off Portland.

Throughout July elaborate arrangements were being made in England. The Earl of Leicester was in supreme command with Norris as his Chief of Staff. The main army, consisting of 1,000 horse and 22,000 foot, was encamped at Tilbury. A subsidiary army, consisting of 2,000 horse and 34,000 foot, for the " protection of Her Majesty's person," under Lord Hunsdon, was located in London, while 20,000 men were stationed at central points along the south coast and at Harwich, to repel the invaders should a landing be effected.[1]

The enemy, as we have seen, had been sighted on the 23rd, and for the next few days a running fight had been carried on up Channel. On the 28th the Spaniards anchored in Calais harbour. That night the English sent fire-ships among the enemy vessels, which were once more driven out into the open sea. The following day the decisive battle was fought and the Spaniards utterly defeated.

Lord Oxford, who, as Camden [2] tells us, had fitted out a ship at his own expense—possibly the *Edward Bonaventure*, for the purchase of which he had been negotiating in 1581 [3]—took part in the fighting during the early days of the encounter, although he missed the decisive battle, as is evidenced by the following letter from Leicester to Walsingham, written from Tilbury Camp on July 28th :

My Lord of Oxford . . . returned again yesterday by me, with Captain Huntly as his company. It seemed only his voyage was to have gone to my Lord Admiral ;. and at his return thither he went yesternight for his armour and

---

[1] Camden, *Annals* (1675), p. 405.
[2] *Annals* (1675), p. 414.   [3] See p. 241, ante.

furniture. If he come, I would know from you what I
should do. I trust he be free to go to the enemy, for he
seems most willing to hazard his life in this quarrel.

Lord Leicester's letter concludes with an amusing
contrast between Oxford's eagerness to fight and the antics
of a certain Sir John Smyth :

Sir, You would laugh to see how Sir John Smyth hath
dealt. Since my coming here he came to me and told me
that his disease so grew upon him as he must needs go to
the baths. I told him I would not be against his health
but he saw what the time was, and what pains he had taken
with his countrymen and that I had provided a good place
for him. The next day he came again, saying little to
my offer then, and seemed desirous for his health to be
gone. I told him what place I did appoint which was a
regiment of a great part of his countrymen. He said
his health was dear to him and desired to take his leave
of me, which I yielded unto. Yesterday being our muster
day he came again to dinner to me, but such foolish and
glorious paradoxes he burst without any cause offered,
as made all that knew anything smile and answer little,
but in sort rather to satisfy men present than to argue
with him. After at the muster he entered again into
such strange tries for ordering of men and for the fight
with weapons as made me think he was not well, and God
forbid he should have charge of men that knoweth so . . .
little as I dare pronounce . . . he doth. I have no more
paper. God keep you. 28th July.
                                   . . . assured,
                                   R. LEYCESTER.[1]

Leicester seems to have been under the impression from
his interview with Oxford on the 27th that the latter had
intended to serve at sea under the Lord Admiral throughout
the campaign. For some reason or another he had been
forced to land, perhaps because his ship had been put out
of action. Hence his application to the Commander-in-
Chief for service with the land forces.

His " voyage to the Lord Admiral," as Leicester put it,
had however included some of the heavy fighting which

[1] S.P. Dom., 213. 55.

occurred during the last week of July between Plymouth and the South Foreland.

The following ballad—perhaps by John Lyly—giving an account of the battle, affords a glimpse of the Lord Admiral and Oxford in action.

When from the Hesperian bounds, with warlike bands,
The vowèd foemen of this happy Isle,
With martial men, drawn forth from many lands,
'Gan set their sail, on whom the winds did smile,
    The rumours ran of conquest, war, and spoil,
    And hapless sack of this renownèd soil.

       .   .   .   .   .

Dictimne, wakened by their bitter threats,   *The goddess of war*
Armed with her tools and weapons of defence,
Shaking her lance for inward passion sweats,
Driving the thought of wonted peace from hence,
    And gliding through the circuit of the air
    Unto Eliza's palace did repair.

As when the flames amid the fields of corn,
With hideous noise awake the sleepy swain,
So do her threatenings seldom heard beforne
Revive the warlike Courtiers' hearts again ;
    So forth they press, since Pallas was their guide,
    And boldly sail upon the ocean glide.

The Admiral with Lion on his Crest,   *Lord Admiral*
Like to Alcides on the strand of Troy,
Armed at assay to battle is addressed ;
The sea that saw his powers waxt calm and coy,
    As when that Neptune with three-forkèd mace
    For Trojans' sake did keep the winds in chase.

De Vere, whose fame and loyalty hath pearst   *Earl of Oxford*
The Tuscan clime, and through the Belgike lands
By wingèd Fame for valour is rehearst,
Like warlike Mars upon the hatches stands.
    His tuskèd Boar 'gan foam for inward ire,
    While Pallas filled his breast with warlike fire.[1]

---

[1] *An answer to the untruths published and printed in Spain in glory of their supposed victory achieved against our English Navy. . . . By I. L. . . .* London 1589. The graphic description of the Earl " standing on the hatches " with the Boar on his helmet " foaming for inward ire " conveys the impression that the ballad was written by someone who actually saw Oxford standing in full armour on the deck of his ship. There could hardly have been a more likely eye-witness than John Lyly, Oxford's private secretary. Lyly always signed his name " Ihon Lyllie," whence no doubt the initials " I. L." of the author of the ballad.

As we have seen, Lord Oxford reported himself to Leicester on the 27th, and on August 1st the latter wrote as follows to Walsingham acknowledging Her Majesty's instructions regarding Oxford's employment :

I did, as Her Majesty liked well of, deliver to my Lord of Oxford her gracious consent of his willingness to serve her; and for that he was content to serve her among the foremost as he seemed. She was well pleased that he should have the government of Harwich, and all those that are appointed to attend that place—which should be two thousand men—a place of great trust and of great danger. My Lord seemed at the first to like well of it. Afterward he came to me and told me he thought the place of no service nor credit ; and therefore he would to the Court and understand Her Majesty's further pleasure ; to which I would not be against. But I must desire you— as I know Her Majesty will also make him know—that it was good grace to appoint that place to him, having no more experience than he hath ; and then to use the matter as you shall think good. For my own part being gladder to be rid of him than to have him, but only to have him contented ; which now I find will be harder than I took it. And he denieth all his former offers he made to me rather than not to be seen to be employed at this time.[1]

After his experiences at sea Lord Oxford must have looked upon the offer of the command of a Naval Base as somewhat of the nature of an anti-climax. He had missed the dramatic episode of the fire-ships on July 28th and the decisive battle of the following day. It is perhaps to this cause that we must attribute the restlessness amounting almost to insubordination that he exhibited during his interview with Her Majesty's Commander-in-Chief. Without question he was a very unsatisfactory subordinate from the point of view of his superiors, but so was Lord Nelson, and the reason was probably the same in both cases. Oxford's views, we may be sure, coincided very closely with those expressed in Nelson's favourite

---

[1] S.P. Dom. Eliz., 214. 1.

Shakespeare quotation from *Henry V* : " If it be a sin to covet honour I am the most offending soul alive."

On Sunday, November 24th, the Queen, accompanied by the Earl of Oxford and the rest of the nobility, went in a procession to St. Paul's, to give thanks for the great victory that had at once freed England and temporarily at least crippled the power of her great adversary. For nearly twenty years the Spanish menace had hung like a pall over the people of England, and now, with this great victory of the English sailors, the bogey of Spanish supremacy was laid for ever. A tremendous wave of enthusiasm and rejoicing swept over the country ; and the Queen decreed that on Sunday, November 24th, she would head a solemn procession to St. Paul's to give thanks to God for the preservation of the country.

An account of this great occasion has fortunately been preserved in the form of an anonymous ballad, which is of interest not only because of its vivid description of the event, but also because it tells us of the part taken by Lord Oxford.[1] It is entitled " A joyful ballad of the Royal entrance of Queen Elizabeth into the City of London, the 24th of November in the thirty-first year of Her Majesty's reign, to give God praise for the overthrow of the Spaniards."

> Among the wondrous works of God for safeguard of our Queen,
> Against the heap of trait'rous foes which have confounded been,
> The great and mighty overthrow of Spaniards proud in mind
> Have given us all just cause to say the Lord is good and kind.
>
> .   .   .   .   .
>
> Our noble Queen and peerless prince did make a straight decree
> That through her land a solemn day unto the Lord should be,
> To yield all laud and honour high unto His glorious Name
> Whose hand upholds our happiness and her triumphant reign.
>
> .   .   .   .   .
>
> Therefore to lovely London fair our noble Queen would go,
> And at Paul's Cross before her God her thankful heart to show ;
> Where Prince and people did consent with joyful minds to meet
> To glorify the God of Heaven with psalms and voices sweet.

---

[1] The ballad was first printed in *Life's Little Day*, pp. 277–281, by A. M. W. Stirling, and published by Messrs. Thornton Butterworth in 1924.

An hundreth knights and gentlemen did first before her ride,
On gallant fair and stately steeds their servants by their side ;
The Aldermen in scarlet gowns did after take their place ;
Then rode her Highness' trumpeters sounding before her Grace.

The noble Lord High Chancellor nigh gravely rode in place ;
The Archbishop of Canterbury before her Royal Grace.
The Lord Ambassador of France and all his gentlemen
In velvet black among the Lords did take his place as then.

The Lord Marquess of Winchester bare-headed there was seen,
Who bare the sword in comely sort before our noble Queen ;
The noble Earl of Oxford then High Chamberlain of England
Rode right before Her Majesty his bonnet in his hand.

Then all her Grace's pensioners on foot did take their place
With their weapons in their hands to guard her Royal Grace ;
The Earl of Essex after her did ride the next indeed
Which by a costly silken rein did lead her Grace's steed.

And after by two noblemen along the Church was led,
With a golden canopy carried o'er her head.
The clergy with procession brought her Grace into the choir ;
Whereas her Majesty was set the service for to hear.

And afterwards unto Paul's Cross she did directly pass,
There by the Bishop of Salisbury a sermon preachèd was.
The Earl of Oxford opening then the windows for her Grace
The Children of the Hospital she saw before her face.

Sir William Segar, in his *Honor Military and Civil* (1602), also gives an account of " The Queen's Majesty's most Royal proceeding in State from Somerset Place to Paul's Church, Ann. 1588."

The Earl Marshal at this time was George Talbot, Earl of Shrewsbury.[1] When we consider the places occupied by Oxford and Shrewsbury in the Procession, as shown on the next page, there can be little doubt that they must have been the " two noblemen " who carried the Golden Canopy[2] over Her Majesty's head as she walked up the

[1] Will of George Talbot, Earl of Shrewsbury (P.C.C. 86 Drury), proved 1590, in which he styles himself " Earl Marshal of England, K.G."

[2] Cp. Samuel Butler, *Shakespeare's Sonnets Reconsidered*, ed. 1927, p. 146, quoting Stow, *Annals*, ed. 1615, p. 750 : " She was, under a rich canopy, brought through the long West aisle to her travers in the quire, the clergy singing the Litany."

Nave of St. Paul's and took her seat in the Choir. Moreover, as Earl Marshal and Lord Great Chamberlain they ranked as the two senior Earls in the realm ; and the only holder of a title higher than that of Earl at this time was the Marquess of Winchester, who carried the Sword of State. It is therefore natural that they should have been selected to " bear the Canopy " over their Sovereign on this great and solemn occasion.

In " the List or Roll of all Estates that were in this Princely Proceeding, according as they were marshalled," we read that the Procession ended as follows :

Sergeants at Arms	Garter King at Arms	The Mayor of London	A Gentleman Usher of the Privy Chamber	Sergeants at Arms
	Lord Great Chamberlain of England	Sword borne by the Lord Marquess	Earl Marshal of England	

THE QUEEN'S MAJESTY IN HER CHARIOT

Gentlemen Pensioners Esquires of the State Footmen	Her Highness' train borne by the Marchioness of Winchester	Gentlemen Pensioners Esquires of the State Footmen
	The Palfrey of Honour led by the Master of the Horse	
	The chief Lady of Honour	
	All other Ladies of Honour	
	The Captain of the Guard Yeomen of the Guard	

BOOK THE THIRD
THE RECLUSE

BOOK THE THIRD

THE RECLUSE

" If Endor's widow had had power to raise,
A perfect body of true temperature,
I would conjure you by your wonted praise,
Awhile my song to hear and truth endure :
Your passèd noble proof doth well assure
Your blood's, your mind's, your body's excellence
If their due reverence may this pains procure,
Your patience—with my boldness—will dispense :
I only crave high wisdom's due defence :
Not at my suit, but for work's proper sake,
Which treats of true felicity's essence,
As wisest King most happiest proof did make :
Whereof your own experience much might say,
Would you vouchsafe your knowledge to bewray."

HENRY LOK, TO THE EARL OF OXFORD, 1597.[1]

" But in these days (although some learned Princes may take delight
in Poets) yet universally it is not so. For as well Poets as Poesie are
despised, and the name become of honourable infamous, subject to scorn
and derision, and rather a reproach than a praise to any that useth it."

LORD LUMLEY, in *The Arte of English Poesie*, 1589.

[1] Henry Lok published a book of verse called *Ecclesiasticus*, which was
printed by Richard Field in 1597. The sonnet Lok addressed to Lord
Oxford seems to have been originally written in manuscript in a gift copy
of his book presented by him to the Earl.

CHAPTER VII

1589–1595

" And in Her Majesty's time that now is are sprung up another crew of Courtly makers [i.e. poets], Noblemen and Gentlemen of Her Majesty's own servants, who have written excellently well as it would appear if their doings could be found out and made public with the rest, of which number is first that noble gentleman Edward Earl of Oxford."

LORD LUMLEY, in *The Arte of English Poesie*, 1589.

" But that same gentle spirit from whose pen
Large streams of honey and sweet nectar flow,
Scorning the boldness of such base-born men,
Which dare their follies forth so rashly throw,
Doth rather choose to sit in idle cell,
Than so himself to mockery to sell."

EDMUND SPENSER, in *The Tears of the Muses*, 1591.

§ I. RETIREMENT

FROM 1589 onwards the life of Lord Oxford becomes one of mystery. We have seen him up till now as a prominent courtier, as a patron of the drama and men of letters, and as the recipient from the Queen of an annuity of £1,000 a year. Although this annuity continued to be paid regularly a veil seems to descend over his life from the day he helped to bear the canopy over Her Majesty on November 24th, 1588. Very little is definitely known as to his movements and activities during the next fifteen years. Let us therefore examine the two quotations at the head of this chapter more closely, in order to see what light they can throw on the Earl's closing years.

The first one, taken from the *Arte of English Poesie*,[1] tells us quite emphatically that Lord Oxford stands first among the aristocratic authors of the time. It also tells

[1] In the *Review of English Studies* (July 1925) I gave reasons for supposing that this anonymous book was written by Oxford's cousin and friend Lord Lumley, and not by one of the Puttenhams, as is generally supposed.

us that he was in the habit of concealing his work, which
may mean that it was either not published at all, or else
that it was brought out anonymously. Elsewhere in the
Arte we read that Oxford shares with Richard Edwards,
late Master of the Children of the Chapel Royal, the
distinction of being the best writer of Comedy and Enterlude, a statement which is further borne out, as we have
seen, by another contemporary, Francis Meres, who,
writing in 1598, places the Earl's name first in a list of
writers of comedies.

Let us compare this evidence with the second quotation
given above. Although Spenser does not specifically
say that he is referring to Lord Oxford, a moment's
examination will reveal that this is almost certainly the
case.[1] He is speaking of some aristocratic author who,
unlike " base-born men," disdains to publish—" throw
forth "—his work. This work is described as " large
streams of honey and sweet nectar," implying not only
a considerable output but also a high standard, the
nature of which may be gathered when we realise that the
stanza comes in that section of the *Tears of the Muses*
which is devoted to Thalia, the Muse of Comedy. So
that in every respect Spenser's " gentle spirit " tallies
exactly with what the author of the *Arte* and Meres have
to tell us about Lord Oxford.

Moreover, in the preceding year (1590) when the *Faery
Queen* was published, Spenser prefaced his poem with
seventeen dedicatory sonnets to the principal members
of the aristocracy. In the sonnet addressed to " The
right honourable the Earl of Oxenforde, Lord High
Chamberlain of England," he again lays emphasis on the
mutual love existing between the Earl and the Muses :

> Receive, most noble Lord, in gentle gree,
> The unripe fruit of an unready wit ;
> Which by thy countenance doth crave to be
> Defended from foul Envy's poisonous bit.

---

[1] The context of this stanza, together with a suggestion as to the identity
of Spenser's enigmatic " Willy," will be found in Appendix D.

> Which so to do may thee right well befit,
>   Sith th' antique glory of thine ancestry
> Under a shady veil is therein writ,
>   And eke thine own long living memory,
> Succeeding them in true nobility :
>   And also for the love which thou dost bear
> To th' Heliconian imps and they to thee,
>   They unto thee, and thou to them most dear :
> Dear as thou art unto thyself, so love
> That loves and honours thee, as doth behove.[1]

It is unquestionably in literature, poetry, and the drama that we shall find the key to Lord Oxford's life of retirement from 1589 to 1604. Nor will it surprise us to find that during this period he published nothing under his own name. This is exactly what we should expect ; for while the author of the *Arte* and Meres are emphatic as to the high quality of his writings, the former expressly adds that he deliberately prefers to conceal his work under the cloak of anonymity.

In 1590 we find Thomas Churchyard, the poet, once more in Lord Oxford's employ. We last met him, it will be remembered, in the Earl's household over twenty years before, when a breach seems to have occurred between them. There is no record as to when Oxford took back his old servant, but on December 24th Churchyard entered into a bond for £25 with a certain Mistress Julia Penn. She was the mother-in-law of Michael Hicks, Lord Burghley's private secretary, and seems to have been in the habit of renting out rooms in her house on St. Peter's Hill in London. The £25 represented the first quarter's rent of some rooms Churchyard had taken at Lord Oxford's orders.

A fortnight later Churchyard wrote as follows to Mistress Penn :

I have lovingly and truly dealt with you for the Earl of

---

[1] The " Heliconian imps " are of course the Muses. From the wording of the second quatrain there is no doubt whatever that Lord Oxford himself has been introduced into the allegory of the *Faery Queen*. I have not, so far, been able to trace which of the " knights " at " Gloriana's Court " is represented by him. It would be interesting to follow up this point.

Oxford, a nobleman of such worth as I will employ all I
have to honour his worthiness. So touching what bargain
I made, and order taken from his Lordship's own mouth
for taking some rooms in your house. . . . I stand to that
bargain, knowing my good Lord so noble—and of such
great consideration—that he will perform what I promised.
. . . I absolutely here, for the love and honour I owe to
my Lord, bind myself and all I have in the world unto
you, for the satisfying of you for the first quarter's rent of
the rooms my Lord did take. And further for the coals,
billets, faggots, beer, wine, and any other thing spent by
his honourable means, I bind myself to answer ; yet
confessing that napery and linen was not in any bargain
I made with you for my Lord, which indeed I know my
Lord's nobleness will consider. . . .[1]

There was evidently some hitch about the payment,
the possibility of which is distinctly foreshadowed in
Churchyard's last sentence ; for in an undated letter
Mistress Penn addressed the Earl as follows :

My Lord of Oxford, The grief and sorrow I have taken
for your unkind dealing with me . . . make me believe you
bereft all honour and virtue to be in your speech and
dealing. You know I never seized an assurance at your
Lordship's hands but Master Churchyard's bond, which
I would be loth to trouble him for your Lordship's sake.
You know, my Lord, you had anything in my house
whatsoever you or your men would demand, if it were in
my house. If it had been a thousand times more I would
have been glad to pleasure your Lordship withal. Therefore, good my Lord, deal with me in courtesy, for that
you and I shall come at that dreadful day and give account
for all our doings. . . . I would be loth to offend your
honour in anything ; I trust I have not been burdensome
to your honour, that I do not know, in anything penned.
But, my Lord, if it please your Lordship to show me your
favour in this I shall be much bound to your honour, and
you shall command me and my house, or anything that is
in it, whensoever it shall please you. By one that prays
for your Lordship's long life and in time to come,

                                        JULYAN PENNE.[2]

[1] Lansdowne MSS., 68. 113.   [2] Ibid., 68. 114.

The indignant landlady also vented her wrath on Churchyard, to which he replied :

I never deserved your displeasure, and have made Her Majesty understand of my bond, touching the Earl ; and for fear of arresting I lie in the sanctuary. For albeit you may favour me, yet I know I am in your danger, and am honest and true in all mine actions. . . .[1]

This ends the correspondence. It may therefore be presumed that Mistress Penn received her money.[2]

The few letters we possess that passed between the Earl of Oxford and Lord Burghley after the death of the Countess show both men to have been on quite friendly terms. In June 1590 Lord Burghley wrote to Attorney-General Popham asking his assistance in a legal matter affecting the Earl. This letter, though it lacks its context, shows us that the Queen was interesting herself in Oxford's behalf :

Sir, For that Her Majesty would be assured that the points contained in the paper enclosed should be duly performed by the patentees for my Lord of Oxford's lands, then such purchasers as by due desire purchased any of his Lordship's lands might not be troubled thereby.

Her Majesty, therefore, before the signing of the book, would have you see to be provided, either by the ground itself or by sufficient bond to that effect to be ordered by the said patentees ; wherefore I pray you to consider how such assurance may be best had for Her Majesty's satisfaction, to be inserted in the book, if the sum be not already expressed therein ; which if it be there would it more amply be countered in the docket of the book or by bond of the patentees, or by any [other ?] means you can devise ; until which assurance I find Her Majesty makes

---

[1] Lansdowne MSS., 68. 115.

[2] It occurs to me that it is possible that the lives of two Thomas Churchyards have been telescoped into one. Are we right in identifying the Thomas Churchyard who wrote the *Welcome Home of the Earl of Essex* in 1599 with the Thomas Churchyard who had been a page to the Earl of Surrey in the reign of King Henry VIII. ? If so, he would have been about eighty when he wrote Essex's *Welcome*, and about seventy when he was engaging rooms for Lord Oxford in Mistress Penn's house.

difficulties, and will not be induced to sign your bill.
And so I commend me heartily to you. From the Court
this 16th of June 1590.

Your very loving friend,

W. BURGHLEY.[1]

In August Lord Oxford appealed to his father-in-law
to help him in the matter of a lawsuit that was costing
him £100 a year :

My very good Lord, Where I mortgaged my lease of
Aveley to Master Herdson, and not as yet redeemed, and
now as well for the supply of my present wants, as also
to have some £300 of ready money to redeem certain
leases at Hedingham, which were gotten from me very
unreasonably for divers years yet enduring, and are of as
good clear yearly value as my said lease of Aveley is : I
therefore most earnestly desire your Lordship to signify
your liking to me in writing, to dispose of the said lease
at my pleasure ; otherwise there is not any will deal with
me for the same nor for any part thereof. Wherein I shall
be greatly beholden unto your Lordship, as I am in all
the rest of my whole estate. The 5th of August.

Your Lordship's to command,

EDWARD OXENFORD.[2]

In September he writes, again on legal matters, to his
father-in-law " whom in all my causes I find mine honourable good Lord, and to deal more fatherly than friendly
with me, for the which I do acknowledge—and ever will—
myself in most especial wise bound." [3]

The next letter, which is dated May 18th, 1591, is most
interesting, because in it Lord Oxford asks Burghley to
obtain the Queen's sanction for him to commute his £1,000
a year for a lump sum of £5,000. Oxford first thanks

---

[1] Egerton MSS. (Brit. Mus.), 2618, fol. 11.

[2] Lansdowne MSS., 63. 71. There is a postscript which deals entirely
with technical legal matters.

[3] Lansdowne MSS., 63. 77. Sir Sidney Lee's pontifical statement in the
Dict. Nat. Biog. that " when the Countess [of Oxford] died on June 6th,
1588 [Burghley] showed little inclination to relieve his son-in-law's neces-
sities " is beneath comment.

Burghley for punishing two of his servants, Hampton and
Amis, who had dealt " unfaithfully " with him.   He then
goes on to state his proposal :

Whereas I have heard Her Majesty meant to sell unto
one Midelsone, a merchant, and one Carmarder, the
domain of Denbighe, which (as I am informed) is £230
yearly rent now as it is ; I would be an humble suitor
to Her Majesty that I might have this burgh, paying the
£8,000 as they should have done, [Her Majesty] accepting
for £5,000 thereof of the pension which she hath given me
in the Exchequer, and the other £3,000 the next term, or
upon such reasonable days as Her Majesty would grant me
by her favour.   And further, if Her Majesty would not
accept the pension for £5,000, that then she would yet take
unto it to make it up [to] that value [of] the total of the
Forest,[1] which by all counsel of laws and conscience is as
good right unto me as any other land in England.   And I
think Her Majesty makes no evil bargain, and I would
be glad to be sure of something that were mine own and
that I might possess. . . .

The effect hereof is : I would be glad to have an equal
care with your Lordship over my children, and if I may
obtain this reasonable suit of Her Majesty, granting me
nothing but what she hath done to others and mean persons
and nothing but that I shall pay for it, then those lands
which are in Essex—as Hedingham, Brets, and the rest
whatsoever—which will come to some £500 or £600 by
year, upon your Lordship's friendly help towards my
purchases in Denbighe, shall be presently delivered in
possession to you for their use.   And so much I am sure
to make of these domains for myself.

So shall my children be provided for, myself at length
settled in quiet, and I hope your Lordship contented,
remaining no cause for you to think me an evil father, nor
any doubt in me but that I may enjoy that friendship
from your Lordship that so near a match, and not fruitless,
may lawfully expect.   Good my Lord, think of this, and
let me have both your furtherance and counsel in this
cause.   For to tell truth, I am weary of an unsettled life,

---

[1] The hereditary claim of Lord Oxford to the custody of the Forest
of Essex was being discussed at this time before Lord Chancellor Hatton.
King James granted it to Oxford in 1603.

21

which is the very pestilence that happens unto Courtiers,
that propound unto themselves no end of their time
therein bestowed.   Thus committing your Lordship to
Almighty God, with my most hearty thanks and commendation, I take my leave, this 18th day of May.

Your Lordship's to command,

EDWARD OXEFORD.[1]

We cannot say whether Lord Burghley laid this proposal
before the Queen.   At any rate, nothing came of it, because
Lord Oxford continued to receive his £1,000 a year.   It
provides, however, an illuminating side-light on his un-
businesslike methods.   That he should attempt, at the
age of forty, to commute an annuity of £1,000 a year
for so small a sum as £5,000, seems most extraordinary.
Well might he say that the Queen would make " no evil
bargain " !   It seems, on the whole, most probable that
Burghley, who knew by bitter experience his son-in-law's
complete ignorance of the value of money, quietly allowed
the matter to drop.

On December 2nd, 1591, the Earl of Oxford alienated the
ancestral home of the de Veres, Castle Hedingham, to his
three daughters and Lord Burghley.   The Castle had
probably remained uninhabited since the day the Earl
and his Countess had buried their four-day-old son in
the parish churchyard in 1583.   By 1591 it had fallen
into sad disrepair, and just before Lord Burghley took it
over Oxford issued a warrant authorising the dismantling
of part of the building and many of the out-houses.   This
perfectly natural precaution has been stigmatised by
historians as a savage act of vandalism !   Their vivid
imaginations have pictured the Earl first selling the Castle
to his father-in-law, and then secretly demolishing the
walls and tearing down the park fences !   Had they taken
the trouble to ascertain the true relations between Oxford
and Burghley—" whom in all my causes I find mine
honourable good Lord, and to deal more fatherly than
friendly with me "—they would have avoided making

---

[1] Lansdowne MSS., 68. 6.

themselves ridiculous by propounding such an absurd theory.[1]

§ II. Mistress Elizabeth Trentham

The quite unusual interest Lord Oxford was displaying in money matters is accounted for by the fact that toward the end of 1591 he married again. His new bride was Elizabeth Trentham, the daughter of Sir Thomas Trentham a Staffordshire landowner. She was one of the Maids of Honour, and evidently a court beauty as the following extract from a gossipy letter tells us :

. . . Mistress Trentham is as fair, Mistress Edgcumbe as modest, Mistress Radcliff as comely and Mistress Garrat as jolly as ever. . . .[2]

The marriage took place between July 4th, 1591, and March 12th, 1592, but I have not succeeded up to date in tracing the entry in any Parish Register.[3]

Perhaps the most interesting thing about this marriage is that it was evidently sanctioned, and probably even encouraged, by the Queen. It had always been a risky proceeding for a courtier to carry off one of the Maids of Honour, as Leicester and Lettice Knollys had found to their cost in 1578 ; but by the nineties it had become an almost certain step to disgrace and even imprisonment. Everyone knows how the Earl of Southampton fell into dire disgrace and was obliged to withdraw from the Court because of his intrigue and subsequent marriage with Elizabeth Vernon ; and Sir Walter Ralegh was sent to the Tower for committing a similar indiscretion with Elizabeth

[1] This theory, unsupported by any evidence, was first started by L. Majendie, *An account of Castle Hedingham* (1796). He has been echoed by Thomas Wright in his *History of Essex* (1836) and others. (See Appendix H.)

[2] J. Farnham to Roger Manners, written from the Court on April 5th, 1582. (Cal. Rutland MSS., I. 134.) Roger Manners was an old courtier who had for many years been an Esquire of the Body to Mary and Elizabeth. He was an uncle of Edward, 3rd Earl of Rutland (1549–87), who had been a Royal Ward in London at the same time as Lord Oxford.

[3] Inquisitions Post Mortem. Chancery Series II. 286. 165.

Throckmorton.   With Lord Oxford, however, it was quite
different.   He suffered no disgrace, and the payment of
his £1,000 was continued punctually and regularly.   This
is only another example of the great favour the Queen
showed him, and how much she sought his welfare and
happiness.   This fondness of the Queen for Lord Oxford
was reciprocated no less by him, as will be seen by his
heart-broken letter to Sir Robert Cecil when she died.

   In 1592 Oxford started a new suit to the Queen in which
he asks for the import monopoly on oils, wools, and
fruits.[1]   The Queen's practice of granting monopolies to
her courtiers has been almost universally condemned by
modern historians.   They were naturally resented by the
people, because once a monopoly was established the
consumer inevitably had to pay more for the article.   In
justice to the Queen, however, it should be pointed out
that necessity drove her to adopt this expedient.   The
difficulty with which she obtained any money at all from
Parliament, especially in the latter half of her reign when
she had the War with Spain and the Irish Rebellion on
her hands, is seldom properly appreciated.   The national
accounts are a sufficient testimony to this fact.   The total
of money voted by Parliament throughout her reign to
meet " extraordinary " war expenses was about 3½ million
pounds.   The expenditure on wars alone during the same
period was estimated in 1603 to have amounted to nearly
5 millions.   These figures put quite a different complexion
on Elizabeth's traditional parsimony.   The deficit obviously had to be met somehow, and it was met with characteristic ingenuity by Her Majesty and her Lord Treasurer.
   Generally speaking, they adopted two methods :
   1. The first method simply involved the selling of
Crown lands, and the auctioning of monopolies to the
highest bidder.   The former needs little or no explanation,
and one example will suffice.   In 1590 the Queen sold land
to the value of over £126,000.   It is impossible to say how

   [1] Lansdowne MSS., 71. 10.

much of this money went to the Privy Purse, and how much was transferred to the Exchequer, because there was practically no distinction between the two. But it is safe to say that a considerable portion was used in one way or another towards the cost of the Spanish War.

The sale of monopolies was rather more complicated. The bidder for a monopoly might, for example, offer a lump sum of money ; or he might propose a percentage to be taken by the Treasury on his profits ; or, again, he might suggest making a fixed annual payment into the Exchequer. To what extent the national revenue profited by these means we cannot now say for certain. It is probable that no two transactions were exactly the same, and the records that have come down to us are very incomplete. Two examples, however, may be given :

(a) In 1592 Sir Henry Neville was given the export monopoly of iron cannon for twenty years. In the famous debate on monopolies held in the House of Commons in 1601 it was asserted that the Queen, which is synonymous for the Treasury, received £3,000 a year from the customs duty on this trade.

(b) In consequence of three Italian merchants having been given the calf-skin monopoly, the price of a pair of shoes had been increased by fourpence. We shall probably never know what proportion of this increase found its way into the Exchequer. But we can at least say for certain that Queen Elizabeth was not fleecing her subjects merely for the personal enrichment of three Italians.

2. The second, or indirect, method is still more obscure from the point of view of actual figures. In practice it simply involved the employment of private wealth in the public service. It is safe to make the general statement that none of Elizabeth's officials—Ministers, Ambassadors, Naval and Military Commanders, etc.—ever received an adequate salary from the Treasury. In some cases the Queen tacitly demanded that their private incomes should defray the difference. For example, the Earl

of Shrewsbury, when appointed custodian of the Queen of Scots, was given a quite inadequate allowance. The indirect contribution he was called upon to make on behalf of the national expenditure was, in effect, precisely the same as if he had been subjected to a regular income-tax.

All Her Majesty's officials, however, were not wealthy men like Lord Shrewsbury. It was a matter of grave concern to a poor man like Francis Walsingham when he was given an appointment such as Ambassador in Paris. Gifts of land did, no doubt, provide partial compensation ; but it is on the whole true to say that no Elizabethan Crown servant was as rich when he relinquished his appointment as when he took it up.

One final example may be quoted to show another aspect of the indirect method of supplementing the national revenue. In 1584 Sir Walter Ralegh was given a commission to discover " remote heathen barbarous lands." At the same time he was given the lucrative monopoly on wine imports and the licensing of taverns. From first to last it is estimated that Sir Walter spent £40,000 in building ships, planting colonies, and fighting the Spaniards ; the money, of course, coming ultimately from the pockets of the wine drinkers in the country.

It was by means of these and similar subterfuges that Elizabeth contrived not only to pay for the war against Spain, but succeeded in staving off the conflict between Crown and Parliament that overwhelmed England a generation after her death. And yet historians persistently denounce her for having given her " favourites " lavish " presents " at the expense of her downtrodden people !

Lord Oxford's suit for the oils, wools, and fruits monopoly failed, no doubt because the Queen was waiting for a higher bid ; but he was still pursuing it next year. We learn this from another interesting letter, which also reveals the fact that for some years past he had been seeking yet another favour from the Queen—the Stewardship, or Custody, of the Forest of Essex. As he was

already the recipient of so munificent an annuity as £1,000
a year from the Exchequer, it is hardly surprising that
Her Majesty was beginning to be exasperated by his
continuous demands for more ! The letter is addressed to
Lord Burghley :

My very good Lord, I hope it is not out of your remembrance how long sithence I have been a suitor to Her
Majesty if she would give me leave to try my title to the
Forest at the law.   But I found that so displeasing unto
her, that in place of receiving that ordinary favour which
is of course granted to the meanest subject, I was brow-
beaten and had many bitter speeches given me.   Nevertheless at length, by means of some of the Lords of the
Council, among which your Lordship especially, Her
Majesty was persuaded to give me ear.

He goes on to give the history of the case, and then
continues :

But now the ground whereon I lay my suit being so
just and reasonable that either I should expect some
satisfaction either by way of recompense or restoration of
mine own, as I am yet persuaded till law hath convinced
me ; these are most earnestly to desire a continuance of
your Lordship's favour and furtherance in my suit which
I made at Greenwich to Her Majesty at her last being
there, about three commodities, to wit, the oils wools,
and fruits, in giving therefore, as then my proffer was.
. . . And thus desiring your Lordship to hold me excused
for that I am so long in a matter that concerneth me so
much, I will make an end.   This 25th October 1593, and
always rest your Lordship's to command,

EDWARD OXEFORD.[1]

It may be remarked, in parenthesis, that Lord Oxford's
request for this monopoly was not quite on all fours with

[1] Harleian MSS., 6996. 22.   It was at this royal visit to Greenwich that
Captain Nicholas Dawtrey, the prototype of Sir John Falstaff, received
a Warrant for " £140 out of the Exchequer " in return for " a little brief
discourse on Ireland " which he delivered " upon Her Highness' commandment " (see *The Falstaff Saga*, by John Dawtrey, 1927, p. 87).   It is
interesting definitely to locate Oxford and Dawtrey together at the Court,
although of course as constant suitors to the Queen they must often have
come into contact with one another there.

Ralegh's wine monopoly mentioned above. Ralegh's was a *gift* from the Queen, in return for which he built ships and fought for her at sea. Oxford was not asking for the oil monopoly as a gift, but was offering to *buy* it. It is obvious how both parties might hope to gain by the transaction : Oxford, by making more out of it than he gave ; the Queen, by parting with something which cost her no more than her signature, and getting a substantial cash payment in return. This " sale of monopolies " was simply a development of the " gift monopolies " of former years.

On July 7th, 1594, the Earl wrote to his father-in-law and made an obscure reference to his " office." It appears, though the details are not specified, that both he and the Queen were suffering from " sundry abuses " which were hindering him in the execution of this " office." He is evidently referring to some work he is doing for Her Majesty, no doubt in return for his £1,000 a year. It is most tantalising that he tells us so much and yet so little ; for he gives no hint—any more than the Queen did in her original warrant—what this work is :

My very good Lord, If it please you to remember that about half a year or thereabout past I was a suitor to your Lordship for your favour : that whereas I found sundry abuses, whereby both Her Majesty and myself were, in my office greatly hindered, that it might please your Lordship that I might find such favour from you that I might have the same redressed. At which time I found so good forwardness in your Lordship that I found myself greatly beholden for the same ; yet by reason that at that time mine attorney was departed the town, I could not then send him to your appointment. But hoping that the same disposition still remaineth towards the justness of my cause, and that your Lordship, to whom my estate is so well known, and how much it standeth me on not to neglect, as heretofore, such occasions as to amend the same as may arise from mine office ; I most heartily desire your Lordship that it will please you to give care to the state of my cause, and at your best leisure admit either my attorney or other of my counsel at law to inform your

Lordship, that the same being perfectly laid open to your Lordship, I may enjoy the favour from you which I most earnestly desire. In which doing I shall think myself singularly beholden in this, as I have been in other respects. This 7th July 1594.

Your Lordship's ever to command,

EDWARD OXENFORD.[1]

The Earl of Oxford and his new Countess settled in the village of Stoke Newington, just north of Shoreditch. It was here, on February 24th, 1593, that a son, Henry, was born. He was christened in the Parish Church on March 31st, and in due course succeeded his father as eighteenth Earl of Oxford. It is curious that the name Henry is unique in the de Vere, Cecil, and Trentham families. There must have been some reason for his being given this name, but if so I have been unable to discover it. It is hardly likely that he would have been named after Lord Henry Howard ! A possible clue is that at this time two Henry's were being sought by Lord Burghley for the hand of Oxford's eldest daughter, Lady Elizabeth Vere. They were Henry Wriothesley, Earl of Southampton, and Henry Percy, Earl of Northumberland. It seems likely that the name Henry may have been derived from one of these. The Earl of Southampton followed Oxford as a Royal Ward in Burghley's household. In later life Henry de Vere and Henry Wriothesley were closely connected as Colonels of two of the regiments raised for special service in the Low Countries in 1624. Perhaps, therefore, Henry Wriothesley was the cause of the name being introduced into the de Vere family.

It was in the winter of 1589–90 that Lord Burghley began to busy himself about the question of a husband for his eldest granddaughter. His choice fell on the Earl of Southampton, then aged seventeen, who had been a Royal Ward since his father's death. The Dowager Countess of Southampton approved the match; but her son, plead-

---

[1] Lansdowne MSS., 76. 74. This letter has been published in facsimile by W. W. Greg, *English Literary Autographs*. (Cf. Appendix H.)

ing his youth, asked to be given a year to make up his mind. It is not clear how the matter stood at the end of the year, but nothing ever came of the proposed marriage. There is, however, a curious story related in a letter written by Henry Garnet, a Jesuit, in 1594. He states that " the young Earl of Southampton refusing the Lady Vere payeth £5,000 of present money." [1] I hardly think this story can be literally true ; but it shows, at all events, that gossip was linking their names together at as late a date as 1594.

However this may be, by 1592 Lord Burghley had turned his attention elsewhere. In a letter from Mary Harding to the Countess of Rutland, written in June, we read that—

Lord Burghley has tried to marry Elizabeth Vere to Lord Northumberland . . . she cannot fancy him.[2]

This proposal also fell through, the reason probably being that Lady Elizabeth had already lost her heart to the man she married three years later. This was Master William Stanley, the second son of the Earl of Derby. So long as his father and elder brother were alive, however, he would have been quite out of the question as a suitor for the hand of the Lord Treasurer's granddaughter. But it so happened that in 1594 he succeeded quite unexpectedly to the title, and three weeks later their engagement was announced openly. This certainly lends colour to the theory that some time previously they had secretly plighted their troth.

We must now digress for a moment and see what manner of man it was who had won the affections of Lord Oxford's daughter.

---

[1] C. C. Stopes, *The Third Earl of Southampton*, p. 86.

[2] Cal. Ancaster MSS. Henry Percy, 9th Earl of Northumberland (1564–1632) was a most interesting character. He was known as the " Wizard Earl " because of his passion for making scientific experiments. He was accused, probably unjustly, of complicity in the Gunpowder Plot, and was imprisoned in the Tower until 1621, where he became intimate with Sir Walter Ralegh.

INTERLUDE: WILLIAM STANLEY, SIXTH EARL OF DERBY

"I dedicate these poems to your favour and protection, as the true Mæcenas of the Muses and judicial in their exercises."

THOMAS LODGE, in dedicating *A Fig for Momus* to the Earl of Derby, 1595.

"There also is (ah no, he is not now)
But since I said he is, he quite is gone,
AMYNTAS quite is gone and lies full lowe,
Having his AMARYLLIS left to mone.
Helpe, o ye shepheards, helpe ye all in this,
Helpe AMARYLLIS this her loss to mourne :
Her losse is yours, your losse AMYNTAS is,
AMYNTAS flowre of shepheards pride forlorne :
He, whilst he livèd, was the noblest swaine,
That ever pipèd on an oaten quill :
Both did he other, which could pipe, maintaine,
And eke could pipe himself with passing skill.
And there, though last not least is AETION,
A gentler shepheard may no where be found :
Whose Muse, full of high thoughts invention,
Doth like himself heroically sound."

EDMUND SPENSER, in *Colin Clouts come home again*, 1595.[1]

IT is a curious coincidence that the same battle that restored the thirteenth Earl of Oxford after his long exile also placed the name of Stanley among the Earldoms of England. When Henry Tudor, Earl of Richmond, with the attainted Earl of Oxford as his first lieutenant, landed in England in 1485 and met the last of the Plantagenets at Bosworth, Thomas Lord Stanley and his followers were ranged on the side of King Richard III. But before

---

[1] "Amyntas" and "Amaryllis" are Ferdinando, Earl of Derby, who died in 1594, and his widow Alice, *née* Spencer, with whom the poet claimed kinship. "Aetion"—from the Greek ἀετός, an eagle—is almost certainly his younger brother William, who succeeded him in the Earldom. The Derby crest was an eagle. (Cf. Professor Abel Lefranc, *Sous le Masque de William Shakespeare*, vol. i, p. 199.)

the battle was over Stanley, who had married Richmond's mother, deserted the King and went over to his son-in-law. After the decisive victory his brother, Sir William Stanley, having recovered the Plantagenet crown from the dead body of King Richard, placed it on the Earl of Richmond's head. And when the latter ascended the throne as King Henry VII. he rewarded Lord Stanley by creating him Earl of Derby.

He was succeeded by his grandson, Thomas, in 1504, who in turn was succeeded by his son, Edward, in 1521. His son, Henry, was born in 1531, and became the fourth Earl of Derby in 1572. Unlike his father, Henry Earl of Derby was a strong Protestant and a vigorous enemy of the recusants. He was made a Knight of the Garter, and was frequently employed by Queen Elizabeth on diplomatic missions to the Continent. In 1555 he married Margaret Clifford, and through her he became a cousin of Queen Elizabeth. He died in September 1593, leaving two sons, Ferdinando and William.

Ferdinando, the elder, was born in 1559. He was styled Lord Strange until his father's death, when he succeeded him as fifth Earl of Derby. Less than seven months later, at the early age of thirty-four, he died in mysterious circumstances, probably of poison.

He was a scholar, a poet, and a patron of the drama. Spenser praised his poetical skill in 1595 under the name of " Amyntas." In the same year the anonymous author of *Polimanteia* eulogised him as a poet and a patron of letters. Nashe in *Pierce Penilesse*, Greene in *Ciceronis Amor*, and Chapman in *The Shadow of the Night*, all acknowledged his literary eminence ; so that although none of his poems or writings survive we have sufficient evidence to realise what a tragedy his early death was to English literature.

He died on April 16th, 1594, and was succeeded by his younger brother. In 1582 William Stanley had undertaken a foreign tour to France, where he visited Paris (in July), Orleans, Blois, Tours, Saumur, and Angers (in

October).[1] One authority asserts that his travels extended as far afield as Spain, Constantinople, and Russia;[2] but it is probable that he has been confused with a renegade adventurer, Sir William Stanley, who, when Governor of Deventer in 1587, betrayed it to the Spaniards. At all events our William Stanley, who does not appear to have been knighted, was back in England by 1587, if not earlier.

On May 9th, 1594, just three weeks after Ferdinando's death, his widow in a letter to Sir Robert Cecil says that she " hears of a motion of marriage between the Earl my brother and my Lady Vere your niece." The Dowager Countess was no friend of the new Earl, as their subsequent quarrels over the Derby estates showed ; and in the letter quoted she adds spitefully, " I wish her a better husband." [3]

In view of Elizabeth Vere's refusal to marry either Southampton or Northumberland it seems not unlikely that she had fallen in love with William Stanley while she was a Maid of Honour at Court as early as 1590 or 1591. If so their patience was rewarded, for we find Lord Burghley giving his consent. And on September 13th, 1594, Lord Derby wrote thus to the Lord Treasurer :

My very honourable good Lord, I understand by my servants Ireland and Doughtye, that according to your Lordship's last speech, they have thoroughly acquainted your Lordship with my estate, and that now it pleaseth your Lordship to partly refer the further speeding to my liking, either now or the next term to be consummated. How grateful the message was unto me I leave your Lordship to conjure. In which case I pray your Lordship to consider my affection to that honourable Lady, the taunting of my unfriends, the gladding of my well wishers, and the investing of me in this estate whereunto Almighty God hath called me. In which, by so honourable a patron,

---

[1] Cal. S.P. Dom., Add. 27, 104, 118. The Court of Navarre was at Blois this year, which may have attracted William Stanley to this place. His Protestant upbringing would naturally have made him sympathetic with Henry of Navarre's heroic struggle against the Catholics.

[2] *A brief account of the travels of the celebrated Sir William Stanley, son of the fourth Earl of Derby.* (Cf. Lefranc, vol. i, p. 104.)

[3] Cal. Hatfield MSS., IV. 527.

with my Lady and mistress to both our contentments, and your Lordship's comfort, God the worker of all goodness may send me a son. Wherefore I wish your Lordship allowance of a present dispatch. Nevertheless, I must and will be wholly directed by your Lordship in this and all other respects, and so humbly take my leave. From my house at Cannon Row this 13th of September 1594. Your Lordship's assured friend to command,

WILL DERBY.[1]

It is evident from this letter that the two lovers were becoming impatient over their deferred marriage. Nor can the delay be entirely attributed to negotiations in connexion with the marriage settlement. It appears that when Ferdinando died Alice, Countess of Derby, was expecting a baby :

The marriage of the Lady Vere to the new Earl of Derby is deferred, by reason that he standeth in hazard to be unearled again, his brother's wife being with child, until it is seen whether it be a boy or no.[2]

Lord Burghley had not unnaturally withheld for the time being his full consent ; but later in the year the Dowager Countess gave birth to a girl. William Stanley's title to the Earldom having been thus secured, the last obstacle to their union was removed.

The marriage took place at Greenwich on January 26th, 1595, in the presence of the Queen and the Court " with great solemnity and triumph." [3]   As was customary at all important weddings, the occasion was marked by feasting and revelry. It is of particular interest that *A Midsummer Night's Dream* was probably performed during these celebrations. It is known that this play was written for a wedding about this time ; and the Lord Chamberlain's company gave a performance that evening.[4]   Shakespeare was then writing for this company, which had been taken under

---

[1] Lansdowne MSS., 76. 76.
[2] Stopes, p. 86. From a letter written by Father Garnet in 1594.
[3] Stowe MSS., 1047, fol. 264 ; cf. Stow, *Annals*, p. 769.
[4] Cf. Chambers, *Elizabethan Stage*, vol. iv, p. 109.

Lord Hunsdon's patronage on the death of its previous patron Ferdinando. It is therefore perhaps not unreasonable to suppose that he may either have written or collaborated in the writing of this comedy for the marriage celebrations of his late employer's brother.

Shortly after the wedding the Earl of Oxford was staying with the newly married couple at their house in Cannon Row, for on August 7th he writes to Lord Burghley that—

> On my coming to Byfleet from Cannon Row the Earl of Derby was very earnest that he might assure £1,000 a year for my daughter, and marvelled that Sir Robert Cecil her uncle, and I her father were so slack to call upon it ; so I desire something may be done therein.[1]

In September 1596 we find Lord Oxford once more staying with his son-in-law at Cannon Row.[2] Some time in this year Lady Oxford bought a house known as " King's Place " in Hackney, the parish adjoining Stoke Newington.[3] Here she lived with her husband until his death in 1604.

In January 1599 Lady Oxford was being entertained by the Derbys at Thistleworth. This transpires in a letter from Lord Derby in which he adds that he intends to accompany the Countess of Oxford back to her home when she returns.[4] He wrote to Sir Robert Cecil " from Hackney " on the 28th, when he was no doubt staying with his father-in-law. He was back at his house in Cannon Row by July ; and in November of the same year (1599) he and his wife were once more staying at King's Place with the Oxfords.[5]

So little is known of the movements of the Oxfords and Derbys at this time that these chance statements that they

---

[1] Cal. S.P. Dom. (1595–7), p. 88. I have remarked elsewhere that the Stanleys were reputed to be the richest family in England, which accounts for the size of this very generous allowance.

[2] Cal. Hatfield MSS., VI. 369.

[3] An interesting account of " King's Place " is to be found in Dr. W. Robinson's *History and Antiquities of Hackney* (1842), p. 100.

[4] Cal. Hatfield MSS., IX. 51.

[5] Hatfield MSS., 74. 107.

were visiting each other in 1595, 1596, and twice in 1599,
argue a close intimacy. It will be worth inquiring into the
nature of this friendship to see if we can discover the bond
that drew the two Earls together.

We know that both of them at this time were living
secluded lives, in spite of the fact that they were still
young men—Oxford being in his forties and Derby in his
thirties. The reason for Derby's seclusion is partly self-
evident. In 1593 a Jesuit plot had been disclosed which
had as its object the dethroning of Elizabeth and the
placing of Ferdinando, who had just succeeded to the
Earldom, on the throne.[1] Ferdinando and William were
descended through their mother, Margaret Clifford, from
Lady Mary Tudor, the younger sister of King Henry VIII.
And although both brothers, by their words and actions,
showed themselves absolutely innocent of any complicity
in this mad project, their very proximity to the throne
rendered them perpetually open to suspicion. Ferdinando's
death has been traced to these Jesuit conspirators, who,
when they discovered his uncompromisingly hostile attitude towards their machinations, hoped perhaps to find
a readier instrument in his brother. In this they were
disappointed, for William proved as loyal to the Queen as
his brother had been. But his position for some years
remained precarious ; and had he dabbled at all in politics
his downfall would almost certainly have been brought
about by his enemies.

With Lord Oxford it was different. His exile from the
Court was from choice, and not from necessity. He had
always despised the Court and its " reptilia," preferring
the seclusion of his " Country Muses." Poetry, the
drama, and music had ever been his chief interests, and we
may be sure that in them we shall find the key to his life
of retirement from 1589 to 1604. And it is natural to
suppose that here too we shall find the key to his friendship
with Lord Derby.

Unsupported supposition, however, should have no

[1] Cal. Hatfield MSS., V. 58.

place in a biography; but in this particular instance confirmatory evidence is forthcoming. I would ask the reader to consider the following statements :

1. In 1598 Francis Meres wrote :

" The best for comedy among us be Edward Earl of Oxford."

2. In 1599, a year in which the Derbys paid at least two visits to the Oxfords at Hackney, George Fanner wrote :

" The Earl of Derby is busied only in penning comedies for the common players." [1]

3. In 1599 John Farmer, in dedicating his *First Set of English Madrigals* to Lord Oxford, said :

" . . . without flattery be it spoke, those that know your Lordship know this, that using this science [i.e. music] as a recreation, your Lordship have overgone most of them that make it a profession."

4. In 1624 Francis Pilkington, in his *Second Set of Madrigals and Pastorals*, printed—

" A *Pavin*, made for the Orpharion, by the right honourable *William* Earle of *Darbie*, and by him consented to be in my Bookes placed." [2]

There need be little doubt that the writing of plays and musical composition led the two Earls to spend their leisure hours together. Such pronounced tastes as these were sufficiently rare among Elizabethan courtiers to bring them together automatically, quite apart from their close alliance by marriage and the fact that they frequently stayed in each other's houses. The " comedies " that the two Earls were writing, probably in collaboration, were presumably acted ; and this brings us to the subject of actors. We have already considered in some detail Lord

[1] Cal. S.P. Dom., 271. 34, 35.
[2] In the British Museum. The Pavane is No. XXVII. in the collection.

22

Oxford's close connexion with the stage since 1580. It
is outside the scope of this work to give a full account of
the various companies of actors that were patronised at
different times by the fourth, fifth, and sixth Earls of
Derby, but a brief outline of the dramatic activities of
Earls Ferdinando and William is perhaps desirable.[1]

Ferdinando Stanley, who was known as Lord Strange
from 1572 to 1593, first took a company of actors under
his patronage in 1576, when he was aged seventeen. Nothing is known of the personnel of this company until 1588
when the Earl of Leicester died and several of his players,
including Will Kempe, George Bryan, and Thomas Pope,
seem to have joined Strange's men.[2] Shortly afterwards
the company amalgamated temporarily with the Lord
Admiral's players, the chief of whom was the great
tragedian, Edward Alleyn.[3] The united company, under
the name of Lord Strange's men, gave six performances
at Court in the winter of 1591–2, followed by a six weeks'
season at the Rose Theatre under Philip Henslowe. In
September 1593, when Ferdinando succeeded to the
Earldom, they assumed the title of the " Earl of Derby's
players." Ferdinando died in April 1594, and in May we
find his company, now called the " Countess of Derby's
players," acting at Winchester.[4] This was Ferdinando's
widow Alice (*née* Spencer), the " Amaryllis " of Spenser's
Tears of the Muses. But she was evidently either unwilling or unable to continue her patronage, for in the
following month the company passed into the service of
Henry Carey, Lord Hunsdon, who was then Lord Chamberlain. The amalgamation with the Lord Admiral's players
was evidently still in force, for we read in Henslowe's
Diary that " the Lord Admiral's men and the Lord

[1] Detailed analysis of these companies will be found in J. T. Murray,
English Dramatic Companies, vol. i ; Professor Abel Lefranc, *Sous le
Masque de William Shakespeare*, vol. i ; and E. K. Chambers, *Elizabethan
Stage*, vol. ii.

[2] Murray, vol. i, p. 73.

[3] Chambers, vol. ii, p. 120.

[4] Murray, vol. i, p. 108.

Chamberlain's men " acted under his direction at Newington Butts from June 3rd to 13th.[1]

This transfer of patronage from the Dowager Countess of Derby to Lord Hunsdon can, I suggest, be accounted for quite simply. Lord Hunsdon's eldest son, Sir George Carey, had married Elizabeth Spencer, the Countess of Derby's sister. It is therefore not unreasonable to suppose that Lady Elizabeth Hunsdon persuaded her father-in-law, who had no players at the time, to take over the patronage of her widowed sister's company. At all events they remained in the service of the Hunsdon family [2] until 1603, when they were taken over by King James and known thenceforward as the "King's players."

It was while they were still in Ferdinando's service that they first gave indications of their future fame. It must have been due largely to Alleyn's talent, as Sir Edmund Chambers says, that they were called upon to give six performances at Court in the winter of 1591–2. But more important still is the fact that early in 1592 they began to act Shakespeare's plays at the Rose.

The début of William Shakespeare as an actor and playwright is closely connected with the fifth Earl of Derby. It has been conjectured that Shakespeare joined the Earl of Leicester's players when they visited Stratford-on-Avon in 1586 or 1587. In July of the latter year the company spent three days at Lathom House, one of the Earl of Derby's seats ; and the following year Ferdinando, then Lord Strange, seems to have taken several of them into his own company. We cannot say for certain whether Shakespeare was one of these ; but we do know that by 1592 he was one of Lord Strange's playwrights. His activities, however, were not confined to his patron's company alone. In 1593 he wrote, or at least worked upon, three plays for Lord Pembroke's men, namely,

---

[1] Chambers, vol. ii, p. 193. There is reason to suppose that they separated once more after this.

[2] Sir George Carey succeeded to the title and the patronage of the company on his father's death in 1596.

The Contention of York and Lancaster, The Taming of a Shrew, and *The True Tragedy of Richard Duke of York.*[1]

Early in 1594 another company—the Earl of Sussex's —acted his *Titus Andronicus* at the Rose.[2] This play has long been a puzzle to critics. Although it was undoubtedly first produced by Sussex's men, its title-page informs us that it was played by " the Earle of Darbie, Earle of Pembroke, and Earle of Sussex their servants." [3] Finally, as we have seen, Shakespeare passed, on Ferdinando's death, via his widow, to the patronage of her sister's father-in-law, Lord Chamberlain Hunsdon.

Meanwhile William Stanley, on his accession to the Earldom, had provided himself with a company of his own.   Their first recorded appearance was at Norwich in September 1594.   None of the personnel of this company are now known to us ; but the fact that they first appear five months after Ferdinando's death lends colour to Sir Edmund Chambers's surmise that some of the latter's men transferred into the service of his brother.[4] If so they must have been the lesser lights, because the principals—Burbage, Phillips, Pope, Kempe, Heminges, and Shakespeare—were all taken on by Lord Hunsdon.   This new company of William Earl of Derby can be traced provincially until 1599.   In 1600–1 they gave four performances at Court.   Thenceforward they are only recorded on tour at intervals until 1618.

There is no doubt that Lord Derby took a keen personal interest in his actors.   In an undated letter to Sir Robert Cecil Lady Derby writes :

Being importuned by my Lord to intreat your favour that his man Browne, with his company, may not be barred from their accustomed playing, in maintenance whereof they have consumed the better part of their substance.   If so vain a matter shall not seem trouble-

---

[1] Chambers, vol. ii, p. 129.

[2] Chambers, vol. ii, p. 95.

[3] *Stationers' Register*, Feb. 6th, 1593–4.   This clearly shows how interrelated the companies were at the time.

[4] Chambers, vol. ii, p. 126.

some to you, I could desire that your furtherance might be a mean to uphold them ; for that my Lord taking delight in them, it will keep him from more prodigal courses.[1]

Sir Edmund Chambers hazards the guess that the " comedies " Lord Derby was " penning " in 1599 were performed by his own men. If so they cannot now be traced ; but no doubt Lord Derby, like his father-in-law Lord Oxford, preferred to conceal his authorship behind the veil of anonymity.

We must now return to Lord Oxford and see what his actors were doing at this time. It will be remembered that he had an adult company which toured the provinces from 1580 to 1590. The records, however, have so far failed to reveal their whereabouts after this date. But in 1600 an anonymous play called *The Weakest goeth to the Wall* was published, containing the information on its title-page that it was acted by the " Earl of Oxford's servants." Next year another anonymous play was published—*The History of George Scanderbeg*—which had also been acted by the Earl's men.[2] No copies of this quarto survive, but the fact that it was played by Lord Oxford's actors has been preserved in an entry in the *Stationers' Register*.

In 1602 the Earls of Oxford and Worcester [3] amalgamated their companies. This transpires in a letter from the Privy Council to the Lord Mayor of London, which may be quoted in full. The personal interest that Lord Oxford took in his company is brought out in this letter ; for in it we see that it is at his express request that the Queen is now " requiring " the Lord Mayor to allot them officially their favourite playing place, the " Boar's Head " :

After our very hearty commendations to your Lordship.

[1] Chambers, vol. ii, p. 127. (From Hatfield MSS.)
[2] Chambers, vol. ii, p. 102.
[3] Edward Somerset (1550–1628) succeeded his father as Earl of Worcester in 1589, when he took over his father's company. His leading actor at this time was Robert Browne, who is mentioned in Lady Derby's letter quoted above. Worcester succeeded the Earl of Essex as Earl Marshal and Master of the Horse after the latter's execution in 1601.

We received your letter signifying some amendment of the abuses or disorders by the immoderate exercise of stage plays in and about the City, by means of our late order renewed for the restraint of them, and withal showing a special inconvenience yet remaining. By reason that the servants of our very good Lord the Earl of Oxford, and of me the Earl of Worcester, being joined by agreement together in one company, (to whom, upon notice of Her Majesty's pleasure at the suit of the Earl of Oxford, toleration hath been thought meet to be granted, notwithstanding the restraint of our said former orders), do not tie themselves to one certain place and house, but do change their place at their own disposition, which is as disorderly and offensive as the former offence of many houses. And as the other companies that are allowed, namely of me the Lord Admiral and the Lord Chamberlain, be appointed their certain houses, and one and no more to each company, so we do straitly require that this third company be likewise to one place. And because we are informed that the house called the Boar's Head is the place they have especially used and do best like of, we do pray and require you that that said house, namely the Boar's Head, may be assigned unto them, and that they be very straitly charged to use and exercise their plays in no other but that house, as they will look to have that toleration continued and avoid further displeasure. And so we bid your Lordship heartily farewell. From the Court at Richmond the last of March 1602.

Your Lordship's very loving friends,

T. Buckhurst	Nottingham
E. Worcester	W. Knollys
John Stanhope	Ro. Cecil
John Fortescue	J. Herbert.[1]

In August the united company was acting at the Rose under Henslowe, and among the actors we find the names of William Kempe and Thomas Heywood, the playwright.[2] They were evidently held in high esteem, for in the autumn of 1603 they were transferred to the patronage of Queen Anne. In March 1604, now known as the " Queen's

---

[1] Chambers, vol. iv, p. 335.   [2] Murray, vol. i, p. 52.

players," they took part in the procession on the occasion of King James's formal entry into London.[1]

It cannot now be said definitely if their habitat—the Boar's Head—is to be identified with the famous Boar's Head tavern in Eastcheap, the traditional house of the tavern scenes in *Henry V*. It is perhaps worth reminding the reader that the Vere crest was a Boar. This may be just a coincidence ; but it seems also possible that the place they were accustomed to play in became known as the Boar's Head in honour of their patron.

We have now completed our survey of the doings of the actors patronised by Lords Oxford and Derby ; and I propose briefly to recapitulate the main facts concerning the two Earls, and their mutual interest in the stage, between the years 1595 and 1602.

1. In 1595, 1596, and 1599 we find them visiting each other. They may have done so at other times as well, but the foregoing occasions are definitely established by documentary evidence.

2. In 1598 Lord Oxford is described as " the best for comedy " ; in 1599 we are told that Lord Derby " is busied only in penning comedies for the common players," and about the same time he is described by Lady Derby as " taking delight in the players."

3. In spite of this, not a single play has come down to us which can be definitely ascribed to them, unless the two anonymous quartos—*The Weakest goeth to the Wall* and *The History of George Scanderbeg*—may be taken as the work of Lord Oxford.

4. Finally, they probably worked either anonymously or pseudonymously,

(*a*) Because of the total absence of any mention of any play bearing their names as authors ; and

(*b*) Because Lord Oxford almost certainly worked in this way in the eighties when he was collaborating with John Lyly in the eight Court Comedies.

A theory has recently been advanced that the Earls

---

[1] Murray, vol. i, p. 186

of Oxford and Derby are in some way connected with the authorship of Shakespeare's plays.[1] It is, of course, well known that Shakespeare collaborated with other dramatists, the hands of Fletcher, Chapman, and others having been traced beyond dispute in some of the plays attributed to him. For two main reasons, however, I have refrained from comment on what the conservative element among literary critics is wont to stigmatise as a "fantastic theory." In the first place, adequate space could not be afforded to the subject without devoting many chapters to its consideration, and, in the second place, the treatment of controversial matters that cannot be definitely settled by contemporary documents and evidence is outside the scope of this biography.

[1] Lefranc, *Sous le Masque* (cit.); and J. T. Looney, *Shakespeare Identified.*

CHAPTER VIII

1597–1604

E xcept I should in friendship seem ingrate,
D enying duty, whereto I am bound ;
W ith letting slip your Honour's worthy state,
A t all assays, which I have noble found.
R ight well I might refrain to handle pen :
D enouncing aye the company of men.

D own, dire despair, let courage come in place,
E xalt his fame whom Honour doth embrace.

V irtue hath aye adorn'd your valiant heart,
E xampl'd by your deeds of lasting fame :
R egarding such as take God Mars his part
E ach where by proof, in honour and in name.

> ANTHONY MUNDAY, in *The Mirror of Mutability*, 1579.

" Far fly thy fame
Most, most, of me belov'd, whose silent name
One letter bounds.   Thy true judicial style
I ever honour, and if my love beguile
Not much my hopes, then thy unvalued worth
Shall mount fair place, when Apes are turnèd forth."

> JOHN MARSTON, in *The Scourge of Villanie* (9th Satire), 1599.[1]

§ I.   THE PASSING OF THE TUDORS

IN August 1597 the Earl and Countess of Pembroke were anxious to promote a marriage between their eldest son, William Herbert, and Lady Bridget Vere, who was then thirteen and living with her grandfather, Lord Burghley.[2]

---

[1] Marston is here speaking of a concealed poet whom he calls " Mutius." The " silent name one letter bounds " may well be a reference to the name Edward de Vere, which begins and ends with the letter E. " Mutius " is evidently one of the anonymous aristocratic poets described in the *Arte of English Poesy*, and would fit no one better than Lord Oxford.

[2] Henry Herbert, 2nd Earl of Pembroke (1534 ?–1601) married (3rdly in 1577) Mary Sidney, sister of Sir Philip Sidney. Their son William Herbert (1580–1630) became 3rd Earl of Pembroke in 1601. His brother, Philip Herbert, married Lord Oxford's youngest daughter, Susan Vere, in 1605. The two brothers were great patrons of the drama, and were " The Incomparable Paire of Brethren " to whom the Shakespeare First Folio was dedicated in 1623.

On September 8th Lord Oxford wrote the following letter to Burghley :

My very good Lord, I have perused these letters which according to your Lordship's desire I have returned. I do perceive how both my Lord and Lady [of Pembroke] do persevere, which doth greatly content me, for Bridget's sake, whom always I wished a good husband, such as your Lordship and myself may take comfort thereby. And as for the articles which I perceive have been moved between your Lordship and them (referring all to your Lordship's wisdom and good liking) I will freely set down mine own opinion according to your Lordship's desire. My Lord of Pembroke is a man sickly, and therefore it is to be gathered he desireth in his lifetime to see his son bestowed to his liking, to compass methinks his offers very honourable, and his desires very reasonable. Again being a thing agreeable to your Lordship's fatherly care and love to my daughter ; a thing which for the honour, friendship, and liking I have to the match, very agreeable to me ; so that all parties but the same thing. I know no reason to delay it, but according to their desires to accomplish it with the convenient speed ; and I do not doubt but your Lordship and myself shall receive great comfort thereby. For the young gentleman, as I understand, hath been well brought up, fair conditioned, and hath many good parts in him. Thus to satisfy your Lordship I have as shortly as I can set down mine opinion to my Lord's desires ; notwithstanding I refer theirs and mine own, which is all one with theirs, to your Lordship's wisdom. I am sorry that I have not an able body which might have served to attend on Her Majesty in the place where she is, being especially there, whither, without any other occasion than to see your Lordship, I would always willingly go.[1] September 8th, 1597.

Your Lordship's most assured,
EDWARD OXEFORD.[2]

The proposed marriage, however, fell through ; and in 1599 Lady Bridget married Francis Norris, grandson of

---

[1] The Queen was staying at Theobalds with Lord Burghley.
[2] S.P. Dom. Eliz., 264. 111.

Lord Norris of Rycote. The latter died in the following
year, when Francis Norris succeeded to the Barony.

On August 4th, 1598, Lord Burghley died. His loss to
the Queen was incalculable. His career as a Minister to
the Crown has never been equalled in English history.
For forty years, without a single break, he was her right-
hand man, serving her first as Principal Secretary and afterwards as Lord Treasurer. It is outside the scope of this
volume to discuss the debt his Sovereign and his country
owed him; but a few words may be said as to his relations
with Lord Oxford.

Up to the present time all historians who have written
about Lord Burghley and his son-in-law have been
unanimous in saying that from the moment the Duke of
Norfolk was executed in 1572 they became bitter and
irreconcilable enemies. The utter falsity of such a view
has been so clearly demonstrated in the preceding pages
that further argument is unnecessary. Again, the entire
blame for the tragedy of 1576 has, without any justification,
been placed wholly on Lord Oxford's shoulders. It is
not too much to say that little or no blame for that unhappy episode attaches to either victim. The poisonous
machinations of the arch-intriguer, Lord Henry Howard,
lay at the root of the whole trouble. It is a matter of
some consolation that in 1581 Lord Oxford was able to
show him up in his true colours, when he exposed the
pro-Spanish plot.

Lord Burghley's unfailing kindness to Lord Oxford,
often in very difficult circumstances, and especially to
the three daughters to whom he was a second father, is
one of the most striking features of this biography. The
way Oxford parted with estate after estate, probably for
a mere song, must have been quite incomprehensible to
his prudent father-in-law, whom we cannot blame. As a
family man Lord Oxford was hopeless. The ruling passion
of his life was poetry, literature, and the drama ; and poets,
as we know, only too often make dead failures of their
domestic lives.

In his will the Lord Treasurer, after leaving the bulk
of his property to his sons, Sir Thomas and Sir Robert,
gives :

to my said son Sir Robert Cecil and to Lady Bridget and
the Lady Susan Vere, the daughters of my deceased
daughter the Lady Anne, Countess of Oxford, all my goods,
money, plate, and stuff that are or shall be remaining at
my death within my bedchamber at Westminster, and in
my two closets, and any chamber thereto adjoining . . .
all which plate, stuff, and money I will shall be divided by
my servant Thomas Bellott and the Dean of Westminster
equally into three parts betwixt my said son Robert Cecil
and the said two ladies.   And that the same be delivered
for the said two young ladies by the order of my daughter
Countess of Derby, the Lady Dennie, and my sister White,
and my Steward, Thomas Bellott, or any two of them.
Saving I will that the value of £1,000 shall be delivered to
the Countess of Derby, and one other thousand pounds
of the said plate and money shall be severed and delivered
to my sons Sir Thomas and Sir Robert Cecil for the charges
of my burial.

In addition certain specified gifts of plate are to be given
to his three granddaughters, who also receive half the
residue of his money ; the other half to be devoted to
" such Godly uses as my executors shall think good." [1]

Lord Burghley was succeeded in the Barony by his
eldest son, Sir Thomas Cecil ; but the mantle of his states-
manship descended to his second son, Sir Robert.   In
1596 the latter had been appointed Principal Secretary,
a post he continued to hold under King James till he
succeeded the Earl of Dorset as Lord Treasurer in 1608.
Sir Robert also took over from his father the guardianship
of his three nieces, Lord Oxford's daughters.   And from

---

[1] *The Life of Lord Burghley, published from the original manuscript wrote
soon after his Lordship's death, now in the library of the Earl of Exeter.* By
Arthur Collins, Esq. (1732).   The will, begun in 1579 and revised several
times (finally in 1597), extends over 18 pages.   Collins estimates that at
his death Burghley was worth £4,000 a year in land, £11,000 in money, and
£15,000 in plate and jewellery.

such correspondence as exists between the brothers-in-law we may judge that they remained friends to the end.

On March 3rd, 1599, Robert Bertie, who was then seventeen and travelling on the Continent, addressed a complimentary letter to his uncle.[1] The "plus serieux affaires" that were then engaging Lord Oxford's attention is probably an allusion to his literary work and his "office" under the Queen.

Monseigneur, Je désire infiniement de vous faire paroistre par quelque effect l'honneur que je vous porte, ayant esté tousjours bien veu de vous ; mais d'autant que je n'ay trouvé encores aucun subject assez digne de vous divertir de vos plus serieux affaires, je n'osoy pas prendre la hardiesse de vous escrire, de peur d'estre trop mal advisé de vous importuner de lettres qui ne mériteroyent pas d'estre seulement ouvertes, si non en ce qu'elles vous asseureroyent de l'éternelle service que je vous ay voué et à toute vostre maison ; vous suppliant très humblement, Monsieur, de l'avoir pour agréable et de me tenir pour celuy qui est prest de reçevoir vos commandemens de telle dévotion que je seray toute ma vie vostre très humble serviteur et neveu.[2]

In July 1600 Lord Oxford addressed a long letter to his brother-in-law, Sir Robert Cecil. In it he begs the latter's assistance to obtain for him the appointment of Governor of the Isle of Jersey :

Although my bad success in former suits to Her Majesty have given me cause to bury my hopes in the deep abyss and bottom of despair, rather than now to attempt, after so many trials made in vain and so many opportunities escaped, the effects of fair words or fruits of golden promises ; yet for that I cannot believe but that there

---

[1] Robert Bertie was the eldest son of Lord Willoughby and Lady Mary, Oxford's sister. He was created Earl of Lindsey in 1628 ; and on the death of the 18th Earl of Oxford without direct heirs, Lindsey laid claim both to the Earldom and to the title of Lord Great Chamberlain. A long dispute ensued with Robert de Vere, the 17th Earl's cousin. Eventually Lindsey was granted the Great Chamberlainship, but the Earldom of Oxford was awarded to Robert de Vere.

[2] Cal. Ancaster MSS., 345.

hath been always a true correspondence of word and intention in Her Majesty, I do conjecture that with a little help that which of itself hath brought forth so fair blossoms will also yield fruit. Wherefore having moved Her Majesty lately about the office of the Isle, which by the death of Sir Anthony Paulet stands now in Her Majesty's disposition to bestow where it shall best please her, I do at this present most heartily desire your friendship and furtherance. First, for that I know Her Majesty doth give you good ear ; then, for that our houses are knit in alliance ; last of all, the matter itself is such as nothing chargeth Her Majesty, sith it is a thing she must bestow upon some one or other. I know Her Majesty hath suitors already for it, yet such as for many respects Her Majesty may call to remembrance ought in equal balance to weigh lighter than myself. And I know not by what better means, or when Her Majesty may have an easier opportunity, to discharge the debt of so many hopes as her promises have given me cause to embrace than by this, which give she must and so give as nothing extraordinary doth part from her. If she shall not deign me this in an opportunity of time so fitting, what time shall I attend which is uncertain to all men unless in the graves of men there were a time to receive benefits and good turns from Princes. Well, I will not use more words, for they may rather argue mistrust than confidence. I will assure myself and not doubt of your good office both in this but in any honourable friendship I shall have cause to use you. Hackney.

Your loving and assured friend and brother,

EDWARD OXENFORD.[1]

But it was Sir Walter Ralegh and not the Earl of Oxford who received the appointment, and in February 1601 Lord Oxford wrote again to his brother-in-law, this time asking for the Presidency of Wales :

At this time I am to try my friends ; among which, considering our old acquaintance, familiarity heretofore, and alliance of house (than which can be no straiter) as of my brother, I presume especially. Wherefore I most earnestly crave that if Her Majesty be willing to confer

[1] Hatfield MSS. (Cal. X. 257).

Although my badd successe, in former sutes to her Mtie, haue
giuene me cause to burye my hopes, in the diepe Abis
and bottome of dispayre, rather then nowe to attempt
after so many tryales made in vayne & so many oportunites
escaped. the effects of fayre woordes or frutes of goulden promisses yet for that, I cannot beleue, but that there hathe bene
alwayes, a trwe correspondencie of woord and intentime
in her Mtie. I doo coniecture, that wythe a lyttell helpe,
that wch of ye selfe hathe brought forthe so fayre blossumes
will also yeld frute. wherfore hauinge moved her Mtie
Lathe about the office of the wch whiche by the deathe of
Sr Antonie Poulet standes nowe in her maiesties dispositime
to bestowe where yt shall best pleas her I doo at this prae-
sent most hartely desire yowre friendship and furtherance
fyrst for yt I know that her Mtie doothe giue yow good
eare, then for yt owre howses are knyt in alliance. last of
all, the matter yt self ys suche, as nothinge chargethe her
Mtie sythe yt ys a thynge she must bestowe up on sume one
or other. I know her Mtie hathe suters abrode for yt. yet
suche as for many respectes her Mtie may call to remembrance
ought in equall ballence to way hygher then my selfe. And
I know not by whatt better meanes or when her maiestie may
haue an easier oportunite to discharge the dept of so many
sutes as her promisses haue giuen me cause to imbrace, then
by this. whiche giue she must & so giue as nothinge extraordi-
narilye doothe part frome her. yf she shall not layne in this
in an oportunite of tyme. sythinge, what tyme shall attend
in a uncerteyne to all men vnles in the graues of men
ther were a tyme to receyve benifites and good turnes frome
prinses. well I will not vse more woordes, for they may
rather argue mistrust then confidence. I will assure my self
and not dout of yowre good office boothe in this but in any
honorable friendshipe I shall haue cause to vse yow. Hakney.

yowre lovinge and assured friend
and brother.

Edward Oxenford

AUTOGRAPH LETTER OF THE EARL OF OXFORD TO
SIR ROBERT CECIL, JULY 1600.

the Presidency of Wales to me, I may assure myself of
your voice in Council.   Not that I desire you should be a
mover, but a furtherer, for as the time is it were not reason.
But if Her Majesty, in regard of my youth, time, and
fortune spent in her Court, and her favours and promises
which drew me on without any mistrust the more to presume in mine own expenses, confer so good a turn to me,
that then you may further it as you may.   I know Her
Majesty is of that princely disposition that they shall
not be deceived which put their trust in her.   This 2nd of
February.[1]

Sir Robert Cecil apparently wrote a favourable answer
without, however, committing himself to a definite assurance ; and the next month Lord Oxford sent another
appeal to his now all-powerful brother-in-law :

My very good brother, I have received by H. Lok your
most kind message, which I so effectually embrace, that
what for the old love I have borne you—which I assure
you was very great—what for the alliance which is between
us, which is tied so fast by my children of your own sister :
what for my own disposition to yourself, which hath been
rooted by long and many familiarities of a more youthful
time, there could have been nothing so dearly welcome
unto me.   Wherefore not as a stranger but in the old
style I do assure you that you shall have no faster friend
or well-wisher unto you than myself, with either in kindness
which I find beyond my expectation in you, or in kindred
whereby none is nearer allied than myself, since of your
sisters, of my wife only have you received nieces.   I will
say no more, for words in faithful minds are tedious ;
only this I protest, you shall do me wrong and yourself
greater, if either through fables, which are mischievous,
or conceit, which is dangerous, you think otherwise of
me than humanity or consanguinity requireth.   I desired
Henry Lok to speak unto you for that I cannot so well
urge mine own business to Her Majesty, that you would
do me the favour, when these troublesome times give
opportunity to Her Majesty, to think of the disposition
of the Presidency of Wales ; that I may understand it by
you, lest neglecting through the time by some mishap I

[1] Hatfield MSS. (Cal. XI. 27).

may lose the suit ; for, as I have understood and have by good reason conceived, I am not to use my friends to move it. So myself having moved it and received good hope I fear nothing but through ignorance when to prosecute it, lest I should lose the benefit of her good disposition on which I only depend.[1]

In February 1601 occurred the disastrous Essex rising. It is impossible to do justice to this dismal tragedy without an exhaustive enquiry which cannot be entered into here.[2] All that concerns us is that the Earl of Oxford took no share whatever either in promoting or suppressing the so-called rebellion. He was summoned from his retirement to act as the senior of the twenty-five noblemen who unanimously declared Essex and Southampton guilty, after the veriest travesty of a trial on February 19th.

Lord Oxford's true feelings on the matter will probably never be known. He never referred to it in any of his subsequent letters to Cecil. Although his relations with his brother-in-law remained as cordial after the event as before, he expressed his feelings against Sir Walter Ralegh, whose share in bringing about Essex's downfall was notorious, in a pun that has gone down to history. The Queen was in the Privy Chamber playing on the virginals when news was brought that the sentence against Essex had been carried into execution. Her Majesty continued to play ; and Lord Oxford, as if in reference to the notes —or " jacks " as they were called—dancing up and down beneath her fingers, glanced at Sir Walter and said bitterly : " When Jacks start up, heads go down." [3]

After the execution of Sir Charles Danvers, one of the Essex faction, the Queen granted his forfeited lands to

[1] Hatfield MSS. (Cal. XI. 152). The letter is only dated March, but it is evident that it refers to 1601. Henry Lok, who seems to have been in Cecil's service, may be the poet who inscribed a sonnet to Lord Oxford in the gift copy of his volume of poems which he presented to the Earl in 1597. The Presidency of Wales was given to Edward, 11th baron Zouch (1556 ?–1625) in 1602.

[2] The reader is referred to E. P. Cheyney, *History of England*, vol. ii, and C. C. Stopes, *Third Earl of Southampton*.

[3] Agnes Strickland, *Life of Queen Elizabeth*.

the Earl of Oxford. Several letters on this subject exist between him and Cecil, in all of which the Earl complains that he cannot get his case, or " book " as it was called, through the law courts. It is of interest that in one of these he says :

I am advised that I may pass my book from Her Majesty, if a warrant may be procured, to my cousin Bacon.[1]

This is the only link that has been established between Lord Oxford and his famous contemporary, Francis Bacon.

In January 1602, nearly a year after he had been granted the Danvers estates, Lord Oxford was still pleading for the matter to be settled. He complains that even Sir Robert Cecil no longer seems to be his friend, adding :

I hope that Her Majesty, after so many gracious words as she gave me at Greenwich upon her departure, will not draw in the beams of her princely grace, to her own detriment.[2]

It is certain that Lord Oxford never got Sir Charles Danvers's lands, for they are not mentioned in the *Inquisition Post Mortem* taken after the Earl's death. The last letter on the subject is from him to Cecil, dated from Hackney, March 22nd, 1602 :

It is now a year since Her Majesty granted me her interest in Danvers' escheat. . . . The matter hath twice been heard before the judges, but their report hath never been made.[3]

After this he seems to have given the matter up in despair.

One of the few specimens of the handwriting of Elizabeth, Countess of Oxford, is to be found in a letter dated from Hackney on November 20th, 1602. It is addressed to Dr. Julius Cæsar, a judge of the High Court :

Master Doctor Cæsar, I should have delivered a request from my Lord unto you concerning a suit depending in

[1] Hatfield MSS. (Cal. XI. 411).   [2] Ibid. (Cal. XII. 39).
[3] Ibid. (Cal. XII. 82).

23

the Court of Requests against an insolent tenant, that for the space of many years hath neither paid any rent nor will show his lease for my Lord's satisfaction. And now being by a late mischance in my coach prevented from the hope of any present opportunity to meet you at the Court, I do earnestly intreat you that whensoever my Lord's counsel shall move against one Thomas Coe of Walter Belchamp for the discovery of his lease and satisfaction of his rent, either yourself or Master Wylbrome will give the cause that expedition as in your favourable justice it shall deserve, and prevent the dilatory pleadings which the injustice of Coe's cause will offer unto you. And thus commending myself very heartily unto you, commit you to the Almighty. From Hackney, this 20th of November, 1602.

Your assured friend,

ELIZABETH OXENFORD.[1]

The reference to her coach is interesting. Coaches were first introduced into England by the Earl of Arundel about 1566, the Queen being one of the first to use one. It will be remembered that Lettice Knollys, after she had married the Earl of Leicester, incurred Her Majesty's further displeasure by driving about London in a richly appointed coach. The appalling state of the roads at that time accounts no doubt for the " late mischance in my coach " complained of by Lady Oxford.

The following March Queen Elizabeth died. A full description of her magnificent funeral procession on April 28th was given in a broadside written by Henry Petowe. But there is one curious omission from an otherwise complete list of those who followed the Queen on her last journey through the streets of London. We are told that there was a canopy over the coffin which was borne by six Earls, but their names are not given. As Lord Oxford's name does not appear elsewhere in the pro-

---

[1] Lansdowne MSS. Sir Julius Cæsar (1558–1636) was the son of an Italian, Cesare Adelmare, who had been physician to Queen Mary and Queen Elizabeth. He was at this time Master of the Court of Requests. He was knighted on King James's accession, appointed Chancellor of the Exchequer in 1606, and Master of the Rolls in 1614.

cession it seems certain that he was one who bore the canopy over the mortal remains of the great Queen he had served so long, as he had borne it on another and happier occasion after the defeat of the Spanish Armada in 1588.

§ II.   The Coming of the Stuarts

Right up to the very day before her death Queen Elizabeth had steadfastly refused to nominate her successor. Her reason for this obstinacy is easy to understand. King Henry VIII.'s matrimonial troubles had left a legacy that threatened to precipitate England into another Succession War.   At one time it looked as if both she and her sister Mary would be excluded from the throne on the grounds of illegitimacy.   Even after her accession had been successfully accomplished her difficulties were far from over.   From the beginning of her reign opinion in the country was divided as to who should succeed her.   Neither the House of Stuart nor the House of Suffolk—the two principal rivals—lacked partisans who were ready to shed their blood on behalf of their leaders.   There is little doubt that had she inclined openly to one or other party a civil war would have ensued.

But although officially she maintained this strictly impartial attitude, her secret wishes, particularly towards the end of her life, became more and more apparent. " My throne," she is reported to have said on one occasion to Lord Admiral Howard, " has been the throne of Kings, neither ought any but he that is my next heir to succeed me."   For some years before her death Sir Robert Cecil, her Principal Secretary and confidential adviser, had been secretly corresponding with the King of Scots.   The gratuities, amounting to many thousands of pounds, and the annuity of £2,500, subsequently raised to £5,000, granted to King James, would have been common knowledge at Court.   But it was not till the day before she died that Lord Keeper Egerton and Secretary Cecil ventured to put the question to her that had been on their minds for so long.   According to them her reply was :

" I will that a King succeed me, and who should that be but my nearest kinsman, the King of Scots ? "

King James was proclaimed without opposition throughout England on March 24th. He quitted Edinburgh on his southward journey on April 5th, and the following day set foot for the first time on English soil. He progressed in leisurely fashion towards London via York ; Belvoir Castle, where he was entertained by the Earl of Rutland ; Burghley, where he was received by Sir Thomas Cecil, now Lord Burghley ; and Theobalds, where he met his secret correspondent, Sir Robert Cecil, for the first time in the flesh. Finally, on May 11th—

the King rode in a coach, somewhat closely, from the Charter House to Whitehall, and from thence he was conveyed by water to the Tower of London, attending on him the Lord Admiral, the Earl of Northumberland, the Lord Worcester, Lord Thomas Howard, and others.[1]

Just before His Majesty reached Theobalds the Earl of Oxford wrote to his brother-in-law to ask what arrangements were being made to receive the King in London. The letter is of great interest, for it shows how deeply he felt the loss of the Queen, and how sincere had been the affection between him and his Royal Mistress. Well might he exclaim that " in this common shipwreck mine is above all the rest " ; and when he voices his apprehension for the future he was thinking no doubt of his " office " and his £1,000 a year, which must have represented a great part of his worldly wealth. But, as we shall see, his fears were ill founded, for James proved to be even more generous than Elizabeth.

Sir, I have always found myself beholden to you for many kindnesses and courtesies ; wherefore I am bold at this present, which giveth occasion of many considerations, to desire you as my very good friend and kind brother-in-law to impart to me what course is devised by you of the Council and the rest of the Lords concerning

[1] Stow, *Annals*, p. 824.

our duties to the King's Majesty ; whether you do expect any messenger before his coming to let us understand his pleasure, or else his personal arrival to be presently or very shortly.   And if it be so, what order is resolved on amongst you either for the attending or meeting of His Majesty ; for by reasons of mine infirmity I cannot come among you as often as I wish, and by reason of my house is not so near that at every occasion I can be present as were fit, either I do not hear at all from you or at least write the latest ; as this other day it happened to me, receiving a letter at nine of the clock not to fail at eight of the same morning to be at Whitehall ; which being impossible, yet I hasted so much as I came to follow you into Ludgate, though through press of people and horses I could not reach your company as I desired, but followed as I might.

I cannot but find great grief in myself to remember the Mistress which we have lost, under whom both you and myself from our greenest years have been in a manner brought up ; and although it hath pleased God after an earthly kingdom to take her up into a more permanent and heavenly state, wherein I do not doubt but she is crowned with glory ; and to give us a Prince wise, learned, and enriched with all virtues, yet the long time which we spent in her service, we cannot look for so much left of our days as to bestow upon another, neither the long acquaintance and kind familiarities wherewith she did use us, we are not ever to expect from another Prince as denied by the infirmity of age and common course of reason. In this common shipwreck mine is above all the rest, who least regarded though often comforted of all her followers, she hath left to try my fortune among the alterations of time and chance, either without sail whereby to take the advantage of any prosperous gale, or with anchor to ride till the storm be overpast.   There is nothing therefore left to my comfort but the excellent virtues and deep wisdom wherewith God hath endued our new Master and Sovereign Lord, who doth not come amongst us as a stranger but as a natural Prince, succeeding by right of blood and inheritance, not as a conqueror but as the true shepherd of Christ's flock to cherish and comfort them.

Wherefore I most earnestly desire you of this favour, as I have written before, that I may be informed from you

concerning those points. And thus recommending myself
unto you, I take my leave.

Your assured friend and unfortunate brother-in-law,
E. OXENFORD.[1]

We do not know when Lord Oxford first met his new
Sovereign, but his next letters to Cecil are written in a more
hopeful frame of mind. We see that his title to the Stewardship of the Forest of Essex, which he had vainly sought
and had given up in despair many years before, has been
laid before the King :

My very good Lord, I understand by Master Attorney
that he hath reported the state of my title to the Keepership of the Forest of Waltham and of the House and Park
of Havering, whereby it appears to His Majesty what
right and acquit is therein. Till the 12th of Henry VIII.
mine ancestors have possessed the same, almost since the
time of William Conqueror, and at that time—which was
the 12th year of Henry VIII.—the King took it for term
of his life from my grandfather ; since which time, what
by the alterations of Princes and Wardships, I have been
kept from my rightful possession ; yet from time to time
both my father and myself have, as opportunities fell out,
not neglected our claim. Twice in my time it had passage
by law and judgment was to have been passed on my side ;
whereof Her Majesty the late Queen, being advertised with
assured promises and words of a Prince to restore it herself
unto me, caused me to let fall the suit. But so it was she
was not so ready to perform her word, as I was too ready
to believe it ; whereupon pressing my title further it was
by Her Majesty's pleasure put to arbitrament ; and
although it was an unequal course, yet not to contradict
her will the Lord Chancellor, Sir Christopher Hatton,
was sole arbiter ; who, after all the delays devised by Sir
Thomas Heneage and the Queen's counsel in law then
being, having heard the cause was ready to make his
report for me, but Her Majesty refused the same and by
no means would hear it. So that by this and the former
means I have been thus long dispossessed. But I hope
truth is subject to no prescription, for truth is truth

[1] Hatfield MSS., 99. 150. Endorsed : " 25/27th April, 1603, Earl of
Oxford to my master."

though never so old, and time cannot make that false
which was once true, and though this three-score years
both my father and myself have been dispossessed thereof,
yet hath there been claims made thereto many times . . .
therefore I shall most earnestly desire your friendship
in this, that you will join with my Lord Admiral, my very
good Lord and friend, to help me to His Majesty's resolution. . . . From Hackney, this 7th of May.

Your Lordship's most assured friend and brother-in-
law to command,

E. OXENFORDE.[1]

There was evidently a close friendship at this time
between Oxford and Lord Admiral Howard, who had been
created Earl of Nottingham in 1597.   In the next three
letters to Cecil he again speaks of the help Nottingham
is according his suit ; and in 1601 Oxford had given him
his proxy when prevented, no doubt because of his infirmity,
from attending the House of Lords.

On June 19th he wrote to his brother-in-law, who had
now been created Baron Cecil of Essendon.   Although
Lord Oxford lived for another year this is the last letter
of his that has come down to us, and therefore I have
given it in full :

My Lord, I understand how honourably you do persevere
in your promised favour to me, which I taking in most
kind manner can at this time acknowledge it but by simple
yet hearty thanks, hoping in God to offer me at some time
or other the opportunity whereby I may in a more effectual
manner express my grateful mind.   I further also understand that this day Master Attorney is like to be at the
Court.   Wherefore I most earnestly desire your Lordship
to procure and end this my suit, in seeking whereof I am
grown old and spent the chiefest time of mine age.   The
case, as I understand by your Lordship, Sir E. Cooke, His
Majesty's Attorney, hath reported the justice thereof ;
I do not doubt but doth appear there remaineth only a
warrant according to the King's last order to be signed by
the six Lords in commission ; whereby Master Attorney
General may proceed according to the course usual.   The

[1] Hatfield MSS., 99. 161.

King, I hear, doth remove tomorrow towards Windsor, whereby if by your Lordship's especial favour you do not procure me a full end this day or tomorrow, I cannot look for anything more than a long delay. I do well perceive how your Lordship doth travail for me in this cause of an especial grace and favour, notwithstanding the burden of more importunate and general affairs than this of my particular. Wherefore how much the expedition of this matter concerns me I leave to your wisdom, that in your own apprehension can read more than I have written. To conclude, I wholly rely upon your Lordship's honourable friendship for which I do vow a most thankful and grateful mind. This 19th of June.

Your most loving assured friend and brother-in-law,

E. OXENFORDE.[1]

The growing optimism displayed in these letters was more than justified. On July 18th the King granted him the Bailiwick, or custody, of the Forest of Essex and the Keepership of Havering House [2]; about the same time he appointed him to the Privy Council; and in the following month he renewed his £1,000 a year from the Exchequer in exactly the same words that Elizabeth had used in the original grant.

Lord Oxford's appointment to the Privy Council has not hitherto been suspected; nor is this surprising, because all the records of the Privy Council between 1602 and 1613 were accidentally burnt in the latter year in a fire at Whitehall. But the authority that he was so appointed is beyond dispute. In a manuscript notice of his death, written in James I.'s reign, we read that he was " of the Privy Council to the King's Majesty that now is." [3] This is a most important fact biographically. Up till now it has been assumed that his years of retirement at Hackney were occasioned by the fact that he was so antiquated and out of date that he was no longer of any service to the Sovereign. But King James's recognition of his talents

---

[1] Hatfield MSS., 100. 108.
[2] Patent Roll, No. 1612, mem. 1 (1603).
[3] Harleian MSS., 41. 89.

and abilities makes the " antiquated " theory no longer tenable.

Of still greater importance is the renewal of his grant of £1,000 a year. Even allowing for the support of his two powerful friends—Secretary Cecil and Lord Admiral Howard—we cannot but help being struck by the King's obvious desire to show him the utmost favour. But if, as I have suggested, Lord Oxford's annuity had been intended primarily as compensation for the money he had spent from 1580 onwards in patronising men of letters and actors, His Majesty's action is quite comprehensible. James was himself a poet and a keen patron of literary men. Nor was he a whit less enthusiastic than his pre-decessor in his love of stage plays and masques. It will be remembered that by 1602 only three companies of actors were licensed to perform in London. These were the Lord Chamberlain's (Hunsdon's), the Lord Admiral's (Howard's), and a united company that had been formed by the merging of Oxford's and Worcester's. On his accession James himself became the patron of the Chamber-lain's men, Queen Anne assumed a like position over Oxford's and Worcester's, while Prince Henry took over the Admiral's. Never, before or since, has the stage stood so high in royal favour. It is not therefore surprising that the courtier who for twenty-three years had main-tained one of the leading companies, and had gained the reputation of being the foremost writer of comedies, should have had special favour shown him by the new sovereign.

On July 25th :

being Monday, and the feast of the Blessed Apostle Saint James, King James of England, first of that name, with the Noble Lady and Queen Anne, were together crowned and anointed at Westminster, by the most Reverend Father in God John Whitgift, Archbishop of Canterbury.[1]

The Earl of Oxford, as Lord Great Chamberlain, claimed the right to attend personally on His Majesty on the

[1] Stow, *Annals*, p. 828.

morning of the ceremony. This claim, together with its sanction by the Lord Steward, is worded as follows :

Edward de Vere, Earl of Oxford, presents to the Court a certain petition in these words. Edward de Vere, Earl of Oxford, asks that as he is Great Chamberlain of England of the fee of our most dread Lord the King, that it should please the King that he should likewise at the Coronation, as formerly he was permitted, to do the said office and services as he and his ancestors have formerly done. That is to say that the said Earl had freedom and entertainment of the King's Court at all times ; and that the said Earl on the day of the said Coronation, on the morning before the King rises, ought to enter into the chamber where the King lies, and bring him his shirt, and stockings, and under-clothing. And that the said Earl and the Lord Chamber-lain for the time being together on that day ought to dress the King in all his apparel. And that he may take and have all his fees, profits, and advantages due to this office as he and his ancestors before him have been used to on the day of Coronation. That is to say, forty yards of crimson velvet for the said Earl's robes for that day. And when the King is apparelled and ready to go out of his chamber, then the Earl should have the bed where the King lay on the night before the Coronation, and all the apparel of the same, with the coverlet, curtains, pillows, and the hangings of the room, with the King's nightgown, in which he was vested the night before the Coronation. He also asks that [he should have the same privileges] as his ancestors [who] from time immemorial served the noble progenitors of our Lord the King with water before and after eating the day of the Coronation, and had as their right the basins and towels and a tasting cup, with which the said progenitors were served on the day of their Coronation, as appears in the records of the Exchequer.

My Lord Steward adjudicates to the aforesaid Earl the fees, services, and fees of presenting water to the Lord the King before and after dinner on the day of the Coronation ; and to have the basins, tasting cups, and towels. And for the other fees the said Earl is referred to examine the records of the Jewel House and the King's Wardrobe.[1]

[1] Cal. S.P. Dom., James I. (July 7th, 1603).

§ III.   " The Rest is Silence "

Lord Oxford only lived to enjoy the benefits conferred
on him by King James for a year.   He died at Hackney
on June 24th, 1604, and on July 6th he was buried in the
Church of St. Augustine.[1]   His grave was marked by no
stone or name ; but in 1612, when his widow died, she
directed in her will that she desired :

to be buried in the Church of Hackney, within the County
of Middlesex, as near unto the body of my late dear and
noble Lord and husband as may be : only I will that there
be in the said Church erected for us a tomb fitting our
degree.[2]

The Earl himself left no will ; but six days before his
death he granted the custody of the Forest of Essex to
his son-in-law, Francis Lord Norris, and to his cousin
Sir Francis Vere, who had just returned to England after
twenty years' continuous campaigning in the Low Countries.
Sir Francis and his brother, Sir Horatio Vere, had always
been Oxford's favourite cousins, and to them he turned
in the hour of his death.   It was under the command of
Horatio, afterwards Lord Vere of Tilbury, that young
Henry learned the art of soldiering in the Netherlands
and the Palatinate when he came of age.   In the campaign
of 1625 he contracted a fever brought on by a wound
received while leading an assault on a fort.   The fever
proved fatal, and he died at the early age of thirty-four.
He had no children, and the Earldom passed to his cousin
Robert ; while the title of Lord Great Chamberlain
descended to Robert Bertie, the eldest son of Oxford's
sister Lady Mary, who had married Lord Willoughby
de Eresby.   Robert Bertie succeeded to his father's
Barony in 1601, and was created Earl of Lindsey in 1626.

[1] Newcombe MSS. in the Hackney Public Library.   In the margin of
the page in the Parish Register in which the entry of his burial occurs
has been written " ye plague."   It may be that his death at the age of
fifty-four was due to this disease.

[2] P.C.C. 10. Capell. The present location of the tomb is discussed
in Appendix E.

The anti-climax presented by the last years of Lord Oxford's life is inevitable. It is almost impossible to penetrate the obscurity surrounding his life at Hackney. There can be little doubt that literature, his main interest in life, occupied the greater part of his time. It is probable that he and his son-in-law Lord Derby amused themselves by writing comedies which were performed by their actors. Music too must have played an important part in the years of retirement. But his secret has been well kept. Indeed, so completely have the last fifteen years of his life been obscured that one is tempted to wonder whether this is due to chance, or whether it may not have been deliberately designed.

In ringing down the curtain on the Earl of Oxford's life, perhaps it may be fitting to close with an epitaph, written by an anonymous contemporary, which is now preserved among the Harleian Manuscripts :

Edward de Vere, only son of John, born the 12th day of April 1550, Earl of Oxenford, High Chamberlain, Lord Bolbec, Sandford, and Badlesmere, Steward of the Forest in Essex, and of the Privy Council to the King's Majesty that now is. Of whom I will only speak what all men's voices confirm : he was a man in mind and body absolutely accomplished with honourable endowments.

APPENDICES

APPENDIX A

THE EARL OF OXFORD AND THE HOUSE OF LORDS (1571–1601)

Lord Oxford only attended intermittently at the House of Lords. He took his seat on April 2nd, 1571, when Parliament was opened by the Queen, although he did not actually come of age till April 12th. A full list of his attendances is given below.

First Session 1571	.	April 2, 4, 6, 7, 9, 10, 11, 12.
		May 7, 28.
Second Session 1572	.	May 8, 12, 15, 17, 21.
		June 3, 6, 10, 24, 26, 30.
Third Session 1581	.	Jan. 19, 26.
		Feb. 23, 27.
		Mar. 2, 18.
Fourth Session 1584/5	.	Nov. 24, 26.
		Feb. 4.
		Mar. 29.
Fifth Session 1586	.	Oct. 29, 30.
		Nov. 10, 19.
Sixth Session 1589	.	Feb. 4, 6, 10, 14, 22.
Seventh Session 1593	.	Feb. 19, 22, 24.
Eighth Session 1597	.	Dec. 14.
Ninth Session 1601	.	No attendance.

In addition to his regular appointment as a trier of petitions from Gascony, Lord Oxford also sat on other committees, viz. :

1571 April 10	.	A committee " touching matters of religion."
1572 May 12	.	A committee " touching the Queen of Scots."
1584	. .	During this and all subsequent sessions, Lord Oxford was appointed one of the " receivers and triers of petitions from Gascony and other lands beyond the seas and from the islands."
1586 Nov. 10	.	A committee appointed to address the Queen on the subject of the sentence of the Queen of Scots.

In 1582 his name was omitted from the list of commissioners for the dissolution of Parliament. This was the only occasion that it was omitted, and is perhaps attributable to his having fallen under the Queen's disfavour at this period.

With reference to the Eighth Session of Parliament, in which only one attendance is recorded, although the name of the Earl of Oxford is not included among the names of peers who attended on Wednesday January 11th, 1598, to which date an adjournment was made from December 20th, 1597, the following quotation from *The Journals of all the Parliaments during the Reign of Queen Elizabeth. Collected by Sir Simonds D'Ewes,* 1682 (p. 535), seems to show that he may have been in his place on that day :

This Wednesday as soon as the Lords were set, it should seem that the Earl of Essex having been created Earl Marshal the 28th day of December last before this instant, took his place according to his said office, viz. next after the Earl of Oxon, Chamberlain of England, and before the Earl of Nottingham, Lord Steward and Lord Admiral.

In 1601, Lord Oxford's health having begun to decline about this time, he was unable to attend the House. He therefore appointed his friend, Lord Admiral Howard, to act as his " proxy " during this Session.

APPENDIX B

THE EARL OF OXFORD'S LANDS (1571–1603)

For generations historians have been echoing one another in saying that when Lord Burghley refused to save the Duke of Norfolk's life at the request of his son-in-law, the Earl of Oxford took the foolish revenge of dissipating his estates in order to ruin his wife, Lord Burghley's daughter. It is, of course, needless to add that not one of the many writers who have so confidently retold the story took any steps whatsoever to verify it. It is therefore of interest to see that a close study of the sales of land effected by the Earl of Oxford proves the " revenge " story to be a pure fabrication.

| Year. | Number of | | Events in Lord Oxford's life. |
	Sales.	Purchases or Grants.	
1571	—	—	Marriage with Anne Cecil.
1572	—	—	Execution of the Duke of Norfolk.
1573	1	1	
1574	—	—	
1575	1	—	Foreign travel.
1576	5	—	ditto
1577	3	—	Investment of £25 in Frobisher's voyage.
1578	2	1	
1579	5	—	Total investments in Frobisher's voyages amount to £2,500.
1580	13	—	Company of actors started.
1581	1	—	Investment of £500 in Fenton's voyage.
1582	4	—	
1583	5	1	
1584	7	2	
1585	2	—	Employed in the Low Countries.
1586	—	—	Annuity of £1,000 a year.
1587	2	1	
1588	1	1	
1591	1	—	Marriage with Elizabeth Trentham.
1592	3	—	
1596	—	1	" King's Place," Hackney.
1603	—	1	Stewardship of the Forest of Essex.

It will thus be seen that of the 56 separate sales during the twenty years 1572 to 1592 no fewer than 24, or nearly half, were effected during the five years 1577 to 1581, when Lord Oxford was engaged in speculating with Martin Frobisher and the other adventurers, and in restarting his father's company of actors. A further 6 sales were màde during the period of foreign travel—no doubt to pay the heavy expenses travelling in those days involved. Moreover, during the three years following execution of the Duke of Norfolk only 2 sales were carried out. It will therefore be seen that the foolish myth that Lord Oxford dissipated his estates in order to " revenge " himself on Lord Burghley has no foundation whatsoever in fact.

NOTE.—This table has been compiled from the Patent Rolls in the Public Record Office. I have not given either the details or the references because the manuscript indexes to the Patent Rolls are arranged chronologically and alphabetically, which makes reference to them an easy matter.

APPENDIX C

THE EARL OF OXFORD'S ANNUITY (1586)

1. THE GRANT

AN annuity of £1,000 a year was granted to the Earl of Oxford on June 26th, 1586, by authority of a Dormant Privy Seal.[1] A Dormant Privy Seal may be defined thus :

Writs of Privy Seal were of two kinds : one which was final directing the payment of a certain sum at a fixed time : the other which directed the several payments to be made from time to time being called a Privy Seal Dormant.[2]

The wording of this writ of Privy Seal is given on page 257.[3]

2. THE PAYMENT OF THE GRANT

This annuity was paid to him quarterly until the death of Queen Elizabeth on March 24th, 1603 ; and the first quarterly payment of £250 that fell due in the reign of King James I. was made on April 16th, 1603, without further question.[4] On August 2nd, 1603, King James issued a fresh writ for the continuance of the annuity in exactly the same words as had been employed in the original grant.[5]

As the Earl of Oxford died on June 24th, 1604, it is clear that he received the annuity continuously from June 26th, 1586, until his death almost exactly eighteen years later.

3. THE EXCHEQUER ROLL OF ISSUE, 1597

The original writs of Privy Seal granted by Queen Elizabeth

---

[1] Teller's Roll Mich. 28 to Easter 29 Eliz. E. 405/145 fol. 50.
[2] *Guide to the Records in the Public Record Office*, 180.
[3] Roll of Issue (Privy Seal Book E. 403/2597).
[4] Pells Issue Book E. 403/1698.
[5] Enrolment of Privy Seals, Pells E. 403/2598.

in 1586 and by King James in 1603 are both missing from the file of Privy Seals, but contemporary copies of the grant occur as quoted above.

Until the year 1527 a Roll of Issue of all Privy Seal writs was kept, but in that year the old Exchequer was abolished and the only check on these payments was contained in the Teller's Rolls, which are the equivalent of receipts for the various payments as they were made.[1] The Roll of Issue was revived in 1597 by Lord Burghley, who had been trying to restore it for some years. The first of the Privy Seal Books containing the Roll of Issue as restored by Lord Burghley is numbered E. 403/2655.

This book contains 78 entries, the 57th entry being a copy of the Dormant Privy Seal of June 26th, 1586, granting £1,000 yearly to the Earl of Oxford.

A second Privy Seal Book containing the revived Roll of Issue is numbered E. 403/2597. This book seems to have been opened simultaneously with E. 403/2655, or at all events very shortly afterwards. The first book appears then to have been discontinued, as it contains no entries subsequent to 1598, whereas the second book continues to the end of the Queen's reign. There are 197 entries in the second book, the Earl of Oxford's grant being item No. 170.

Both books were kept by " Chidiock Wardour, clerk of the pells for the restoring of the Pell of Exitus," [2] and are in his handwriting. It seems probable, therefore, that the two books between them give all the payments made from the Exchequer during the last six years of Elizabeth's reign.

If this supposition is correct we shall be able to compare the salary of the Earl of Oxford with other salaries or pensions paid during the same period. The following is a table of the principal gratuities, salaries, and annuities paid from the Exchequer during the period in question. If we omit the large grants made for political reasons to the King of Scots (Items 15, 22, 26, 27) it will be seen that the grant to the Earl of Oxford is larger than any of the other grants or annuities, with the exception of the sum of £1,200 a year paid to Sir John Stanhope, the Master of the Posts, " for ordinary charges."

[1] *4th Report of the Deputy Keeper of the Public Records*, Appendix II., 179.
[2] E. 403/2597, fol. 25. (Entry No. 51).

TABLE OF ANNUITIES, ETC.

NOTE.—The following abbreviations are made use of :

I.	.	Privy Seal Book E. 403/2655.
II.	.	ditto E. 403/2597.
O	.	Ordinary Privy Seal.
D	.	Dormant Privy Seal.
G	.	Gratuity.

No.	Class.	Date.	To whom paid.	Amount.	Reference.
1	D	1.12.80	Sir Henry Lee, Master of the Armoury	£400 a year	I. 34 & II. 168
2	D	26.6.84	The Earl of Oxford	£1000 a year	I. 57 & II. 170
3	D	15.7.90	Sir John Stanhope, Master of the Posts	£1200 a year " for ordinary charges "	I. 10 & II. 171
4	D	6.2.94	Robert Bowes, Ambassador in Scotland	40/- a day	I. 14
5	D	4.4.95	The four daughters of Francis Dacres	£50 a year each	I. 60 & II. 147
6	D	13.4.95	Lady William Howard	£400 a year	I. 58
7	D	13.5.95	Lady Margaret Neville	£50 a year	I. 59
8	D	9.4.96	The Lieutenant of the Tower	£100 a year	I. 36
9	D	27.9.96	Sir Robert Cecil (secret service money)	£800 a year	II. 139
10	O	5.11.96	George Guilpin, Ambassador to the Low Countries	20/- a day	I. 75 & II. 176
11	D	22.9.97	Thomas Edmunds, Secretary in Paris	40/- a day	I. 12 & II. 20
12	O	24.12.97	John Wroth and Stephen Lesieure, Queen's Messengers in Germany	20/-a day each	I. 72
13	D	11.1.98	Edmund Tylney, Master of the Revels	£200 a year	I. 62 & II. 29
14	O	4.2.98	Sir Robert Cecil, during embassy to France	£4 a day	I. 71
15	G	19.4.98	The King of Scots	£3000	II. 52
16	O	2.7.98	The two daughters of the Countess of Desmond	Annuity of £33.6.8 each	II. 64
17	O	24.7.99	Lord Henry Howard, as long as the lands of the late Earl of Arundel are in the Queen's hands	£200 a year	II. 146
18	O	26.9.99 13.4.02	Stephen Lesieure, sent to Denmark	30/- a day	II. 87 & 120
19	D	18.10.99	Sir Nicholas Parker, Captain of the new fort at Falmouth, for 50 men	£46.13.4 a month	II. 179

TABLE OF ANNUITIES, ETC.—*continued.*

No.	Class.	Date.	To whom paid.	Amount.	Reference.
20	D	8.2.00	Lady Arabella Stuart, for maintenance	£200 a year	II. 142
21	G	4.7.00	Captain Nicholas Dawtrey, for acceptable service	£200	II. 95
22	G	25.10.01	The King of Scots	£2000	II. 114
23	O	9.1.02	James Croft, Gentleman Pensioner	£100 a year	II. 106
24	D	13.3.02	Sir Thomas Parry, Ambassador in Paris	£3.6.8 a day	II. 102
25	D	9.6.02	William Pearse, on account of wounds	2/- a day for life	II. 155
26	D	28.6.02	The King of Scots	£2500 a year	II. 152
27	D	4.1.03	The King of Scots	£5000 a year	II. 190

APPENDIX D

" WILLY " AND THE " GENTLE SPIRIT " IN SPENSER'S " TEARS OF THE MUSES "
(1591)

THE following well-known stanzas occur in Spenser's *Tears of the Muses* in the section devoted to Thalia, the Muse of Comedy:

> And he the man, whom Nature selfe had made
> To mock her selfe, and Truth to imitate,
> With kindly counter under Mimick shade,
> Our pleasant *Willy*, ah is dead of late :
> With whom all joy and jolly meriment
> Is also deaded and in dolour drent.
>
> In stead thereof scoffing Scurrilitie,
> And scornfull Follie with Contempt is crept,
> Rolling in rymes of shameles ribaudrie
> Without regard, or due Decorum kept,
> Each idle wit at will presumes to make,
> And doth the Learneds taske upon him take.
>
> But that same gentle Spirit, from whose pen
> Large streames of honnie and sweete Nectar flowe,
> Scorning the boldnes of such base-borne men,
> Which dare their follies forth so rashly throwe ;
> Doth rather choose to sit in idle Cell,
> Than so himselfe to mockerie to sell.

1. EDMUND MALONE'S IDENTIFICATION

Malone tells us that Dryden and other famous poets thought that Spenser was referring to William Shakespeare. His own opinion, however, is definitely against this identification. He says : " Spenser's description, I have no doubt, was intended for John Lyly." [1]

2. " WILLY " AND THE " GENTLE SPIRIT "

Before we go on to consider this identification that Malone advances so confidently, let us examine the three stanzas. In

[1] James Boswell, *Life of William Shakespeare, by the late Edmund Malone*, pp. 176–181.

the first Spenser laments the recent death of a certain " Willy," who may be either a poet, a playwright, or a comedian. In the second he deplores the rise since " Willy's " death of certain idle wits whose " rhymes of shameless ribaldry " are very unfavourably contrasted with the work of " Willy " and other "learneds." From this it seems likely that " Willy " is a poet. Lastly, in the third stanza, he refers to a " gentle Spirit "—evidently some aristocratic poet then living—whose verses he describes as " large streams of honey and sweet nectar." This " gentle Spirit," unlike " base-born men," refuses to " throw forth " (i.e. publish) his writings ; and is living the life of a recluse in " idle cell."

This, as I read it, is the straightforward meaning of these stanzas. But some critics, led astray apparently by the adjective " same "—" that *same* gentle Spirit "—have assumed that " Willy " and the " gentle Spirit " are identical.[1] The stumbling-block, however, to this line of argument is that whereas " Willy " is *dead*, the " gentle Spirit " is *alive*, and engaged at the present moment in producing " large streams of honey and sweet nectar." It is a curious thing that this obvious flaw in the argument does not seem to have been detected by any previous critic, because whether we consider " Willy " as *physically* dead, or only dead in a *literary* sense, he cannot surely in the same breath be described as someone

from whose pen
Large streams of honey and sweet nectar flow !

I think most people who read the three stanzas will agree with me that we have every reason for supposing " our pleasant Willy " and the " gentle Spirit " to be two entirely different people. I propose therefore to examine each in turn.

3. " WILLY "

During Elizabeth's reign the name " Willy," denoting a " shepherd," or poet, occurs in three separate poems only.[2]

[1] The following use of the word " same " as an adjective is quoted from *N.E.D.* : " Pleonastically emphasising a demonstrative, used absol. or with ellipsis of substantive : 1588 *L.L.L.* ' What Lady is that same ? ' "

A similar example is to be found in the March eclogue of the *Shepherd's Calendar* (quoted on p. 362, *post*) : ' Seest not thilke same Hawthorne studde ? ' This is the first mention of ' Hawthorne ' in the poem, so that ' same ' is obviously pleonastic, and is not meant to refer back.

[2] There *may*, of course, be other instances of which I am not aware.

It appears first in Spenser's *Shepherd's Calendar* (1579), in the eclogues entitled March and August. We next come across it in an *Eclogue made long since upon the death of Sir Philip Sidney*, in which Sidney, who died in 1586, is mourned as "Willy." This eclogue was not printed until 1602, when it appeared over the initials "A. W." in Davison's *Poetical Rhapsody*. Finally it is used once more by Spenser in the stanzas already quoted from the *Tears of the Muses* in 1591.

Now I have little doubt in my own mind that these three "Willys" are one and the same person, and that person Sir Philip Sidney. The eclogue in the Rhapsody affords incontrovertible proof that Sidney was known as Willy; but the idea seems to have got about that "Willy" was a name applied promiscuously to many poets at this time. Mr. R. W. Bond, for example, says: "'Willy,' as Malone points out, is a frequent pastoral name for a shepherd, and a shepherd is poetic for a poet "—giving as his authority Boswell's *Malone's Shakespeare*. An examination of this authority cited by Bond reveals the following paragraphs:

As shepherd was a common appellation for any of the poetical tribe, so *Willy* was a common name for a shepherd; hence probably this denomination was sometimes applied by the writers of Shakespeare's age to poets who had no claim to the Christian name of William. Thus in an ancient song, probably of the time of James I.

> As *Willy* once essay'd
> To look for a lamb that was stray'd, etc. . . .

And in an eclogue on the death of Sir Philip Sidney (as Dr. Farmer formerly suggested to me) which was written not long after that event, perhaps by Arthur Warren, a poet very little known, we find the celebrated author of the *Arcadia* lamented in several stanzas by the name of Willy. On this ground therefore alone "our pleasant Willy, ah! is dead of late" might mean—our spritely *poet* is of late as silent as the grave, and wholly unemployed.[1]

As Malone gives no context and no reference to "the ancient song," beyond saying it was probably of the time of James I., we cannot now say for certain whether any particular individual is meant. But it is worth remarking that the poet William

[1] Boswell, op. cit., p. 198.

Browne (born 1591) definitely calls himself " Willy " throughout his *Britannia's Pastorals* (1613–16). Is it not highly likely that the " Willy " of Malone's ancient Jacobean song is quite simply and naturally the Jacobean pastoral poet William Browne ?

I think the reader will agree that Mr. Bond's extraordinary statement that " Willy " is a frequent pastoral name for a poetic shepherd will not bear looking into for a moment. The plain truth is that from such evidence as we possess the pastoral name of " Willy " was applied to two poets only :

(*a*) Sir Philip Sidney, who died in 1586.

(*b*) William Browne, who was born in 1591.

4. SIR PHILIP SIDNEY

I propose now to give my reasons for supposing that the " Willy " in the *Shepherd's Calendar* and the *Tears of the Muses* is Sir Philip Sidney.

In the first place it is noteworthy that the " shepherds " (i.e. poets) who are introduced into " A. W.'s " eclogue—Thenot, Cuddy, and Perin—are identical with three of the " shepherds " in the *Calendar* [1]; and since " A. W.'s " " Willy " is unquestionably Sidney we are confronted by a strong *prima facie* case for supposing that " Willy " of the *Calendar* is also Sidney.

But there is yet further proof ; and I propose to take the three unidentified " Willies," viz.,

(*a*) In the March eclogue of the *Calendar*,

(*b*) In the August eclogue of the *Calendar*,

(*c*) In the *Tears of the Muses*,

and examine each in turn.

(*a*) In the March eclogue of the *Calendar* the following lines occur :

> WILLYE : Seest not thilke same Hawthorne studde,
> How bragly it beginnes to budde,
>   And utter his tender head ?
> Flora now calleth forth eche flower,
> And bids make ready Maias bowre,
>   That newe is upryst from bedde.
> Tho we shall sporten in delight,
> And learne with *Lettice* to wexe light,
>   That scornefully lookes askaunce,

---

[1] In the *Calendar* they are Thenot, Cuddy, and *Perigot* ; but the latter I take to have been corrupted into *Perin* by " A. W."

> Tho will we little Love awake,
> That nowe sleepeth in Lethe lake,
>   And pray him leaden our daunce.

THOMALIN : Willye, I wene thou bee assott :
> For lustie Love still sleepeth not,
>   But is abroad at his game.

WIL : How kenst thou that he is awoke ?
> Or hast thy selfe his slomber broke ?
>   Or made previe to the same ?

THOM : No, but happely I hym spyde,
> Where in a bush he did him hide,
>   With wings of purple and blewe.
> And were not, that my sheepe would stray,
> The previe marks I would bewray,
>   Whereby by chaunce I him knewe.

WIL : Thomalin, have no care for thy,
> My selfe will have a double eye,
>   Ylike to my flocke and thine :
> For als at home I have a syre,
> A stepdame eke as whott as fyre,
>   That dewly adayes counts mine.

In the " Gloss " we find the following note :

> Lettice, the name of some country lass.

Now, I suppose nobody imagines that " Lettice " was really some obscure farm girl living in a country hamlet. Spenser, when he wrote the *Calendar*, was living in Leicester House, and moving in court circles with his friends Sidney, Dyer, and Greville. For example, two " shepherds " who appear in the July eclogue—" Morrell " and " Algrin "—are unquestionably John Aylmer, Bishop of London, and Edmund Grindal, Archbishop of Canterbury. I suggest that " Lettice " is an obvious allusion to Lettice Knollys, the widow of the Earl of Essex, who had married the Earl of Leicester on September 21st, 1578. Leicester, moreover, had adopted Sidney and had made him his heir ; so that if " Willy " is Sidney his remark " at home I have a sire " might very well refer to the Earl and Leicester House.[1] As for his " stepdame " who is " as hot as fire," this description would seem to be peculiarly applicable to

[1] Of course Sidney's father, Sir Henry, was alive at this time. But he was Lord Deputy of Ireland, and at the time the *Calendar* was written his son Philip was living at Leicester House, which was in every sense of the word his " home."

Lettice, Countess of Leicester. The Earl and his Countess, although their marriage was by way of having been a love match, never seem to have been on happy terms. The following quotation, taken from Miss Violet Wilson's *Queen Elizabeth's Maids of Honour*, is significant :

The differences between the Earl of Leicester and his wife were common property, so that the country generally favoured the story that Leicester had prepared a poisoned draught for Lettice " which he willed her to use in any faintness." She, not suspecting its properties, gave him a drink of the supposed cordial when he came to Cornbury and of the results whereof he died.[1]

(*b*) I have dealt with the " Willy " in the August eclogue of the *Calendar* elsewhere.[2] It only remains therefore to say here that, in my opinion, Sidney fits this particular " Willy " better than anyone else.

(*c*) With regard to the " Willy " of the *Tears of the Muses* little need be said. He is described as " dead of late," and Sidney had died in 1586. We know that Spenser had spent many happy days at Leicester House, and it is therefore not surprising to find him mourning the death of his generous friend and patron. It is natural, moreover, to find his death lamented by Thalia, the Muse of Comedy, because his great work, the *Arcadia*, published the year before the *Tears of the Muses*, was a romantic love story.

5. RICHARD TARLETON

Although it seems to me that there is no real reason to doubt that " our pleasant Willy " of the *Tears of the Muses* is Sir Philip Sidney, a theory has arisen in the past identifying him with Richard Tarleton (died 1588), who was the leading comedian of the Queen's company of players. At the outset we are confronted with the difficulty of reconciling his Christian name with " Willy." There is at least some phonetic resemblance between " Phil " and " Will," but none between " Richard " and " Willy."

The case for Tarleton rests mainly on the evidence of a contemporary note in a copy of Spenser's works dated 1611, which

[1] Page 166. Miss Wilson gives instances of Lettice's quick temper and arrogance.

[2] See p. 182, *ante*.

was once in the possession of Halliwell-Phillipps.[1] Dr. C. M.
Ingleby, who examined this book, tells us that the name Tarleton is written in a contemporary hand in the margin opposite the stanza in which "our pleasant Willy" occurs.[2] Now, this evidence might have some validity if we were aware of the identity of the author of the note ; but as we are not it must be admitted that it carries very little weight. The word "contemporary," when applied to handwriting, leaves a wide margin of dates ; and since the writer must have made the entry at least twenty-four years after Tarleton's death, the supposition seems more probable that his note was purely conjectural and made on the grounds that Tarleton was a famous comedian who died in 1588, and that "Willy's" death, which occurred some time before 1591, happens to be mourned by the Muse of Comedy.

But Sir Edmund Chambers, who appears to incline to the Tarleton identification, finds support for the theory in the evidence provided in a ballad [3] preserved in the Bodleian Library. In my opinion, for reasons I shall give, this evidence entirely negatives the case in favour of Tarleton. The ballad is entitled "A pretie new ballad intituled willie and peggie, to the tune of tarleton's carroll." It is a lament for the death of an actor called Willie, evidently a famous comedian, who was made a Groom of the Chamber by the Queen, and who leaves behind him a wife or lover called Peggie.[4] So far this would fit Tarleton quite well, for the Queen's Company were all made Grooms of the Chamber. But the poem concludes with the subscription : "finis qd Richard Tarleton." Surely this is the clearest possible proof that from whatever source Rawlinson obtained the ballad it was unmistakeably signed by Tarleton as the author, and written by him to go to the tune of his "carroll"![5]

---

[1] Chambers, *Elizabethan State*, vol. ii, p. 343.

[2] *Notes and Queries*, 6th Series, vol. xi, p. 417.

[3] Rawlinson Poetical MSS., 185, f. 10.

[4] Compare the following lines : "his like behind him for merth is not left " . . . "none would be wery to see him on stage " . . . "A groom of the chamber my Willie was made " . . . "ay me what comfort may Peggie now have."

[5] Chambers (op. cit., vol. ii, p. 342) cites another ballad written on October 5th, 1570, which is signed : "Qd Richard Tarleton." The word "quod," or "quoth," followed by the name, was a common method for an Elizabethan poet to sign his verses. It seems absolutely certain that Tarleton himself wrote both these ballads.

Who, then, is the " Willie " of this ballad ? It appears that there was an actor William Knell, who was a member of the Queen's Company, and who died before 1588. He left a widow, Rebecca, who married John Heminges 10th March, 1588.[1] Both he and Tarleton were evidently very popular with Elizabethan audiences as the following anecdote shows :

An excellent Jest of Tarlton suddenly spoken. At the Bull of Bishops-gate was a Play of Henry the fift, wherein the Judge was to take a box on the eare, and because he was absent that should take the blow, Tarlton himselfe (ever forward to please) tooke upon him to play the same Judge, besides his owne part of the Clowne : and Knel then playing Henry the fift, hit Tarlton a sound boxe indeed, which made the people laugh the more because it was he : but anon the Judge goes in, and immediately Tarlton (in his Clownes cloathes) comes out, and askes the Actors what newes ; O (saith one) hadst thou been here, thou shouldest have seene Prince Henry hit the Judge a terrible box on the eare. What man, said Tarlton, strike a Judge ? It is true y faith, said the other. No other like, said Tarlton, and it could not be but terrible to the Judge, when the report so terrifies me, that me thinkes the blow remaines still on my cheeke, that it burnes againe. The people laught at this mightily : and to this day I have heard it commended for rare.[2]

There can be little doubt that William Knell was the " Willie " whose death was mourned by Tarlton in the ballad we are considering. His name was William ; he belonged to the Queen's Company and was therefore a Groom of the Chamber ; he left a widow called Rebecca, whose pet name may well have been Becky or Peggy ; and we have seen that the audience of the Bull Inn " laughed mightily " at a piece of

[1] Chambers, vol. ii, p. 327.

[2] *Shakespeare's England*, vol. ii, p. 259, quoting from *Tarleton's Jests* (1611). It is interesting to find Tarleton and Knell, both members of the Queen's Company, acting in a play about King Henry V. at the Bull in Bishopsgate Street, where, it will be remembered, the Queen's Company was licensed to act by the City authorities on November 28th, 1583. The play undoubtedly was the anonymous *Famous Victories of King Henry V.*, which Shakespeare drew upon for his trilogy 1 & 2 *Henry IV.* and *Henry V.* The author of the *Famous Victories*, whoever he may have been, was evidently one of the playwrights of the Queen's Company ; while the play itself would almost certainly have been produced at Court during one of the winter seasons between 1583–4 and 1587–8.

horse-play between himself and his fellow comedian.   Is it not
perfectly natural, then, to find Tarleton composing his elegy?
The superficial attempt to impose the nick-name of " Willy "
on to Richard Tarleton completely breaks down on closer
scrutiny.[1] This, coupled with the overwhelming evidence in
favour of Sidney, seems to me to make it a moral certainty
that he (and not Tarleton) is the " Willy " of Spenser's *Tears
of the Muses*.

6. The " gentle Spirit "

But it is immaterial to my next argument whether or not
Sir Philip Sidney should be identified with " our pleasant
Willy." In any case " Willy " cannot be the " gentle Spirit "
of the third stanza quoted at the beginning of this Appendix,
because Spenser here is obviously referring to someone who is
alive.

As I have already said, Malone, and following him Mr. Bond,
have put forward the view that Spenser was referring to John
Lyly.[2] It is true that they included " Willy " in their argument,
which we have seen to be inadmissible. I propose, therefore, to
consider their arguments as if they applied only to the " gentle
Spirit."

7. John Lyly

In some respects Lyly fits the case very well. He was the
author, or at any rate the reputed author, of eight Court
Comedies.[3] The fact that these plays were notably free from
" shameless ribaldry " is a distinct point in his favour. And
we know that at least seven, if not all, of Lyly's plays had been
acted by 1590 ; so that there is nothing apparently incongruous
in his being described in 1591 as " sitting in idle cell."

But in another respect Spenser's " gentle Spirit " is entirely
at variance with what we know of Lyly. In 1589 Lyly published

---

[1] Unless, of course, one is disposed to accept the evidence of the
" contemporary " marginal note made at least twenty-four years after
Tarleton's death !

[2] Feuillerat, *John Lyly*, p. 226, notes both Malone's and Bond's identification, but disagrees : " La chose est loin d'être évidente ; en réalité,
rien ne permet d'avancer semblable hypothèse."

[3] I must refer the reader to page 274, where I have argued at some length
that Lord Oxford, Lyly's employer, collaborated with him in the writing
and production of these well-known plays.

a pamphlet called *Pap with a hatchet*.[1] It was his contribution, written on the side of the anti-Martinists, in the famous Marprelate controversy. This controversy was a scurrilous paper campaign of abuse and vituperation which began in 1588 and lasted several years.

Such of the Queen's Protestant subjects [writes Strype] that laboured for a new reformation of this Church, both of the government of it by Bishops, and of the Divine Service by the Book of Common Prayer, did at this time mightily bestir themselves, by publishing divers books and libels full of scurrilous language and slanders, chiefly against the hierarchy : but those of Martin Marprelate made the greatest noise.[2]

Nearly all the leading literary hack-writers were drawn in, either directly or indirectly, including Harvey, Nashe, and Greene. It is hardly necessary to say that Spenser had no share whatever in these proceedings ; and when he speaks in 1591 of the recent appearance in print of " scoffing scurrility," " scornful folly," and " shameless ribaldry," there is little doubt that he is referring to the Marprelate and anti-Marprelate tracts. It seems to me quite out of the question that in the next stanza of the *Tears of the Muses* he can possibly mean the author of *Pap with a hatchet* when he speaks of that—

> gentle Spirit from whose pen
> Large streams of honey and sweet nectar flow :

adding the descriptive information that he—

> Scorning the boldness of such base-born men,
> Which dare their follies forth so rashly throw ;
> Doth rather choose to sit in idle cell,
> Than so himself to mockery to sell.

Whoever the " gentle Spirit " may have been there seems no doubt whatever that he cannot, by any stretch of the imagination, be John Lyly, the author of *Pap with a hatchet*.

---

[1] There is no name on the title-page, but Gabriel Harvey, in *Pierces Supererogation*, says : " Would God Lilly had alwaies bene Euphues and never Pap-hatchet " ; which shows that Harvey at any rate considered him the author of this pamphlet. (Grosart, *Works of Gabriel Harvey*, vol. ii, p. 124.)

[2] John Strype, *Annals of the Reformation*, vol. ii, part ii, chap. xix, p. 93.

8. The Earl of Oxford

To my mind the description of the "gentle Spirit" fits Lord Oxford far better than anybody else. He was admittedly the author of comedies, and probably collaborated with his private secretary, John Lyly, in the composition of Lyly's eight Court Comedies. He took no part whatever in the Marprelate controversy, and, indeed, had published none of his writings—plays or poems—under his own name since 1576. He could most aptly be described in 1591 as " sitting in idle cell," as those who have followed his life in the preceding pages will readily agree. He was "gentle" as opposed to "baseborn " in the true sense of the word. Further, Spenser, in one of his dedicatory sonnets in the *Faery Queen* (1590), which was addressed to Lord Oxford, refers explicitly to the mutual love existing between the Earl and the Muses. Finally, what more likely than that Spenser, in *The Tears of the Muses*, should connect in his mind Oxford and Sidney, those two brilliant court poets whose rivalry provided the theme of the August eclogue in his own *Shepherd's Calendar* ? All these facts are surely convincing that nobody fits the " gentle Spirit " so accurately and truly as the Earl of Oxford.

25

APPENDIX E

THE EARL OF OXFORD'S TOMB

" The earth can yield me but a common grave."

Sonnet No. LXXXI.

THE Earl of Oxford was buried on July 6th, 1604, on the north side of the chancel in the Church of St. Augustine, Hackney; and his widow was buried beside him in 1612.

A monument was at some subsequent date erected to mark the spot. We know that this monument was not erected until after the death of the Countess, for in her will dated November 25th, 1612, she writes :

I joyfully commit my body to the earth from whence it was taken, desiring to be buried in the Church of Hackney, within the County of Middlesex, as near unto the body of my said late dear and noble Lord and husband as may be, and that to be done as privately and with as little pomp and ceremony as possible may be. Only I will that there be in the said Church erected for us a tomb fitting our degree, and of such charge as shall seem good to mine executors.

John Strype, who was lecturer in the Church of St. Augustine from 1689 to 1723, thus describes what must have been the Oxford tomb in his *Continuation of Stow's Survey* (1721) :

On the north side of the chancel, first an ancient Table Monument with a fair grey marble. There were coats-of-arms on the sides, but torn off. This monument is concealed by the schoolmaster's pew.

In 1721 the Church was falling into disrepair and was partially restored, but the growth of Hackney as a suburb of London in the course of the eighteenth century necessitated a larger Parish Church. In 1790 an Act of Parliament (30 Geo. III. cap. 71) was passed authorising the demolition of the old Church and the construction of a new one—the present Church of St. John-at-Hackney. The old tower standing at the west end of the Church of St. Augustine was the only portion of the old

Church that was not dismantled.   It still stands, a prominent
landmark, some 24 feet square and 90 feet high at the north end
of Mare Street, and a representation of it has been adopted as
the Arms of the Borough of Hackney.

From Strype's evidence quoted above, and from *The Diary
and Correspondence of Ralph Thoresby . . . now published from
the original MSS. by the Rev. Joseph Hunter* (1830), in an entry
dated June 8th, 1712, it is possible accurately to locate the
position occupied by the Oxford monument.   The monument
itself has disappeared, but a drawing of it made at some time
during the eighteenth century exists in the Hackney Public
Library.   This drawing shows the place occupied by the two
coats-of-arms, probably those of Vere and Trentham.

The evidence of Ralph Thoresby in 1712 confirms the evidence
of Strype as to the position of the monument and also shows that
it contained no inscription at the time of his visit.   Whether
the inscription was defaced when the brasses were removed, or,
which is more likely, that it never contained any identification
beyond the two coats-of-arms, cannot now be positively stated.
Its location on the ground can be fixed from two upright stones,
set up to mark the north-east and south-east corners of the
Church.   Starting from the north-east stone, mark off six yards
towards the south-east corner, and from this point mark off
seven and a half yards westward.

NOTE.—See articles by the late Mr. Waldron Clarke in the *Hackney
Spectator*, dated January 18th and October 24th, 1924.

APPENDIX F

AN ELIZABETHAN COURT CIRCULAR

NOTE.—The following lists of Queen Elizabeth's Ministers, Officials, Ambassadors, etc., have been collected from various printed and manuscript sources. They do not claim to be exhaustive, but are intended primarily to give a bird's-eye view of the *milieu* in which the Earl of Oxford lived. I have endeavoured to make them as accurate as possible, but it is necessary to warn the reader that even contemporary authorities at times disagree as to the exact date on which an appointment was made. Indeed, while we find numerous references in the State Papers to the " Lieutenant of the Tower," the " Warden of the East Marches," etc., it is the exception rather than the rule to find the name of the holder mentioned as well. This frequently leads to confusion, and it is often impossible to tell when a change actually took place. Finally, it will be noticed that there is sometimes a lapse of many years even in such important billets as those of Lord Steward, Vice-Chamberlain, and Principal Secretary. It seems probable that Queen Elizabeth deliberately left them vacant for reasons of economy ; and that the duties, which obviously had to be carried out, were performed temporarily by junior officials in addition to their own. (Cf. in this respect " Chancellors of the Exchequer.") The lists should therefore be regarded as a general guide only, and should not be accepted as definite without verification from documentary evidence.

The following abbreviations are employed :

> d. = died.
> ex. = executed.
> imp. = imprisoned.

§ I. THE ROYAL HOUSEHOLD

LORDS GREAT CHAMBERLAIN

John de Vere, 16th Earl of Oxford	.	1539–1562 d.
Edward de Vere, 17th Earl of Oxford	.	1562–1604 d.
Henry de Vere, 18th Earl of Oxford	.	1604–1625 d.

MASTERS OF THE HORSE (out-doors)

Sir Henry Jernegan . . .	.	1557–1558
Lord Robert Dudley (cr. Earl of Leicester, 1564) . . .	.	1559–1587
Robert Devereux, 2nd Earl of Essex	.	1587–1601 ex.
Edward Somerset, 4th Earl of Worcester		1601–1616

LORDS STEWARD (downstairs)

Henry FitzAlan, 12th Earl of Arundel .	1558–1564
William Herbert, 1st Earl of Pembroke	1567–1570 d.
(Vacant : run by the Lord Chamberlain)	
Henry Stanley, 4th Earl of Derby [1] .	1585–1593 d.
Robert Dudley, Earl of Leicester . .	1587–1588 d.
Charles Howard, Earl of Nottingham .	1597–1618

LORDS CHAMBERLAIN (upstairs)

William, Lord Howard of Effingham .	1558–1573 d.
Thomas Radcliffe, 3rd Earl of Sussex .	1573–1583 d.
Charles, Lord Howard of Effingham .	1584–1585
Henry Carey, Lord Hunsdon . .	1585–1596 d.
William Brooke, Lord Cobham . .	1596–1597 d.
George Carey, Lord Hunsdon . .	1597–1603 d.
Thomas Howard, Earl of Suffolk . .	1603–1614

VICE-CHAMBERLAINS

Sir Henry Jernegan	–1558
Sir Edward Rogers	1558–1559
Sir Francis Knollys	1559–1570
(Qy. Vacant : 1570–1577)	
Sir Christopher Hatton . . .	1577–1588
Sir Thomas Heneage	1588–1595 d.
(Qy. Vacant : 1595–1601)	
Sir John Stanhope (cr. Lord Stanhope 1605)	1601–1613

MASTERS OF THE REVELS (£10)

Sir Thomas Cawarden. . . .	1544–1559 d.
Sir Thomas Benger	1560–1572
John Fortescue . . . . ⎫	
Henry Seckford . . . . ⎬ 1572	
Thomas Blagrave . . ' .	1578–1578
Edmund Tilney	1579–1610 d.
Sir George Buck	1610–1622

[1] But in October 1591 Lord Buckhurst is shown as " Lord High Butler " (cf. *Acts of the Privy Council*).

MASTERS OF THE TENTS AND TOILS (£30)

Sir Thomas Cawarden	–1559 d.
Henry Seckford [1]	} 1559–1569
John Tamworth	
Henry Seckford	1569–1610 d.

CLERK OF THE REVELS (£12 3s. 4d.)

Thomas Philips	–1560
Thomas Blagrave	1560–1603 d.

CLERKS COMPTROLLER OF THE REVELS (£12 3s. 4d.)

Richard Lee	1550 ?–1570
Edward Buggin	1570–1584
William Honing	1584–1596
Edmund Packenham	1596–1603

MASTERS OF THE CHILDREN

St. Paul's Cathedral

Sebastian Westcott	1559?–1582 d.
Thomas Gyles	1582–1590 ?
(The Paul's Boys were suppressed about 1590 on account of their share in the Marprelate Controversy)	
Edward Piers	1597 ?–1605 ?
(About 1605 they were renamed the " King's Revels Children ")	
Edward Kirkham	1605–1609

The Chapel Royal (£40)

Richard Bower	1545–1561
Richard Edwards	1561–1566 d.
William Hunnis	1567–1597 d.
Nathaniel Giles	1597–1605
Edward Kirkham	1605–1609
(About 1605 they were renamed " Queen's Revels Children ")	

[1] Henry Seckford (appointed Groom of the Chamber before 1587; knighted after 1593; died 1610) was a brother of Thomas Seckford (appointed Master of the Court of Requests 1558; died 1588). His niece, Frances, married Edmund Packenham, Clerk Comptroller in the office of the Revels. His son, Charles Seckford (died 1592), married Mary, the daughter of Frances de Vere, widow of the poet Earl of Surrey, by her second husband, Thomas Steyning, of Woodford, Suffolk.

St. George's Chapel, Windsor

Richard Farrant	1564–1580 d.

COMPTROLLERS OF THE HOUSEHOLD

Sir Thomas Parry	1558–1559
Sir Edward Rogers	1559–1567 d.
John Skynner	1567–1570
Sir James Crofts	1570–1590 d.
Sir Francis Knollys	1590–1596 d.
Sir William Knollys	1596–1600
Sir Edward Wotton (cr. Lord Wotton, 1603)	1603–1617

TREASURERS OF THE HOUSEHOLD

Sir Thomas Cheyney	1558–1559 d.
Sir Thomas Parry	1559–1560 d.
Sir Francis Knollys	1572–1596 d.
Roger, Lord North	1596–1600 d.
Sir William Knollys (cr. Lord Knollys, 1603)	1600–1614 ?

TREASURERS OF THE CHAMBER

Sir John Mason	1558–1565 d.
Lady Mason	1565–1566
Sir Francis Knollys	1566–1569
Sir Thomas Heneage	1569–1592
Lady Heneage (widow of the 2nd Earl of Southampton)	1592–1595
William Killigrew	1595–1596
Sir John Stanhope (cr. Lord Stanhope, 1605)	1596–1617

MASTERS OF THE GREAT WARDROBE

Sir Edward Walgrave	1558–1559
Sir John Fortescue	1559–1603
Sir George Home (cr. Earl of Dunbar, 1605)	1603–1606

COFFERERS OF THE HOUSEHOLD

Thomas Weldon	1558–1567 d.
Richard Warde	1567–1578
Anthony Crane	1579–1582 d.
Gregory Lovell	1582–1596 d.
Sir Henry Cocke	1596–1610

CAPTAINS OF THE BODYGUARD (£50)

Sir Edward Rogers	1558–1559
Sir Francis Knollys	1559–1572
Sir Christopher Hatton	1572–1588
Sir Walter Ralegh	1588–1603 imp.

§ II. THE QUEEN'S MINISTERS

LORDS CHANCELLOR [1]

Sir Nicholas Bacon*	1558–1579 d.
Sir Thomas Bromley	1579–1587 d.
Sir Christopher Hatton	1587–1591 d.
Sir John Puckering *	1592–1596 d.
Sir Thomas Egerton (cr. Lord Ellesmere, 1603) *	1596–1614

LORDS TREASURER

William Paulet, 1st Marquess of Winchester	1550–1572 d.
William Cecil, Lord Burghley	1572–1598 d.
Thomas Sackville, Lord Buckhurst (cr. Earl of Dorset, 1604)	1599–1608 d.

PRINCIPAL SECRETARIES OF STATE (£100)

Sir William Cecil (cr. Lord Burghley, 1571)	1558–1572
Sir Thomas Smith	1572–1577 d.
Sir Francis Walsingham	1573–1590 d.
Dr. Thomas Wilson	1578–1581 d.
William Davison	1586–1587
(Qy. Vacant : 1590–1596)	
Sir Robert Cecil (cr. Baron Essendon and Viscount Cranborne, 1603, and Earl of Salisbury, 1605)	1596–1608

[1] Those marked with an asterisk (*) took the title of " Lord Keeper of the Great Seal."

CHANCELLORS OF THE EXCHEQUER (£200)

Sir Richard Sackville	1558–1566 d.
Sir Walter Mildmay [1]	1566–1589 d.
Sir John Fortescue	1592–1603
Sir Julius Cæsar	1606–1626 ?

LIEUTENANTS OF THE TOWER (£200)

Sir Henry Bedingfield	1556
Sir Edward Warner [2]	1556 ?–1558
Sir Richard Blount	1559–1564
Sir Francis Jobson	1564–1570
Sir Owen Hopton	1570–1590
Sir Michael Blount (son of Sir Richard Blount)	1590–1595
Sir Drue Drury	1595–1597
Sir Richard Berkeley . . .	1597–1598
Sir John Peyton	1598–1603
Sir George Harvey	1603–1605
Sir William Waad	1605–1613

LORDS WARDEN OF THE CINQUE PORTS

Sir Thomas Cheyney	1558–1559 d.
William Brooke, Lord Cobham .	1559–1597 d.
Henry Brooke, Lord Cobham .	1597–1603 imp.

MASTERS OF THE POSTS (£66 13s. 4d.)

Sir John Mason	1544–1566 d.
Thomas Randolphe	1567–1590 d.
Sir John Stanhope	1590–1618

MASTERS OF THE ROYAL WARDS

Sir Nicholas Bacon	1546–1558
Sir Thomas Parry	1558–1560 d.
Sir William Cecil (cr. Lord Burghley, 1571)	1561–1598 d.
Sir Robert Cecil (cr. Earl of Salisbury, 1605)	1599–1612 d.

[1] Sir Walter Mildmay was appointed " Under Treasurer " vice Sir Richard Sackville in 1566 ; and it is probable that Sir John Fortescue, another of the Under-Treasurers, was acting Chancellor during the vacancy 1589–92.

[2] Sir Robert Oxenbridge was " Constable of the Tower " from 1556 to 1558. This appointment was dropped on Queen Elizabeth's accession.

ROYAL WARDS

Edward de Vere, 17th Earl of Oxford .	1562–1571
Edward Manners, 3rd Earl of Rutland .	1563–1570
Edmund, 3rd Lord Sheffield . .	1568–1585
Edward, Lord Zouch . . .	1569–1577
Philip Howard, Earl of Surrey . .	1572–1578
Robert Devereux, 2nd Earl of Essex .	1576–1587
Henry Wriothesley, 3rd Earl of South-ampton	1581–1594

§ III. NAVAL AND MILITARY COMMANDERS, ETC.

EARLS MARSHAL

Thomas Howard, 4th Duke of Norfolk	1558–1572 ex.
George Talbot, 6th Earl of Shrewsbury .	1573–1590 d.
Charles, Lord Howard of Effingham ⎫ William Cecil, Lord Burghley ⎬ Henry Carey, Lord Hunsdon ⎭	1592–1596
Robert Radcliffe, 5th Earl of Sussex .	1597
Robert Devereux, 2nd Earl of Essex .	1597–1601 ex.
Robert Radcliffe, 5th Earl of Sussex .	1601

MASTERS OF THE ORDNANCE (£133 6s. 8d.)

Sir Richard Southwell . . .	1553–1560
Ambrose Dudley, Earl of Warwick .	1560–1590 d.
Robert Devereux, 2nd Earl of Essex .	1597–1601 ex.
Charles Blount, Lord Mountjoy (cr. Earl of Devonshire, 1604) . . .	1603–1606 d.

MASTERS OF THE ARMOURY (£66 13s. 4d.)

Sir Richard Southwell . . .	1553–1561
Sir George Howard	1561–1580
Sir Henry Lee	1580–1610 d.

LORDS ADMIRAL (£133 6s. 8d.)

Edward Fiennes de Clinton, Lord Clinton (cr. Earl of Lincoln, 1572) . .	1557–1585 d.
Charles, Lord Howard of Effingham (cr. Earl of Nottingham, 1596)[1] . .	1585–1618

[1] In 1599 Nottingham was appointed " Lieutenant-General of all England as well by sea as by land."

TREASURERS OF THE NAVY (£66 13s; 4d.)

Benjamin Gonson	1549–1577 d.
John Hawkins	1577–1585
Sir Francis Drake	1585
Sir John Hawkins	1585–1595 d.
Roger Langford	1596–1598
Sir Fulke Greville	1598–1603
Sir R. Mansell	1604–1617

LORDS DEPUTY OF IRELAND

Thomas Radcliffe, 3rd Earl of Sussex .	1555–1564
Sir Henry Sidney	1565–1571
Sir William FitzWilliam . . .	1571–1575
Sir Henry Sidney	1575–1578
Sir William Drury	1578–1579 d.
Arthur, Lord Grey de Wilton . .	1580–1582
Sir John Perrott	1583–1588 imp.
Sir William FitzWilliam . . .	1588–1594
Sir William Russell	1594–1597
Thomas, Lord Burgh	1597–1598 d.
Robert Devereux, 2nd Earl of Essex .	1599
Charles Blount, Lord Mountjoy . .	1600–1603

LORDS PRESIDENT OF THE NORTH (H.Q. YORK) (£1,000)

Henry Neville, 5th Earl of Westmorland	1558–1559
Thomas Howard, 4th Duke of Norfolk .	1559–1560
Thomas Young, Archbishop of York .	1561–1568 d.
Thomas Radcliffe, 3rd Earl of Sussex .	1568–1572
Henry Hastings, 3rd Earl of Huntingdon	1572–1595 d.
Matthew Hutton, Archbishop of York .	1595–1599
Thomas Cecil, Lord Burghley . .	1599–1603
Edmund, Lord Sheffield . . .	1603–1619

WARDENS OF THE EAST MARCHES (H.Q. BERWICK) (£424)

Thomas Percy, 7th Earl of Northumberland	1558–1559
William, Lord Grey de Wilton . .	1560–1562 d.
Francis Russell, 2nd Earl of Bedford .	1564–1567
Henry Carey, Lord Hunsdon . .	1568–1596 d.
Sir Robert Carey	1596–1598
Peregrine Bertie, Lord Willoughby de Eresby	1598–1601 d.

WARDENS OF THE MIDDLE MARCHES (H.Q. ALNWICK)

Thomas Percy, 7th Earl of Northumberland	1558–1559
Sir John Forster [1]	1560–1592
Ralph, Lord Eure	1592–1597
Sir Robert Carey	1598–1603

WARDENS OF THE WEST MARCHES (H.Q. CARLISLE)

William, Lord Dacre	1558–1560 d.
William, Lord Grey de Wilton . .	1560–1562 d.
Henry, Lord Scrope	1563–1592 d.
Thomas, Lord Scrope	1593–1603 ?
Sir Robert Carey	1593–1595

GOVERNORS OF BERWICK

Sir James Crofts	1559–1560
William, Lord Grey de Wilton . .	1560–1562 d.
Francis Russell, 2nd Earl of Bedford .	1564–1567
Henry Carey, Lord Hunsdon . .	1568–1596 d.
Peregrine Bertie, Lord Willoughby de Eresby	1598–1601 d.

§ IV. RESIDENT AMBASSADORS

ENGLISH AMBASSADORS IN FRANCE (£1,200)

Sir Nicholas Throckmorton [2] . .	1559–1564
Sir Thomas Smith	1562–1566
Sir Thomas Hoby	1566 d.
Sir Henry Norris (cr. Lord Norris of Rycote, 1572)	1567–1570
Francis Walsingham	1570–1573
Dr. Valentine Dale	1573–1576
Sir Amias Paulet	1576–1579
Sir Henry Cobham [3]	1579–1583
Sir Edward Stafford	1583–1591
Sir Henry Unton	1591–1592
Thomas Edmondes [4]	1592–1596

[1] Temporarily suspended 1586–8 owing to charges of maladministration.

[2] Placed under restraint in France by King Henri II., 1562–4.

[3] *Alias* Brooke. He was the seventh son of George Brooke, Lord Cobham (died 1558).

[4] " Secretary of the French Tongue " to Queen Elizabeth. He seems to have been Resident Ambassador at this time, but it is possible that he was only sent over to France periodically on special embassies.

ENGLISH AMBASSADORS IN FRANCE—*cont.*

Sir Henry Unton	1596 d.
Sir Anthony Mildmay	1596–1597
Sir Henry Neville	1599–1600
Sir Thomas Parry	1601–1605

FRENCH AMBASSADORS IN ENGLAND

Antoine de Noailles	1553–1556
François de Noailles	1556–1557
Gilles de Noailles	1558–1559
Michel de Seure	1560–1562
Paul de Foix	1562–1566
Pasquier Bochetel de la Forest . .	1566–1568
Bertrand de Salignac de la Mothe Fénelon	1568–1575
Michel de Castelnau, Seigneur de Mau-vissière	1575–1585
Claude de l'Aubespine Chasteauneuf .	1585–1588
Henri de la Tour, Vicomte de Turenne .	1590
M. de Morlaas	1593
Antoine de Loménie, Seigneur de la Ville-aux-Clercs	1593 ?–1595
de Sancy	1596
André Paul Hurault, Seigneur de Maisse	1597–1598
Thumier de Boissize	1598–1601
Christophe de Harlay, Seigneur de Beaumont	1601–1605
Antoine Lefèvre, Seigneur de la Boderie	1606–1612

NOTE.—Owing to the Civil War and the disputed succession after the assassination of King Henri III. in 1589 it is difficult to follow exactly the French Resident Ambassadors in England from this date onwards.

ENGLISH AMBASSADORS IN SPAIN

Anthony Browne, Viscount Montague .	1560
Sir Thomas Chamberlain . . .	1560–1562
Sir Thomas Challoner	1562–1565 d.
Dr. John Man (expelled by King Philip II)	1566–1568
(Vacant : 1568–1575)	
Sir Henry Cobham	1575
Sir John Smith	1576
Thomas Wilkes	1577
William Waad	1584
(Vacant until 1604 owing to the War)	

SPANISH AMBASSADORS IN ENGLAND

Count de Feria	1558–1559
Alvaro de Quadra, Bishop of Aquila .	1559–1563 d.
Gusman de Silva, Canon of Toledo .	1564–1568
Guerau Despes (expelled by Queen Elizabeth)	1568–1572
(Vacant : 1572–1578)	
Bernardino de Mendoza (expelled by Queen Elizabeth)	1578–1584
(Vacant until 1604 owing to the War)	

[NOTE.—Where information is available I have inserted the annual salary of the appointment in brackets. These figures, however, are apt to be misleading unless one exercises judgment in their interpretation. For example, the Lord Admiral's salary as shown in the Exchequer accounts was £133 6s. 8d., but the appointment was worth over £3,000 a year (see p. 258). Again the Lord President of the North and the English Ambassador in Paris were paid on a contract basis, which included the upkeep of their Headquarters and Staffs. The same, no doubt, is true of the Lord Warden of the East Marches. On the other hand the Mastership of the Revels must have been worth considerably more than £10 a year. The holder seems to have been given £1 a day during Court Performances, and he was also entitled to a commission for censoring plays.]

APPENDIX G

A LONDON AND WESTMINSTER DIRECTORY

NOTE.—The following abbreviations are employed:

d. = died.
ex. = executed.
imp. = imprisoned.

Bacon, Sir Nicholas	York House, Strand [1]	1560–1579 d.
Bertie, Peregrine, Lord Willoughby de Eresby	Willoughby House, Barbican	1580–
Carey, Henry, Lord Hunsdon	King's Place, Hackney	1578–1583
	Hunsdon House, Blackfriars	–1596 d.
Cecil, William, Lord Burghley	Cecil House, Strand	1561–1598 d.
Clinton, Henry, Earl of Lincoln	Lincoln House, Cannon Row	
Devereux, Robert, 2nd Earl of Essex	Essex House, Strand (renamed from Leicester House)	1588–1601 ex.
Drury, Sir William	Drury House, Drury Lane	–1579 d.
Dudley, Robert, Earl of Leicester	Leicester House, Strand (renamed from Paget House)	1563–1588 d.
FitzAlan, Henry, 12th Earl of Arundel	Arundel House, Strand	1552–1580 d.
Hatton, Sir Christopher	Ely Place, Holborn	1576–1590 d.
Herbert, Henry, 2nd Earl of Pembroke	Baynard's Castle, Blackfriars	1559–1601 d.
Herbert, William, 3rd Earl of Pembroke	Baynard's Castle, Blackfriars	1601–
Howard, Charles, Lord Howard of Effingham and Earl of Nottingham	King Street, Westminster. Arundel House, Strand	–1603 1603–1607
Howard, Philip, Earl of Surrey and Earl of Arundel	Arundel House, Strand	1580–1589 imp.

[1] York House appears to have been let by the Archbishops of York to the Lords Chancellor. Sir John Puckering died here in 1596, and Lord Ellesmere in 1617. Francis Bacon was born here in 1561, and occupied it during the tenure of his Chancellorship from 1617 to 1621.

Howard, Thomas, 4th Duke of Norfolk	Charterhouse, Aldersgate	1565–1572 ex.
Howard, Thomas, Lord Howard de Walden and Duke of Suffolk	Charterhouse, Aldersgate	1603–1611
Howard, Thomas, 2nd Earl of Arundel	Arundel House, Strand	1607–1646
Lumley, John, Lord	Lumley House, Tower Hill	1595–1609 d.
Paget, William, Lord	Paget House, Strand	1537–1563 d.
Radcliffe, Thomas, 3rd Earl of Sussex	Sussex House, Cannon Row	1562
	Bermondsey House, Bermondsey	1577–1583 d.
Ralegh, Sir Walter	Durham House, Strand	1583–1603 imp.
Seymour, Edward, Earl of Hertford	Hertford House, Cannon Row	1583–1621 d.
Stanley, William, 6th Earl of Derby	Derby House, Cannon Row	1595–
Suffolk, Catharine, Duchess of	Willoughby House, Barbican	–1580 d.
Vere, Edward de, 17th Earl of Oxford	Cecil House, Strand	1562–1571
	Oxford Court, London Stone	1571–1591
	Fisher's Folly, Bishopsgate	
	King's Place, Hackney [1]	1596–1604 d.
Wriothesley, Henry, 3rd Earl of Southampton	Southampton House, Holborn	

[1] Elizabeth, Countess of Oxford, continued to live at King's Place until 1609, when she sold it to Fulke Greville, Lord Brooke, who renamed it Brooke House.

NOTE.—The information contained in this Appendix is chiefly derived from *London Past and Present*, by H. B. Wheatley. I have only included the more important people mentioned in this *Life*. The dates must be regarded as approximate only. For example, the Earl of Sussex was living in Cannon Row in 1562, and by 1577 he was established in Bermondsey; but we do not know when he moved from one to the other.

APPENDIX H

ANNOTATED BIBLIOGRAPHY

APART from casual references in the histories of Camden and
Stow, what is probably the first allusion to Lord Oxford
after his death occurs in

Fragmenta Regalia, by Sir Robert Naunton. *c.* 1630.

Sir Robert, who was only thirteen years younger than the Earl,
gives us forty seven thumb-nail sketches of the " servants of
Queen Elizabeth's state and favour," but Lord Oxford is not
included, the only allusion to him being an incidental one.
This omission, however, is accounted for in the last paragraph
of the book :

Modesty in me forbids defacements of men departed, whose
posterity yet remaining enjoys the merit of their virtues, and do
still live in their honour.   And I had rather incur the censure
of abruption, than to be conscious and taken in the manner
of eruption, and of trampling upon the graves of persons at
rest, which living we durst not look in the face, nor make our
addresses to them otherwise than with due regard to their
honours and renown of their virtues.

It looks as if Naunton must have been thinking of Lord Oxford
when he wrote this.   So prominent a courtier and favourite
as the Earl had been could hardly have been omitted from a
list of 47 of the Queen's " servants " without good reason.
Probably Naunton, whose daughter married the Earl's grandson,
felt that Oxford's life could not be written without some allusion
to the Arundel accusations of 1581.   Under the circumstances
it seemed better to say nothing at all, as the mere allusion
would have had the effect of reviving scandalous gossip.

Royal and Noble Authors, by Horace Walpole.   1758.

Contains a short but favourable life of Lord Oxford.   In

26   385

that section of the volume devoted to another great Elizabethan scholar, the Earl of Dorset, the following sentence occurs :

[The Earls of] Tiptoft and Rivers set the example of borrowing light from other countries, and patronised the importer of printing, Caxton. The Earls of Oxford and Dorset struck out new lights for the drama, without making the multitude laugh or weep at ridiculous representations of Scripture. To the two former we owe PRINTING, to the two latter TASTE— what do we not owe perhaps to the last of the four ? Our historic plays are allowed to have been founded on the heroic narratives in the *Mirror for Magistrates* : to that plan, and to the boldness of Lord Buckhurst's new scenes, perhaps we owe SHAKESPEARE.

Curiosities of Literature, by Isaac D'Israeli. 1791.

One of the items in this volume, entitled *The Secret History of Edward Vere, Earl of Oxford*, is a fantastic piece of fiction of no historical value whatever. It is clear that Isaac D'Israeli was actuated more by the desire to give the public something sensational than by motives of veracity. We are told that the Earl lived in Italy for seven years in a state of prodigality which threw the Court of Tuscany into the shade. We are also told that during this period he spent more than £40,000. And there is a preposterous story of how the Earl came to go abroad, which, though absolutely devoid of truth, no doubt helped the sale of the book.

An Account of Hedingham Castle in the County of Essex, by Lewis Majendie, Esq., F.R.S., F.S.A. 1796.

A folio volume of 15 pages containing plans, sections, and elevations of Hedingham Castle, together with a short account of the de Vere family. There are several references to a " terrier " in the possession of the author, describing the property as it existed in 1592 when alienated to Lord Burghley by his son-in-law.

The historic value of the work, however, is greatly reduced by the author's persistent attempt, unsupported by any documentary evidence, to advance the theory that Lord Oxford deliberately destroyed Castle Hedingham in order to spite Burghley. We now know that this theory is utter nonsense, the evidence all going to prove that Oxford and Burghley were on excellent terms at the time.

An Account of the most ancient and noble family of the De Veres,
    Earls of Oxford.

This is an anonymous manuscript volume of about 160 pages,
written in 1825 or 1826, and preserved in the Borough Library
at Colchester.   It contains much valuable historical material,
and shows that the de Vere family had settled in England before
the Norman Conquest.

The History and Topography of the County of Essex, by Thomas
    Wright.   1836.

The de Vere family and Hedingham Castle are dealt with in
volume i, pages 507 to 524 of this work.   A short biography of
the 17th Earl is given on page 516, and as it is a good example of
the persistent calumny that has pursued his memory ever since
the time of Charles Arundel's unfounded charges, it is quoted
below in full :

Edward the seventeenth Earl succeeded his father : he
wasted and nearly ruined his noble inheritance.   For, having a
very intimate acquaintance with Thomas Howard, Duke of
Norfolk, with cruel injustice condemned for his attachment to
the Queen of Scots, he most earnestly interceded with Sir
William Cecil, Lord Chancellor [sic] Burghley, to save the life
of his friend ; and failing in his attempt he swore he would
ruin his estate at Hedingham, because it was the jointure of his
first wife, Anne, Lord Burghley's daughter.   According to
this insane resolution, he not only forsook his lady's bed, but
sold and wasted the best part of his inheritance ; he began to
deface the Castle, pulled down the out-houses, destroyed all
the pales of the three parks, wasted the standing timber, and
pulled down the walls that inclosed the Castle.   The father
of the Lady Anne, by stratagem, contrived that her husband
should, unknowingly, sleep with her, believing her to be another
woman, and she bore a son to him in consequence of this
meeting.   The lady died in 1588.   His second wife was Elizabeth, daughter of Thomas Trentham, Esq., who when her
husband was about to sell the Castle and estate at Hedingham,
contrived to purchase and preserve it for the family.   He died in
1604, and was buried in a private manner at Hackney.

Neither the " insane resolution " attributed to Lord Oxford,
nor the " stratagem " alleged to have been contrived by Lord
Burghley have, it need hardly be pointed out to readers of the
present *Life,* any historical foundation whatever.   These two so-

called " facts " have been accepted hitherto, however, without question, and the latter forms the foundation of the belief that Oxford was the original of Bertram in *All's Well that Ends Well*. Oxford and Bertram were certainly both Royal Wards, both married into families of lower social prestige than their own, and both decided for a time to live apart from their wives. But it by no means necessarily follows that every detail connected with Bertram has its counterpart in actual events in Lord Oxford's life. It is much more likely in the case of the " stratagem " that this particular episode in the play was transferred to Lord Oxford, in view of the general similarity of his character to that of Bertram, than that the episode was transferred from Oxford to the play.

The Philosophy of Shakespeare's Plays unfolded, by Delia Bacon. 1857.

This book was one of the earliest which set forth the argument against the Stratfordian authorship of the Shakespeare plays. Miss Delia Bacon contends that a secret society existed, the head of which was Sir Walter Ralegh, and its philosopher Francis Bacon, including amongst others the Earl of Oxford, Lord Paget, and Lord Buckhurst. This society, the authoress claims, was responsible for the Shakespeare Drama.

During the nineteenth century many brief lives or mentions of Lord Oxford appeared, notably :

Lives of Eminent Englishmen, by G. C. Cunningham. 1837.
Dormant and Extinct Peerages, by B. Burke. 1883.
Memorials of St. John-at-Hackney, by R. Simpson. 1882.
Official Baronage of England, by J. E. Doyle. 1886.
Complete Peerage, by G. E. C. 1887.
A History of English Poetry, by W. J. Courthope. 1897.

All of these, however, were content to quote from previous printed authorities without adding anything original.

Miscellanies of the Fuller Worthies' Library, Vol. IV., edited by Rev. A. B. Grosart. 1872.

A collection of 23 poems by the Earl of Oxford, 15 of which had been published during his lifetime. The remainder are taken from manuscript sources in the Bodleian Library. In a brief

" Memorial-Introduction " Dr. Grosart says significantly of Lord Oxford : " An unlifted shadow somehow lies across his memory."

The Dictionary of National Biography. 1898.

When the late Sir Sidney Lee wrote the life of the Earl of Oxford for the *D.N.B.* it was by far the most comprehensive biography so far attempted. Unfortunately Sir Sidney was unable to make use of the numerous manuscript sources, but was of necessity confined to the scandal, gossip, and hearsay of printed records. Lord Oxford is convicted unheard on the evidence of the traitor Charles Arundel ; we are told that he " is said " to have planned the murder of Sir Philip Sidney ; his character, according to Sir Sidney, was " wayward, violent, extravagant, and boorish."

Sir Sidney, however, fully appreciated his worth as a poet, stating that " he evinced a genuine interest in music, and wrote verses of much lyric beauty."

John Lyly, by A. Feuillerat. 1909.

M. Feuillerat, in his able study of Lyly's life and works, devotes a chapter to Lord Oxford, who employed Lyly as his private secretary and actor manager for ten years or more. He thinks it absurd to suppose—in view of Lyly's social position—that any of his plays could possibly contain allegorical references to court affairs. It has been suggested, for instance, that Sapho and Phao stand for Queen Elizabeth and the Duc d'Anjou. M. Feuillerat considers this to be quite out of the question, and if Lyly was the author he is undoubtedly right. His original researches about the Earl are mostly confined to the Knyvet affray. Unfortunately the Professor has allowed his imagination to run away with him, and he has magnified this incident out of all proportion. The London streets are described as " running with the blood " of the two protagonists' followers ; and the episode is likened to the famous family quarrel between the Montagues and the Capulets.

Sous le Masque de William Shakespeare . William Stanley, 6me Comte de Derby, by Abel Lefranc. Payot et Cie, Paris, 1919.

Professor Lefranc, who has recently been elected a member of the French Academy, advances the theory that Lord Oxford's son-in-law, William Stanley, 6th Earl of Derby, was the real author of the Shakespeare plays. He gives a portrait of the Earl of Oxford, with a short account of his company of actors.

Shakespeare Identified, by J. Thomas Looney. Cecil Palmer, 1920.

A long and carefully worked out argument, in which the author claims most of the Shakespeare plays and poems for the Earl of Oxford.

The Poems of Edward de Vere, by J. Thomas Looney. 1921.

In addition to the 23 poems published by Dr. Grosart in 1872, Mr. Looney includes 13 of the songs contained in the 1632 edition of Lyly's plays, and 11 poems which appeared in *England's Helicon* (1600 and 1614) signed " Ignoto." With regard to the latter it seems more probable that the pseudonym " Ignoto " belongs not to Lord Oxford, but to his cousin and friend Lord Lumley. (Cf. my article on the authorship of the *Arte of English Poesie* in the *Review of English Studies*, vol. i, No. 3, page 284.)

The Mystery of Mr. W. H., by Colonel B. R. Ward, C.M.G. Cecil Palmer, 1923.

Following up Mr. Looney's hypothesis, Colonel Ward not only confirms Sir Sidney Lee's identification of the famous " Mr. W. H." of the dedication of Shakespeare's Sonnets, but sets forth arguments to show that they were written by the Earl of Oxford at King's Place, Hackney. This book is the first to uphold what may be called the Oxford-Derby theory.

The Elizabethan Stage. By Sir E. K. Chambers. 4 vols. 1923.
This is the most complete and detailed history of the Elizabethan Stage that has been attempted hitherto. One section (vol. ii, pp. 99–102) is devoted to the Earl of Oxford's actors, and another (pp. 118–27) to those of his son-in-law the Earl of Derby.
In the opening chapter of Volume I. Sir E. Chambers emphasises the paramount importance of the Queen and her Court in connexion with the Drama :

It will be manifest in the course of the present treatise, that the Palace was the point of vantage from which the stage won its way, against the linked opposition of an alienated pulpit and an alienated municipality. . . . It is worth while, therefore, to attempt to recover something of the atmosphere of the Tudor Court, and to define the conditions under which the presentation of plays formed a recurring interest in its bustling many-coloured life.

An Appendix is devoted to a detailed Court Calendar, an item which by itself makes the book indispensable to students of the period.

Sir E. Chambers gives but short shrift to the originators of the Oxford-Derby theory of Shakespeare authorship, as will be seen from the following quotations :

J. T. Looney, *Shakespeare Identified* (1920), gives him (i.e. Lord Oxford) Shakespeare's plays, many of which were written after his death. . . . I do not accept Mr. James Greenstreet's theory that W. Stanley was the real W. Shakespeare.[1]

The Golden Hind, January 1924. Chapman and Hall.

An article in the first number of this quarterly magazine, connecting the episode of the rivalry of the Earl of Oxford and Sir Philip Sidney for the hand of Anne Cecil with certain scenes in *The Merry Wives of Windsor*.

Shakespeare through Oxford Glasses, by Captain H. H. Holland, R.N. 1924.

This book is another sequel to Mr. Looney's hypothesis, and in it many apparently inexplicable topical allusions in the Shakespeare plays are explained as references to Lord Oxford.

English Literary Autographs, edited by Dr. W. W. Greg. Part I. Dramatists, 1550–1650. 1925.

This is a collection of specimens of the handwriting of all English dramatists who lived between 1550 and 1650 whose holographs exist. The famous signatures of William Shakespeare have been omitted in order to avoid controversy. Place has been found, however, for examples of the handwriting of the Earls of Oxford and Derby on account of their " close connexion

[1] Vol. iii, p. 503 ; vol. ii, p. 127.

with the stage." The second Oxford letter reproduced by Dr. Greg is dated July 7th, 1594, and is of interest on account of an allusion to an " office " held by the writer, an allusion which not unnaturally puzzled Dr. Greg. " It does not appear," he writes, " what was the ' office ' to which he alludes, but the affair may possibly have had to do with the import monopoly for which he was petitioning in 1592."

It is most unlikely that Oxford is here alluding to an import monopoly—which, moreover, he did not succeed in obtaining. Dr. Greg was, however, unaware when he advanced this theory that Oxford was at this time in receipt of an allowance of £1,000 a year from the Exchequer. The precise duties which he had to perform in return for this salary must be a matter for research supplemented by inference and conjecture. The following is the opening sentence of the letter in question, and one fact at least stands out clearly, namely, that the " office " was one in which Queen Elizabeth was very closely concerned. " My very good Lord [he writes to Lord Burghley], if it please you to remember that about half a year or thereabout past, I was suitor to your Lordship for your favour, that whereas I found sundry abuses, *whereby both Her Majesty and myself were in mine office greatly hindered*, that it would please your Lordship that I might find such favour from you that I might have the same redressed."

Dr. Greg summarily dismisses Oxford at the time of his death in 1604 as " the antiquated type of the Italianate Englishman." Readers of this *Life* will, however, be aware that King James I., in the first year of his reign, continued Lord Oxford's salary of £1,000 a year that had been granted by Elizabeth, and in addition appointed him to his Privy Council. It is permissible to suppose that *he* at least did not share Dr. Greg's view that the Earl was too antiquated to be of further use to his country !

A Hundreth Sundrie Flowres, edited by B. M. Ward. 1926.

This is a reprint of what is commonly called the " first edition " of George Gascoigne's works. It was originally published in 1573. The argument is put forward that Lord Oxford was the editor of the volume, which is known to have been brought out during Gascoigne's absence abroad, and that 16 of the lyrics were contributed by the Earl himself.

Axiophilus : or Oxford alias Shakespeare, by Eva Turner Clark.
  The Knickerbocker Press, New York, 1926.

An attempt firstly to identify Lord Oxford with the poet
alluded to as " Axiophilus " by Gabriel Harvey, and secondly
to find an anagram in the pseudonym connecting it with
Shakespeare. The identification is quite possible, but the
anagram is not convincing.

The First English Translators of the Classics, by C. H. Conley,
  Ph.D.   Yale University Press, 1927.

A study of the translations from the Classics into English
during the first fifteen years of Elizabeth's reign. On pages
39 and 40 the author gives a table showing the persons chosen
by the translators as patrons.   Queen Elizabeth heads the list
with 9 dedications, closely followed by Burghley and Leicester,
who each receive 8.   The Earls of Oxford and Bedford come
next, with 3 each.

The group to which Oxford belonged, which included his
guardian Lord Burghley and his friend and cousin the Duke of
Norfolk, received 18 dedications as against 16 offered to the
Leicester *coterie*.   The book represents an important piece of
research work on a comparatively neglected period ; and shows
that Elizabethan dedications were by no means the formal and
conventional documents they have hitherto been assumed to be.

By drawing attention to the close connexion between the
literary activity and the political and religious movements of
the time, the author has given real assistance to students of the
period ; and has shown what valuable results may be anticipated
from a similar study of the latter period of Queen Elizabeth's
reign.

The Shakespeare Mystery, by Georges Connes, Professor of
  English in the University of Dijon.   Translated by a
  Member of the Shakespeare Fellowship.   1927.

A comprehensive examination of the various theories that
have arisen from time to time as to the authorship of the
Shakespeare literature.   The following claims are examined as
they have been expounded by their several advocates : William
Shakespeare of Stratford, Francis Bacon, Roger Manners,
5th Earl of Rutland, William Stanley, 6th Earl of Derby, and
Edward de Vere, 17th Earl of Oxford.

In the final chapter Professor Connes argues that all these claimants were intimately acquainted with one another, and shows that if we add Robert Devereux, 2nd Earl of Essex, Henry Wriothesley, 3rd Earl of Southampton (Shakespeare's patron), and William and Philip Herbert (the " Incomparable paire of Brethren " of the First Folio of 1623), we find a group of Elizabethans who were nearly all closely inter-related by marriage ties. This group comprised all the most important leaders of the Essex faction, to which " Shakespeare " indubitably belonged. M. Connes more or less accepts the " Group Theory," and assumes that as all the members of this group were well acquainted with one another there is no adequate reason for awarding the authorship of the plays and poems to one rather than another. He therefore inclines to the traditional view that William Shakespeare of Stratford, who is assumed to have been on intimate terms with them all, was the actual author.

APPENDIX K

" HE IS BUT A LITTLE FELLOW "

THE description by Thomas Nashe of the Earl of Oxford as
" a little fellow . . . who hath one of the best wits in England " [1]
is strikingly confirmed by the reproduction of Hollar's engraving
of the Earl opposite page 192.

This engraving, which represents the last two figures in a
procession of sixty Knights of the Garter and other Courtiers,
was made in 1666 from the original drawn by Marcus Gheeraedts
the elder in 1578. The procession is on its way to St. George's
Chapel, Windsor, on the 18th June 1572, on the occasion of
the installation of the Duc de Montmorenci as a Knight of the
Garter.[2]

The Sword of State was carried in all processions by the
senior nobleman present, as for instance on the occasion of
the Armada Thanksgiving Procession in 1588 when it was
carried by the Marquess of Winchester.[3]

On the 18th June 1572 the senior nobleman in England was
John Paulet, 2nd Marquess of Winchester, who, at the age of
about fifty-five, had succeeded his father just three months
previously.

As Lord Great Chamberlain the Earl of Oxford took precedence of all other Earls, and was therefore the next nobleman
in point of seniority.[4] The figure shown bearing the Sword of
State in the engraving is that of a young man wearing a
moustache but no beard. When Oxford was painted in Paris
by a Flemish artist in 1575 [5] he is similarly represented. All
the other figures in the procession are wearing beards as well
as moustaches, as was the almost universal fashion of the time.
The figure is unquestionably that of a young man—certainly
not of one between fifty and sixty years of age. We may there-

[1] See pp. 191–192.
[2] See pp. 56–57.
[3] See pp. 294 and 295.
[4] See p. 52.
[5] See Frontispiece and p. 104.

395

fore take it as quite certain that it is not a portrait of the 2nd
Marquess of Winchester, and with equal certainty that it represents the seventeenth Earl of Oxford, who at the time of the
procession (1572) was twenty-two years old, and when the
drawing was made (1578) was twenty-eight.

Wenceslaus Hollar (1607–1677) was one of the greatest
engravers who ever lived. We may therefore feel with some
confidence that his portrait of the Earl of Oxford accurately
follows the drawing by the well-known artist Gheeraedts,
and that in this picture of Queen Elizabeth and Lord Oxford
we have a faithful representation of the Earl " in the prime of
his gallantest youth " when he was, as Fulke Greville tells us,
" superlative in the Prince's favour." [1]

Of the two figures that of Queen Elizabeth is, if anything,
the taller; and we know that she was by no means a tall woman.
Of the other figures in the procession there are none shorter
and many taller than the sprightly and self-confident " little
fellow " who is here seen bearing the Sword of State before his
Royal Mistress.

[1] See pp. 158, 169. It is worth mentioning that Queen Elizabeth's
features in this picture bear a most striking resemblance to the same
artist's painting of her, now No. 200 in the National Portrait Gallery. We
may therefore assume that in Gheeraedts' original drawing the figure of
Lord Oxford was definitely a portrait.

INDEX

Printed in Great Britain by
Hasell, Watson & Viney, Ld., London and Aylesbury.